# CONTENTS

## 3  Values and Prejudice   49

# Social Psychology of Prejudice

**Melinda Jones**

*University of Memphis*

Upper Saddle River, New Jersey 07458

Library of Congress Cataloging-in-Publication Data

Jones, Melinda,
    Social psychology of prejudice / Melinda Jones.
        p. cm.
    Includes bibliographical references and index.
    ISBN 0-13-028771-7
    1. Prejudices.   2. Social psychology.   I. Title.

HM1091 .J66 2001
303.3'85—dc21

                            2001035076

VP/Editorial Director: Laura Pearson
Managing Editor (Acquisitions): Sharon Rheinhardt
VP/Director of Production & Manufacturing:
    Barbara Kittle
Senior Managing Editor (Production): Mary Rottino
Production Editor: Kathleen Sleys
Prepress & Manufacturing Manager: Nick Sklitsis
Prepress & Manufacturing Buyer: Tricia Kenny
AVP/Director of Marketing: Beth Gillett Mejia
Executive Marketing Manager: Sheryl Adams
Cover Art Director: Jayne Conte
Cover Design: Bruce Kenselaar
Cover Art: Roxana Villa

DEDICATION

**To my parents,
Gary and Val,
And to my brother,
Michael**

© 2002 by Pearson Education
Upper Saddle River, New Jersey 07458

Printed in the United States of America

ISBN 0-13-028771-7

Pearson Education LTD.
Pearson Education Australia PTY, Limited
Pearson Education Singapore, Pte. Ltd
Pearson Education North Asia Ltd., Hong Kong
Pearson Education Canada, Ltd., Toronto
Pearson Educacíon de Mexico, S.A. de C.V.
Pearson Education—Japan, Tokyo
Pearson Education Malaysia, Pte. Ltd
Pearson Education, Upper Saddle River, New Jersey

# 4 Cognitive Components of Prejudice: Stereotyping and Categorization 75

# 5  *Individual Differences in Prejudice*  111

# 6  *Intergroup Relations*  129

# PREFACE

During the course of writing this book—literally on the cusp of the 21st century between 1998 and 2000—widespread intergroup conflict and violence erupted, both internationally and nationally. In the late 1990s, for instance, "ethnic cleansing" occurred in Kosovo, as Serbs waged war on ethnic Albanians, killing thousands and forcing a million people from their homes. Meanwhile, almost half a world away in Rwanda, an entire nation continued to struggle with the aftermath of genocide, in which an estimated 800,000 Tutsis were systematically murdered by the majority Hutus within a span of 100 days during 1994.

Here in the United States, hate crimes reached a record level during this period. Many of these incidents were cases in which majority group members attacked minority group members, but in many also minority group members attacked members of the majority or members of other minority groups. Consider a sample of highly publicized hate crimes that occurred between 1998 and 2000. In June 1998, James Byrd Jr., a Black man, was beaten unconscious by three White men and then chained to a pickup truck and dragged to his death in Jasper, Texas; in October 1998, two young men murdered University of Wyoming college student Matthew Shepard because he was gay; in July 1999, a gunman with ties to a White supremacist church fired shots into a group gathered outside a Korean church in Bloomington, Indiana, killing Won Joon Yoon, a student at Indiana University; in August 1999, Buford O. Furrow opened fire at a Jewish community center, wounding five people, and later said that he wanted his act to be "a wake-up call to America to kill Jews"; and in March 2000, a Black man went on a racially motivated rampage killing three Whites and wounding two others in Wilkinsburg, Pennsylvania.

Events such as these serve as tragic reminders that prejudice based upon race, ethnicity, religion, and sexual orientation continues to exist, and sadly, continues to be expressed in horrific ways. How can we make sense of such hatreds and rivalries between groups of people? What factors give rise to antipathy toward members of certain groups? Are certain "types" of people more likely to be prejudiced? And perhaps the most important question, What can be done to prevent, or at least reduce, prejudice?

These questions lie at the heart of any course that focuses on prejudice and discrimination. Building on a tradition of research in stereotyping and intergroup conflict, social psychologists have much to offer in terms of identifying the origins of prejudice and recommending strategies for its reduction.

## ➤ GOALS OF THIS BOOK

*Social Psychology of Prejudice* is conceived as a textbook to accompany upper-division psychology courses in prejudice and discrimination. Because of a growing multicultural perspective in psychology, many departments are responding by offering specialty courses in the psychology of prejudice. Very few textbooks appropriate for this audience currently exist, and those that do emphasize Black–White relations in the United States. Although elements of this analysis certainly may be generalized to prejudice against other groups, taking a broader perspective in approaching the topic of prejudice is advantageous for two reasons. First, social psychologists are increasingly addressing other forms of prejudice: ethnic prejudice (e.g., against Latinos, Asians), sexism, antigay prejudice, and antifat prejudice, to name just a few. The unique aspects of these types of prejudice have yet to be addressed in an undergraduate text. This book attempts to fill that void.

Second, research on prejudice and discrimination is burgeoning not only in the United States, but also in other countries. Researchers in European countries especially have contributed greatly to our understanding of the extent that identification with a social group underlies prejudice and intergroup discrimination. A focus on Black-White relations in the United States would ignore much of the research in these countries.

The overall goals of this book are to describe the various theories of prejudice, to explore the common psychological processes that maintain prejudice of many kinds (i.e., stereotyping and other cognitive mechanisms), and to address issues of intergroup relations and social identity as sources of prejudice. Additionally, this book focuses on how marginalized individuals cope with prejudice, and how prejudice affects one's sense of identity and self-worth. Finally, methods to reduce prejudice will be considered, and the inevitability of prejudice will be addressed.

## ➤ ACKNOWLEDGMENTS

Certain people were instrumental in the initial phases of the writing project. Eric Stano, psychology acquisitions editor at Longman, believed in this project and offered unlimited encouragement. I owe a great deal of thanks to colleagues at the University of Pittsburgh–Bradford. I am especially grateful to Warren Fass for his support—and for sharing his journal collections with me, sparing me numerous trips to the library. Thanks also go to Michael Klausner for his helpful sociological ideas and insights. Also, I would like to thank one of my psychology students, LaDawn Ishman, for providing invaluable assistance with library research and teaching-related duties.

My staff in the University Honors Program at the University of Memphis, Patrick Perry and Tallulah Campbell, were supportive throughout the lengthy writing process and shielded me from minor distractions in the office so I could meet looming deadlines. Daniel Avant, our resident Honors student, assisted with library research, read sections of the manuscript, and provided much-needed reactions from a student's perspective. I am also grateful to Trent Pitts for putting together the references.

I am also indebted to the following colleagues who provided thoughtful comments and suggestions on one or more chapters: Kimberly Barrett, University of Washington; Nyla Branscombe, University of Kansas; Lisa M. Brown, University of Florida; Victoria Esses, University of Western Ontario; Stephen Fein, Williams College; Stephanie Goodwin, Boston College; Elizabeth Salierno, University of Central Florida; Glenda H. Sehested, Sociology Department, Augustana College; Eugene Sheehan, University of Northern Colorado; Ted Singelis, California State University–Chico; Marshall Stevenson, Dillard University; and William Wooten, University of Central Florida.

In conclusion, I must recognize those debts that have a much longer history. Many thanks go to my intellectual and emotional mentor, Jeff Topping. And there is Lori Varlotta, who suggested that I write this book. Many an hour we spent discussing how to shape various chapters, and I'm grateful for her insights. And finally, I express my gratitude to my parents, Gary and Val, and my brother, Mike, who have always supported my life choices.

# 1

# Introduction to Prejudice and Discrimination

➤ INTRODUCTION

Although our universities today are more culturally diverse, campuses remain deeply divided along lines of race, ethnicity, gender, sexuality, and other differences. This is partly due to students' reluctance to talk openly about prejudice and discrimination. These are such painful topics for many college students, evoking emotional responses such as guilt or anger, that they do not want to discuss them. In fact, Arthur Levine (1998), a leading scholar on higher education, suggests that students are more comfortable talking about the intimate details of their sex lives than about diversity on campus. He argues that "the dirty words on college campuses now are no longer four letters: they are six-letter words like 'racist' and 'sexist'—and 'homophobic,' which is even longer" (p. 15).

A close examination of prejudice is thus more crucially important than ever. As educational institutions are becoming more multicultural in terms of their student bodies, faculties, and staff, and as corporate America is attempting to promote diversity through workshops and seminars, as well as through hiring and retaining members of diverse groups, contact with people who are different from oneself (e.g., with regard to race, ethnicity, and sexual orientation) is virtually inevitable. For some of us, we may welcome these differences in cultures because they enrich our lives in exciting and unexpected ways. For others, these cultural collisions can be threatening.

Because of the differences that exist between groups of people, many have become personally acquainted with prejudice and discrimination; if asked to do so, most individuals can recall an incident in their lives in which they either treated someone poorly on the basis of their group membership or were themselves targets of

1

prejudice. And most of us realize that prejudice comes in many forms—prejudices against others on the basis of skin color, religion, sexual orientation, as well as prejudices against overweight people, the disabled, the elderly, and the mentally ill. Consider a few recent examples of prejudice:

March 11, 1996. Peeter Kopvillem writes in *Maclean's* that the Supreme Court of Canada upheld the conviction of James Keegstra, who spread anti-Semitic beliefs while teaching at an Alberta school. The case began in 1982 when one parent found the following examination answer in her son's notebook: "Moles only come out in the dark when no one is watching. Jews only do their deeds when no one is watching. A mole when mad will strike back and have no mercy when disturbed. Jews strike at any time and have NO mercy." One former student, who asked to remain anonymous, said in reference to Keegstra, "He was so strong about it that I believed what he believed. You basically accepted what you were being taught."

November 25, 1996. In *Newsweek*, Jolie Solomon describes how a scandal over racial slurs forces Texaco to pay over $115 million in reparations. The settlement came quickly after transcripts of a 1994 meeting were released that showed corporate officials laughing about Black employees. One senior executive referred to minority employees as "black jelly beans." Another executive, in complaining about multiculturalism said, "I'm still struggling with Hannukkah, and now we have Kwanzaa...Poor Saint Nicholas, they s—tted all over his beard." The executives go on to mock the symbols of Kwanzaa and the African-American anthem "Lift Every Voice."

February 25, 1997. Alice Green writes in the *Panama City News Herald* about Charisse Goodman's experiences growing up fat. Goodman said that when she was five, she realized that people saw her differently from other children. According to Goodman, "People make assumptions about others based on their size. They automatically assume that fat people are lazy, sloppy, and ugly." Goodman said she recognizes the prejudice against fat people, because she is Jewish. "I don't understand why people will get upset if someone is mistreated because of being Jewish but not because of being fat."

October 1998. Matthew Shepard, a 21-year-old gay student at the University of Wyoming, met some people at a campus bar one evening. One of two men, reportedly upset because he thought Shepard was making passes at him, allegedly decided to teach him a lesson. Pretending to be gay, the men drove Shepard to the end of town, pistol-whipped him into a coma, and left him lashed to a fence post. Shepard died while on life support. At Shepard's funeral, anti-gay protestors carried signs that said "No Fags in Heaven" and "No Tears for Queers."

September 21, 2001. Shortly after the World Trade Center had been toppled by a terrorist attack, a number of troubling instances of discrimination against Arab Americans unfolded across the United States. In seven separate incidences in cities including Minneapolis, Tampa, San Antonio, and Orlando, men of Arab descent were expelled from domestic flights simply because of their ethnicity. Ashraf Khan, a Pakistani-American passenger removed from a Delta Air Lines flight, said that he was deeply saddened by the terrorist attack, but "just because the people who did this were Muslims does not mean that all the Muslims are bad."

As these anecdotes suggest, prejudice is a ubiquitous phenomenon that may apply to any identifiable group that departs from the "cultural default." Smith and

Zarate (1992) suggest that male gender, White racial identity, nondisabled status, heterosexual orientation, and young age are the expected person attributes in Western cultures. Thus, given no other information, the word "person" immediately brings to mind a White, heterosexual, able-bodied, youthful man. From this perspective, then, a person can be outside the cultural default values in one or more ways. A young Asian male who is able-bodied and heterosexual departs only from the "racial norm," but an elderly Black lesbian who relies on her walker departs from all default categories. Interestingly, departures from these cultural default values are linguistically marked; people typically say "Black doctor," "female pilot," "lesbian therapist," but not "White doctor," "male pilot," or "heterosexual therapist."

Nevertheless, any deviations from these cultural default categories attract scrutiny and form the basis of a stigmatizing condition. Thus prejudice includes the many "isms" to which we have become acquainted (e.g., racism, sexism, heterosexism, ageism and so on), as well as other conditions that are perceived negatively (e.g., obesity, disfigurement, disability, religious affiliation). Prejudice is not only targeted at racial, ethnic, and religious groups, but at stigmatized people in general.

Our analysis of prejudice begins with an examination of the nature of "prejudice" and "discrimination." Although often used interchangeably, these two terms actually have quite different meanings. Second, we'll also broaden our understanding of stereotypes and discuss their contribution to prejudice and discrimination. Third, we will explore the nuances of social stigmatization and compare certain stigmas to other forms of prejudice (e.g., racial or ethnic bigotry) that have caused so much strife throughout human history. Finally, because it has been the subject of some debate among social psychologists, we'll pose the question of whether prejudice is an inevitable consequence of being human. Before moving forward with our examination of these complex issues, let's define the basic concepts of prejudice, stereotypes, and discrimination.

➤ ## PREJUDICE, STEREOTYPING, AND DISCRIMINATION

### What Is Prejudice?

Although many of us have no difficulty recognizing prejudice as we experience it in our own lives, social psychologists have debated the meaning of the term. Consider these different definitions of prejudice:

- "an antipathy based upon a faulty and inflexible generalization" (Allport, 1954, p. 10)
- "an emotional, rigid attitude . . . toward a group of people" (Simpson & Yinger, 1965)
- "an unreasonable negative attitude towards others because of their membership in a particular group" (Fishbein, 1996, p. 5)
- "differential evaluations that are based solely on category membership" (Jackson, 1992, p. 164)

These definitions of prejudice suggest several specific features. First, prejudice is generally considered to be an *attitude* toward others because of the groups to which they belong. Although prejudice is usually thought of as a negative attitude toward the members of specific groups, it can also be positive. As an example, most people can easily recognize that a negative attitude directed toward members of other groups (i.e., out-groups) is prejudice. But at the same time that people view out-group members unfavorably, they also view members of their own social group (i.e., in-group) more favorably. By definition, such positive attitudes toward the in-group are prejudice too.

Second, prejudice is directed toward people solely because of their group memberships. For example, it would not be prejudice if you were to dislike someone simply because he or she is mean-spirited, but it would be prejudice if your view of that person was based upon the group to which that person belongs. Prejudice is not just a "garden-variety" positive or negative attitude toward someone due to their personal characteristics; rather, **prejudice** is a positive or negative attitude directed toward people simply because they happen to be members of a specific group.

Because prejudice is an attitude, Victoria Esses and her colleagues (1993) argue that it is appropriate to study prejudice as one would study any attitude. Attitudes are evaluations (e.g., good-bad, approve-disapprove) that are based upon affect, cognition, and behavior (Eagly & Chaiken, 1993). Thus, attitudes toward social groups can be based upon three sources of information: (1) *affective information* or feelings toward members of a group, (2) *cognitive information* or beliefs about the characteristics of members of a group, and (3) *behavioral tendencies* or overt acts that treat individuals differently depending upon their group membership.

Viewing prejudice as an attitude provides a way to integrate such related constructs as stereotyping and discrimination. How does this conceptualization of prejudice-as-attitude incorporate stereotyping and discrimination? Whereas prejudice represents the affective or emotional reaction to social groups, stereotypes are the cognitive manifestation of prejudice, and discrimination is the behavioral manifestation of prejudice. Using this model, then, a person's negative attitude toward a group (e.g., Group X) may be conceptualized as:

**Negative Stereotype:**  *Members of Group X are lazy, unreliable, and slovenly,* which *may lead to*

**Prejudiced Attitude:**  *I don't like Group X* which *may lead to,*

**Discrimination:**  *I prefer to exclude them from the neighborhood, avoid hiring them, etc.*

Thus, *disliking* members of Group X is prejudice, *believing* them to be lazy, unreliable, and slovenly is stereotyping, and *behaving* toward them in an exclusionary fashion is discrimination. Notice, too, that stereotypes *may* lead to prejudice, and that prejudice *may* lead to discrimination. Quite frankly, stereotyping does not always lead to prejudice, nor does prejudice always lead to discrimination. Later in this chapter we will discuss some of the difficulties associated with attempting to predict when stereotyping leads to prejudice, and when prejudice leads to discrimination.

Thus far, we have learned that prejudice, like any other attitude, contains affective, behavioral, and cognitive components. To better understand prejudice, let's examine more fully each of these components.

## Prejudiced Attitudes: The Affective Component

When most people think about prejudice, they typically focus on the affective, or emotional, component. Prejudice is clearly associated with emotions directed toward social groups, but not all emotions are the same. Many researchers suggest that different social groups may elicit different emotions (Esses et al., 1993; Smith, 1993; Stangor, Sullivan, & Ford, 1991; Vanman & Miller, 1993), and to complicate matters even more, individuals may experience both positive and negative emotions toward a single group (Katz, 1981; Zanna, 1994). For instance, Dijker (1987) examined the role of emotion in intergroup attitudes by asking residents of Amsterdam to report what emotions (e.g., positive mood, irritation, anxiety, concern, or worry) they experienced when they had contact with three immigrant groups in the Netherlands: Surinamers, Turks, and Moroccans. In addition to assessing emotional reactions, the questionnaire also asked respondents their overall attitudes toward the target groups.

In general, respondents who reported more favorable attitudes toward the groups also reported being in a more positive mood when they had contact with members of these ethnic minorities. However, respondents reported different emotions associated with different groups. Although respondents felt anxiety toward all three groups, they also reported greater irritation and concern toward Turks and Moroccans than toward Surinamers. In addition, respondents reported not only a more positive mood, but also more favorable attitudes toward Surinamers than Turks and Moroccans. These differences in attitudes and emotions directed toward the groups perhaps are due to perceived differences between the Dutch majority and the immigrant groups. Surinamers, according to Dijker, are more culturally similar to the Dutch majority group than are Turks and Moroccans; unlike immigrants from Turkey and Morocco, Surinamers speak Dutch and share cultural customs similar to the Dutch respondents.

A study described by Mark Zanna (1994) also demonstrates how different social groups may elicit different emotional responses. College students at the University of Waterloo were asked to provide their attitudes toward several target groups (French Canadians, Aboriginals/Native Indians, Pakistanis, and Homosexuals), in addition to the feelings or emotions they experience when they see, meet, or think about typical members of those groups. A content analysis of the students' responses indicated that the affective tonality differed among the groups. For example, in response to indigenous peoples, subjects reported feelings of anger, uneasiness, and pride, whereas homosexuals elicited feelings of disgust, discomfort, and confusion.

Why might different social groups evoke different emotions? Eliot Smith (1993) suggests that prejudice is a social emotion that is linked to the nature of the groups in question. Perceivers do not simply *like* or *dislike* an out-group, according to Smith; instead the nature of the relations between the out-group and one's own group may evoke qualitatively different emotional responses. For instance, members of a dominant group might appraise Group X as pushy and illegitimately demanding preferential treatment, so the predominant emotional reaction to Group X may be anger, hostility, and resentment. Similarly, Group Y might be seen as violating standards of morality, so the predominant emotion evoked by members of Group Y might be disgust or revulsion. Attitudes toward lesbians and gay men often fall into this category. In a recent survey of 15- to 19-year-old males, for instance, 89 percent of the respondents believed that sex between two men was "disgusting" (Marsiglio, 1993).

Viewing prejudice in terms of a "social emotion" (Smith, 1993) accounts not only for the degree of favorability in attitudes toward various social groups, but also behavioral reactions toward the groups. Put simply, perceivers may react differently toward groups that they find disgusting than toward groups they fear.

In sum, emotional reactions toward various social groups seem to play a powerful role in determining attitudes toward those groups. But as we shall see, negative beliefs about a group and its members also contribute to prejudicial attitudes.

## Stereotypes: The Cognitive Component of Prejudice

Think about the following groups: librarians, bodybuilders, Asians, accountants, beauty pageant participants, lesbians. If you were asked to ascribe traits to these groups, would you have difficulty? Probably not. You might very easily describe librarians as meek, Asians as good in math, bodybuilders as dumb. If such traits spontaneously come to mind, then you are using stereotypes. A **stereotype** is a set of beliefs or expectations that we have about people based solely on their group membership. Thus, stereotypes represent the cognitive component of prejudice. Many people's attitudes toward Italians, for example, are not based just upon whether they like or dislike Italians; they also include beliefs about Italians—that they "talk with their hands," are "great singers," or "belong to the Mafia" (Helmreich, 1997).

Social psychologists have found it useful to make a distinction between "individual stereotypes" and "cultural stereotypes" (Ashmore & Del Boca, 1979; Stangor & Schaller, 1996; Tajfel, 1981). *Individual stereotypes* are one's idiosyncratic beliefs about a social group that have developed over time through experience with individual group members. *Cultural stereotypes,* on the other hand, are culturally shared beliefs about the traits that are characteristic of a given group. For example, an individual may share the popular belief that women are nurturant (cultural stereotype), but may also believe that they are stubborn (individual stereotype), a trait for which there is less agreement. Cultural stereotypes are especially pernicious, because they are socially shared and deeply embedded within the cultural fabric. As Gardner (1973, p. 134) suggests, a stereotyped group member "may be somewhat chagrined to find that a few individuals in the larger community have beliefs about the characteristics of the group of which he is a member, but it has major implications...when such beliefs are relatively widespread in a community."

Social psychologists have devoted considerable attention to stereotyping, primarily because stereotypes have an enormous impact on our perceptions of others, our memory for their behavior, and ultimately, our judgments about their behavior. Stereotypes are essentially frequently used *schemas*—that is, cognitive structures that affect how information is processed (Fiske & Taylor, 1991). If you have a stereotype about a particular group, for example, the stereotype will influence what you notice about group members, how you interpret their behavior, and how you organize this information in your memory (Fiske & Neuberg, 1990; Biernat, Manis, & Nelson, 1991; Jussim, Nelson, Manis, & Soffin, 1995).

Juror simulation research offers strong support for this view of how stereotypes shape our perceptions of others. Potential jurors, for instance, may render different verdicts depending on whether the crime is stereotypically consistent or inconsistent with the defendant's group membership (Gordan, 1990; Jones, 1997). In one study designed to show how stereotypes bias our processing of information, Galen Bodenhausen (1988) asked college students to read a court case about a defendant accused of a crime. Half the students learned that the defendant, Carlos Ramirez of Albuquerque, New Mexico, was accused of assault, a crime consistent with the stereotype of Hispanics as aggressive. The other students read that Robert Johnson, of Dayton, Ohio—presumably an ethnically nondescript name—was accused of the same crime. However, Bodenhausen also manipulated the timing of stereotype activation, such that half the students learned the defendant's name prior to the presentation of the evidence, whereas the other students learned his name afterwards.

What effect did the timing of stereotype activation have on judgments? Bodenhausen predicted that students whose stereotypes about the defendant were activated *prior* to processing the evidence would be more likely to judge the Hispanic defendant guilty, because these students would pay greater attention to, and have greater recall for, stereotype-consistent information presented in the court case. Consistent with this reasoning, the students were more likely to judge Carlos Ramirez guilty than Robert Johnson, but only before receiving the evidence. Apparently, once a stereotype is activated, we have a tendency to notice and remember information that is consistent with our stereotypes and to ignore information that is inconsistent with our stereotypes.

At this point, it is important to note that stereotypes may be positive or negative. Although we typically think of stereotypes in terms of negative traits, stereotypes may also be complimentary to different groups (e.g., "women are caring and gentle," "African Americans are good athletes"). Is there anything wrong with holding such positive views of social groups, you might ask? Two lines of evidence suggest that seemingly positive stereotypes about groups may be problematic. First, sociologist Thomas Wilson (1996) doubts whether benign stereotypes are genuinely complimentary. In a recent article on Jewish stereotypes, Wilson points out that there are two sorts of Jewish stereotypes. The first is blatantly anti-Semitic, portraying Jews as pushy, grasping, money-loving, and ruthless. The second kind of stereotype is ostensibly complimentary, characterizing Jews as financially successful, ambitious, hardworking, and able to get ahead. However, a survey of attitudes toward Jews indicated that holders of benign Jewish stereotypes also expressed blatant anti-Semitic attitudes, leading Wilson to conclude that benign stereotypes are subtle expressions of underlying prejudice.

A second reason "complimentary" stereotypes may be problematic is based upon how they may constrain the stereotyped individual's behavior. Consider this story from a journalist who adopted a son from Korea:

David . . . was 5 months old when he arrived. That did not stop even some otherwise sophisticated friends from volunteering that he would no doubt be a good student. Probably

a mathematician, they opined, with a tone that uncomfortably straddled jest and prediction. I tried to take it all with good humor, this idea that a 5-month-old who could not
yet sit up, speak a word or control his bowels was already destined for academic great-
ness. Even his major seemed foreordained (Gup, 1997).

This excerpt demonstrates that stereotypes contain descriptive and prescriptive
beliefs (Terborg, 1977; Fiske, 1993). *Descriptive* stereotypes provide information
about the alleged behavior, preferences, and competencies of group members. People
may believe, for instance, that women generally make good secretaries, but men
make good physicians. But stereotypes may also be *prescriptive*, suggesting how people ought to behave, how certain groups should think and feel. If group members fail
to conform to stereotypes, they may be ostracized or otherwise penalized (Eagly,
Makhijani, & Klonsky, 1992).

A recent sex discrimination case before the U.S. Supreme Court illustrates
how individuals who fail to conform to stereotypes may be penalized (Fiske, 1993).
Ann Hopkins, a top manager at Price Waterhouse, a Big Eight accounting firm, was
denied promotion to partner. Although Hopkins was number one in the amount of
business she brought to the company and was well liked by clients, she was not accepted as a partner because she needed a "course at charm school," and needed to
"talk more femininely, dress more femininely." The Supreme Court decided that
Price Waterhouse acted on the basis of gender and subsequently ruled in Hopkins'
favor.

In short, stereotypes—whether positive or negative—deny people their individu-
ality and constrain their opportunities. For these reasons, Susan Fiske (1993) argues
that stereotypes have a controlling impact on the behavior of the stereotyped group.

## Discrimination: The Behavioral Component of Prejudice

Which of the following are examples of discrimination (adapted from Goldstein,
1997)?

- A police department requires that applicants for a position be 5'9" or taller.
- A real estate agency steers Black clients to houses in minority or racially
  mixed neighborhoods.
- Employees of a particular university are allowed free tuition, as are their
  spouses.
- A mayoral election is held on the third floor of a building without elevators.
- An Asian storeowner dislikes Blacks, but treats all customers courteously.

These examples differ in many ways. However, social psychologists usually define **discrimination** as a negative *action* toward a social group or its members on
account of group membership (Allport, 1954; Mackie & Smith, 1998). Although discrimination is a term used by some to connote an unfavorable action, the term also
may be used to refer to actions that are favorable to a particular group or its members.
For example, a university's positive act such as preferentially admitting children of
alumni, even if their SAT scores are lower than a child of a nonalumnus, represents
discrimination.

Other examples mentioned above represent discrimination too. Requiring applicants to meet a certain height requirement that is unnecessary for competent job performance may, in fact, discriminate against women. Universities that offer free tuition to employee *spouses* discriminate against gay and lesbian employees who are not legally able to marry. This definition of discrimination as a favorable or unfavorable act also rules out simply disliking certain group members, such as the example given of the Asian storeowner who dislikes Blacks but remains courteous. By definition, discrimination is behavior.

Discrimination may vary widely in terms of form and severity (Allport, 1954). For example, mild forms of discrimination may involve verbally expressing antipathy or avoiding individuals who belong to a disliked group. More intense expressions of discrimination involve excluding group members from certain types of employment, housing, or other social privileges. Examples of these forms of discrimination have captured attention in national headlines. In 1994, Denny's restaurant chain was ordered to pay millions of dollars to African-American customers who were discriminated against in its restaurants (Kohn, 1994). Because of the specific beliefs employers had about Blacks as customers (e.g., how they would behave, how much they would tip, whether they would leave without paying), employees were instructed to systematically mistreat Black customers in order to keep them to a minimum. Specific actions included seating Whites ahead of Blacks, seating Blacks in the rear of the restaurant, purposefully providing poor service, and requiring Blacks to make minimum purchases. Other recent examples of discrimination include a consistent pattern of bias against women and African Americans by car sales personnel in the Chicago area (Ayres, 1991), and the differential encouragement given to boys and girls in the classroom, putting the girls at a disadvantage (Sadker & Sadker, 1994).

In its most extreme form, discrimination may involve acts of aggression against group members (such as beatings, bombings), and even genocide. The systematic murder of 6 million Jews by the Nazis, the lynchings of Blacks in the Old South, and the "ethnic cleansing" in the former Yugoslavia are horrendous examples of discrimination. Such acts of violence are not limited to racial and ethnic minorities, however. According to the *Intelligence Report,* a newsletter published by the Southern Poverty Law Center (1997), hate crimes against gays and lesbians increased 260 percent from 1988 to 1996.

Although it is tempting to define discrimination in relation to prejudice, the two are conceptually distinct. A person who harbors prejudice may choose not to act overtly on those attitudes. For example, laws against discrimination may prevent overt discrimination, but as South African researcher John Duckitt (1992-1993) points out, subtle discrimination may still be present (e.g., voice tone, less eye contact, less friendliness, less verbal interaction).

Just as a prejudiced individual may not behave in a discriminatory fashion, so too may discriminatory acts not be based necessarily on prejudicial attitudes. For instance, the employment manager who implements a minimum height requirement of 5'9" for a job may not actually be prejudiced against women, but in effect, has discriminated against women. Similarly, the owner of a garage, who believes that women can do as good a job as men, may hire a male mechanic over an equally qualified female, only because he feels that customers may be reluctant to patronize a garage that has a female mechanic. This, too, is a case of discrimination without prejudice. Although these examples demonstrate that discrimination may occur without prejudice, such actions are hardly benign. In fact, discrimination (with or without prejudicial intent) is clearly illegal.

According to the U.S. Commission on Civil Rights (1981), discrimination may be classified according to two types: individual and institutional. **Individual discrimination** involves actions carried out by an individual, which may be either intentional (e.g., a landlord who refuses to rent to persons of color) or unintentional (e.g., the employment manager who arbitrarily sets a height requirement for a job position). **Institutional discrimination,** in contrast, is a systematic discrimination against a particular group of people. In the case of institutional discrimination, the institutions themselves become structured against certain groups of people. Institutional discrimination also may be either intentional (e.g., segregation of schools, or real estate agencies that steer Black homebuyers away from White housing areas) or unintentional (e.g., holding elections in a building without wheelchair accessibility).

## ➤ RELATIONSHIPS AMONG STEREOTYPING, PREJUDICE, AND DISCRIMINATION

Recognizing that stereotypes, prejudice, and discrimination are distinct constructs, social psychologists recently have become concerned with examining the relationships among these phenomena (Dovidio, Brigham, Johnson, & Gaertner, 1996; Stangor, Sullivan, & Ford, 1991; Eagly, Mladinic, & Otto, 1994). The general questions raised by these researchers are: How are stereotypes related to prejudice and discrimination? And how is prejudice related to discrimination?

Traditionally, researchers have assumed that stereotyping promotes prejudice, which promotes discrimination (Dovidio et al., 1996). In other words, beliefs about members of a social group are assumed to arouse liking or disliking for the group, which in turn dictates behavior toward group members. This way of viewing the relationships among stereotypes, prejudice, and discrimination certainly makes sense. However, judging from what we know about links between attitudes and behavior, perhaps links between stereotypes, prejudice, and discrimination are much more complex.

Attitude researchers have long known the difficulties of predicting behavior from attitudes. Quite frankly, researchers have not always found consistent relations between beliefs, attitudes, and behavior, prompting them to try to understand why and how such inconsistencies arise. Researchers in the areas of stereotyping, prejudice, and discrimination are now turning to the domain of attitude theory to account for the relationships among these constructs. Diane Mackie and Eliot Smith (1998a; 1998b) for instance, argue that there are many parallels between the conceptualizations of stereotypes, prejudice, and discrimination and the conceptualizations of beliefs, attitudes, and behaviors. As we shall see, this approach provides us with new insights as to links among stereotyping, prejudice, and discrimination.

### How Are Stereotypes Related to Prejudice and Discrimination?

Researchers who have studied stereotypes traditionally have assumed that our beliefs about social groups are a powerful determinant of our attitudes and behaviors toward members of these groups. As R.C. Gardner (1994, p. 16) aptly summarizes this position, "stereotypes are often considered the language of prejudice." Despite this assumption, surprisingly little empirical research has been devoted to studying the importance of stereotypes to understanding prejudice and discrimination.

In recent studies that have examined the relationship between stereotyping and prejudicial attitudes, researchers have considered not only the stereotypical traits associated with various social groups, but also whether the ascribed traits are evaluated positively or negatively (Esses et al., 1993; Stangor et al., 1994; Eagly et al., 1994). In one study, for example, Alice Eagly and her colleagues (1994, Experiment 1) asked participants to indicate their attitudes toward one of four target groups (women, men, Republicans, Democrats) along with 10 additional groups (e.g., Europeans, teenagers). The participants then were asked to list up to 10 characteristics they believed were typical of members of the group, and to evaluate each of the characteristics they had listed on a 7-point good-bad scale. The results showed that the participants' attitudes toward women, men, Democrats, and Republicans were significantly predicted by the evaluative content of their stereotypes about these groups.

A study by Victoria Esses and her colleagues (1993) also suggests that whether stereotypical beliefs are positively or negatively evaluated plays a significant role in determining prejudicial attitudes. These researchers asked students at the University of Waterloo to indicate their attitudes toward the group to which they belonged (English Canadians) and four out-groups: French Canadians, Aboriginals/Native Indians, Pakistanis, and Homosexuals. Not surprisingly, participants rated their own group most favorably ($M = 81.42$), followed by French Canadians ($M = 69.07$), Aboriginals/Native Indians ($M = 66.20$), Pakistanis ($M = 58.88$), and Homosexuals ($M = 44.13$).

In addition to providing their attitudes, students were asked to list the characteristics they associate with typical members of these groups. The students then were asked to rate the valence of each characteristic on a 5-point scale ranging from "very negative" (–2) to "very positive" (+2). Similar to Eagly et al., Esses and her colleagues found a significant relation between stereotypic beliefs and prejudice.

So what can we conclude from these studies? Stereotypes and prejudice do appear to be positively associated: In general, the more positively stereotypes are viewed, the more favorable attitudes are toward social groups.

Although social psychologists have examined the link between stereotypes and prejudice, John Dovidio and his colleagues (1996) point out that surprisingly little research has focused on the link between stereotypes and discrimination. The traditional assumption concerning a stereotype-behavior link has been that stereotypes influence the way people perceive others, which subsequently may guide interpersonal behaviors. According to Dovidio et al., however, research examining the relationship between stereotypes and racial discrimination has found only a modest relationship (if at all) between Whites' stereotypes of Blacks and measures of discrimination. They point out that certain features of the situation, such as norms, may be an important overriding factor that influences whether people act in accord with their stereotypic beliefs.

Thus, very little research demonstrates that stereotypes cause discrimination. Interestingly, however, Jost and Banaji (1994) recently proposed that stereotypes may be a consequence, rather than a cause, of discrimination. They argue that stereotypes stem from **system justification,** which they define as "the psychological process by which existing social arrangements are legitimized" (p. 2). In this view, then, disadvantaged groups are stereotyped in ways that justify their social position. For instance, women may be stereotyped as "nurturant" because of their role as child-bearers; similarly, Blacks may be stereotyped as "lazy" to explain their disadvantaged social status.

Although stereotypes may tell us a great deal about the relations between groups in society, the extent to which individuals' stereotypes relate to their behavior is modest at best. Perhaps this finding is not surprising in light of research that has examined the relationship between prejudice and discrimination.

## How Is Prejudice Related to Discrimination?

Just how important is prejudice as a cause of discrimination? When we typically think about the relationship between prejudice and discrimination, we commonly view the two as going hand in hand. However, as suggested earlier, prejudicial attitudes may not necessarily result in discriminatory behavior.

A classic study by LaPiere (1934) demonstrates dramatically that discrimination does not always follow from prejudice. Recognizing that anti-Asian sentiment was quite high in the early 1930s, LaPiere, a White male, decided to investigate the correspondence between prejudiced attitudes and actual behavior (i.e., discrimination). In a 3-month period, LaPiere traveled 10,000 miles around the United States with a Chinese couple, visiting 66 hotels and 184 restaurants. Only once were they ever refused service. Six months later, LaPiere sent a letter to each establishment asking whether they would serve Chinese patrons. Only about half of the establishments responded, and of those who did, 92 percent stated they *would not* accept Chinese as guests.

Why would prejudice be linked to discrimination at some times, but not others? In the actual situations, many elements come into play. First, other values—the desire to avoid seeming unkind or to avoid economic difficulty—may have outweighed the prejudice. Second, situational factors may have been influential in determining the proprietors' behavior. The fact that the Chinese couple was accompanied by a White man or that the couple did not fit the negative stereotype might also be reasons that the couple was not refused service.

A number of investigators have pursued this issue within the broader context of attitude-behavior discrepancy, and many psychologists and sociologists have questioned the assumption that attitudes influence behavior (e.g., Blumer, 1955; Deutscher, 1966; Kutner, Wilkins, & Yarrow, 1952). Moreover, many of these investigations assessed Whites' attitudes toward Blacks, which were then correlated with their behavior. In a study conducted during the 1950s, DeFleur and Westie (1958) asked prejudiced and nonprejudiced White students to participate in a nationwide campaign for racial integration by having their photograph taken with a Black person of the opposite sex, ostensibly to be distributed widely during the campaign. The study showed that prejudice was positively related to discrimination (i.e., unwillingness to sign the release form for the photographs to be used). However, a substantial number of the nonprejudiced persons refused to sign the release form, whereas a similar number of prejudiced persons did sign the release form. Similar studies support this finding that individuals' verbal attitudes do not necessarily predict their behaviors (Green, 1972; Linn, 1965; Rokeach & Mezei, 1966).

After extensively reviewing relevant studies on the attitude-behavior link, Wicker (1969) concluded that there is only a modest relationship between attitudes and behavior. In fact, Wicker found few studies in which the correlation between attitudes and behaviors exceeded +0.30, leading him to conclude that the link between attitudes and behavior is a weak one at best.

Challenged by Wicker's critique, many researchers have attempted to determine why attitudes may not necessarily correspond to behaviors. Fishbein and Ajzen (1975) have argued that the ability to predict behaviors from attitudes is determined partly by how the attitudes and behaviors are measured. For example, using general attitudes (e.g., attitudes toward Blacks) to predict specific behaviors (e.g., discrimination in housing) is not nearly as useful as using specific attitudes (e.g., attitudes toward Blacks moving into the neighborhood) to predict such behavior. Similarly, accuracy in predicting attitudes from behaviors is improved if more than one behavior is measured. Prejudice, for example, may be represented by a class of behaviors (e.g., not voting for minority candidates, not selling property to minorities, not hiring minorities, etc.), not just one single act.

It is not surprising, then, that generalized attitudes, such as prejudice toward Chinese persons, are not predictive of specific behaviors, such as refusing service to a well-dressed, well-spoken Chinese couple who happened to be accompanied by a distinguished-looking White man. Thus, prejudiced attitudes do not always lead to discrimination.

Now consider another possibility. Perhaps discrimination sometimes leads to prejudice. The notion that people often change their attitudes in response to how they have already behaved has received strong support in social psychological research (Eagly & Chaiken, 1993), and there is every reason to believe that this principle also applies to the correspondence between prejudice and discrimination. According to this perspective, discriminatory behaviors breed prejudice, largely because the prejudiced attitudes develop to rationalize or justify discrimination (Pettigrew, 1980; Raab & Liset, 1959). For example, Stanley Gaines and Edward Reed (1995) make explicit this assumption by arguing that prejudice and racism do not begin with false generalizations, but with the exploitation of a people or peoples:

> In the case of racism in the United States, a diverse group of peoples was stripped forcibly of home, property, and to some extent, culture and family . . . and brought into the cauldron of slavery. . . . This was not a simple mental process of erroneous generalization combined with aggressive feelings but rather a very real historical process of social, economic, and physical exploitation (p. 99).

Laboratory experiments reveal just such a connection between unfavorable actions and negative attitudes. For example, Worchel and Andreoli (1978) found that, compared to participants who were instructed to reward a man for right answers on a learning task, participants who instead delivered electric shocks for incorrect responses were more likely to dehumanize him. Not only were they less likely to remember individuating information about him, such as his name and physical characteristics, but they were more likely to depersonalize him by remembering group-related characteristics like his religion and race.

On a societal level, discriminatory practices do appear to determine prejudicial attitudes. Sociologist John Farley (1995) points out that the most dramatic changes in racial prejudice in the United States have occurred in the South since World War II. This effect, he suggests, is due to federal legislation and court orders that prohibited *overt* discrimination, which ultimately resulted in attitudes changing to become consistent with behavior. In short, a reduction in discrimination can cause a reduction in prejudice.

This leads us to the question, What came first, prejudice or discrimination? If prejudices develop to rationalize exploitation and oppression of less powerful groups, then prejudice is not "the" cause of discriminatory behavior; prejudice is merely a supporting mechanism. In reality, it is likely that cause and effect runs in both directions (Bobo, Kleugal, & Smith, 1997). Thus, to understand fully prejudice and discrimination, larger societal forces that shape majority-minority relations must be examined.

## ➤ MAJORITY AND MINORITY GROUPS

To whom are prejudice and discrimination typically directed? Frequently, minority groups are the targets of prejudicial beliefs and discriminatory behaviors. A **minority group** can be defined as any group that maintains a subordinate position in society, with less than its share of power and/or social status. In a classic definition, Louis Wirth (1945, p. 347) explicitly defined a minority group as "a group of people who, because of their physical or cultural characteristics, are singled out from others in the society in which they live for differential and unequal treatment and who therefore regard themselves as objects of collective discrimination." Thus, Wirth's definition emphasizes group consciousness and differential treatment.

The term "minority group" implies the existence of a **majority group,** a dominant group in society that enjoys greater privilege and more than its proportional share of power and/or social status. A majority group is usually in a position to exercise power over other groups in society.

In discussing majority and minority groups, a number of important points should be made. First, the physical or cultural traits upon which a minority is based is socially defined, indicating that these traits are perceived as socially relevant criteria in distinguishing among people. Thus, as Tajfel (1978) suggests, there is a difference between a "social group" and a "social category." For instance, red-haired people occupy a social category in which their defining feature is socially neutral and does not allow us to draw conclusions (rightly or wrongly) about them. However, if red hair were considered a meaningful distinguishing feature, such that red hair was deemed less desirable than blond, black or brown hair, then red-haired people might be singled out and treated differently. In this example, then, red-haired people would occupy the "social group" of minority.

Second, social psychologists define majority and minority groups in terms of *social power*, not group size. For this reason, some social scientists prefer to use the terms **dominant group** and **subordinate group,** rather than majority and minority group, to reflect this difference in social power. Although minority groups may sometimes be numerically smaller, this is not always the case. Two examples are readily apparent. Blacks in South Africa represent one example of a numerical majority that lacks social power. Over 80% of South Africans are Black, yet until recently, the White numerical minority controlled the political system. Blacks in South Africa today still occupy the lower occupational positions and have little economic power. Moreover, there is every reason to believe that the White minority will continue to have a disproportionate share of wealth and influence for many years.

Women in the United States represent another example of a numerical majority that is actually considered a minority. Women make up slightly more than half the population in the United States, yet the power structure of the United States remains heavily male dominated. Men earn, own, and control most of the wealth in the United States, and the overwhelming majority of high elected officials in the United States are men (Richardson, 1988). In 2000, for instance, women held 65, or 12.1%, of the 535 seats in the 106th U.S. Congress—9 of the 100 seats in the Senate and 56 of the 435 seats in the House of Representatives (Center for the American Woman and Politics, 2000).

Evidence of gender inequality also can be found in incomes. In 1998, women earned 73 percent of the income of similarly educated working men. At all levels of education between some high school and bachelor's degree, women were paid between 68 and 71 percent of men's earnings. Women with professional degrees earned about 61 percent of the pay of men (U.S. Bureau of the Census, 1999). Thus, from a social psychological point of view, women can be regarded a minority group.

Finally, another point to keep in mind in discussing majority and minority groups is this: The term "minority" can be applied to a variety of social groups. A minority group may be defined not only on the basis of race, ethnicity, or gender, but may also include other factors, such as sexual orientation, physical disability, age, and religion. Consequently, most of the principles of majority-minority relations can be applied to these groups. All of these groups, for example, have been targets of differential treatment in such areas as employment and housing. And members of these groups share a perception that they are somehow "different" from the dominant group, meeting the psychological criteria of "shared group consciousness" that defines a minority group (Tajfel, 1978; Wirth, 1948).

➤ STIGMAS

Prejudice and discrimination are directed toward stigmatized persons in general, which includes not only those groups that conventionally have been considered minorities (i.e., racial, ethnic, and religious groups), but also individuals who possess (or are believed to possess) some characteristic that is devalued in a particular context (Crocker, Major, & Steele, 1998). In a classic analysis, Erving Goffman (1963), a sociologist, traces the meaning of the word stigma to its Greek origins, whose meaning denotes "bodily signs designed to expose something unusual and bad about the moral status of the signifier" (p. 1). These signs were cut or burnt into the body to signify that the bearer was a criminal or a slave, someone to be avoided. Similarly, in Nazi Germany the "undesirables" were forced to wear emblems, such as the Star of David for Jews or the pink triangle for homosexuals, on their outer garments to signify their less than human status. Jews, homosexuals, gypsies, political dissidents, and other groups were stigmatized by the Nazis, and these emblems were the outward signs of this stigma.

Today the current meaning of the term **stigma** defines a person as "deviant, flawed, limited, spoiled, or generally undesirable" (Jones et al., 1984, p. 6) and serves to discredit the person in the eyes of others. Stigmas may or may not be physical: They may be "embedded in behavior, biography, ancestry, or group membership" (Jones et al., 1984, p. 6).

Goffman (1963) suggested that there are three broad types of stigmatizing conditions: (a) *tribal stigmas,* such as membership in devalued racial, ethnic, or religious groups, (b) *abominations of the body,* including physical deformities and disabilities, and (c) *blemishes of individual character,* such as addiction, homosexuality, and imprisonment.

As you can see, in our society numerous qualities can trigger stigmatization processes. A person who deviates from the cultural default of White, male, and heterosexual is commonly stigmatized, but so too are people who are disfigured, extremely unattractive, obese, addicted, mentally ill or retarded, or terminally ill. For these individuals, their stigmatizing condition may become a "master status," in which the person is defined in terms of that characteristic and treated accordingly. Put simply, once an individual is labeled as having a master status, the person is perceived only in terms of the stigma. Thus, the college student who happens to be deaf may never be described simply as "a student," but instead may be referred to as "the deaf student," or even "the deaf one." In our society, race, sex, and sexual orientation are master statuses along which all members can be categorized.

## ► THE RELATIONSHIP BETWEEN STIGMA AND PREJUDICE

How might processes relating to stigmatization compare to prejudice in general? There is no doubt that the stigmatized share many aspects in common with groups that are conventionally considered minorities (i.e., racial and ethnic minority groups). Both "minorities" and the stigmatized are often devalued in society, labeled deviant, and frequently are targets of stereotyping, prejudice, and discrimination (Goffman, 1963; Jones et al., 1986; Major & Crocker, 1993). In fact, sociologist Ruth Glass (1964) described minorities as being part of society, yet "not-belonging or not-quite-belonging" (p. 141). The same observation could be made of the stigmatized, particularly those visibly stigmatized like women and the disabled. In fact, a good deal of what has been written about racial minorities can also be applied to women, gay men and lesbians, and the disabled. Similar to racial minorities, all of these groups tend to elicit negative stereotypes and have experienced discrimination in such areas as employment and housing (Frable, 1993).

Researchers have generally assumed that stereotypes and prejudice directed toward one group are generalizable to another, and this assumption is reflected in their methodology. When researchers have studied prejudice, their focus typically has been on attitudes toward one group, whether the group is defined according to race, ethnicity, gender, age, sexual orientation, or disability. The reasoning behind this approach is that the processes of stereotyping and prejudice are similar and can be generalized to all groups (e.g., Taylor, 1981). But is this a valid assumption?

Gertrude Stein's famous dictum, "A rose is a rose is a rose" notwithstanding, not all prejudices are alike. Although prejudices are primarily intergroup and typically involve stereotypes, some stigmas (e.g., abominations of the body) may be more interpersonal and not critically involve stereotyping. Moreover, attitudes toward certain stigmatizing conditions—for example, obesity, terminal illnesses such as AIDS, disability, or mental illness—may differ uniquely from attitudes toward racial or ethnic groups. In the case of AIDS-related stigma, for example, part of the negative evaluations may stem from beliefs about the deviance of homosexuality and IV drug use, rather than concerns about the spread of the disease (Crandall et al.,1997; Devine, Plant, & Harrison, 1999; Herek, 1999; Herek & Capitanio, 1999). Social norms about expression of prejudice (Blanchard, Crandall, Brigham, & Vaughn, 1994; Monteith, Deneen, & Tooman, 1996), and the amount of experience with the groups (Pettigrew, 1997; Stephan & Stephan, 1984) are other variables that potentially may influence the nature of prejudice toward deviant groups in general.

Another characteristic that might differentiate among various forms of prejudice is whether the stigma is a "simple" stigma or a more "complex," ambivalent stigma. For example, Neuberg et al. (1994) notes that the male homosexuality stigma is "simple" in that it generally elicits negative affect and social discomfort. The disability stigma, in contrast, is considerably more complex in that it elicits a combination of social discomfort and sympathy (Goldstein & Johnson, 1997; Katz, Wackenhut, & Glass, 1986). As we shall see in Chapter 3, we are frequently ambivalent about some stigmatized groups (e.g., racial minorities, the disabled), but not others (e.g., the obese; Crandall, 1994). Thus, it is important to keep in mind that not all stigmatized groups are perceived as being equally negative. In fact, negative connotations of stigmatized groups are often reflected in perceptions of responsibility, providing an explanation for why criminals and homosexuals are perceived more negatively than the blind, the elderly, and amputees (Frable, 1993).

Finally, although racial and ethnic minorities and other stigmatized groups may elicit negative affect, the *type* of negative affect may be different. For example, someone who is prejudiced against Blacks may experience negative affect, but the affect may be "anger" or "hate" depending on the person and the social context. Negative affect evoked by certain other stigmatizing conditions (e.g., obesity, facial disfigurement, dwarfism) may be a different sort of affect, perhaps disgust, repugnancy, and revulsion. In fact, Smith (1994) suggests that the nature of the emotion experienced in the presence of stigmatized group members provides information about the intergroup context. For example, the disabled may evoke feelings of guilt, because of the benefits the dominant group receives; homosexuals may evoke feelings of disgust, because the dominant group is concerned with the expression of superiority; and finally, subordinate groups that demand favored treatment may evoke feelings of anger and resentment.

Nonetheless, stigmatizing others may serve functions similar to those served by stereotyping and prejudice in general (Snyder & Miene, 1994). Identifying a person with a particular category allows us to reduce complex social information to a manageable size. Of course, this categorization can occur along multiple dimensions, including race, gender, age, religion, and social class. But people are especially stigmatized when their membership in a category pervades all aspects of their social interactions, such that their category membership essentially assumes a "master status." Moreover, just as stereotypes serve a self-protective function by allowing perceivers to feel better about themselves, the stigmatization of others serves a similar function. In explaining the stereotypes of the elderly, for instance, Snyder and Miene (1994) argue that the tendency to blame the elderly themselves for their deficiencies protects young people from the realization that a similar fate will happen to them, assuming they live long enough. This notion is quite similar to Jones et al.'s (1984) description of the danger dimension of stigma (i.e, the anxiety the stigma evokes about our own vulnerability):

> The emaciated and dying cancer patient may make us starkly and disagreeably aware that a similar fate can befall us. The paraplegic blocked by stairs or the disoriented and confused blind person places upon us the burden of intervention and rescue. In fact, marked persons always seem to pose some form of threat, and it may be that danger, in its many forms, is the most fundamental characteristic of stigmatizing interactions (p. 66).

Similarly, Goffman (1963) writes:

> The stigmatization of those with a bad moral record clearly can function as a means of formal social control; the stigmatization of those in certain racial, religious, and ethnic groups has apparently functioned as a means of removing these minorities from various avenues of competition; and the devaluation of those with bodily disfigurements can perhaps be interpreted as contributing to a needed narrowing of courtship decisions (p. 139).

Thus, the stigmatization of others, like stereotypes, serves many functions, and may be associated with prejudice, discrimination, and oppression.

## ➤ IS PREJUDICE INEVITABLE?

In a course on the psychology of prejudice, students at some point in the class will ask, "Isn't it perfectly normal to be prejudiced toward someone or some group?" Students are not alone in asking this question. In recent years this issue of whether prejudice is inevitable has been raised by social scientists in many disciplines. One view is that prejudice is normal, necessary, and universal for all human beings. This viewpoint is reflected in two camps: Those researchers who argue that prejudice is rooted in our evolutionary history and those researchers who suggest that prejudice is an automatic and inevitable result of social categorization. The opposing perspective is that prejudice is not inevitable, and that people can circumvent prejudicial thinking by making a conscious decision to do so. Briefly, let's consider both viewpoints, beginning with the perspective that prejudice is a natural consequence of being human.

## Viewpoint One: Prejudice Is Inevitable

In a highly controversial article published in 1992, anthropologist Robin Fox argued that prejudice is a universal condition of humans, an adaptive response that has allowed us to survive as a species. Proceeding from a Darwinian framework, Fox suggests that stereotyping is a rapid form of reasoning that has been favored by natural selection: Such "prejudgement" is essential to decision making in uncertain circumstances.

Basically, Fox claims that (a) stereotyping is an intuitive mode of thought, and (b) that the intuitive mode often leads to adaptive judgments. To support his argument, Fox turns to a real-life example of rapid-fire reasoning in an uncertain situation. Bernhard Goetz (the White New Yorker who opened fire on Black youths who demanded money from him in the subway), Fox suggests, operated on the basis of a racial stereotype. Fox describes Goetz as "faced with alien warriors in a provocative situation" and choosing to attack because he was prejudiced. Fox continues with this vivid example by reminding us that Goetz is alive and that "his antagonists are in various states of disarray" (p. 146).

Fox hastens to add that he does not intend to justify Goetz's action, but that this tendency to "trust the familiar, suspect the unfamiliar" is deeply rooted in our evolutionary history. Unlike animals, however, human culture provides different ways of identifying "us" from "them," primarily through language, clothing, hairstyles, and yes, skin color.

From this perspective, then, stereotypes are viewed as automatic, built-in, even "natural," and our evolutionary history makes it inevitable that we will be prejudiced:

> The whole point of this argument has been to show that we have no choice but to think in stereotypes. That is what a lot of basic thinking is. . . . We have to come to terms with the idea that prejudice is not a form of thinking but that thinking is a form of prejudice (Fox, 1992, pp. 149, 151).

Psychologist Harold Fishbein (1996) concurs with this evolutionary viewpoint, arguing that prejudice and discrimination are rooted in the nature of primate and human subsistence groups. He argues that because "we are fundamentally tribal beings" we identify tribal members by the "badges" (language, dialect, dress, etc.) they display (p. 261). Consequently, we are genetically predisposed to favor in-group members over out-group members, which makes intergroup tensions likely to occur. Although acknowledging that this viewpoint suggests that prejudice and discrimination will always exist, Fishbein cautions that prejudice is not necessarily inevitable. Because our genetic/evolutionary heritage provides only a *predisposition* toward prejudice and discrimination, Fishbein reasons that we probably can overcome prejudicial tendencies, albeit with much effort. Fishbein goes on to say, however, that "the underlying pressures for prejudice and discrimination will always be with us" (p.268).

Other researchers agree that prejudice is inevitable, but for very different reasons. Cognitive psychologists have suggested that stereotyping and prejudice may be inevitable consequences of social categorization. According to this social-cognitive approach, categorization is a necessary feature of human functioning that allows us to simplify the complexities of our world. Just as biologists classify plants and animals into categories on the basis of certain criteria, so do we categorize persons we encounter on the basis of social features. In fact, many researchers suggest that we spontaneously attend to such salient features as race, gender, and age (Allport, 1954; Billig, 1985; Brewer, 1988; Hamilton, 1981; Stangor, Lynch, Duan, & Glass, 1992), and these physical features automatically form the basis of our social categories. Why do we automatically categorize individuals on the basis of these physical characteristics, but not others (e.g., styles of clothing)?

Rothbart and Taylor (1992) provide an interesting answer to this question. They suggest that categories that are perceived to be based on innate, biological differences are assumed to be unalterable, and as a result, are routinely and automatically used in perceiving others. Nonetheless, once we categorize someone as "disabled," "Black," or "female," stereotypes are then likely to be activated automatically, which in turn may influence our perceptions and interaction with that person (Macrae, Milne, & Bodenhausen, 1994). According to this view, then, prejudice stems from basic cognitive processes and appears to be inevitable. As Michael Billig (1985) succinctly summarized this perspective, "people will be prejudiced as long as they continue to think" (p. 81).

## Viewpoint Two: Prejudice Can Be Controlled

Not surprisingly, a number of social psychologists have questioned this pessimistic analysis of prejudice as "natural" and therefore inevitable (Fiske, 1992; Jackson, 1992). Patricia Devine (1989) believes that as a result of socialization in a society that is saturated with prejudice, we have knowledge of cultural stereotypes. But *knowledge* of a stereotype does not invariably lead to prejudice. Blacks, Devine argues, may be well acquainted with the stereotypes of African Americans, but this does not imply that they endorse such a view of their social group. Similarly, feminists may be aware of the stereotypes of women, but this does not by definition lead to prejudice against women. Thus, according to Devine, prejudice is not an inevitable result of socialization.

Devine argues against the inevitability of prejudice by drawing upon a critical distinction, often made by cognitive psychologists, between automatic and controlled processes (Posner & Snyder, 1975; Schneider & Shiffrin, 1977). *Automatic processes*, which are largely involuntary, involve the spontaneous activation of well-learned information from memory. *Controlled processes*, in contrast, involve voluntary, deliberative judgments that frequently relate to decision making and problem solving.

Devine, like other psychologists, recognizes that stereotypes may be automatically activated once we categorize someone along a particular dimension, such as race or gender (Dovidio, Kawakami, Johnson, Johnson, & Howard, 1997; Fazio, Jackson, Dunton, & Williams, 1995; Fiske, 1992). For example, when White Americans encounter an American Indian, American-Indian stereotypes may spontaneously come to mind, without an intention on their part.

Such spontaneous stereotypic reactions occur very rapidly, in milliseconds actually, and are not controllable because of our well-learned stereotypes about various social groups. Thus, in the presence of a member of a minority group, we may be unable to control our split-second reactions—perhaps, for example, thoughts linking that social group to criminal activity may spontaneously come to mind. But such a spontaneous initial reaction does not always influence subsequent judgments. In fact, what happens immediately *after* the automatic activation of a stereotype is indeed under our control (Fiske, 1992; Dovidio et al., 1997). Quite frankly, there are times that we might go beyond this automatic, stereotyped reaction and invoke controlled processes that "correct" for our initial stereotypic beliefs, and there are times that we might be content with our initial negative reaction.

To explain when people might be likely to "correct" for their spontaneously activated stereotypes, Devine suggests that people's *personal beliefs* are a crucial factor in determining whether the automatic activation of a stereotype leads to prejudice. If people's personal beliefs are discrepant from the stereotype, then they may consciously decide to inhibit and control the activation of the stereotype. Specifically, Devine proposes that individuals who are low in prejudice—those whose personal beliefs are inconsistent with the stereotype—are more motivated to control and suppress their initial, automatic reactions. For individuals high in prejudice, however, their personal beliefs are congruent with the automatically activated stereotypes. Consequently, high-prejudiced people will be unlikely to "correct" for their initial, negative judgments, leading them to respond to a minority member in a way consistent with the cultural stereotype.

From Devine's perspective, then, prejudice is like an overlearned response that can be unlearned. But much like breaking a bad habit, inhibiting prejudicial thinking requires conscious and deliberate attention. The implication of Devine's perspective is this: Although individuals may be aware of stereotypes due to their socialization in a racially divided society, individuals may consciously decide that prejudice is personally unacceptable and deliberately renounce prejudicial thinking and responding.

In his book *The Racist Mind*, psychologist Raphael Ezekiel (1995) eloquently expresses sentiments similar to Devine's:

> Imagine growing up next to a cement factory, and imagine the cement dust inevitably becoming a part of your body. As we grow up within a society that is saturated in white racism, year after year we pass through interactions in which white racist conceptions are an unspoken subtext.... We cannot live from day to day without absorbing a certain amount of white racism into our thoughts.... It is important to discover the subtle ways our culture's racism has affected our thinking: to identify those habits of thought and learn how to keep them from influencing us (p. 322).

## ➤ CONCLUSION

Writing about the complexities of prejudice in his classic book *The Nature of Prejudice* (1954), Gordon Allport noted that:

It required years of labor and billions of dollars to gain the secrets of the atom. It will take a still greater investment to gain the secrets of man's irrational nature. It is easier, someone has said, to smash an atom than a prejudice (p. xv).

Despite the difficulty of the challenge, social psychologists have continued to address the following fundamental questions: Why does prejudice exist? What social conditions foster such negative views of others? And perhaps most importantly, how can prejudice be eradicated?

These are questions that cannot be answered definitively in this first chapter. But in the chapters that follow, we will heed Gordon Allport's advice and view prejudice through many different lenses: historical, cultural, and psychological, to name just a few. Because prejudice has multiple causes, Allport (1954, p. 208) reminds us "there is no master key. Rather, what we have at our disposal is a ring of keys, each of which opens one gate of understanding."

In Chapter 2, we will use an historical and sociocultural lens to examine three forms of prejudice—racism, sexism, and antigay prejudice. By taking on this perspective, we'll learn how visibly identifiable characteristics, such as race and gender, and a less salient characteristic, such as sexual orientation, have become defining criteria upon which individuals are excluded from various social opportunities.

# 2

# Racism, Sexism, and Antigay Prejudice

➤ INTRODUCTION

Suppose you meet a 70-year-old White woman who owns a condo along the gulf coast of Florida. She speaks with a strong Southern accent, dresses expensively but conservatively, and wears glasses. Any of these distinguishing qualities may influence your perception of this person—for example, you easily may categorize her on the basis of her gender, race, age, clothing style, or perceived social class. But which distinguishing features will be most influential in your impressions?

Several factors may influence why you may attend to some dimensions, but not others. Obviously, easily visible surface features will exert some influence on a perceiver's judgments about a person. Research suggests that we do spontaneously categorize individuals on the basis of immediately apparent features (Stangor, Lynch, Duan, & Blass, 1992). Because age, sex, and skin color are highly salient features, these features are almost always attended to and remembered, even without explicit instructions to do so (Brewer, 1988; Fiske & Neuberg, 1990; Stangor & Lange, 1994). But why do we attend to these features, and not other equally visible features, such as clothing style? Put simply, age, sex, and skin color are perceived to be more informative about the underlying personality of individuals, because we generally assume that people who share a social category are similar to each other in many respects.

In addition, any characteristics about individuals that make them "stand out" in some way will attract increased attention (Fiske, 1980; Taylor & Fiske, 1978). For example, in a group of elderly men, the gender of the 70-year-old woman may be the distinguishing feature that influences your impression, rather than her age or her Southern accent. Or if our hypothetical woman is in a crowd of relatively young women, her age will predominate over the categories "Southern" or "female." Thus, to some extent, how we categorize and subsequently form impressions of others may depend upon the salience of their characteristics.

Finally, whether a person belongs to an unusual social group may determine which characteristics are especially attended to and remembered. According to Smith and Zarate (1992), certain person characteristics may be perceived as the norm within a particular culture, and these dimensions are used as a basis on which to categorize others who deviate from that norm. They argue that White racial identity, male gender, heterosexual orientation, young age, and nondisabled status are the "cultural default values" in our society, and that any departure from these categories will attract attention and form the basis of categorizing others. Simply categorizing others on dimensions in which they differ from the "White male norm" is not prejudice. However, such categorization easily may lead to stereotypic judgments, prejudicial attitudes, or discriminatory treatment.

In American society certain deviations from the perceived norm traditionally have been associated with prejudice and discrimination at both an individual and a societal level. Cultural and social factors shape the meaning that is given to both visibly distinguishing characteristics, such as race and gender, or less salient characteristics like sexual orientation. All of us can be categorized according to our race, sex, and sexual orientation, but it is only for those whose categorization deviates from the cultural norm that their "difference" becomes socially meaningful. Thus, being Black may be perceived as less "normal" than being White, due to the numerical infrequency of Blacks relative to Whites and the historical dominance of Whites in our society. Consequently, race will be a more defining feature for Black individuals than for Whites. Similarly, being female or being gay may be perceived as less "normal" than being male or heterosexual. Once individuals are classified as deviant or generally undesirable, they are stigmatized in the larger society and everything about them is interpreted in terms of their "master status" (Frable, 1993).

The primary objective of this chapter is to explore three different forms of prejudice based upon departures from the "cultural default": **racism,** which is prejudice based upon race; **sexism,** which is prejudice based upon sex; and **antigay prejudice,** which is prejudice based upon sexual orientation. In discussing each of these forms of prejudice, this chapter will draw upon other disciplines, such as history and anthropology, to place contemporary conflicts over race, gender, and sexual orientation in context.

The issue of racism will be addressed first, with a focus on defining "race," "racism," and distinguishing between individual, institutional, and cultural racism. Embedded within this discussion is an acknowledgement that race is a social construction. Following this discussion of racism, we will examine sexism, with a particular emphasis on how gender is socially constructed. We will review contemporary beliefs about women and men and discuss whether women as a group are devalued relative to men. Finally, we will consider antigay prejudice, with an examination of the social construction of sexuality, and then we will focus on attitudes toward gays and lesbians, discrimination against gays and lesbians, and gay people's struggle for their civil rights.

➤ UNDERSTANDING RACISM

> *"The world is basically run by White people. If you're trying to move up in the world, it's hard when the person you have to go to thinks you're going to steal and not work hard for what you get."*
>
> *Levin & Dyer (1998)*

Those are the words of a 16-year-old Black high-school junior who recently participated in a focus group, comprised of Black and White teenagers in Pittsburgh, Pennsylvania, on race relations. Both White and Black teens agreed on many issues. All participants, regardless of race, shared the beliefs that the news media tend to show negative images of Black people, or that job opportunities are better for Whites than Blacks. But some perceptions were split along racial lines. For example, the perception that Whites are biased against people of color, that Blacks are unfairly stereotyped, and that Blacks are not treated as courteously as Whites in stores was a familiar theme that emerged among the Black participants in the focus group. The White teens, however, perceived racism as something that happened in the past, before and during the Civil Rights years, such as when a state governor personally blocked the doorway of a university to prevent the admission of a Black student or when crosses were burned on the lawns of Black persons as a perilous warning.

The Black teens who participated in this forum on racial issues perceived racism as something that continues to occur in the present. Most of the Black teens were acquainted with racism at a personal level, in terms of prejudicial remarks or behaviors directed toward them. Perhaps because of their young age, few of these teens identified racism at a macro-level, which includes institutional practices—within schools, businesses, and other organizations—that subordinate individuals of a given race.

To better understand the nature of racism in all of its forms, let us begin at the most basic level by considering what is meant by the term race. Ironically, this is a term that most of us are acquainted with, but few of us fully understand.

## What Is Race?

Susie Guillory Phipps, the wife of a White businessman in Louisiana, went to court in the 1980s to change her racial classification on her birth certificate from "colored" to "White." Phipps, who "appears" White, is the descendant of a Black woman and an 18th-century White plantation owner. The state of Louisiana defines race on the basis of "blood"; that is, a person is considered Black if he or she is one-thirty-second Black by blood. What this means is that if a person is the descendant of one ancestor who was classified as Black as far back as five generations ago, then that person, by law, is designated as Black. In Phipps's case, that small amount of African ancestry was enough to warrant her classification as Black; she lost her case against the state of Louisiana (Marcus, 1983).

This example illustrates the elusiveness of the concept of race. In popular usage, the term race has been used to categorize a wide range of people—from the entire species (the "human race"), to a group of people based upon religion and culture (the

"Jewish race"), to a group of people based upon skin color (the "Caucasian race"), or to those Adolf Hitler referred to as the racially pure (the "Aryan race"). None of these examples of "race" are truly accurate, because as we shall see, race is a social, rather than a biological, construct.

RACE AS A BIOLOGICAL CONSTRUCTION    Many individuals erroneously assume that race is an immutable biological given, defined by physical characteristics such as skin color, hair texture, eyelid form, and other facial features. The concept of "race" is so ingrained in our society that if you were to tell a neighbor that race is a myth, you would be readily dismissed as a fool. But the attempt to classify people on the basis of purely physical or biological concepts has been all but abandoned by scientists today, largely because of the ambiguities inherent in the term "race."

Traditionally, the concept of race has been approached from a biological perspective, assuming that humans may be classified on the basis of physical characteristics that distinguish one group of people from another. However, this notion that human beings can be partitioned into discrete types based upon certain hereditary characteristics has proved futile for two reasons. First, geneticists, anthropologists, and other scientists have been unable to agree on the physical characteristics that determine the racial categories, resulting in the selection of differing physical characteristics that are said to be the markers of racial classifications. Depending upon who is doing the classifying, the racial taxonomies historically have emphasized anatomical features (e.g., skin color, hair texture, and facial structures), blood composition (e.g., distribution of ABO blood types), physical stature, and even brain size (Marks, 1995). Thus, selection of physical traits to demarcate groups of people is purely arbitrary, resulting in disagreement among social and biological scientists about something as basic as a definition of the term "race."

Also adding to the confusion over the term "race" is the fact that physical differences that may be used to define race are not discrete, but in reality, often blur or overlap. In the United States, skin color is often viewed as the defining trait of race. But skin color, which is based upon the combination of four or five genes, comes in varying shades on a light-dark continuum. As evident in the example of Susie Guillory Phipps, some "Black" people have skins as light or lighter than some "White" people. Recognizing this fact, racial classification based upon skin color (and any other physical characteristics for that matter) can be confusing and, it seems, quite arbitrary.

This disagreement among scientists about which biological features constitute race, combined with the fact that the physical characteristics between the races are not sharply defined, contributes to a lack of agreement among experts as to how many so-called races there are in the human population. Estimates of the number of racial groups have varied widely from the popular notion of three—Caucasoid, Mongoloid, and Negroid—to perhaps four or five, or to as many as 37 (Loehlin, Lindzey, & Spuhler, 1975; Stringer & McKie, 1996). In fact, summarizing decades of anthropological research, Steve Molnar (1992) concludes:

The number of races and their boundaries remains a subject of dispute partially because of the lack of agreement on which traits identify a person's racial identity. Just what constitutes a race is a difficult question to answer, because one's classification usually depends on the purpose of the classification (p. 21).

This excerpt illustrates an important fact: Race, as a purely biological concept, is virtually meaningless.

RACE AS A SOCIAL CONSTRUCTION    Although from the biological and anthropological view the concept of race has no scientific meaning at all, Marks (1995) argues that Americans retain a cultural tendency to "see" discretely different races: "whites" (Caucasians), "blacks" (African Americans), "yellows" (Asian Americans), and perhaps "reds" (Native Americans). But the fact that we retain an interest in classifying people on the basis of physical dimensions demonstrates that race has enormous cultural significance. In the words of Yolanda Moses, past president of the American Anthropological Association, "everyone believes that races exist, and we all function as if they did" (Bronner, 1998). This suggests an important fact: *Race is a socially constructed concept,* with the physical characteristics used to classify people into racial types varying from one society to another.

In the United States, a person is socially—and in some states, legally—defined as "Black" if he or she has a traceable amount of Black ancestry. What is considered a "traceable amount" may vary depending upon who is doing the classifying, but a typical definition of many states (like Indiana and Missouri) was that a person is defined as Black if one great-grandparent was Black, regardless of how that person looks. What this means, of course, is that one-eighth of Black ancestry is enough to define one as Black, whereas seven-eighths of White ancestry is insufficient to define one as White!

This "one drop of blood rule" represents the American folk concept of "blood," and falls under a classificatory strategy called *hypodescent* (Hirschfeld, 1996). According to hypodescent, children of mixed parentage are always assigned the status of the subordinate parental category. For instance, children of one "White" parent and one "Black" parent—regardless of their physical appearance—are considered "Black" in the United States. That hypodescent tells us little about the physical appearance of a person, but more about the power and social status of the parent, is made explicit by Madison Grant, a leader in the eugenics movement, in his 1916 book, *The Passing of the Great Race:*

> The cross between a white man and an Indian is an Indian: the cross between a white man and a negro is a negro; the cross between a white man and a Hindu is a Hindu; and the cross between any of the three European races and a Jew is a Jew (p. 16).

Perhaps the clearest way to demonstrate that race is a social construction is to contrast the American racial classification strategy with that of Brazil, a society that has a much more complex system of classification. Although the American folk taxonomy uses hypodescent to classify race, in the absence of information about ancestry, people in the United States rely upon skin color as a marker for race. In Brazilian society, however, the pigment of a person's skin is not the single determinant of racial classification. In addition to skin color, other physical features such as eye color and hair texture are used to describe the "tipos" (the Portuguese word that corresponds to "races"). Thus, numerous racial terms are used in Brazilian society to describe a series of physical features. Proceeding along the light to dark continuum, for example, a *loura* is a person with very light skin color, blond hair, blue or green eyes, and a narrow nose and lips. *Branca* is the term for "white," but many Brazilians who are classified as such in Brazil are often surprised that they are considered "non-White" in the United States. A *branca* has light skin color, eyes of any color, and hair of any color and texture except tight curly. A *morena* has dark eyes, dark wavy or curly hair, tan skin, and a nose and lips that are full. A *mulata* has tight curly hair, and darker hair colors and skin colors, whereas a *preta* looks very much like a *mulata* but has darker brown skin, broad nose, and thick lips. Other terms that may be used include *sarara* (light-skinned, tight curly blond or red hair, broad nose, thick lips) and *cabo verde* (straight black hair, dark skin, dark eyes, narrow nose and lips).

The differences in racial categorizing between Brazilian and American societies demonstrate the arbitrariness of racial categorizing. In a wonderful metaphor, psychologist Jefferson Fish (1995) argues that race is like an avocado, which may be classified as a vegetable or fruit, depending upon who's doing the classifying. People in the United States classify an avocado as a vegetable, he says; it is primarily eaten in salads. Brazilians, in contrast, insist the avocado is a fruit; they eat it for dessert topped with sugar. In a similar way, Fish suggests that some people, who perhaps may be classified as Black in the United States, may change their racial classification by getting on a plane and going from the United States to Brazil, which has a more nuanced racial taxonomy that acknowledges the subtleties of people's physical features. Like the avocado, a person's physical appearance does not change, but the classification does.

## Why Is Skin Color Socially Marked?

> "The first difference which strikes us is that of colour. And is this difference of no importance? Is it not the foundation of a greater or less share of beauty in the two races?"
>
> Thomas Jefferson, Notes on the State of Virginia (1787)

This focus on the differences between American and Brazilian racial taxonomies brings us to the following question: Why are some physical characteristics, such as skin color, considered crucial in distinguishing among groups of people in the United States, whereas other characteristics, such as eye color, seldom are? And we can ask this same question about other differences that have been considered critical in categorizing people. Why might religion be an important distinguishing factor? Why ethnicity? Why sexual orientation?

Clearly these questions cannot be answered strictly in biological terms; instead they require historical and sociological analyses. In the case of skin color, the pigment of a person's skin has no inherent meaning. But skin color has become "marked" in our society. According to Morris (1996), after the institution of New World slavery, skin color became the principal means of distinguishing between persons of European and African origin—in essence, skin color became a mark of "free" (White) and slave (Black). Linked to skin color was a theory about the psychological and behavioral differences between Europeans and Africans. This is not surprising because once a dominant group exploits another group of peoples, the dominant group develops a theory of group differences that *justifies* why it is only "natural" for the subordinate group to be exploited. In justifying the enslavement or oppression of another group, the dominant group attaches social meaning to the differences that exist between their group and the subordinate group (Gaines & Reed, 1995; Smedley, 1997). To justify slavery, for example, Europeans depicted Africans as "primitive," even subhuman, and in every way inferior beings. Thomas Jefferson (1782), who held anti-slavery sentiments but also was a slaveowner, was a prolific writer about the inferiority of Africans that justified their harsh treatment:

> They secrete less by the kidneys, and more by the glands of their skin, which gives them a very strong and disagreeable odour . . . They are more ardent after their females: but love seems with them to be more an eager desire, than a tender delicate mixture of sentiment and sensation . . . in memory they are equal to whites, in reason much inferior . . . in imagination they are dull, tasteless, and anomalous . . . I advance it therefore . . . that the blacks, whether originally a different race, or made distinct by time and circumstances, are inferior to whites.

As we shall soon see, such beliefs in the inherent superiority and inferiority of different groups based upon their genetic inheritance form the basis of racism. But before turning to this issue, let's consider a concept closely related to race.

## What Is Ethnicity?

Ethnicity is a relatively new concept, and according to Nathan Glazer and Daniel Moynihan (1975), the term did not even appear in standard English dictionaries until the 1960s. W. Lloyd Warner was perhaps the first social scientist to use the term "ethnicity" to refer to a group of people, recognized by themselves or others as a distinct social group, on the basis of cultural characteristics (Feagin & Feagin, 1996). Thus, ethnicity traditionally has been defined on the basis of such cultural characteristics as nationality, language, customs, and religion (Van den Berghe, 1967), whereas race usually has been defined on the basis of immutable physical characteristics.

More recently, social scientists question whether "race" and "ethnicity" are as easily distinguished from each other as is commonly assumed. For example, populations with similar physical appearances may have different ethnic identities (Serbs and Croats in Bosnia, Hutus and Tutsis in Rwanda, Catholics and Protestants in Ireland). Conversely, populations with different physical appearances may have a common ethnic identity. For example, many Caribbean Islanders have ancestral roots in different parts of Africa, Asia, or Europe, yet everyone on a particular island is considered, for example, a Jamaican or a Trinidadian, and so on.

Also blurring the distinction between race and ethnicity is the fact that many groups now defined as ethnic groups were once defined as races. In the early twentieth century in the United States, many immigrant groups representing different nationalities or religions (e.g., Poles, Italians, Jews, Romanians) were thought to be racial groups that were distinct from the majority White population. Today, of course, these groups are now seen as ethnic groups that are included in the majority White population.

As a result of the conflicting usage of the terms race and ethnicity, and the fact that race as a biological concept lacks scientific validity, many social scientists now recommend dispensing entirely with the term "race" in favor of "ethnicity" (Montagu, 1963; Phinney, 1996). Interestingly, the American Anthropological Association (AAA) recently advocated that the U.S. Government phase out the use of the term "race" in the collection of federal data (Overbey, 1997). Because the concept of race is a social construction with no basis in biology, the AAA recommends simply eliminating the term "race" and replacing it with a more correct term, such as "ethnic origins."

For the purposes of this book, then, the term **ethnic group** will be used in a broad manner to define groups characterized by a common language, religion, customs, and perhaps most importantly, ancestral origins. Thus, African Americans, Asian and Pacific Islander Americans, Latinos, and Native Americans most accurately represent different ethnic groups of color, rather than different races per se. However, keep in mind that these broad ethnic groupings can be expanded by dividing the Hispanic and Asian ethnic groups into subgroups. For instance, "Asian Americans" is a broad grouping, comprised of people from different countries of origin (e.g., Japan, Korea, Vietnam, etc.) reflecting multiple languages and customs. Similarly, "Hispanic" represents people from numerous countries (e.g., Mexico, Cuba, Panama, etc.), who speak various languages and have significantly different customs.

## What Is Racism?

**Racism** may be defined as any attitude, action, or institutional arrangement that results in the subordination of another group based ostensibly upon group-linked physical characteristics. Thus, racism involves prejudice and/or discrimination and is defined primarily in terms of the consequences to the subordinated group. If the consequence of a particular action is that one ethnic group is favored over another, then that action, whether it was intentional or unintentional, may appropriately be described as racist.

Racism as an ideology, or belief system, rests upon the following assumptions:

1. Humans differ on the basis of their genetic inheritance.
2. These biological differences are directly linked to intellectual and psychological characteristics.
3. Because of these biologically based differences, some groups are innately superior to others.

Thus, such racist ideology assumes that differences among ethnic groups are innate and reflected in intellectual and personality differences between groups. This type of reasoning is based upon **biological essentialism,** which purports that racial differences are the inevitable consequences of differences in biology. This idea is clearly reflected in a statement made by anthropologist Vincent Sarich. According to Sarich (Selvin, 1991), referring to supposed differences in athleticism between the races:

"There is no white Michael Jordan, one of the greatest basketball players ever to play the game, nor has there ever been one." Presumably this anthropologist is implying that Blacks as a group are naturally superior to Whites in basketball, yet such reasoning is clearly rooted in a racist belief system. It is only a short journey from making claims about a group's natural *superiority* to making claims about a group's natural *inferiority*.

Frequently, racist ideology has been elevated to a science by scholarly writers who have attempted to prove empirically that some ethnic groups are, in fact, biologically inferior to others. In the 19th century, this "scientific racism" proliferated in the field of craniometry—literally the measuring of skulls. Dr. Samuel Morton, the scientist who founded the field, published many studies on the sizes of human skulls, offering "evidence" that matched the prejudices of his day: The Negro had a smaller brain than Whites, with Indians in the middle. Moreover, Morton argued that a similar ranking of brain sizes was possible within the White group, with Anglo-Saxons on top, Jews in the middle, and Hindus at the bottom (Gould, 1981).

Although such arguments may seem far-fetched today, some scientists are still debating "who's on top, who's on bottom." Recently psychologist J. Philipe Rushton (1995, 1996), who argues that there is an indisputable correlation between brain size and intelligence, has calculated the average brain sizes of different races while controlling for body weight. In general, Rushton argues that his calculations have affirmed the innate intellectual superiority of Whites over Blacks. In contrast to earlier studies but in harmony with popular stereotypes about intelligence, Rushton calculated that the average brain size of Asian males exceeds that of Whites. Rushton also reported that women have smaller average brain size than men, even though women do not have lower average IQs. Needless to say, Rushton's arguments have provoked a storm of protest from other psychologists. Rushton's detractors have called into question both his analyses (Peters, 1995) and his interpretations (Yee, Fairchild, Weizmann, & Wyatt, 1993). Regarding Rushton's analyses, some researchers have pointed out that brain size correlates not only with body weight, but with age and nutrition, which Rushton failed to take into consideration (Marks, 1995; Peters, 1995). And, of course, some critics have questioned Rushton's interpretations of his findings (Marks, 1995; Stringer & McKie, 1996; Yee et al., 1993). For example, can brain size really be equated with intelligence in humans? And what benefits necessarily accrue from larger brains? In the words of anthropologist Jonathan Marks (1995), "for all we know, the sole advantage to a human of having a big skull over a small skull would come in a head-butting contest" (p. 272).

As you can imagine, Rushton's arguments are highly controversial and have not been well received in the scientific community. But it appears that ideological racism continues to masquerade as science even today.

## Types of Racism

Racism manifests itself in many ways: overtly and covertly, intentionally and unintentionally, and importantly, individually and collectively. Accordingly, social scientists find it useful to distinguish between several forms of racism.

INDIVIDUAL RACISM   **Individual racism** refers to attitudes, behaviors, and beliefs of individuals that result in unequal treatment of individuals on the basis of their racial or ethnic group. Individual racism, as a concept, focuses on attitudes and behaviors at an individual level. For example, a person who believes in the superiority of his or her own ethnic group, based on presumed biological differences, would be considered a racist.

INSTITUTIONAL RACISM   Stokely Carmichael and Charles Hamilton (1967) distinguished between individual racism and **institutional racism,** which is a pattern of racism embodied in the policies and practices of social institutions—the educational system, the legal system, the economic system, family, state, and religion—that has a negative impact upon certain ethnic groups:

> When White terrorists bomb a church and kill five Black children, that is an act of individual racism . . . But when in the same city—Birmingham, Alabama—five hundred Black babies die each year because of lack of proper food, shelter and medical facilities, and thousands more are destroyed and maimed physically, emotionally, and intellectually because of conditions of poverty and discrimination in the Black community, that is a function of institutional racism (p. 4).

This concept of institutional racism, then, shifts the focus from the individual to societal practices that have negative consequences for the subordinated group. Institutional racism, like individual racism, may be intentional or unintentional, overt or covert, but it functions to dominate, exploit, and systematically control members of the oppressed group.

What are some examples of institutionalized racism today? Security officers at airports often scrutinize Middle-Eastern passengers because they meet the "profile" of a terrorist. Mortgage loan discrimination, unemployment and underemployment for people of color, and more severe law enforcement policies for people of color are just a few examples of how social institutions play a critical role in continuing racial and ethnic inequality.

CULTURAL RACISM   Cultural racism, according to James Jones (1988), contains elements of both individual and institutional racism. **Cultural racism** refers to a devaluation of another racial or ethnic group's culturally different values and modes of behavior. Such cultural racism is reflected in beliefs that the subordinate group's problems (i.e., lower educational attainment, higher unemployment, lower socioeconomic status, etc.) can be attributed to their "inferior" cultural characteristics. Albert Ramirez (1988), for example, argues that Latinos are often viewed as responsible for their plight—that members of the dominant group believe that if Latinos would adopt Euro-American values (i.e., become more success-oriented, achievement-oriented, future-oriented, etc.), then their problems would cease. This belief that "our way is the best way" (Jones, 1988, p. 132) is also reflected in a tendency to ignore the achievements and contributions of another ethnic group in education.

## Summary

In summary, these three kinds of racism demonstrate that racism is not simply an individual problem, but a societal problem stemming from institutional policies and practices designed to maintain racial and ethnic inequality. Racism is multifaceted and manifests itself in myriad ways: overtly and covertly, intentionally and unintentionally, and individually and collectively.

Building upon analyses of race relations in the United States, many researchers have attempted to compare the plight of other social groups, such as women, to minority ethnic groups such as African Americans. Are there similarities in the nature of discrimination among these groups? Are racism and sexism similar processes?

➤ ## UNDERSTANDING SEXISM

If by *minority group* we refer to any group that maintains a subordinate position in society, with less than its share of power and/or social status, then females might be considered a minority group even though they constitute a numerical majority. This is the case because women have been excluded from political and economic power and have been subject to discrimination in such areas as employment and education.

Although overt sex discrimination is illegal in many countries, subtle forces continue to operate that disadvantage women. A comparison of women's to men's earnings show that overall women earn only 73 cents for every dollar paid to men (U.S. Bureau of the Census, 1999). Women from ethnic minorities fare even worse: In 1998 African-American women earned 63 cents for every dollar paid to men, and Hispanic women averaged just 54 cents (U.S. Department of Labor, 1999). Thus, women of color experience racial discrimination along with gender discrimination.

When controlling for education and length of service, men still earn more money than women (Reskin & Padavic, 1994; Stroh, Brett, & Reilly, 1992), and they are more quickly promoted even when they receive lower performance evaluations than their female counterparts (Gupta, Jenkins, & Beehr, 1983). The power structure of the United States remains heavily male-dominated, with men holding nearly all of the highest positions in both the public and private sector. Women, as a group, are concentrated in clerical, nursing, or service positions, all of which are low-paying, low-prestige jobs (Martin, 1992). Even in these female-dominated occupations, men may be paid more. For example, a recent study showed that the 1998 median salary for female nurses was $38,168 and for male nurses, it was $40,248 (U.S. Department of Labor, 1995). The consequence of such exclusion is gender inequality, with the result that men enjoy greater power, prestige, and wealth than women do.

In some ways, perhaps, **sexism**—which may be defined as any attitude, action or institutional arrangement that subordinates a person on the basis of his or her sex—has been around longer than any other form of prejudice. Although there are some important parallels between sexism and racism, there also are some important differences. First, let's consider some of the similarities between racism and sexism, in terms of how gender, like race, is a social construction and how science has been used to justify and rationalize inequality between the sexes.

## Gender as a Social Construction

The terms *sex* and *gender* are often used interchangeably, but social scientists prefer to make a distinction between these two concepts (Deaux, 1998; Richardson, 1988; Unger & Crawford, 1998). The term **sex** refers to characteristics of an individual that are rooted in biology, such as the chromosomal and anatomical structures that characterize the categories of male and female. In contrast, **gender** refers to the culturally agreed-upon characteristics that are considered appropriate for men and women. Gender is achieved by a host of behaviors and cues, such as styles of clothing, nonverbal behaviors, occupational preferences, and social roles. Thus, sex is a biological construction, whereas gender is a social construction.

There are many reasons why social scientists believe gender is socially constructed. First, we "do" gender everyday without thinking about it, and the enactment of gender will often vary according to the social context. Consider how you displayed gender today. If you are female, did you dress in "feminine" clothes today, wear cosmetics and jewelry? And if you are male, did you open a door for a woman today? And while you are reading now, are your legs apart rather than crossed at the knee? As males and females, are there some instances when you're more concerned about your gender presentation than usual? Perhaps when you're wanting to make a good impression on a date? Because people choose to vary their gender-related behaviors with social circumstances, gender is a dynamic, rather than static, phenomenon.

Further, the fact that cultures have different conceptions about gender supports this view of gender as a social construction. Although some cross-cultural similarities exist in beliefs about gender (Best & Williams, 1990), gender constructions do differ across cultures. In Western cultures, gender has been divided into two categories, male and female, based upon biological attributes. Other cultures, like several northwestern American Indian societies, recognize another gender category, *berdache*. According to Williams (1986), the berdache are individuals who, although biologically male, dress or engage in activities of the other gender. The berdache are accorded special status within their society, often performing important ceremonial roles in many Native-American religions. Thirty-three North-American Indian groups recognized females who assume the third gender role. Dubbed "amazons" (Williams, 1986) or "Two-Spirits" (Bonvillain, 1998) by many anthropologists, these biological women dressed as men, married women, and also performed spiritual duties for their community.

The Navajo, in particular, recognized many gender categories: male, female, males who act like females, females who act like males, and intersexed (male and female) people (Martin & Voorhies, 1975). Although intersexed people are no new phenomenon, Anne Fausto-Sterling (1998) notes that Western culture is so committed to the idea there there are only two sexes that any deviations are immediately treated surgically.

And finally, beliefs about the nature of males and females vary across cultures. In Western cultures, for example, we believe that men are more aggressive than women. But in many societies, like that on Vanatinai, a small island off the coast of New Guinea, sex differences in aggression do not exist (Lepowsky, 1993).

These examples illustrate that the meanings attached to being male or female—in terms of beliefs about men and women and their activities and personality traits—are socially constructed and not necessarily rooted in biological differences. Nonetheless, as Sandra Bem (1993) points out, certain beliefs about women and men have prevailed throughout the history of Western culture: that men and women are fundamentally different from each other, that men are inherently superior to women, and that these differences are natural (i.e., biological in origin). These beliefs about women's inferiority are reflected in the Judeo-Christian tradition, beginning with the biblical story of creation, in which Adam was created first, and Eve was created as a "helpmate." Thus, the Adam and Eve story (particularly Eve's role as temptress which led to their fall from grace) can be perceived as a rationale for women's subordination. Additionally, Bem argues that Western culture has turned from the language of religion to the language of science to rationalize the existing status inequalities between the sexes.

## Biological Essentialism: The Form of Scientific Prejudice

Science, supposedly objective and value-free, is a human endeavor and, as such, is subject to the same biases that characterize human beliefs and interpretations. As we learned earlier in this chapter, science has been used to legitimize social inequalities between various ethnic groups. Not surprisingly, science has been employed in much the same manner to explain women's supposed innate biological inferiority. The belief that any differences between men and women are rooted in biology, rather than culture, reflects biological essentialism. And, as we shall see, such biological theorizing makes women's subordinate position inevitable.

Sandra Bem (1993), in her account of the scientific search for a biological basis of male-female differences, presents many examples of how scientific explanations portray women as deficient. Bem notes that biological theorizing about men and women intensified in the second half of the 19th century, amidst a period of great social change. During this time, feminists like Susan B. Anthony, Elizabeth Cady Stanton, and Lucretia Mott challenged the social and legal inequalities between the sexes, and increasing numbers of universities began to open their doors to women. In response to these social changes, scientists such as Edward Clarke theorized that higher education is dangerous to a woman's reproductive system. Why? Nineteenth-century physicians believed that the nervous system had a limited amount of energy or "vital force," and overindulgence in any single activity would leave little energy for other pursuits. Thus, Clarke reasoned that any energy a woman spent on the development of her mind would divert energy away from more important parts of the body, such as her reproductive system. This idea that higher education might be dangerous to a woman's reproductive system was supported by many accomplished scholars in the late nineteeth and early twentieth centuries, including American psychologist G. Stanley Hall and British philosopher Herbert Spencer.

Similarly, Fausto-Sterling (1992) comments that neuroanatomists of that time determined that the frontal lobes were clearly the seat of higher intellectual functioning, and reports quickly began appearing that documented female brain deficiencies. Women, relative to men, were "discovered" to have smaller frontal lobes, but relatively larger parietal lobes. But later, near the turn of the century, the parietal lobe was believed to be the seat of the intellect, and inevitably studies began to appear that showed that women's frontal lobes were not, in fact, smaller than men's, but that their parietal lobes were.

Perhaps by now, you're ready to proclaim, "But that was back in the 1800s!" Such biological theorizing, however, continues today. Rather than focusing on brain size, the focus of research in recent years has been on hemispheric specialization, which refers to the degree to which particular functions (i.e., verbal ability, visual-spatial ability) are localized in one hemisphere of the brain. Some research suggests that the female brain is "less specialized" than that of the male (i.e., verbal and spatial functions are equally represented in both hemispheres) and concludes that the presumed inferiority of women in visual-spatial skills is because such tasks require hemispheric specialization (Levy, 1972), which supposedly is the case for males. As Carol Tavris (1992) reminds us, the language of science once again describes women's deficiencies. Women's brains are said to be "less specialized," but as Tavris points out, researchers could have easily described men's brains as "less integrated."

Before leaving the topic of brain specialization, however, keep in mind that this research is highly inconclusive. Neurophysiologist Ruth Bleier (1984) points out that the research on brain lateralization is conflicting and arbitrary. Some researchers have found that women are less specialized, some have found that women are more specialized, and others have found no sex differences in brain specialization. Given the inconclusiveness of research findings, Bleier cautions us about jumping to any conclusions about sex differences in brain organization.

What is important to remember is that science is a product of its social/cultural context; consequently, science may affirm societal prejudices. Such scientific explanations of group differences explain women's inequality in society not in terms of prejudice and discrimination, but in terms of biological differences that inevitably reinforce women's subordinate position in society.

## Beliefs About Men and Women

Traditionally, psychologists have focused on the content of gender stereotypes to explain prejudice and discrimination against women. Early studies that examined gender stereotypes showed a definite bias in how men and women are perceived. Perhaps the most commonly cited research is a series of studies conducted by Paul Rosenkrantz and his colleagues in the late 1960s and early 1970s (Rosenkrantz et al., 1968; Broverman et al., 1972). These investigators identified a large number of traits that people typically ascribe to women and men. Overall, two dimensions emerged that comprised beliefs about men and women. The *agentic* dimension, which is regarded as the core of the male stereotype, includes such traits as aggressiveness, dominance, independence, ambitiousness, and self-confidence. The *communal* dimension, which is regarded as the core of the female stereotype, includes such traits as emotionality, expressiveness, talkativeness, and awareness of others' feelings. Because a larger number of agentic traits than communal traits were rated more positively by respondents, many scholars concluded that the male stereotype is more favorable than the female stereotype.

But is this necessarily true almost 30 years later, particularly in light of women's greater participation in the workforce? Alice Eagly and her colleagues (Eagly & Mladinic, 1989; Eagly & Mladinic, 1994; Eagly, Mladinic, & Otto, 1991) suggest that, at least among college students in North America, contemporary stereotypes about women are actually *more* favorable than that of men, and that recent questionnaire studies reveal that positive attitudes toward women prevail.

What are we to make of this "women-are-wonderful effect" (Eagly & Mladinic, 1994), as Eagly calls it? Two issues deserve consideration: (a) Why are women evaluated more favorably than men in contemporary stereotyping research?, and (b) Does this change in attitudes toward women indicate that people are not prejudiced against women?

In addressing the issue of the overall favorability of the contemporary stereotype of women, Eagly and her colleagues argue that the reason women are evaluated more favorably than men today is because of the highly positive communal qualities that are typically ascribed to women. After all, traits like *kind, warm and expressive,* and *sensitive to others* really are wonderful human qualities. But why are these traits deemed to be more characteristic of women than men?

To explain why women are perceived to possess more communal qualities than men, we must keep in mind that stereotypes about women and men do not exist in a social vacuum. As we have already seen, culture shapes and molds our perceptions of males and females, and to some extent, these perceptions are based upon a culture's sexual division of labor. Many psychologists suggest that biology and culture interact to determine the sexual division of labor (S. Bem, 1993; Eagly, 1987; Williams & Best, 1982).

The division of labor in modern Western societies is still one where women's primary roles are played out in the domestic sphere (i.e., homemaking and childcare). Men's primary roles, on the other hand, are within the public sphere (i.e., occupations). According to Eagly (1987; Eagly & Steffen, 1984), these differing social roles underlie the content of gender stereotypes. In other words, the reason that men are primarily perceived as agentic and women as communal is due to the distribution of males and females into differing social roles. An experiment by Eagly and Steffen (1986) demonstrates this point. In this study, college students read a brief description of a stimulus person (male or female) who was described as either a full-time employee, part-time employee, or homemaker. In the control condition, the occupational role description was omitted. After reading the description, participants were asked to rate the stimulus person on several agentic attributes (e.g., competitive, dominant) and communal attributes (e.g., understanding, warm). Their results revealed that when occupational information was provided, men and women were perceived similarly. That is, both male and female homemakers were perceived as more communal than agentic, whereas both male and female full-time employees were perceived as more agentic than communal. In the absence of occupational role information, men and women were perceived stereotypically: Women were described as communal and men were described as agentic. Thus, this study demonstrates the power of social roles in shaping out stereotypical perceptions of men and women.

Perhaps the most important issue related to this increased favorability in attitudes toward women is whether it is accompanied by a corresponding decrease in prejudice against women. We will concentrate on this issue in the next section.

## Are People Prejudiced Against Women?

Although recent research (Eagly et al., 1994; Haddock & Zanna, 1994) has discovered that women are evaluated more favorably than men, sexism may still exist in some contexts. One manifestation of sexism is a subtle tendency to devalue women's work. In a now classic study, Philip Goldberg (1968) asked female students to evaluate six articles that were supposedly written by male or female authors in different fields. One-third of the articles represented traditionally masculine fields (law and city planning), one-third represented traditionally feminine fields (dietetics and education) and the remaining third represented gender-neutral fields (linguistics and art history). For each article, half of the students were told the author was a male (e.g., John T. McKay), and for the remaining students, they were told the author was a female (e.g., Joan T. McKay). In general, the articles presumably authored by a male were evaluated more favorably. However, bias against women was not evident for all articles. The tendency to devalue women's work occurred only for the two articles about traditionally masculine fields and one gender-neutral field. For articles about the two traditionally feminine fields and one gender-neutral field, the preference for male-authored articles did not emerge.

Not surprisingly, Goldberg's highly influential article is frequently cited as evidence of gender bias and that even women are prejudiced against women (e.g., Paludi & Bauer, 1983; Wallston & O'Leary, 1981). More recent studies, however, have questioned whether there is a pervasive tendency to devalue women's achievements. Janet Swim and her colleagues (Swim, Borgida, Maruyama, & Myers, 1989) provided a quantitative review of 123 studies using Goldberg's experimental paradigm and found, contrary to the original study, negligible differences in ratings of men's and women's work. Similarly, Eagly et al. (1994) report "the most accurate overall conclusion about Goldberg-paradigm experiments is that they have not demonstrated an *overall* tendency to devalue women's work" (p. 19).

So does this mean that gender bias has faded? Eagly et al. suggest that this is not necessarily the case. They argue that prejudice against women persists in certain circumstances, such as when women attain leadership roles. Although men and women do not differ overall in leadership effectiveness (Eagly, Karau, & Makhijani, 1995), people may react more negatively to female leaders than their male counterparts, perhaps because women's leadership is unexpected. In an experimental study of reactions to women and men who occupy leadership roles, Butler and Geis (1990) had male and female college students participate in a four-person discussion in which either a male or female confederate assumed leadership. Unbeknownst to the participants, their nonverbal responses to the confederates were observed. This study revealed that female leaders received more negative responses (e.g., furrowed brow, tightening of the mouth) and fewer positive responses (e.g., smiling, nodding of the head) than males offering the identical suggestions and arguments.

Equally disturbing is the fact that female leaders, though perhaps as effective as their male counterparts, may actually be devalued in leadership roles (Rudman & Kilianski, 2000). For example, Eagly and her associates (Eagly, Makhijani, & Klonsky, 1992) provided a quantitative review of experiments that varied the sex of the leader while holding the leadership behaviors constant. The studies included in their review typically presented written vignettes of leadership behavior or used confederates who had been trained to lead in a particular style. Overall, Eagly et al. found only a slight tendency to evaluate female leaders less favorably than male leaders. However, the devaluation of female leaders was considerably more pronounced when leaders occupied male-dominated roles (e.g., military officer) or when their leadership style was stereotypically masculine (e.g., autocratic or directive).

Overall, then, the increasingly favorable stereotypes of women, portraying them as warm and caring individuals, do not necessarily lead to favorable outcomes for women. These positive stereotypes may not serve women well in work settings, especially in occupational roles that are thought to require characteristics stereotypically ascribed to men. Moreover, recent evidence suggests that women in high-status positions who do exhibit agentic qualities may be respected, yet disliked (MacDonald & Zanna, 1998). This subtle antifemale bias may limit the achievements of women, particularly those who enter traditionally male-dominated professions.

## Summary

Overall, we have seen many similarities between the processes of sexism and racism. Like racism, sexism rests on a belief system that subordinates a person on the basis of presumed biological differences. Despite the fact that race and gender are said to be biologically based, in actuality, both race and gender are socially constructed.

And like racism, sexism is structured in institutional arrangements, including work, family, mass media, and education. Ethnic groups and women share a history of exclusion from prestigious communities (e.g., universities, the military, community organizations, and clubs), and both continue to be placed in a subordinate position with respect to wealth, income, and power.

Finally, prejudice against women, like racial prejudice, has become increasingly more covert in recent years (Swim, Aikin, Hall, & Hunter, 1995). Most people today do not openly admit their biases against women, but such subtle biases still linger.

Although there are significant parallels between racism and sexism, some notable differences exist. One important distinction is the amount of contact between the racial groups and between the sexes. It is entirely conceivable that a White person may live his or her life without forming a personal relationship with someone from another ethnic background. In contrast, men and women are not segregated in the same way; rather, the socialization of men and women ensures that their lives will be intertwined in a way unsurpassed by different ethnic groups.

Perhaps another distinction between racism and sexism lies in the emotional responses to members of these groups. Glick and Fiske (1994, 1997) argue that attitudes toward women may be more accurately described as affectively ambivalent than attitudes toward ethnic minority groups. Sexism, they argue, encompasses both hostile and benevolent attitudes toward women. Attitudes toward ethnic groups, in contrast, may have fewer positive components.

Although racism and sexism represent different forms of oppression, these forms of oppression may intersect for some individuals. The challenges and issues faced by African American and Hispanic women, for instance, are uniquely different from those faced by most White, non-Hispanic women. Racism and sexism, while affecting different groups of people in different ways, are part of a system of oppression that advantages a dominant group at the expense of others.

## ➤ UNDERSTANDING ANTIGAY PREJUDICE

There is no doubt that prejudice and discrimination directed toward gay men and lesbians are widespread in our culture. So strong are these prejudices that a number of communities have attempted to deny or abolish equal rights for gays and lesbians. In 1992, a state-wide referendum in Colorado (Amendment 2) was passed by popular vote that explicitly denied civil rights to lesbians and gay men, although it was later declared unconstitutional by the U.S. Supreme Court. Sexual intimacy between persons of the same sex remains illegal in many states, and in every state and community, gay men and lesbians are denied the legal right to marry. Gay and lesbian employees in the federal government have routinely been denied security clearances on the basis of their sexual orientation (Herek, 1990), and homosexuality has been grounds for dishonorable discharge in the armed forces. Historically, the U.S. Department of Defense has viewed homosexuality as incompatible with military service, because gay people were thought to pose a security risk and not competent to perform their duties (Herek, 1993). When President Bill Clinton took office in 1993, he announced his intention to stop excluding gays and lesbians from military service. His plan triggered a firestorm of controversy, with intense opposition voiced by military leaders, conservative Republicans, and religious fundamentalists. The result of the controversy was the "don't ask, don't tell" compromise in which gay men and lesbians may serve in the military as long as they do not reveal their sexual orientation. Although military leaders may no longer ask recruits their sexual orientation, anyone who openly acknowledges his or her homosexuality is still discharged.

The most extreme expression of antigay prejudice occurs in hate crimes, which involve words or actions intended to harm or intimidate individuals because of their membership in a minority group. Antigay hate crimes, involving physical attacks against lesbians and gay men, appear to have increased in recent years (Herek, 1989), and in 1996, at least 21 men and women were murdered because of their sexual orientation (Southern Poverty Law Center, 1997). According to Herek (2000), a total of 1,102 hate crimes based on sexual orientation were reported to law-enforcement authorities in 1997. In some surveys, as many as 92 percent of lesbians and gay men report that they have been verbally harassed because they were gay (Herek, 1991), and as many as one-fourth report being victims of physical assaults because of their sexual orientation (Herek, Gillis, & Cogan, 1999).

Such antigay prejudice and discrimination must be understood in terms of a cultural ideology that permeates our social institutions. **Heterosexism** is an ideological system that denies, denigrates, and stigmatizes any nonheterosexual form of behavior or identity (S. Bem, 1993; Herek, 1990). Like racism and sexism, heterosexism manifests itself in social practices and institutions that privilege heterosexuality and marginalize homosexuality. In Gregory Herek's (1990) words, "heterosexism is like the air that we breathe: It is so ubiquitous that it is hardly noticeable" (p. 316).

So how does heterosexism manifest itself? Some examples of institutional manifestations of heterosexism are: (1) laws banning sexual relations between people of the same sex have been upheld as recently as 1986, when the U.S. Supreme Court ruled in the *Bowers v. Hardwick* case to uphold Georgia's antisodomy law; (2) marriages are by definition heterosexual, which denies gay men and lesbians spousal benefits that accrue to heterosexual married couples; (3) openly homosexual individuals are not allowed to serve in the military; (4) many religious organizations condemn homosexuality and refuse to allow gay people to join the clergy; (5) media portrayals of gay people are infrequent and typically negative. As these examples show, societal institutions and practices convey that heterosexuality is normal, natural, and desirable; any nonheterosexual behavior is deviant, unnatural, and undesirable.

## Social Construction of Sexuality

To fully understand the origins of heterosexism as a cultural ideology, sexual orientation must be situated within historical and cultural contexts. Gregory Herek (1993), a leading scholar on antigay prejudice, argues that the concept of sexual orientation, like racism and sexism, is a cultural construction. To support this social constructionist view of sexuality, scholars typically analyze sexuality from an historical and cross-cultural perspective.

By all accounts, homosexual practices have existed throughout history. But the idea that a person may be defined as a homosexual has a relatively recent history. In their history of sexuality, D'Emilio and Freedman (1988) describe the mid- to late-19th century as a time of rapid social change when opportunities for sexual expression expanded. Urbanization and industrialization pulled men and women away from their family homes into cities, allowing greater anonymity to explore sexuality outside of the marital context. By the late nineteenth century, a rudimentary homosexual subculture began emerging in many cities. Some urban districts also became a sexual marketplace, with pornography and prostitution taking economic root. Not surprisingly, social reformers became increasingly concerned about sexuality outside of a marital context and began organizing crusades against these sexual practices. The medical profession too became interested in regulating nonprocreative sexual expression by mounting an attack on masturbation, birth control, abortion, and individuals whom they termed "sexual inverts." Sexual inversion was a broad, all-encompassing term that referred to anyone who deviated from the traditional gender scripts. Included in the category of sexual inverts were feminine men, masculine women, cross-dressers, individuals with same-sex erotic attractions—and even feminists (S. Bem, 1993). At that time, the concepts of *heterosexuality* and *homosexuality* as we know them today had not yet been articulated. This does not mean, of course, that same-sex sexual acts did not come into existence until the nineteenth century, but rather until then sexuality was not considered a predominant feature that defined a person's identity.

D'Emilio and Freedman (1988), for instance, note that although 19th-century Americans had no concept of homosexuality as an *identity* per se, they did acknowledge homosexual behavior. Americans during this time recognized sodomy, which they defined as anal intercourse between men, as well as other nonprocreative sexual acts (e.g., oral sex, masturbation). Sodomy was first condemned from a religious perspective (i.e., as sinful behavior), and later condemned from a legal perspective (i.e., as a crime). Sodomy was defined during that period not in terms of a homosexual-heterosexual distinction, but on the basis of whether the sexual act was procreative or nonprocreative.

By the end of the nineteenth century, however, members of the medical community began separating same-sex sexual activity from other sexual inversions, largely because of the growing threat that same-sex relationships posed for marital, reproductive heterosexuality. Thus, homosexual behavior was reconceptualized not as a moral issue or a legal issue, but as a medical issue. In the process, medical professionals began describing same-sex eroticism as a disease or mental illness. According to Sandra Bem (1993), physicians and scientists now employed a medical language to privilege heterosexual behavior by pathologizing homosexual behavior.

Due to this pathologizing of homosexual behavior, the concept of the homosexual was finally invented in the late 1800s. The terms "homosexual" and "heterosexual" were not just adjectives describing sexual behaviors, but they became nouns, ascribing mutually exclusive identities (S. Bem, 1993; D'Emilio & Freedman, 1988). As Michel Foucault (1978) summarized this development of sexual orientation as a construct, "the sodomite had been a temporary aberration; the homosexual was now a species" (p.43). In other words, homosexual behaviors, which once were considered sporadic, individual acts of which one could repent, now indicated a particular class of people—people with a mental illness.

Cross-cultural comparisons of sexual behavior also demonstrate that "sexual orientation" is a cultural construction. In terms of sexuality, modern-day Westerners tend to "see" two kinds of people, homosexuals and heterosexuals, who are defined on the basis of their sexual behavior. In other cultures, these same sexual behaviors have a very different symbolic meaning. The best example comes from perhaps the most studied group, the Sambians in New Guinea (Herdt & Boxer, 1995). Among the Sambia, boys leave their family home around the age of seven and are expected to spend the next 10 years living with males. During this time, boys regularly perform oral sex on older males, because ingesting semen is believed to transform young boys into strong and virile men. When the boys reach puberty, they reverse roles, becoming semen donors to younger initiates. When it comes time to marry and father children in their late teens and early twenties, the Sambian males become exclusively heterosexual. The sexual behaviors that Sambian males exhibit are ones that we would call homosexual. Sambian males, however, do not develop a homosexual identity, because homosexual acts are considered a natural progression toward heterosexual behavior.

As another example of how sexual orientation is a cultural construction, consider how some cultures define who is and who is not a homosexual. Sexuality in our culture is based solely on the sex of one's partner. In other cultures, sexuality is based on the roles people play or the positions they assume. In Mexico, Brazil, Greece, and Morocco, for instance, it is not uncommon for men to engage in anal intercourse or oral sex with members of the same gender. However, the crucial determinant of a homosexual classification is based upon the role performed during the sexual act. In these countries only the partner who is penetrated is regarded as homosexual (Carrier, 1980; Kulick, 1997).

These examples of sexuality in different cultures and in different historical periods allow us to see that "homosexual" and "heterosexual" are culture-bound notions. As Jeffrey Weeks (1977) summarizes this social constructionist perspective,

> homosexuality has existed throughout history. But what has varied enormously are the ways in which various societies have regarded homosexuality, the meanings they have attached to it, and how those who were engaged in homosexual activity viewed themselves. . . . As a starting point we have to distinguish between homosexual behavior, which is universal, and a homosexual identity, which is historically specific (pp. 2–3).

As we have just seen, defining people on the basis of mutually exclusive categories, heterosexuals and homosexuals, led people to see homosexuality as a pathological condition and homosexual people as mentally ill. In fact, homosexuality was included as a psychological disorder in the American Psychiatric Association's *Diagnostic and Statistical Manual* (DSM-I), which was first published in 1952, and later updated and republished in 1968 as DSM-II. The unfortunate consequence is that during the twentieth century the medical profession subjected gay men and lesbians to many medical treatments intended to provide a "cure" for their condition: psychoanalysis, aversion therapies, hormone treatments, electroconvulsive therapy, and even castration, clitorectomies, and lobotomies. According to Jonathan Katz (1976), the treatment of lesbians and gay men by the medical establishment represented "one of the more lethal forms of homosexual oppression" (p. 129).

Ironically, at the height of the McCarthy-era witchhunt against communists and homosexuals, several scientists began to challenge this view of homosexuality as a mental illness. The first challenge came from Alfred Kinsey's (1948) survey of Americans' sexual behaviors. Kinsey's data showed that about 37 percent of men and about 13 percent of women had had at least one homosexual experience to orgasm. This statistic sparked a furor, revealing that homosexual behavior might not be as statistically infrequent as commonly thought.

A second challenge came from Evelyn Hooker's (1957) study showing that heterosexual and homosexual males could not be distinguished on the basis of any psychological tests. This finding that homosexuals were as well adjusted as heterosexuals provided the impetus for depathologizing homosexuality. Finally, on December 15, 1973, the American Psychiatric Association voted to remove homosexuality from its official listing of mental disorders. With the stroke of a pen, a "disease" was cured.

## Contemporary Attitudes Toward Gay Men and Lesbians

Following the APA decision and the gay rights movement, have attitudes toward gay men and lesbians improved? Recent surveys suggest that attitudes toward homosexuality remain largely negative. Concerning attitudes toward the morality of homosexuality, Table 2.1 shows that although disapproval rates have dropped in the 1990s,

*Table 2.1      Attitudes Toward Homosexuality*

Are sexual relations between
adults of the same sex:

| | Percentage of Sample | | | |
| --- | --- | --- | --- | --- |
| | 1973 | 1980 | 1990 | 1996 |
| Always wrong | 70% | 70% | 73% | 56% |
| Almost always wrong | 6% | 6% | 5% | 5% |
| Sometimes wrong | 7% | 6% | 6% | 6% |
| Not wrong at all | 11% | 14% | 12% | 26% |

*Source: Yang, A.S. (1997). The Polls—Trends: Attitudes Toward Homosexuality.* Public Opinion Quarterly, 61, 477–507.

56 percent of American adults polled in 1996 believe that homosexual relations are *always* wrong. In a 1994 survey, 46 percent believed that homosexuals should not be hired as elementary school teachers and 26 percent believed a homosexual man should not be allowed to teach in a college. And finally, although 45 percent support the decriminalization of homosexual relations between consenting adults, the majority of individuals remain opposed to gay marriage (64%) or adoptions (65%).

Recently social scientists have begun looking at the characteristics of people who hold antigay attitudes. This research shows that a variety of social and demographic variables are correlated with extremely negative attitudes toward gay men and lesbians. In general, heterosexuals who strongly endorse antigay attitudes tend to:

1. Be male rather than female (Kite & Whitley, 1998; Whitley & Kite, 1995)
2. Hold traditional views regarding gender roles (Agnew, Thompson, Smith, Gramzow, & Currey, 1993; Herek, 1994)
3. Hold conservative attitudes toward sex in general (Simon, 1995)
4. Believe homosexuality is "caused" by social factors, rather than biological factors (Herek & Capitanio, 1995; Whitley, 1990)
5. Belong to traditionally conservative religions (Agnew et al., 1993; Herek & Capitanio, 1995)
6. Be racially prejudiced and authoritarian (Altemeyer, 1996; Haddock & Zanna, 1998; Haddock, Zanna, & Esses, 1993; Altemeyer, 1996)
7. Have few gay acquaintances or friends (Agnew et al., 1993; Herek & Capitanio, 1996)

Of particular theoretical interest is why heterosexual men generally hold more negative attitudes toward homosexuality than heterosexual women. Mary Kite and Bernard Whitley (1996) quantitatively integrated 112 studies of attitudes toward homosexuality and found sex differences on several dimensions. First, their review indicated that men generally had more negative attitudes toward homosexuals, particularly toward gay men. In contrast, the sexes did not differ in attitudes toward lesbians. Second, men were more negative than women toward homosexual behavior, even though men hold more permissive attitudes toward sexuality in general. And finally, their review indicated that, overall, men and women do not differ in attitudes toward gay people's civil rights. However, Whitley and Kite (1998) suggest that sex differences do emerge on gender-role related issues, such as gays serving in the military.

Overall, this comprehensive review of attitudes toward gay men and lesbians indicates that heterosexual men hold more negative attitudes than heterosexual women toward homosexuality in general and toward gay men in particular. It is interesting to note, however, that men and women do not differ in their attitudes toward lesbians. Why do heterosexual men perceive homosexuality more negatively than heterosexual women? Numerous theoretical explanations have been offered.

Perhaps the most compelling explanation for sex differences in attitudes toward homosexuality is rooted in beliefs about the appropriate roles for men and women (S. Bem, 1993; Whitley & Kite, 1993). Put simply, any deviation from stereotypical gender roles may make a person sexually suspect. Consider, first, that gay men are widely stereotyped as effeminate, and lesbians as masculine (Herek, 1984; Kite & Deaux, 1987). Thus, men possessing stereotypically feminine characteristics and women possessing stereotypically masculine characteristics are more likely to be judged homosexual than individuals who possess gender-congruent characteristics (Deaux & Lewis, 1984). Consider, also, that gender roles are more narrowly defined for men. As a result, men who deviate from prescribed gender roles are often judged more negatively than women who violate the traditional female gender role (Jackson & Cash, 1985). Because of greater pressure to conform to culturally prescribed gender roles, men may be more likely to view homosexuals negatively, since they are perceived as violating norms of gender. Gay men especially may be perceived to violate traditional gender scripts, perhaps explaining why both sexes are more tolerant of lesbians.

Psychodynamic theories, in contrast, propose that heterosexuals' abhorrence of homosexuality stems from a denial of sexual attraction to same-sex individuals. From this perspective, repressed homosexual impulses produces irrational, intense dislike of homosexuals. Although relatively little research has explicitly examined the relationship between antigay prejudice and repressed homosexual impulses, a recent study (Adams, Wright, & Lohr, 1996) demonstrated that homophobic men showed greater physical arousal to male homosexual activity than did nonhomophobic men, suggesting that homophobic men were indeed repressing their attraction to homosexual activity.

Finally, another theoretical explanation for sex differences in antigay attitudes specifically addresses the finding that heterosexual men view gay men significantly more negatively than they do lesbians. Louderback and Whitley (1997) suggest that heterosexual men have more positive views of lesbians because lesbianism holds greater erotic value for them. This sexualization of lesbianism, they argue, may contribute to heterosexual men's lesser negativity toward lesbians.

## But Are Gay Men and Lesbians <u>Really</u> a Minority Group?

The struggle for equality for gay men and lesbians has been a major issue for many American communities since the gay rights movement emerged in the 1960s. The movement has focused primarily on changing laws and policies in order to secure basic civil rights for gays and lesbians. Gay rights advocates have sought protection from discrimination in employment and housing, the repeal of sodomy laws, the attainment of domestic partner employment benefits, and the legalization of same-sex marriage (Button et al., 1997). Additionally, gay rights advocates have pushed for sexual orientation to be included in civil rights legislation that bans discrimination on the basis of race, ethnic background, sex, disability, age, and religion. In the process, gays and lesbians have compared their status to other minorities (e.g., racial groups, women) deserving of legal protection. But are gay men and lesbians really a minority group?

According to political scientist James Button and his colleagues (1997), a defining criterion for a group in need of civil rights protection is a history of systematic discrimination. They argue that the civil rights movement for African Americans was sparked by evidence that Blacks were widely discriminated against in employment, housing, education, and other institutions. Whether a similar pattern of oppression against gays and lesbians exists is crucial in determining whether gays should have protected-class status.

Historically, victimization of gay men and lesbians has been widespread. In fact, up until the nineteenth century, laws against homosexual acts often included the death penalty. In 1656, for instance, the New Haven Colony published a body of laws that prescribed the death penalty for lesbianism and male homosexuality. In the eighteenth century, no one was actually executed for homosexual acts, but men and women who were convicted of such behavior received severe whippings, burning with a hot iron, imprisonment, and fines (D'Emilio & Freedman, 1988; Katz, 1992). Tens of thousands of homosexuals or suspected homosexuals were killed during the Holocaust (Plant, 1986), perhaps making this group second only to Jews in the highest death rate. Recent studies suggest that antigay violence continues today in the form of physical assault, verbal abuse, and vandalized property (Southern Poverty Law Center, 1997). And according to Button et al. (1997), several surveys between 1980 and 1991 revealed that between 16 and 44 percent of respondents reported discrimination in employment on the basis of their sexual orientation, and 8 to 32 percent experienced housing discrimination.

Based upon national opinion polls (Yang, 1997) and the recent antihomosexual laws in several states (e.g., Colorado, Oregon) that have attempted to ban civil rights protection on the basis of sexual orientation, the majority of Americans do not believe that gays and lesbians are a minority group that should be protected from discrimination. One key factor that influences attitudes toward extending civil rights protection to gay men and lesbians is beliefs about the origin of sexual orientation. Opponents of such legal protection tend to believe that homosexuality is not biologically based, but is a choice freely made (unlike race, sex, and disability). Thus, from this point of view, individuals who choose to subject themselves to stigma do not require legal protection.

There are a couple of problems with this argument. First, there is a growing body of evidence for a biological contribution (Gladue, 1994; Levay, 1993) that may actually interact with early experience to influence sexual orientation (D. Bem, 1996). And second, even if homosexuality is a choice "freely made," other choices (i.e., religion) *are* protected in the legal arena.

The debate on the origin of sexual orientation is clearly beyond the scope of this book, and scientists do not know what causes sexual orientation. Actually, it might be best to think about homosexuality in the plural rather than in the singular, acknowledging that there might be many different "kinds" of homosexuals. Indeed, psychologist Alan Bell (Bell & Weinberg, 1978) has suggested that, rather than referring to "homosexuality," we should instead refer to "the homosexualities." Thus, for some individuals, sexual orientation may be genetically influenced (Hamer & Copeland, 1994) and be as immutable as race, which is a protected category in civil rights legislation. And for others, sexual orientation may be as much a matter of choice as one's religion, which is also a protected category (Rosenbluth, 1997). Regardless, for most individuals, their sexual orientation is not volitional—people do not choose their sexual orientations as they would select food in a buffet line. Sexual orientation evolves through a complex array of biological and social factors.

Even if one does not accept the claim that homosexuality exists in the plural, it is still the case that gay men and lesbians are entitled to protection of their civil liberties based upon a history of victimization and discrimination. Thus, the important question to ask is not what causes sexual orientation, but what can be done to ensure protection against discrimination in employment, housing, and other basic institutions.

## Summary

In recent years, the concepts of majority and minority groups have been applied to a wide variety of groups, including those based upon sexual orientation. As with minorities defined on the basis of race and gender, it is clear that gay men and lesbians have been widely discriminated against in American society. There are, however, important differences among these forms of prejudice. First, race and gender are visible characteristics, but sexual orientation is less obvious. Faced with prejudice and discrimination, many gay men and lesbians have concealed their sexual identities. But such self-concealment comes with a high personal cost: Closeted individuals must live with a painful dishonesty about an important part of their identity. Moreover, concealing one's sexual orientation has other negative emotional and psychological consequences. In a recent study of lesbians and bisexual women, self-concealment was associated with increased depression and negative affect (DiPlacido, 1998).

Second, although racism and sexism exact a heavy economic and psychological toll on individuals personally affected by these social oppressions, they do not deny aspects of one's identity. For gay men and lesbians, however, the message often received from others is that they will be tolerated as long as they "don't flaunt it" and remain firmly closeted. Such admonitions render gay people invisible and deny them their identity.

## ➤ CONCLUSION

In this chapter, we have seen that visibly identifiable characteristics, such as race and gender, and a less salient characteristic, sexual orientation, are the criteria by which some individuals are excluded from various social opportunities. Sociopolitical and historical factors determine which characteristics are important for distinguishing among various groups in society, and the selection of those defining characteristics is inevitably made by those groups that occupy positions of dominance within a society. For instance, race as a biological concept of classification was created in the 19th century to justify why it was only "natural" for Africans to be enslaved. Similarly, the concept of "the homosexual" was created in the 19th century to privilege reproductive marital sexuality at a time when male and female cultural scripts were threatened by social change. Once certain characteristics are deemed valued over others, a built-in system of privilege develops. The experiences of the dominant group become institutionalized, designed to benefit the various groups making these differences so important in the first place.

The categorization of individuals—male versus female, Black versus White, heterosexual versus homosexual—is ultimately a categorization of *us* versus *them*. But this is a false dichotomy. Each individual in society derives varying amounts of privilege and penalty, due to the intersection of race, gender, sexual orientation, religion, social class, and other defining dimensions. Recognizing this fact should prevent us from entering contentious debates about whose stigmatized group is most oppressed. To attempt to rank oppressions is counterproductive, given the interlocking facets of oppression that characterize our lives.

# 3

# Values and Prejudice

## ➤ INTRODUCTION

In the last 40 years, sweeping changes in the area of race relations have occurred within the United States. In 1954, the U.S. Supreme Court *Brown v. Board of Education* case held that racial segregation in public schools was unconstitutional. This historic decision effectively reversed the "separate but equal" doctrine that had prevailed since the Supreme Court's *Plessy v. Ferguson* decision in 1896 that provided for "separate but equal facilities" for Whites and Blacks. In 1964, Congress passed the strongest civil rights law in United States history, providing measures for ensuring equal rights for all Americans to vote, to work, and to use public accommodations and facilities. In 1965, President Lyndon B. Johnson established "affirmative action" in an executive order that required federal contractors to ensure racially fair employment practices. During the early 1970s the federal government not only expanded affirmative action policies to other organizations doing business with the federal government, but also extended affirmative action in such a way as to include hiring and promotion goals for Blacks, women, and other minorities.

"What has been the effect of such legislative activism on the racial attitudes of White Americans?" we may ask. In his classic work, Gordon Allport (1954) suggested that such legislation ultimately would have beneficial effects on racial attitudes:

> The establishment of a legal norm creates a public conscience and a standard for expected behavior that check *overt* signs of only its open expression...when expression changes, thoughts too, in the long run, are likely to fall into line (pp. 469–470).

The implication here is that a link exists between attitudes and behavior, such that attitudes not only precede behavior, but also follow behavior. Thus, Allport suggested that one way to change prejudice is to legislate changes in behavior, with the hope that individuals' hearts and minds will follow. This line of reasoning concurs with a statement later made by Martin Luther King, Jr. (1962, p. 49): "While it may be true that morality cannot be legislated, behavior can be regulated;" accordingly, "the habits, if not the hearts, of people are being altered every day by Federal action."

At the beginning of the 21st century, the United States remains at a crossroads over the issue of race. For this reason, Chapter 3 addresses prejudice from an individual-level perspective, with a primary focus on Whites' racial attitudes toward Blacks in the United States. There is another reason for a focus on Black-White prejudice, however. Because of the historical significance of Black-White relations in the U.S., researchers have analyzed Black–White relations more extensively than any other form of racial prejudice.

Our purpose in this chapter is threefold. First, we will examine White Americans' racial attitudes toward Blacks that show a shift from an "old-fashioned" racism to what has been called a "new" racism. This "new" racism is a more subtle, covert expression of underlying prejudice. Then we will consider four contemporary theories of racism, each of which describes this new racism in terms of fundamental contradictions in White America's racial attitudes. The final section explores how these theories of racism have been used to develop a broader model of out-group prejudice. Specifically, many premises of the racism theories have been used to understand antagonism toward other groups in society, such as women, persons with disabilities, fat people[1] and gay people.

To better understand the nature of racism, let us begin by considering whether the racial attitudes of White Americans reflect less racism in the 1990s compared to 40—or even 20—years ago.

## ➤ HAVE RACIAL BELIEFS CHANGED?

White Americans' reported racial attitudes have indeed changed dramatically in the last 40 years. In general, surveys of Whites' racial attitudes indicate greater tolerance and acceptance of other racial groups (Schuman, Steeh, & Bobo, 1985). For example, 88 percent of Whites surveyed in the 1970s believed that Blacks should have the right to live wherever they want to, compared to only 65 percent in the 1960s. When asked whether there should be laws against intermarriage, 71 percent of Whites opposed such laws in the 1970s, compared to 38 percent in the 1960s. Similarly, 33 percent of Whites in the 1970s reported that they *approved* of interracial marriage, compared to only 4 percent in the 1960s.

This trend toward egalitarianism in Whites' racial attitudes has been viewed with skepticism by some researchers (Bobo et al. 1997; Katz, Wackenhut, & Hass, 1986; McConahay, 1986). Although overt expressions of prejudice—or what has been termed **old-fashioned racism** (McConahay, 1986)—indeed may have declined, a more subtle or **modern racism** lingers. In the past, many White Americans felt no hesitancy in openly expressing animosity toward Black Americans. For example, studies of racial stereotyping often revealed that Whites believed Blacks were lazy, ignorant, and superstitious (Katz & Braly, 1933; Karlins, Coffman, & Walters, 1969). In general, such blatant expressions of negative stereotypes have declined (Dovidio & Gaertner, 1991), but does this mean that Whites really have become less prejudiced?

Some social psychologists argue that Whites' racial attitudes have simply changed form, resulting in conflicting and complex components (Katz & Hass, 1988;

---

[1]Following Christian Crandall's (1994) lead, the term *fat* is used, rather than *obese* or *overweight*, because the latter imply a medical condition.

Kinder & Sears, 1981; Gaertner & Dovidio, 1986; McConahay, 1986). Today, Whites may be sympathetic to the plight of Blacks, yet Blacks are often criticized for not doing enough to help themselves (Bobo, 1988). From these conflicting beliefs emerges a paradox: Many White Americans *endorse equal rights,* but do not necessarily endorse governmental policies aimed at providing *equal opportunity* (Schuman et al., 1985; Sears & Jessor, 1996; Tuch & Hughes, 1996). The number of Whites who believed the government should spend more on improving the conditions of Blacks declined from 27 percent in the 1960s to 18 percent in the 1970s. When asked whether the government should see to it that Black and White children go to the same schools, 42 percent of Whites positively endorsed such a policy in the 1960s, compared to only 25 percent in the 1970s. Similar sentiments about curtailing the role of the government in promoting racial equality have been expressed more recently, in 1996, when the state of California passed Proposition 209, a highly controversial initiative that effectively banned affirmative action policies in that state.

## ➤ CONTEMPORARY THEORIES OF RACIAL PREJUDICE

A number of current theories attempt to address the conflicting values that characterize this new racism. These theories share many common features. Each proposes that a different form of racism has emerged, one that is represented by fundamental value contradictions in White Americans. These value contradictions suggest a "two factor" model of prejudice: one factor tends to promote prejudice, the other to inhibit it (Biernat, Vescio, Theno, & Crandall, 1996). The theories also share the belief that negative attitudes persist (perhaps unconsciously) in people who consider themselves to be nonprejudiced—a result of their life-long socialization in a racially divided society.

The theories described include *symbolic racism* (Kinder, 1986; Kinder & Sears, 1981; Sears, 1988), *modern racism* (McConahay, 1986; McConahay & Hough, 1976), *ambivalent racism* (Katz & Hass, 1988; Katz et al., 1986), *aversive racism* (Dovidio & Gaertner, 1991; Gaertner & Dovidio, 1986), and *compunction theory* (Devine, 1989; Devine, Monteith, Zuwerink, & Elliot, 1991). These theories, developed originally to highlight the complexity of racial attitudes, have recently been extended to a variety of other out-groups. The applicability of racism theories in explaining other forms of prejudice will be addressed, with a view toward providing a general model of how values underlie prejudice.

### Symbolic and Modern Racism Theories: Values Violation

David Sears and his colleagues (Sears, 1988; Sears & Kinder, 1970) suggest that racial prejudice, like a virus mutating into a more resistant strain, has changed from a simple dislike of Black people to a more complex, multifaceted form of hatred. Sears believes that as a result of their socialization, White individuals may retain a residue of negative attitudes toward African Americans that may be evoked by appropriate political symbols. **Symbolic racism,** the term used to describe this phenomenon, can be conceptualized in three ways (Sears, Van Laar, Carrillo, & Kosterman, 1997). First, this form of racism is described as "symbolic" because it is viewed as an abstract, ideological resentment toward Blacks as a group, rather than toward particular Black individuals. Second, symbolic racism contains beliefs that Blacks should expend greater effort to succeed in life; that Blacks are making excessive demands for special treatment; and that Blacks as a group have gained more than they truly deserve. Finally, symbolic racism is hypothesized to be based on a blend of anti-Black affect and the traditional American values embodied in the Protestant ethic. In the words of Donald Kinder (1986), symbolic racism "is the *conjunction* of racial prejudice and traditional American values"; it "is neither racism, pure and simple, nor traditional values, pure and simple, but rather the blending of the two" (p. 154).

This belief that Blacks contradict Whites' moral codes represents the basis of symbolic racism. According to Sears, many Whites are genuinely committed to the Protestant work ethic and believe that anyone, regardless of his or her racial group, can succeed in life through hard work. Thus, symbolic racists, who are defined as well-educated political conservatives, attribute inequalities between Whites and Blacks to Blacks violating cherished American values, such as individualism, self-reliance, work ethic, discipline, and obedience. This abstract, moralistic resentment of Blacks finds its strongest expression in opposition to policies designed to foster racial equality. For instance, symbolic racists may not personally acknowledge negative feelings toward Blacks, but they often express intense opposition to social policies such as welfare and affirmative action, which they perceive as benefiting Blacks at the expense of Whites.

Somewhat surprisingly, symbolic values appear to be a better predictor of Whites' attitudes and behaviors than old-fashioned racism (Kinder & Sears, 1981; Sears & Citrin, 1985). Research reveals that survey items designed to measure symbolic values (e.g., "It is wrong to set up quotas to admit Black students to college who • don't meet the usual standards") are a better predictor of whether Whites will support school busing or vote for a Black candidate than survey items designed to measure old-fashioned racism (e.g., "Black people are generally not as smart as Whites"; "It is a bad idea for Blacks and Whites to marry one another").

Moreover, symbolic values often are a better predictor of political attitudes than Whites' own self-interest. Support for this possibility comes from a survey designed to determine whether symbolic values are related to Whites' anti-Black voting behavior. The 1969 and 1973 mayoral elections in Los Angeles both featured a contest between White conservative Samuel Yorty and Black liberal Thomas Bradley. Kinder and Sears (1981) wondered whether the voting behavior of Whites would be predicted better by their degree of symbolic racism or personal threats to their self-interest (e.g., Blacks moving into the neighborhood). Interestingly, the study revealed that personal threats to self-interest did not predict preference for the White candidate, but measures of symbolic racism did. Similarly, in another study, Sears and Kinder (1985) found that whether a parent opposed school busing is dependent more on the parent's symbolic values than whether the parent's own children are likely to be affected by the policy.

Similar to Sears's concept of symbolic racism, John McConahay and his colleagues (McConahay & Hough, 1976) use the term **modern racism** to refer to Whites' beliefs that Blacks violate traditional American values "derived from the secularized versions of the Protestant ethic: hard work, individualism, sexual repression, and delay of gratification" (p. 41). Instead of using the label "symbolic racism," McConahay

(1986) prefers the label "modern racism" to emphasize the contemporary nature of beliefs in this post-civil rights era.

McConahay (1986) describes the major tenets of modern racism as: (a) denial that there is continuing discrimination against Blacks, (b) antagonism toward Blacks' demands for equal rights, and (c) resentment over preferential treatment given to Blacks. According to McConahay, modern racists truly do not perceive themselves as racist. Racism, in the view of these modern racists, is typified by beliefs associated with old-fashioned racism: beliefs in the inherent inferiority of Blacks, as well as support for segregation and other discriminatory practices. Modern racists believe racism is bad, and they do not define their beliefs as racist. From the perspective of modern racists, their beliefs that discrimination is a thing of the past and that Blacks are receiving preferential treatment at the expense of Whites represent *empirical* facts, not racist ideology.

To measure modern racism, McConahay developed the Modern Racism Scale, a seven-item self-report instrument designed to tap the major tenets of modern racism (see Table 3.1). According to McConahay, the scale was designed to be a nonreactive measure of racial prejudice; that is, the wording of the items is such that respondents may endorse them because they do not consider the statements to be racist.

Support for the assumption of the nonreactivity of the Modern Racism Scale comes from a study by McConahay, Hardee, and Batts (1981). In this study White male undergraduates completed a questionnaire entitled "Student Opinions" that contained items measuring either modern racism or old-fashioned racism. The questionnaire was administered by either a White or Black experimenter. For participants who completed the survey measuring old-fashioned racism, it was expected that the presence of the Black experimenter would cause them to moderate their racial

---

**Table 3.1    *Measuring Modern Racism***

*Denial of continuing discrimination (Sample items)*

1. It is easy to understand the anger of Black people in the United States. *
2. Discrimination against Blacks is no longer a problem in the United States.

*Antagonism toward African Americans' demands (Sample items)*

3. Blacks have more influence upon school desegregation plans than they ought to have.
4. Blacks are getting too demanding in their push for equal rights.
5. Blacks should not push themselves where they are not wanted.

*Resentment about special favors for African Americans (Sample items)*

6. Over the past few years, the goverment and news media have shown more respect to Blacks than they deserve.
7. Over the past few years, Blacks have received more economically than they deserve.

Note: The item with an asterisk requires reverse scoring.
*Adapted from: McConahay, J.B. (1986), Modern Racism, Ambivalence, and the Modern Racism Scale. In J.F. Dovidio & S.L. Gaertner (Eds.), Prejudice, Discrimination, and Racism (pp. 91–125). Orlando, FL: Academic Press.*

attitudes because participants would not risk offending her. In contrast, the presence of a Black experimenter was not expected to affect participants who completed the items measuring modern racism, presumably because these modern racism items would not be perceived as racist. The results confirmed these predictions, providing support for the scale's nonreactivity. More recently, however, the presumed non-reactivity of the Modern Racism Scale has been challenged (e.g., Bargh & Chen, 1996; Fazio, Jackson, Dunton, & Williams, 1995).

There are many commonalities between Sears's notion of symbolic racism and McConahay's modern racism. First, both of these theories suggest that blatant racism is on the wane, yet it is being replaced by a new racism that is more subtle and diffi-cult to detect. These theories assume that because racism is now considered socially undesirable, people express racial prejudice in more disguised ways. Second, both con-ceptions of this contemporary form of racism assume that Whites are unaware of their prejudices. According to McConahay (1986), modern racists do not acknowledge their negative attitudes toward Blacks; instead, they rationalize their negative feel-ings in such a way as to protect their egalitarian self-image. Similarly, Sears's sym-bolic racists rationalize their negative feelings toward Blacks by pointing to abstract political issues, like affirmative action, that they deem as giving unfair advantage to Black people. Third, the symbolic racism and modern racism perspectives suggest that this new racism is characterized by the belief that Blacks do not emulate cher-ished values. And what are these cherished values? For Kinder and Sears (1981) and McConahay (1986), these values are those embodied by the Protestant ethic: individu-alism, self-reliance, hard work, and discipline. And finally, both theories emphasize the abstract quality of this new racism: Anti-Black attitudes have little to do with personal negative experiences or threats, but are a result of socialization in a racist society.

Where the two theories differ, perhaps, is in the perception of discrimination in society. McConahay's modern racist believes that discrimination in American society is a thing of the past, and that just as many opportunities exist for Blacks as for Whites. In contrast, this perception that discrimination no longer exists is not part of Sears's definition of the symbolic racist.

Not surprisingly, many criticisms of the modern and symbolic racism perspec-tives have been voiced recently. Perhaps the most vocal critics of these perspectives are Paul Sniderman and his colleagues (Sniderman, Piazza, Tetlock, & Kendrick, 1991; Sniderman & Tetlock, 1986a, 1986b), who criticize these theories on both con-ceptual and empirical grounds. One fundamental issue raised by these researchers is whether modern and symbolic racism theories confound prejudice and political con-servatism. For example, political conservatives are less likely than liberals to support governmental policies such as affirmative action, but is this lack of support for such policies due to racism, as implied by the symbolic and modern racism theories, or due to genuine conservative values like "equity" and taking a "color-blind" approach to fairness? Sniderman et al. (1991) argue that political conservatism is not a function of racism and that under certain circumstances conservatives may actually be more sup-portive of governmental assistance for Blacks, primarily when it appears that Blacks have acted in accord with traditional values of discipline and self-reliance. More re-cently, however, this notion that people who oppose policies such as affirmative ac-tion do so, not because of racism, but because of their "principled conservatism" (i.e., the belief in a truly color-blind society) has been challenged (Meertens & Pettigrew, 1997; Sears et al., 1997; Sidanius, Pratto, & Bobo, 1996).

Despite the controversial nature of symbolic and modern racism theories, few researchers would argue that Whites' racial attitudes today are simple and rooted entirely in beliefs about the inherent inferiority of Blacks. Instead, these theories accentuate the complexity of Whites' racial attitudes as they emerge covertly in policy-related issues like affirmative action. Clearly, more research is needed to examine the interface between racism, conservatism, and attitudes toward social policies designed to remediate racial inequality.

## Racial Ambivalence Theory: Conflicting Emotions

Irwin Katz and his colleagues (Katz, Glass, & Cohen, 1973; Katz & Hass, 1988; Katz, Wackenhut, & Hass, 1986) also acknowledge the complexity of White America's racial attitudes and have concluded that "ambivalence" best describes Whites' attitudes toward Blacks. This ambivalence stems from two competing core values in American society: *individualism* as embodied in the Protestant ethic, which emphasizes devotion to work and self-reliance; and *humanitarianism-egalitarianism*, which stresses equality and sympathy for those less fortunate.

These conflicting values result in complex attitudes toward Blacks. On the one hand, because many Whites endorse egalitarian values, they perceive Blacks as being truly disadvantaged in society and empathize with their plight. Such genuine pro-Black sentiments are reflected in Whites' support of racial equality and their belief that steps should be taken to help the oppressed in society. On the other hand, however, any social policies that are perceived to give preferential treatment to Blacks are vehemently opposed by Whites, because these policies violate the principles of individualism and self-reliance. As a result, anti-Black sentiments, such as "Blacks aren't doing enough to help themselves" may be aroused.

To determine whether there is a relationship between these value orientations and racial attitudes, Katz and Hass (1988) developed the following four scales: Humanitarian-Egalitarianism, Protestant Ethic, Pro-Black, and Anti-Black. As the sample items from Table 3.2 show, the Humanitarian-Egalitarianism and the Protestant Ethic scales provide separate measures of these core values, and the Pro-Black and Anti-Black scales provide measures of racial attitudes.

Katz and Hass (1988) also demonstrated the link between racial prejudice and these conflicting core values. To make salient college students' value orientation, they presented participants a questionnaire that either measured their humanitarian-egalitarian values or another questionnaire that measured their Protestant ethic values. After completing the questionnaire, participants were given a second questionnaire that measured their degree of racial prejudice. Katz and Hass's rationale for this "priming technique," as such a procedure is called, is that activating one set of values can arouse other related concepts. If these core values are indeed related to racial attitudes, then priming participants' Protestant ethic values should increase pro-Black attitudes. The results confirmed this prediction. When egalitarian values were made salient, participants' racial prejudice scores were decreased. On the other hand, when Protestant ethic values were made salient, participants' racial

**Table 3.2    *Racial Ambivalence and Conflicting Core Values***

*Protestant Ethic (Sample items)*

1. Most people who don't succeed in life are just plain lazy.
2. If people work hard enough, they are likely to make a good life for themselves.
3. Our society would have fewer problems if people had less leisure time.

*Humanitarianism-Egalitarianism (Sample items)*

1. One should be kind to all people.
2. One should find ways to help others less fortunate than oneself.
3. There should be equality for everyone—because we are all human beings.

*Anti-Black Attitudes (Sample items)*

1. The root cause of most of the social and economic ills of Blacks is the weakness and instability of the Black family.
2. On the whole, Black people don't stress education and training.
3.  Most Blacks have the drive and determination to get ahead. *

*Pro-Black Attitudes (Sample items)*

1. Black people do not have the same employment opportunities that Whites do.
2. It's surprising that Black people do as well as they do, considering all the obstacles they face.
3. Most Blacks are no longer discriminated against. *

Note: Items with asterisk require reverse scoring.
Adapted from: Katz, I. & Hass, R.G. (1988). Racial Ambivalence and American Value Conflict: Correlation and Prime Studies of Dual Cognitive Structures. Journal of Personality and Social Psychology, 55, 893–905.

prejudice scores were increased. Thus, these value orientations do appear related to racial prejudice.

Thus far, we have seen how these simultaneously conflicting feelings of liking and disliking, sympathy and resentment directed toward Blacks result in ambivalence. What are the behavioral implications of this ambivalence? Katz and his colleagues believe the ambivalence creates a tendency toward psychological discomfort and behavioral instability, such that reactions toward particular Black individuals are extremely favorable or unfavorable, depending upon the situational context. In general, any negative cues in the social context or socially undesirable behaviors on the part of a Black individual may lead Whites to react more negatively toward that Black person than toward a similar White. Conversely, any positive situational cues or socially desirable behaviors on the part of a Black individual may lead Whites to react more positively toward that Black person than toward a similar White. This tendency for responses to be more extreme when feelings of liking and disliking of Blacks coexist is termed **ambivalence amplification.** Such amplified responses are viewed as an attempt by the ambivalent person to discredit the contradicted component of the ambivalent attitude. Thus, for example, when a Black person behaves competently, ambivalent persons will suppress anti-Black feelings in order to defend against self-accusations of bigotry and, simultaneously, enhance sympathetic feelings. In contrast, when a Black person behaves incompetently, ambivalent persons will suppress sympathetic feelings to support their self-image as a person who is discerning and, simultaneously, enhance unfavorable feelings.

A study on cross-racial evaluations (Hass, Katz, Rizzo, Bailey, & Eisenstadt, 1991) provides an excellent example of this ambivalence-amplification process. In this study, small groups of undergraduates jointly played a quiz game, called "Trivia Challenge," in which they would be able to compete for prizes. Participants were told to draw lots to determine who would be team captain.

Unbeknownst to the participants, the drawing was rigged so that either a White or a Black male confederate, posing as a research participant, was chosen as the captain. As the game progressed, the team captain was always plainly responsible for the team's success or failure. After the game ended, the remaining group members were asked to complete a questionnaire that called for evaluations of the captain. Consistent with the predictions of ambivalence-amplification, when the captain was responsible for the team's success, the Black confederate received more favorable evaluations than the White confederate. Presumably this positive encounter with the Black confederate threatened the negative, anti-Black component of the participants' ambivalent attitude, and so to reduce this threat, the positive response was amplified. When the captain was responsible for the team's failure, however, the Black confederate received less favorable evaluations than the White confederate. Again, this amplified response occurred because the negative encounter with the Black confederate threatened the positive, pro-Black component of the ambivalent attitude, and the negative response was amplified to reduce the threat.

Another study conducted by Katz and his colleagues (Katz, Cohen, & Glass, 1975) illustrates the role of ambivalence in determining the extremity of Whites' responses to a Black individual. In this experiment, White male college students were asked to give what they thought were painful shocks to a Black male confederate as feedback for incorrect responses on a learning task. The participants' levels of prejudice and sympathy toward the plight of Blacks were measured one month prior to the experimental session. According to the ambivalence-amplification notion, participants who were ambivalent toward Blacks (i.e., scored high on prejudice and high on sympathy) were expected to be most likely to denigrate the Black victim. The results of the study did indeed confirm this hypothesis.

Knowing this tendency toward an amplified response to Black individuals, can you predict the outcome of Linville and Jones's (1980) study that examined how people evaluate two applicants, one White and one Black, for admission to a graduate program? Picture this scenario: An all-White admissions committee at a law school must consider applications from two top-notch students—one student is White, the other is Black. In this example, which student would be evaluated more favorably? According to Katz's ambivalence-amplification theory, the Black applicant should be judged more positively, because having desirable qualities accentuates greater positivity toward Black than White applicants. In contrast, what would you predict in a situation in which the Black and White applicants are equally poor students? Here again, evaluations of the Black applicant should be more extreme, but this time in a negative direction. Under conditions in which the target demonstrates negative behavior, ambivalence leads evaluators to judge Blacks more negatively than similar Whites.

In sum, Katz and his colleagues' research suggests that many individuals hold conflicting feelings toward Blacks, characterized by simultaneous feelings of sympathy and disdain. These ambivalent feelings are said to result from two contradictory values: beliefs in the individualistic Protestant ethic and humanitarianism-egalitarianism. These contradictory feelings result in an arousal state that leads to an exaggeration of positive or negative responses to Black individuals, depending upon the situational context. This model of prejudice is perhaps one of the broadest that we will discuss in this chapter, because as we will see later, ambivalence amplification was developed originally to account for attitudes toward stigmatized groups in general. Similar amplification responses have been documented toward disabled persons (Katz, Glass, Lucido, & Farber, 1979; Katz et al., 1986), and the mentally ill (Gergen & Jones, 1963).

## Aversive Racism Theory: Egalitarian Values and Prejudiced Beliefs

Consistent with the previous theorists, Samuel Gaertner and John Dovidio (1986) acknowledge the subtlety of racial prejudice today. Rather than positing a distinction between "old-fashioned" racism and "modern" racism, however, they distinguish between two forms of racism. *Dominative* racists display explicit, blatant expressions of racial antipathy, and Dovidio and Gaertner (1991) estimate, represent about 20 percent of Whites in the United States. However, the remaining White Americans are not free of negative feelings and beliefs toward African Americans. Largely because of their socialization in a historically racist culture and the almost unavoidable cognitive biases that influence group perceptions, these aversive racists also have negative attitudes toward Blacks. But what distinguishes *aversive* racists from their dominative counterparts is their commitment to egalitarian values. Aversive racists

> sympathize with the victims of past injustice; support public policies that, in principle, promote racial equality and ameliorate the consequences of racism; identify more generally with a liberal political agenda; regard themselves as nonprejudiced and nondiscriminatory; but almost unavoidably, possess negative feelings and beliefs about blacks (Gaertner & Dovidio, 1986, p. 62).

Similar to Katz and his colleagues, Gaertner and Dovidio view aversive racists as "ambivalent" or conflicted. But unlike Katz's ambivalent racists who experience conflict due to their coexisting pro-Black and anti-Black attitudes, Gaertner and Dovidio argue that aversive racists experience conflict due to their strong egalitarian value system and their unacknowledged negative feelings and beliefs toward Blacks. The unacknowledged feelings that aversive racists have for Blacks is not hostility or hatred, as would be typical of dominative racists, but rather discomfort, uneasiness, perhaps even fear—feelings that tend to motivate avoidance of Blacks rather than intentional, aggressive acts directed toward Blacks.

Due to their egalitarian self-image and their politically liberal leanings, aversive racists perceive themselves as truly nonprejudiced, yet they may discriminate in sub-

tle ways. When are aversive racists most likely to discriminate? According to Gaertner and Dovidio, whether aversive racists exhibit positive or negative responses toward Blacks depends upon the normative features of the social context. For instance,
if the situation clearly calls for a nonprejudiced standard of behavior, such that prejudiced behavior would not be easily rationalized or justified, then aversive racists will
go out of their way to appear nonprejudiced. On the other hand, if the situation is ambiguous in respect to social norms for appropriate conduct, and aversive racists can
generate plausible justifications for their actions, then their unconscious anti-Black
sentiments are likely to be manifested.

To test their predictions regarding when aversive racists would be most likely to
exhibit discriminatory behaviors, Gaertner and Dovidio (1986) have relied largely on
experiments that focus on interracial helping. Their reason for using such helping par-
adigms is that Whites should be less likely to help someone from another race if they
can attribute their nonhelpful behavior to factors other than race. An early study by
Gaertner and Dovidio (1977) clearly demonstrates this point. In this study of bystander behavior, White female college students were exposed to an unambiguous
emergency involving either a White or Black female victim. Additionally, the participants were led to believe that they were either the only witness or that there were
two other witnesses to the emergency. By including other bystanders to the emergency, Gaertner and Dovidio provided an opportunity for the participant to rationalize or justify their failure to help—for example, the participants might think, "I don't
have to help; one of these other people will intervene." As predicted, when participants were the only bystander to the victim's plight, the Black, as opposed to White,
victim was slightly more likely to be helped (94 percent versus 81 percent). This amplified positive response to the Black victim is consistent with aversive racism theory, suggesting that aversive racists will go out of the way to appear nonprejudiced
when there is a clear norm defining appropriate behavior. However, when responsibility for helping was diffused across additional bystanders, participants were less likely
to help the Black than the White victim (38 percent versus 75 percent).

In another study, Frey and Gaertner (1986) examined whether social norms influence the interracial helping behavior of Whites. In this study, White female college
students worked on a task with either a White or Black female partner (in actuality,
the partner was a confederate). Participants received a request for help from their partner, who needed assistance either because the partner had not worked very hard (internal cause) or due to the unusual difficulty of the task (external cause). Frey and
Gaertner found that when there was a clear norm for helping, as exists in the situation in which the task was unusually difficult, participants helped the Black and
White partners equally. However, in the condition in which the partner needed assistance because of her failure to work hard, a racial bias in helping emerged, with
Blacks receiving less help than Whites. Apparently, when it seems that potential victims have created their own problem—through lack of foresight or laziness—these
conditions provide Whites a handy reason for not helping a Black person, allowing
them to attribute their nonhelpful behavior to factors other than race.

Using a different experimental paradigm, Dovidio and Gaertner (2000) investigated changes over a ten-year period in Whites' self-reported prejudice and discrimination in hiring recommendations. Two comparable student samples at a Northeastern
liberal arts college, the first sample in 1988–89 and a subsequent sample in 1998–99,

completed identical questionnaires that measured racial prejudice and decisions in a simulated employment context. First, in a mass pretesting session, participants were administered several surveys, one of which measured their racial attitudes. Later, during an experimental session, participants were asked to evaluate a candidate for a peer counseling program on the basis of an excerpt from the candidate's interview. These written transcripts of the interview were systematically varied to manipulate the candidate's perceived qualifications. Participants read an excerpt that reflected either clearly strong qualifications, ambiguous qualifications, or clearly weak qualifications. In addition, the race of the candidate was manipulated by including information about his campus involvement. In some cases, the candidate listed membership in the Black Student Union, whereas in other cases, the candidate listed fraternity membership (which was almost exclusively White on this campus).

Based upon the aversive-racism framework, Dovidio and Gaertner hypothesized that although racial prejudice may have declined over a ten-year period, subtle bias in Whites' hiring recommendations persists. In fact, they predicted that Whites would not be likely to discriminate against the Black candidate when his qualifications were clearly strong or weak, because such discrimination would be obvious to themselves and others. However, Dovidio and Gaertner predicted that in cases in which the candidate's qualifications were ambiguous and discrimination could then be rationalized, Whites would exhibit greater bias against the Black candidate.

The results confirmed these predictions. In both samples, Black and White candidates were recommended equivalently often in the strong-qualifications (91 percent versus 85 percent) and weak-qualifications (13 percent versus 6 percent) conditions, but Blacks were recommended significantly less often in the ambiguous-qualifications condition (76 percent versus 45 percent). As these findings suggest, Whites may give ambiguously qualified White candidates the "benefit of the doubt" while not granting the same benefit to Black candidates.

Although Gaertner and Dovidio (1986) suggest that the aversive racist is, by definition, a political liberal, relatively few studies have directly explored the link between political liberalism and prejudice. In an early study, however, Gaertner (1973) identifed liberals and conservatives residing in Brooklyn, New York on the basis of their political party membership. Using the "wrong number technique," Gaertner had Black or White confederates call the households, explaining that their car was disabled and they were trying to reach a garage. The confederates went on to say that they did not have any more change for another phone call, and then asked the participants to relay a message to the mechanic.

The results of this study were quite revealing. Overall, liberals were more likely to hang up prematurely (i.e., before the request for help was made) on Black callers than White callers. Presumably the participants who hung up prematurely could rationalize their behavior as a justifiable response to a wrong number, rather than to the race of the caller. Of participants who remained on the phone long enough for the request for help to be made, however, conservatives were significantly less helpful to Blacks than to Whites. Liberals, in contrast, helped Black and White callers equally. This finding suggests that when the norms for appropriate behavior are salient, liberals are not likely to discriminate against Blacks, because to do so would be a threat to their egalitarian self-image.

More recently, Monica Biernat and her colleagues (Biernat, Vescio, Theno, & Crandall, 1996) report a study in which they "primed" egalitarian or Protestant ethic values to determine the effect on liberals' and conservatives' reactions to Black and White employees. After listening to an audiotaped speech designed to make salient either egalitarian or Protestant ethic values, research participants examined an employee file that contained evaluations written by supervisors. The employee was either White or Black (as depicted in a photograph that accompanied the file), and described as either a good, responsible worker or as a lazy, irresponsible worker. After reading the file, participants were asked to evaluate the employee along several dimensions (e.g., "this person appears to be likeable"; "I would like to have this person as a friend"), and to make a recommendation to fire or retain the employee.

As you might expect, both liberals and conservatives were more negative toward the employee that violated the Protestant work ethic values. However, the priming manipulation had an interesting effect on reactions to the employee, depending upon the participants' political orientation. When they were primed to think of work ethic values, no differences emerged in how political liberals and conservatives evaluated the Black and White employees. However, when egalitarian values were primed, liberals evaluated the Black employee more favorably than the White employee. Conservatives who also received the egalitarian prime, on the other hand, evaluated the Black and White employees similarly. This finding that egalitarian primes affect liberals' (but not conservatives') responses to White versus Black persons is relevant to aversive racism theory: It provides direct support for Gaertner and Dovidio's contention that liberals are more likely to be characterized as aversive racists and that egalitarian convictions form the basis of their self-concept.

## Compunction Theory: Conflicting Beliefs and Behavior

A final theory that is relevant to understanding racial prejudice is the model posited by Patricia Devine (1989), which suggests that the conflict White Americans feel regarding African Americans is rooted in the distinction between *stereotypic knowledge* and *personal beliefs*. According to Devine, Whites, as a result of life-long socialization in a historically racist culture, are very much aware of the stereotypes about Blacks. However, Whites differ in the extent to which they personally endorse such negative stereotypes.

As you might recall from Chapter 1, the distinction between automatic and controlled processes is central to Devine's analysis of prejudice. Automatic processes are those that occur spontaneously and unintentionally, and research indicates that stereotypes may be automatically activated in the presence of members of a stereotyped group. Moreover, this involuntary activation of stereotypes may occur in all people, regardless of their level of prejudice (Blair & Banaji, 1996; Devine, 1989; Dovidio et al., 1997; Fazio et al., 1995). Thus, upon meeting someone of a different racial or ethnic group, even nonprejudiced people may experience spontaneously activated stereotypes.

Low-prejudiced and prejudiced people differ, however, in what happens after a stereotype unintentionally comes to mind. In contrast to automatic processes, controlled processes are intentional, deliberate, and conscious, and low-prejudiced people are more likely to invoke controlled processes to counteract their initial, biased reactions. Low-prejudiced responses, then, involve consciously inhibiting the activated stereotype and deliberately activating nonprejudiced beliefs. Low-prejudiced individuals, having decided that prejudice is personally unacceptable for them, must activate nonprejudicial beliefs consistent with their rejection of the stereotype. Prejudiced people, in contrast, do not reject the stereotype, and so they are not motivated to avoid responding in a prejudicial manner.

Because stereotypes have been so frequently activated in the past, and because people must have the time and cognitive capacity to use controlled processes to respond consistently with their nonprejudicial beliefs, people who have made a deliberate decision to renounce prejudicial thinking may sometimes fail (Devine & Monteith, 1993). Thus, like the previous theorists that we've discussed, Devine too believes that Whites experience conflict, but the conflict is between their nonprejudiced beliefs and their actual prejudiced responses (Devine, Monteith, Zuwerink, & Elliot, 1991).

When low-prejudiced people experience discrepancies between their personal standards and their actual behavior, they experience compunction, or feelings of guilt or self-dissatisfaction. High-prejudiced people, on the other hand, experience significantly less compunction, perhaps because their personal standards do not differ significantly from their prejudiced responses.

To determine how people experience prejudice-related inconsistencies between their beliefs and behavior, Devine et al. (1991, Study 1) presented White college students (who were predominately low-prejudiced) with hypothetical situations and asked them to imagine being in those situations. For example, participants were asked to imagine how they would feel if a Black couple moved in next door, or if a Black boarded the bus and sat next to them. Participants first were asked to indicate the extent to which they *should* feel uneasy about their interactions with the Black individual, and then they were asked to indicate the extent to which they actually *would* feel uneasy in that situation. Of particular interest to Devine et al. was how the participants felt about the *should-would* discrepancies. The findings from this preliminary study revealed that although low-prejudiced people are prone to responding in prejudiced ways, they do experience guilt and self-criticism for violating their nonprejudiced beliefs.

Due to the relatively few high-prejudiced people in the sample, Devine et al. were unable to determine how high-prejudiced persons respond to *should-would* discrepancies. Therefore, in a second study, Devine et al. used homosexuals as the target group. Using similar scenarios, high- and low-prejudiced individuals were asked to imagine how they should respond in various interactions with a gay person (e.g., going for a job interview and discovering that the interviewer is gay), and then indicate how they *would* respond in the same situations. As one would expect, high-prejudiced people, compared to low-prejudiced people, reported more prejudiced responses to how they should behave and how they would behave. But similar to low-prejudiced people, high-prejudiced people reported that they would respond more negatively than they *should*. Additionally, a key finding from this study was that both high- and low-prejudiced individuals were aware of the discrepancies between their personal beliefs and responses, and the greater the discrepancy, the more negative affect experienced. However, the type of negative affect differed according to participants' level of prejudice. When low-prejudiced people considered the inconsistency between how they should respond and how they would respond, they reported feeling guilty and critical of themselves. In other words, low-prejudiced people experienced "prejudice with compunction." High-prejudiced people, in contrast, reported negative affect as well, but it was directed toward homosexuals rather than toward themselves. Thus, high-prejudiced people generally experienced "prejudice without compunction."

What are the implications of these findings? First, Devine and her associates (Devine & Monteith, 1993; Devine et al., 1991; Monteith, 1993, 1996; Monteith, Zuwerink & Devine, 1994) suggest that guilt appears to be a key factor in reducing prejudice. Their studies show that inconsistencies between beliefs and behaviors threaten low-prejudiced people's self-concepts. Consequently, they are more motivated to reduce such inconsistencies by using controlled processes to inhibit their prejudiced responses. Second, it is important to note that "breaking the prejudice habit"—like breaking any undesirable habit—represents an ongoing process. With repeated attempts at controlling unwanted prejudicial responses, low-prejudiced people may effectively break the prejudice habit (Devine & Monteith, 1993; Lepore & Brown, 1997)

The implications for reducing prejudice among high-prejudiced persons are less clear, however. The fact that high-prejudiced individuals experience "prejudice without compunction" indicates that guilt and self-recriminations do not characterize their psychological landscape. Instigating prejudice-inhibition responses in high-prejudiced people might entail heightening their level of guilt, perhaps by making salient the discrepancy between their egalitarian values and prejudiced personal standards (Monteith, 1996; Monteith et al., 1994). However, the success of this approach may depend on how high-prejudiced individuals construe egalitarianism.

Some high-prejudiced individuals conceptualize egalitarianism in terms of equality of opportunity (i.e., equality exists when people have equal resources and opportunity), whereas other high-prejudiced individuals define egalitarianism in terms of individualism (i.e., equality exists when hard work accounts for people's success). Defining egalitarianism in terms of equality of opportunity has implications for prejudice reduction efforts. High-prejudiced individuals who conceptualize egalitarianism in terms of equality of opportunity are more likely to report a greater moral obligation to temper their prejudice than those who endorse an individualistic interpretation of egalitarianism (Monteith & Walters, 1998). Nonetheless, additional theorizing and research is needed to determine how best to encourage high-prejudiced people to renounce prejudicial thinking.

In summary, Devine's compunction theory, like the other theories discussed, provides an individual-level analysis of prejudice. Her model focuses upon the internal conflict experienced by individuals at differing levels of prejudice, and the emotional consequences that result from discrepancies that often arise between one's personal beliefs and actual behaviors. Like Katz's response amplification theory, Devine assumes that people are aware of their prejudiced responses, sometimes painfully so, and this is what motivates low-prejudiced people to attempt to consciously inhibit their prejudiced responses. In general, Devine's model of prejudice has broad applicability—although research coming out of her laboratory has focused predominantly on prejudice against Black people (Devine et al., 1991; Zuwerink et al., 1992) and gay people (Monteith et al., 1993), the research findings should hold for other stereotyped groups.

## ➤ EVALUATING CONTEMPORARY THEORIES OF RACIAL PREJUDICE

Although many researchers have documented a shift in the racial attitudes of White Americans, suggesting that blatant racism is on the wane, other researchers find negative racial attitudes are still quite common. For example, contrary to the commonly championed belief that negative stereotyping of Blacks is on the decline, a recent study showed that consistent, highly negative stereotypes of Blacks persist (Devine & Elliot, 1995). Moreover, studies suggest that Whites' racial attitudes are strongly related to their opposition to affirmative action (Sidanius et al., 1996), school busing (Sears & Citrin, 1985), and Black political candidates (Kinder & Sears, 1981; Abramowitz, 1994). It appears, then, that racism is more widespread in American society than previously believed (Sears et al., 1997), but whether there is indeed a "new racism" (i.e., more covert, more disguised) is debatable (Sniderman et al., 1991).

Nonetheless, we have just reviewed several theories of contemporary prejudice toward Blacks. Generally, all of these conceptualizations of prejudice propose that White Americans possess contradictory beliefs or values, such that one belief facilitates prejudiced responses and the other inhibits prejudiced responses. Moreover, all of these theories of prejudice attempt to explain why, like dinner guests that have overstayed their welcome, prejudiced responses linger, even among individuals who may not perceive themselves as prejudiced. So how do the theories differ? Basically, the theories differ in terms of (a) which beliefs or values are likely to be implicated in prejudice, (b) whether Whites are aware of their prejudices, and (c) to whom the theory applies.

According to the theories of symbolic racism (Sears & Kinder, 1981) and modern racism (McConahay, 1986), Whites experience ambivalence in their reactions toward Blacks due to their perception that Blacks violate traditional values of individualism, as embodied in the Protestant ethic. Although Whites strongly endorse beliefs in abstract principles of justice (i.e., equality, fairness), they also possess strong negative feelings about Blacks, largely due to a negative socialization about African Americans. Whites are unaware of these negative feelings, however. They maintain a nonprejudiced self-image, largely because they reject traditional racist beliefs of Black inferiority and segregation. Nonetheless, these theories suggest, negative feelings toward Blacks remain and are expressed in abstract, ideological principles that are evoked by appropriate political symbols. According to Sears and Kinder (1981) and McConahay (1986), these theories are most applicable to those Whites who are political conservatives.

Gaertner and Dovidio's (1986; Dovidio & Gaertner, 1991) aversive racism theory suggests that Whites experience ambivalence due to a conflict between their egalitarian values and their prejudiced beliefs about Blacks. They suggest that most White Americans endorse egalitarian beliefs, but as a result of their socialization, they also harbor strong negative feelings about Blacks. To protect their egalitarian self-concept,

Whites do not acknowledge their anti-Black attitudes. However, their behaviors may reflect this unconscious prejudice, primarily when the situation provides a rational, justifiable reason for responding negatively to a Black person. Gaertner and Dovidio's theory is unique in that an emphasis is placed on the normative context; that is, they have shown that when norms for situationally appropriate behavior are clear, Whites do not display discriminatory behavior. In contrast to the theories of modern racism and symbolic racism, Dovidio and Gaertner's aversive racist tends to be politically liberal.

According to Katz's (Katz, 1981; Katz & Hass, 1988; Katz et al., 1986) theory of racial ambivalence, ambivalence arises from two conflicting value orientations that White Americans are socialized to hold: individualistic values and humanitarian-egalitarian values. These contradictory value orientations give rise to both pro-Black and anti-Black attitudes, resulting in more extreme positive or negative evaluations of Blacks, relative to Whites. Katz suggests that this theory is applicable to most Whites, and that these individuals are indeed conscious of their anti-Black attitudes.

And finally, Devine's (Devine et al., 1991) compunction theory also acknowledges Whites' awareness of their prejudices, because such awareness leads to feelings of guilt for low-prejudiced individuals and feelings of hostility toward the stereotyped group for high-prejudiced individuals. However, the source of the ambivalence stems from individuals' knowledge of the cultural stereotype of Blacks and their personal beliefs about Blacks. Thus, Devine argues, the conflict that Whites experience is between how they believe they should respond and how they actually would respond to members of various out-groups. In contrast to the other theories, Devine's model of prejudice is applicable only to low-prejudiced individuals; how this theory applies to high-prejudiced individuals is not yet clear.

After reviewing the distinctions between these theories of racial prejudice, you are probably wondering, so which theory is correct? Rather than viewing these theories as competing, perhaps it is better to view the theories as complementary. As suggested by Margo Monteith (1996), each of these conceptualizations of prejudice represent unique forms of prejudice that are conceptually distinct. It may be, as Dutch psychologists Gerard Kleinpenning and Louk Hagendoorn (1993) argue, that these different forms of prejudice represent differing stages of racial tolerance. For example, Kleinpenning and Hagendoorn suggest that *biological* or old-fashioned racism, which reflects a belief in the biological inferiority of the out-group, represents zero-level tolerance of another group. Symbolic or modern racism reflects somewhat greater acceptance of the out-group, yet there is still a belief in the cultural superiority of the in-group (particularly in terms of core values) and a concern about benefiting disadvantaged groups at the expense of the in-group. Aversive racism is the next step toward greater tolerance, which is characterized by greater egalitarian ideals, but aversive racists' unacknowledged negative feelings toward Blacks prevent them from responding in a truly egalitarian manner.

Although Kleinpenning and Hagendoorn did not include Katz's racial ambivalence theory and Devine's compunction theory in their analysis of racism, Katz's theory may represent the next step toward greater acceptance. Because Katz's ambivalent racists possess negative attitudes toward Blacks, along with genuinely positive attitudes, they are unable to make a firm commitment toward nonprejudiced responses. But the fact that Katz's theory posits genuine pro-Black attitudes indicates greater acceptance than Dovidio and Gaertner's aversive racism theory (which posits no genuine pro-Black attitudes, but rather egalitarian ideals). And finally, Devine's theory represents still closer movement toward racial acceptance, at least for low-prejudiced individuals. For individuals who are low in prejudice, they have truly embraced egalitarian ideals and have made a firm commitment toward nonprejudiced beliefs and behaviors. When they fall short of their ideals, they experience guilt and this motivates them to eliminate prejudiced responses.

## ➤ PREJUDICE AND VALUES

> *"The most important categories a man has are his own personal set of values. He lives by and for his values. Seldom does he think about them or weigh them; rather he feels, affirms, and defends them."*
>
> Gordon Allport, The Nature of Prejudice (1954, p. 24)

As you can see from the previous discussion of current theories of racial prejudice, there is a common underlying theme of values and how they relate to racism. The values that appear to be central to racial prejudice in the United States are individualism, as expressed in the Protestant ethic, and egalitarianism/humanitarianism. In general, individualistic values encourage prejudiced responses toward Blacks, because Blacks as a group are perceived to deviate from the values of hard work, discipline, and self-reliance. Egalitarian-humanitarian values, in contrast, encourage nonprejudiced responses, because these values reflect the democratic ideals of equality, justice, and concern for others' welfare.

Recently, social psychologists have attempted to extend the various theories of racism to other stereotyped groups in society in hopes of discovering a unified theory of prejudice. From the perspective of these researchers, the general premises of racism theories—the emphasis on egalitarian and individualistic ideals and their implications for attitudes toward Blacks—may be applicable to other groups in society that are perceived as violating these cherished values. To this end, researchers have begun examining prejudice toward women, persons with disabilities, fat people, and gay people in terms of how values are implicated in prejudice toward these groups.

### Prejudice Against Women

It is not difficult to see how values that contribute to racism may also apply to sexism. As researchers (Swim, Aikin, Hall, & Hunter, 1995; Tougas, Brown, Beaton, & Joly, 1995) point out, many similarities exist between racism and sexism. Women, like Blacks, often face overt discrimination in the workplace, higher education, and government (Heilman, Block, & Lucas, 1992). And women, like Blacks, have been the subject of strongly held stereotypes (Bergen & Williams, 1991). Another similarity between racism and sexism lies in the public expression of prejudice; similar to racism, prejudice and discrimination against women have become increasingly covert and subtle. Due to these similarities, researchers believe that the values that underlie modern racism also underlie what Janet Swim calls "modern sexism" (Swim et al., 1995) or what Francine Tougas dubs "neosexism" (Tougas et al., 1995).

As you may recall from McConahay's (1986) theory, the basic tenets of modern racism are: (a) denial of continuing discrimination, (b) resentment about special favors, and (c) anatagonism toward African Americans' demands. Swim et al. and Tougas et al. believe that these same beliefs apply to women. Many people, they argue, believe that discrimination against women is a thing of the past, and that women as a group are given preferential treatment in hiring decisions and admission to universities. Thus, these researchers argue, these symbolic values are reflected in bias against women.

To determine whether beliefs said to underlie racism also underlie sexism, Swim et al. used McConahay's (1986) Modern Racism Scale and Old-Fashioned Racism items to develop a similar measure of old-fashioned and modern sexism (see Table 3.3 for sample items). Because previous research indicated that modern racism influences voters' preferences for a White or a Black candidate (Sears, 1988), Swim et al. reasoned that modern sexism should be predictive of voting preference for a male or a female candidate. To test this idea, Swim et al. took advantage of a senatorial election in Pennsylvania between a Republican male (Arlen Specter) and a Democratic female (Lynn Yeakel). They found that modern sexism significantly predicted voting preferences, such that preference for the female candidate was associated with lower modern sexism scores.

Along similar lines, Francine Tougas and her colleagues (Tougas et al., 1995) developed the Neosexism Scale, which is also based on the basic tenets of modern

---

*Table 3.3*    *Measuring Modern and Old-Fashioned Sexism*

---

**Old-Fashioned Sexism** (Sample items)

1. It is more important to encourage boys than to encourage girls to participate in athletics.
2. I would be equally comfortable having a woman as a boss as a man.*

**Modern Sexism** (Sample items)

*Denial of continuing discrimination*

1. Discrimination against women is no longer a problem in the United States.
2. It is rare to see women treated in a sexist manner on television.

*Antagonism toward women's demands*

1. It is easy to understand the anger of women's groups in the United States.*
2. It is easy to understand why women's groups are still concerned about societal limitations of women's opportunities.

*Resentment about special favors for women*

1. Over the past few years, the government and news media have been showing more concern about the treatment of women than is warranted by women's actual experience.

---

Note. Items with an asterisk require reverse scoring.
*Adapted from: Swim, J.K., Aikin, K.J., Hall, W.S., & Hunter, B.A. (1995). Sexism and Racism: Old-Fashioned and Modern Prejudices.* Journal of Personality and Social Psychology, 68, 199–214.

**Table 3.4      Measuring Neosexism (Sample Items)**

1. Discrimination against women in the labor force is no longer a problem in Canada.
2. Over the past few years, women have gotten more from the government than they deserve.
3. I consider the present employment system to be unfair to women.*
4. Universities are wrong to admit women in costly programs such as medicine, when in fact, a large number will leave their jobs after a few years to raise their children.

Note: The item with an asterisk requires reverse scoring.
*Adapted from: Tougas, F., Brown, R., Beaton, A.M., & Joly, S. (1995). Neosexism: Plus ça change, plus c'est pareil.* Personality and Social Psychology Bulletin, 21, 842–849.

racism (see Table 3.4 for sample items). In their study of Canadians' attitudes toward gender-related policies, scores on the Neosexism Scale proved to be a reliable predictor of opposition to affirmative action policies.

Although sexism and racism are indeed both prejudices, sexism probably is characterized by greater emotional ambivalence than racism. Although racist attitudes appear to be strongly negative, sexist attitudes are not. For this reason, Peter Glick and Susan Fiske (1996) make a distinction between **hostile sexism**, in which people hold negative views of women and overtly discriminate against them, and **benevolent sexism**, which places women in stereotypical and restricted roles, and on the surface, appears to be positive. For example, a benevolent sexist might believe that a woman should be placed on a pedestal, and cherished and protected by her man. No matter how well intentioned such beliefs about women are, they serve to restrict and limit women's social roles and opportunities.

To measure the existence of both positive and negative attitudes about women, Glick and Fiske (1996) developed the Ambivalent Sexism Inventory. As Table 3.5

**Table 3.5      Measuring Ambivalent Sexism**

*Hostile Sexism (Sample items)*

1. Women seek to gain power by getting control over men.
2. Many women are actually seeking special favors, such as hiring policies that favor them over men, under the guise of asking for "equality."
3. When women lose to men in a fair competition, they typically complain about being discriminated against.

*Benevolent Sexism (Sample items)*

1. Women should be cherished and protected by men.
2. Every man ought to have a woman whom he adores.
3. A good woman should be set on a pedestal by her man.
4. Women, compared to men, tend to have a superior moral sensibility.

*Adapted from: Glick, P., & Fiske, S.T. (1996). The Ambivalent Sexism Inventory: Differentiating Hostile and Benevolent Sexism.* Journal of Personality and Social Psychology, 70, 491–512.

shows, the scale measures hostile sexism and benevolent sexism separately and provides an overall measure of ambivalence. This scale has been administered to over 15,000 men and women in 19 nations, and according to Glick and Fiske (2001), hostile and benevolent sexism are complementary, cross-culturally prevalent ideologies that serve as justifications for gender inequality.

As you have probably noticed, Glick and Fiske's ambivalent sexism approach shares some similarities with Katz's (Katz & Hass, 1988) analysis of racial ambivalence. First, both theories predict that ambivalence, whether directed toward Blacks or women, should polarize responses to members of the target group. That is, just as responses toward Blacks may be extremely exaggerated, depending upon the situational context, so too should responses toward women be more extreme than those toward men. It remains for future research, however, to determine whether such predictions hold for ambivalent sexism.

Second, like Katz's analysis that posits genuine pro-Black attitudes, as well as anti-Black feelings, ambivalent sexism also contains genuinely positive views about women. Unlike Katz's racial ambivalence analysis, Glick and Fiske suggest that the positive views are not rooted in egalitarian beliefs per se, but rather in paternalistic beliefs.

The modern sexism and ambivalent sexism analyses show the subtlety present in prejudice against women. The general premise of these two analyses of sexism is similar to contemporary conceptualizations of racial prejudice. Sexism, like racism, has become increasingly covert in recent years. Moreover, symbolic values also appear to underlie sexism. The modern sexist, like the modern racist, views discrimination as a thing of the past and resents special favors given to the disadvantaged group.

## Prejudice Against Persons with Disabilities

As mentioned earlier, Katz's (Katz et al., 1973; Katz et al., 1986) ambivalence theory was developed originally to account for negative attitudes toward stigmatized groups in general. One group in particular that has been the focus of Katz's research program is the physically disabled. Similar to attitudes toward Blacks, attitudes toward individuals with disabilities are best described as ambivalent. On the one hand, people have strong feelings of sympathy and compassion for individuals with disabilities, but at the same time, aversion is felt toward the disabled (Carver, Glass, & Katz, 1978; Katz et al., 1986; Snyder, Kleck, Strenta, & Mentzer, 1979; Soder, 1990).

Robert Kleck and his associates (Kleck, Ono, & Hastorf, 1966) conducted one of the earliest studies that documented this contradictory reaction to individuals with disabilities. In face-to-face encounters with either a disabled or nondisabled person, research participants evaluated the disabled person more favorably and agreed more with his opinions. But the participants' behaviors belied their uncomfortableness in the interaction. Those who talked to the disabled person exhibited greater motoric inhibition, demonstrated less variability in their behavior, and terminated the interaction sooner.

This apparent contradictory reaction to persons with disabilities provides an excellent test for Katz's ambivalence theory. Perhaps you recall Katz's experiment (Katz et al., 1973) in which White college students were induced to deliver either a mild or painful electric shock to either a White or Black confederate. Following this unintentional harm-doing, the students denigrated the Black victim more than the White one, presumably because ambivalence heightened feelings of guilt. In a similar study, Katz and colleagues (Katz et al., 1977) had college students administer either mild or noxiously loud noise signals to a female confederate working on a learning task, as feedback for incorrect answers. For half the participants the confederate was seated in a wheelchair, and for the other half she apparently was nondisabled. As you might expect, denigration of the victim was greatest when participants delivered noxious noise to the disabled victim. This successful replication of the earlier experiment that varied the race of the victim suggests that both individuals with disabilities and Blacks are viewed ambivalently, providing support for Katz's ambivalence theory.

In a study demonstrating how ambivalence might amplify responses to persons with disabilities, Frederick Gibbons and his colleagues (1980) had college students work with a confederate on anagram tasks. The confederate, who either appeared with crutches or apparently was nondisabled, was always selected as team captain. Through the course of the task, it became apparent that the confederate's performance directly determined whether the team succeeded or failed. Following completion of the task, the students were asked to rate the confederate on a number of dimensions. Consistent with ambivalence theory, participants who succeeded evaluated the confederate more favorably when she was disabled than when she was not. In contrast, participants who failed evaluated the confederate less favorably when she was disabled than when she appeared nondisabled.

In explaining response amplification processes in terms of underlying values, Katz and his colleagues primarily have focused on reactions toward Blacks. However, in one article, Katz et al. (1986) suggest a link between egalitarian values and pro-disabled attitudes, and Protestant ethic values and anti-disabled values, respectively. For example, people who strongly endorse egalitarian values may be more likely to express sympathy, compassion, and friendly sentiments toward persons with disabilities. On the other hand, people with strong Protestant ethic values may be more critical, and perhaps even resentful, of disabled persons, because they view them as using their disability for unfair advantage. To test these ideas, Katz et al. constructed scales that measured pro- and anti-disability attitudes and correlated these scales with measures of Protestant ethic and egalitarian-humanitarian values. They found that, similar to attitudes toward Blacks, endorsement of Protestant ethic values was related to negative attitudes toward persons with disabilities, whereas egalitarian values were associated with favorable attitudes toward the disabled.

In general, research on the attitudes toward individuals with disabilities strongly support Katz's ambivalence theory, and closely replicate the findings of earlier studies that used Blacks as the stigmatized target group. Despite obvious differences between these two groups, both Blacks and individuals with disabilities are regarded ambivalently, and this ambivalence is rooted in two general value orientations, Protestant work ethic and egalitarianism.

## Prejudice Against Fat People

Jennifer Crocker and her colleagues (Crocker, Cornwell, & Major, 1993; Crocker & Major, 1994) suggest that of all the stigmatizing conditions that exist, the obesity stigma may be the most debilitating. In terms of Goffman's (1963) analysis of stigma, obesity is both an *abomination of the body* (i.e., viewed as aesthetically displeasing), and a *blemish of individual character* (i.e., viewed as a moral failure). Moreover, unlike some stigmatizing conditions that are concealable, such as homosexuality, obesity is immediately visible to others and has the potential to determine the course of social interactions (Miller, Rothblum, Barbour, Brand, & Felicio, 1990; Miller, Rothblum, Brand, & Felicio, 1995).

That strong antifat attitudes exist has been documented by many researchers. In general, the obese are viewed as unattractive (Harris, Harris, & Bochner, 1982), lazy and unable to control themselves (Brink, 1988), alienated from their sexuality (Millman, 1980), and weak-willed and self-indulgent (Allon, 1982). Amazingly, these stereotypes are shared by health care professionals, including physicians (Monello & Mayer, 1963) and nurses (Maroney & Golub, 1992). Fat people are often the target of discrimination also. Fat people are less likely to be hired (Roe & Eickwort, 1976), and once hired, are less likely to be promoted (Larkin & Pines, 1979). Even parents discriminate against their own children, because heavyweight daughters are less likely to receive financial support from their parents for their college education (Crandall, 1995).

Why do such strong antifat sentiments exist? Christian Crandall and colleagues (1994; Biernat et al., 1996; Crandall & Biernat, 1990), borrowing from the elements of symbolic racism, suggest that much of the uniformly negative attitudes directed toward fat people stems from the perception that they violate the principle of individualism. Crandall (1994) notes that the stereotypes of fat people are remarkably similar to those of Blacks: Both groups are regarded as lazy, lacking discipline, and unable to defer gratification. In other words, both groups are perceived as violating the Protestant work ethic.

To demonstrate that the same values underlying racism also underlie antifat attitudes, Crandall (1994) first developed a questionnaire that measures prejudice against fat people (see Table 3.6). He then correlated respondents' antifat attitudes with other attitudes and beliefs, such as political ideology, that consistently have been found to relate to racism.

In his studies, Crandall reports many similarities between antifat attitudes and racism. First, persons embracing politically conservative ideology tend to have more negative attitudes toward both Blacks (Lambert & Chasteen, 1997) and fat people (Crandall, 1994; 1995). Second, greater political conservatism is also associated with a tendency to hold people responsible for their fate. In fact, Kinder and Sears (Kinder, 1986; Kinder & Sears, 1981) suggested that one component of anti-Black attitudes is the belief that Black people are responsible for their own economic fate. Similar reasoning is often associated with explanations for obesity: People who possess antifat attitudes believe fatness is due to a lack of willpower and discipline, rather than a genetic or metabolic predisposition. Thus, prejudiced persons tend to view both Blacks and fat people as responsible for their own plight. Finally, anti-Black attitudes and antifat attitudes are correlated with greater authoritarianism (i.e., conventional beliefs, submissiveness to authority, and intolerance for others).

**Table 3.6**   *Measuring Antifat Attitudes*

*Dislike of Fat People (Sample items)*

1. If I were an employer looking to hire, I might avoid hiring a fat person.
2. I don't have many friends that are fat.

*Fear of Becoming Fat (Sample items)*

1. I feel disgusted with myself when I gain weight.
2. I worry about becoming fat.

*Belief in the Controllability of Weight (Sample items)*

1. Some people are fat because they have no willpower.
2. Fat people tend to be fat pretty much through their own fault.

*Adapted from: Crandall, C. S. (1994). Prejudice Against Fat People: Ideology and Self-Interest.* Journal of Personality and Social Psychology, 66, 882–894.

Interestingly, Crandall (1994) suggests one crucial difference between antifat and anti-Black attitudes. Whereas racism is thought to have become more covert and subtle in recent years, antifat attitudes remain overt and widely expressed. Apparently, social norms inhibit the public expression of racism (Blanchard, Crandall, Brigham, & Vaughan, 1994; Blanchard, Lilly, & Vaughn, 1991), but similar norms do not yet exist for the public expression of "fatism."

## Prejudice Against Gay Men and Lesbians

In a recent study, Alan Yang (1997) reports that, in general, attitudes toward homosexuality have become more positive during the 1990s. Between 1973 and 1991, a stable 70 percent of people polled believed that sexual relations between two adults of the same sex was wrong. In 1996 the disapproval of same-sex sexual relations dropped to 56 percent of people, indicating a significant change in public opinion. However, when measuring attitudes toward homosexuals as a group, the polls show considerable antigay prejudice. Although the average "feeling thermometer"[2] ratings for gays and lesbians have increased—from an average of 30 in 1984 to an average of 39.9 in 1996—they were still among the lowest averages for any social groups measured (Yang, 1997). In fact, Sherrill (1996), who used the feeling thermometer for several social groups, including gays and lesbians, reported that "only illegal aliens . . . rival lesbians and gay men in this regard . . . No other group of Americans is the object of such sustained, extreme, and intense distaste" (p. 470).

_____

[2]A "feeling thermometer" is a survey technique used to measure affective responses to a target group. Using a 100-point scale, respondents provide a number between 0 and 100 to indicate "how favorable and warm" they feel toward the target group. The extreme ends of the scale, 0 and 100, are labeled *not favorable, don't care too much for,* and *feel favorable and warm.*

In accounting for prejudice against various groups—Blacks, women, fat people, for example—the focus has been on the symbolic values that underlie negative attitudes toward these groups. Given this focus on values, which values matter when it comes to antigay prejudice?

One explanation for antigay prejudice is that gays are often perceived as violating "family values." Gregory Herek (1988), for instance, suggests an association between religiosity and negative attitudes toward gays and lesbians. He argues that homosexuals might be perceived as violating "God's laws" or traditional values concerned with respect for family, which may result in extremely negative views of gays and lesbians. To determine if such symbolic beliefs underlie antigay prejudice, Geoffrey Haddock and his colleagues (Haddock, Zanna, & Esses, 1993; Esses, Haddock, & Zanna, 1993) asked college students at the University of Waterloo to list the values, customs, and traditions that they believed are blocked or facilitated by members of several target groups, including homosexuals. In general, this study revealed that college students, especially those high in authoritarianism, viewed themselves as differing from homosexuals in terms of the values that guide their lives. Specifically, students who were high in authoritarianism viewed homosexuals as blocking the attainment of the traditional family.

Other values that might be implicated in prejudice toward gays and lesbians are those associated with prejudice toward other groups. For example, Biernat et al. (1996) report a study in which participants listened to a mock radio interview, in which either a homosexual or heterosexual widowed father discussed his adjustment following the loss of his wife. The father's sexual orientation was manipulated within the context of talking about dating. To manipulate support or violation of family values, the father was presented in such a way that he appeared to be either a "good" father (e.g., the father was concerned with placing his son's needs above his own, and did not want his son to witness his displays of affection to the dating partner), or a poor father (e.g., the father was concerned about getting on with his life, and described how the son witnessed him engaging in sex with his dating partner). After listening to the interview, participants rated the father on several dimensions.

Not surprisingly, Biernat et al. found evidence that, overall, the homosexual father was perceived more negatively than the heterosexual father, whether he violated traditional family values or not. Additionally, they examined the role of participants' egalitarian-humanitarian values in influencing their perceptions of the fathers. Similar to attitudes toward other groups—Black Americans, individuals with disabilities, and fat people, for instance—egalitarian-humanitarian values were implicated in prejudicial responses. Put simply, greater endorsement of egalitarian beliefs was associated with reduced levels of prejudice toward each of these groups.

➤ CONCLUSION

> "In the end, antiblack, antifemale, and all forms of discrimination are equivalent to the same thing—antihumanism."
>
> *Shirley Chisholm*, Unbought and Unbossed (1970)

As you can see from this chapter, the contemporary theories of racism suggest that values play a central role in prejudice. Moreover, some compelling evidence indicates that these same values—the Protestant work ethic and humanitarianism/egalitarianism—are implicated in other forms of prejudice. Specifically, Protestant work ethic values facilitate prejudice toward Blacks, persons with disabilities, gays and lesbians, and fat people, whereas egalitarian values suppress prejudice toward these groups (Biernat et al., 1996). It may be, in the words of Weigel and Howes (1985), that "prejudice is not target specific, but rather is a generalized hostility towards a number of outgroups" (p. 126). If so, this explains why different forms of prejudice—racism, sexism, and so on—tend to coexist within the same individuals (Bierly, 1985; Altemeyer, 1994).

Will social psychologists be able to find an all-encompassing theory of prejudice that can account for the nuances in different types of prejudice? Although different forms of prejudice share many commonalities, it is highly unlikely that any single theory can account for all prejudices. In fact, Young-Bruehl (1995), who examines the four major types of prejudices, based on race, gender, sexual orientation and religion (i.e., anti-Semitism), argues that these forms of prejudice are based on different psychological processes. Understanding racial prejudice, she says, does not necessarily lend itself to understanding anti-Semitism.

This line of reasoning, in some ways, resonates with that of Allport (1950), who suggests that prejudice should be examined through a series of lenses that include lenses of an historical, cultural, and psychological nature. Prejudice is such an enigmatic and enduring phenomomenon that a multiplicity of approaches is required to fully capture the role that history, culture, and society play in it.

Keep in mind that the theories we have covered in this chapter are *individual-level* theories, in that the primary focus has been on the internal conflict that people experience between their egalitarian beliefs and their prejudiced responses. This is but one lens in which to view prejudice. Other lenses might offer a more *societal/intergroup-level* perspective. Before moving toward the societal/intergroup approach, however, we will continue with this individual-level analysis in Chapter 4 when we consider the cognitive components of prejudice.

# 4

# Cognitive Components of Prejudice: Stereotyping and Categorization

➤ INTRODUCTION

In 1998, Green Bay Packers defensive lineman Reggie White was invited to speak before the Wisconsin State Assembly. His speech stunned many lawmakers, largely because he blatantly stereotyped many ethnic groups. In his speech, White said that he had thought about why God created different races, and it is because each race has certain gifts. According to White, "Black people are gifted at worship and celebration," while Whites are good at structure and organization, adding that they "know how to tap into money"; Asians are gifted with invention, "they can turn a television into a watch"; Hispanics have a gift for family and "can put 20 or 30 people in one home"; and American Indians are gifted in spirituality. Moreover, White added, they were never enslaved because "they knew how to sneak up on people."

As you might expect, White's comments were offensive to many people. He later issued an apology, saying that his remarks were meant to be complimentary and that his intent was not to demean anyone. For many reasons, though, this example demonstrates why stereotyping is problematic. First, stereotypes are never true for all group members. Clearly, not all American Indians are spiritual, nor are all Asians intellectually gifted. At best, stereotypes are generalizations about a group of people, and inevitably there are individual group members who do not fit the stereotype of their group. Consequently, the use of stereotypes may lead us to ignore individual differences among group members.

Second, stereotypes exaggerate group differences. When we define people on the basis of their group memberships, we tend to view them as if they are more similar to some people (other group members) and more different from others (members of other groups) than they really are. Consequently, we may perceive that we have little in common with individuals from different social groups, which certainly does not bode well for harmonious intergroup relations.

In this chapter, we will examine more closely how stereotypes function, how they are formed, and how they are measured by psychologists. We will also broaden our understanding of stereotyping by analyzing the consequences of stereotyping for both the perceiver and the target. Finally, we will explore factors that may influence when individuals are more likely to stereotype others. Before we analyze these issues, let us define stereotypes and discuss their functions for the perceiver.

## ➤ WHY DO PEOPLE STEREOTYPE OTHERS?

Journalist Walter Lippman (1922) first coined the term "stereotype" to refer to our beliefs about groups. He borrowed this term from the printing process in which a "stereotype" literally was a metal plate that made duplicate copies of a printed page. Lippman believed this term aptly describes how we continuously reproduce the "pictures in our heads" that we have about a group whenever we encounter members of that group. In other words, Lippman recognized the human tendencies to categorize people into groups, and then to see individual members as a reflection of that group, rather than as the unique persons they are.

As we learned in Chapter 1, **stereotypes** are a set of beliefs about the personal attributes of a group of people (Ashmore & Del Boca, 1981). Although stereotypes may be products of individual cognitive processes, they also may be consensually shared within a society. Collectively held stereotypes may be especially pernicious as they are often widespread in a society. As an example of this important distinction between individual and collective stereotypes, suppose you are a member of Group X who has been denied employment because the employer assumes that your group is intellectually inferior to the dominant group. While this would undoubtedly be a frustrating experience for you, you may easily be able to find employment elsewhere. However, if this belief that your group is intellectually inferior is widely accepted within a society, finding employment may prove challenging indeed. Thus, it is the widespread acceptance of particular stereotypic beliefs about a social group, rather than an individual's idiosyncratic beliefs about the group, that is more problematic (Stangor & Schaller, 1996).

We also learned in Chapter 1 that stereotypes may be positive (e.g., "Asians are the model minority") or negative (e.g., "Irish are heavy drinkers"). But even complimentary stereotypes are not as benign as they initially appear, because they are equally exaggerated generalizations. A person who accepts seemingly positive stereotypes as factual may be prone to readily accept the less positive ones as well.

Nonetheless, if stereotypes represent inaccurate or distorted generalizations, why do they persist over time? For example, during the days of American slavery,

Blacks were stereotyped as intellectually inferior, unevolved, primitive, and apelike (Plous & Williams, 1995). Beliefs about innate physical differences (e.g., Blacks are less sensitive to pain than Whites; Blacks have thicker skulls than Whites) and innate abilities (e.g., Blacks are innately more athletic and rhythmic than Whites) were commonplace among Whites in the United States and Europe during the 18th and 19th centuries. Sad to say, these stereotypes persist today. In a telephone survey of White and Black residents of central Connecticut, S. Plous and Tyrone Williams (1995) found that the majority of respondents (58.9%) endorsed at least one stereotypical difference in inborn ability. Whites, for example, were more likely than Blacks to be viewed as superior in intellectual ability, whereas Blacks were more likely than Whites to be viewed as superior in athletic and musical ability. Moreover, nearly half (49%) of those surveyed believed at least one stereotypical anatomical difference between Whites and Blacks: Almost one-third of respondents believed that Black skin is thicker than White skin; 20% believed that Blacks have thicker skulls than Whites; and 14% believed Whites were more sensitive to pain than Blacks.

Surprisingly, Blacks were somewhat more likely than Whites to endorse racial stereotypes. That these racial stereotypes resulting from the legacy of slavery endure in American society, even among African Americans, is perplexing. The crucial question is: Why?

If pressed to do so, most people easily acknowledge that not all Blacks are rhythmic or athletic, not all Jews are good with money, not all women are submissive and nurturant, not all Latinos are family oriented, to name a few popular stereotypes. Still, many people stubbornly cling to these assumptions, and some researchers suggest they do so because stereotypes serve important psychological functions, both at an individual level and a group level.

## Individual-Level Functions of Stereotypes

Considering the individual-level analysis first, Snyder and Meine (1994) propose that stereotypes serve three distinct functions for the individual: (a) a cognitive function, (b) an ego-defensive function, and (c) a social function. These three functions are described as follows:

COGNITIVE FUNCTION In their cognitive function, stereotypes allow the individual to simplify and reduce complex information to a manageable size. In fact, Gilbert and Hixon (1991) suggest that stereotypes are "cognitive tools" that save people the trouble of thinking about each new person they encounter. Upon encountering someone for the first time and knowing little about that person except for his or her group membership, we may rely upon stereotypes to infer that person's interests and attitudes. After being told that someone is a feminist, for example, we may make assumptions about that person's views on abortion, affirmative action, and sexual harassment policies.

Fitting a person to a category also works in the opposite manner, however. People may compare an individual's behavior to a prevailing stereotype in order to determine the person's membership in a social group. For example, knowing that Dennis is a hairstylist who has lived with the same man for several years may lead us to predict his group membership (e.g., "Is he gay?"). In short, stereotypes are energy-saving devices that allow us to compress information about others in a rapid fashion (Macrae, Milne, & Bodenhausen, 1994).

EGO-DEFENSIVE FUNCTION   Stereotypes also serve an ego-defensive function, in which stereotyping others helps us to feel better about ourselves. One way that we defend against threats to our personal self-esteem may be to derogate others. Imagine, for instance, that you have just been given an intelligence test, and your self-esteem is later deflated when the experimenter informs you (falsely) that you have scored poorly on the test. The experimenter then asks you to complete a "social judgment task" in which you read about Greg, a 31-year-old struggling actor living in New York City, who you infer to be gay. Would you be more likely to evaluate Greg consistently with the gay stereotype if you had just received negative feedback about your intelligence than if you had not received any negative feedback?

According to a study by Steven Fein and Steven Spencer (1997), the answer is "yes." Compared to subjects in the control group who were not given failure feedback, subjects who were told they scored poorly on the intelligence test were more likely to perceive a gay male target in a stereotypical fashion (e.g., as more sensitive, feminine, passive, etc.) than subjects who had not received negative feedback. In addition to perceiving the target stereotypically, subjects whose self-esteem was threatened by negative feedback were also less inclined to like the gay target than subjects who were not given negative feedback.

That stereotypes serve an ego-defensive function may also explain why most stereotypes are primarily negative. For example, stereotypes about Blacks, Latinos, women, the elderly, people with disabilities, gay men and lesbians, American Indians, and many other groups may differ in actual content, but what these stereotypes have in common are predominantly negative characterizations. Speaking disparagingly of others may allow people to feel better about themselves. Apparently, one way to boost self-esteem may be through denigrating others.

SOCIAL FUNCTION   Finally, stereotyping may serve a social function by helping us to fit in and identify with our own groups. Shared stereotypes among group members may foster loyalty to the group and help to demonstrate in-group identification (Worchel & Rothgerber, 1997). In fact, Nyla Branscombe and colleagues (1995) suggest that derogating the out-group may be one method of demonstrating loyalty to the in-group, particularly for group members who are insecure of their status. In one study of fraternities and sororities, for example, pledge and active members were asked to evaluate members of their own group as well as members of different fraternities (male subjects only) or sororities (female subjects only). In addition, subjects believed that their ratings would be confidential (private condition) or shared later with in-group members (public condition). Pledges, who are in the process of being initiated into the group but are not fully accepted as group members, are less secure in their group membership than are active members. Because of their insecurity, pledges were more likely than active group members to hold very negative views of the out-groups, but only when they believed their opinions would be shared with other in-group members. Thus, it appears that stereotyping and openly derogating out-group members serves the important social function of gaining the acceptance of in-group members.

## Group-Level Functions of Stereotypes

Stereotypes not only serve the individual, but they serve the group interest as well. At times, stereotypes may serve the group by positively differentiating the in-group from out-groups. At other times, stereotypes may serve the group by justifying the exploitation of other groups.

GROUP-JUSTIFICATION FUNCTION    According to Henri Tajfel (1981), stereotypes must be understood within the context of intergroup relations, because stereotypes protect not just the individual's ego, but the status of the group as a whole. This group-justification function (Jost & Banaji, 1994) is rooted in Tajfel's **social identity** theory, which suggests that we derive part of our self-esteem from our group memberships. If we feel good about the groups to which we belong, our self-esteem is enhanced; conversely, if we feel bad about the groups to which we belong, our self-esteem is deflated. Thus, our social identity forms the basis of our *collective* self-esteem.

At times we may seek to enhance our collective self-esteem by bolstering our social identity. Consequently, we often exaggerate differences between our group and another group in order to strengthen our social identity. How we distinguish ourselves from other groups occurs in two ways: (a) We hold positive stereotypes of our in-group; and (b) we hold negative stereotypes of the out-group (Hogg & Abrams, 1988; Mullen, Brown, & Smith, 1992). Just as we might be predisposed to stereotype or derogate others when we experience threats to our *personal* self-esteem, social identity theorists suggest we may be prone to out-group derogation when our *collective* self-esteem is threatened as well (Rubin & Hewstone, 1998). That is precisely what Branscombe and Wann (1994) found when they threatened their subjects' collective self-esteem. Several weeks prior to their participation in the experiment, subjects were given a questionnaire that established the extent to which they identified with the in-group "Americans." Once the researchers identified subjects who were high or low in their degree of identification with Americans, subjects were asked to watch a boxing segment from the film *Rocky IV*, in which American Rocky Balboa faces his Russian opponent Ivan Drago. For subjects in the threatening condition, they saw a segment in which the Russian opponent defeated Rocky. Subjects in the unthreatening condition, in contrast, saw a segment in which Rocky defeated the Russian boxer.

Following the film clip, subjects were given the opportunity to evaluate a variety of out-groups, including Russians. As you might expect, highly-identified, but not low-identified subjects, showed significantly lower collective self-esteem and were more willing to derogate Russians after watching Rocky lose the match than they did after he won. Thus, as predicted by social identity theory, individuals who are closely identified with their in-group are more likely to defend their group against threats by derogating the out-group. Derogating the out-group, in turn, boosts individuals' collective self-esteem. We will have more to say about the group-justification function of stereotypes in Chapter 6 when we focus on intergroup relations and prejudice.

SYSTEM-JUSTIFICATION FUNCTION    Stereotypes also serve another function, namely to maintain the status quo. John Jost and Mahzarin Banaji (1994) argue that stereotypes serve ideological functions by rationalizing or justifying existing intergroup relations. In describing the system-justification function of stereotypes, they suggest that stereotypes develop to explain prevailing economic, social, and political arrangements. Consider, for example, the historical roots of stereotypes pertaining to several groups. Dehumanizing stereotypes of Blacks in the United States emerged partly because of the need of Whites to rationalize the systematic exploitation of Blacks under slavery (Gaines & Reed, 1995; Plous & Williams, 1995). Gender stereotypes arose in order to rationalize or explain the sexual division of labor (Eagly & Steffen, 1984; Hoffman & Hurst, 1990). Likewise, demeaning stereotypes of Japanese, Koreans, and Vietnamese emerged in the United States during periods of war in order to justify large-scale conflicts.

What is unique to this system-justification approach is that it explains the phenomenon of *negative* self-stereotyping that cannot be adequately accounted for by the group-justification function of stereotyping. The group-justification function of stereotypes, you will recall, suggests that individuals engage in positive self-stereotyping and negative stereotyping of out-groups in order to enhance their social identity. But research suggests that groups may sometimes endorse negative stereotypes about their *own* group. Studies have shown, for instance, that men and women possess similar gender stereotypes (Banaji & Greenwald, 1994; Broverman et al., 1972), and that Blacks and Whites also have similar racial stereotypes (Bayton, McAlister & Hamer, 1956; Judd et al., 1995). Remember Plous and Williams's (1995) study of racial stereotypes that have their roots in slavery? It probably surprised you to learn that African-American respondents were more likely to endorse negative stereotypes about Blacks than White respondents. Why might individuals endorse pejorative stereotypes of their own group?

Because "the ideas of the dominant tend to become the ideas of the dominated" (Jost & Banaji, 1994, p. 10), the system-justification approach suggests that people may justify existing social arrangements that are actually disadvantageous to them. This means that stereotypes allow people—both members of the dominant group and members of the subordinate group—to provide an account for why things are the way that they are. Thus, members of the dominated group may form ideas about their own inferiority, which in turn, may limit their achievements (Croizet & Claire, 1998; Steele, 1997).

Before concluding our discussion of stereotypes and how they serve important functions for both the individual and society, we should consider the implications of this analysis. At an individual level, stereotypes might serve quite different underlying functions depending upon the situation. For instance, sometimes we might stereotype others in order to feel better about ourselves, and at other times we might stereotype in order to demonstrate loyalty to our social group. On a broader level, stereotypes tell us much about the relations between groups in society. What we have to keep in mind is that stereotypes are not constants; rather, they are responsive to the broader intergroup relations context. Thus, changes to the existing social arrangements will also produce changes in stereotype content. War, for instance, can very dramatically change the stereotypes that groups have of each other. In the next section, we will consider the content of stereotypes and how they have changed over the years within the context of stereotype measurement. As you will see, stereotypes have been measured in diverse ways, and each method has its own advantages and shortcomings.

## ➤ HOW ARE STEREOTYPES MEASURED?

How stereotypes influence our perceptions of members of social groups has been a concern to social psychologists since Lippman (1922) first defined stereotypes as "pictures in our heads." Early research on stereotyping initially focused on identifying the content of those "pictures" by examining the traits and characteristics attributed to different social groups. In this section, we will consider several techniques designed to measure the content of stereotypes about different social groups. In addition, recent use of these stereotype measurement methodologies will be presented, along with some of the relevant findings regarding stereotype content.

### Adjective Checklist Approach

In 1933, Katz and Braly asked 100 White male college students at Princeton University to provide their beliefs about 10 ethnic groups: Germans, Italians, Irish, Jews, (White) Americans, Chinese, Turks, Japanese, English, and Negroes. Respondents were presented with a list of 84 adjectives (e.g., intelligent, conservative, quick-tempered, etc.) and instructed to select those 10 adjectives that they believed best described each of the target groups. Once they had completed the checklist for all 10 groups, respondents were asked to select the five adjectives that seemed to them most characteristic of each group.

These college students demonstrated a high level of consistency in their stereotypes. For example, White Americans were described as industrious, intelligent, materialistic, and ambitious; Jews were viewed as shrewd, mercenary, industrious, and grasping; and Negroes were seen as superstitious, lazy, happy-go-lucky, and ignorant. Widely shared stereotypes of the other target groups included: Germans, scientifically-minded and industrious; Italians, artistic and impulsive; Turks, cruel; English, sportsmanlike and intelligent; Irish, pugnacious and quick-tempered; Japanese, intelligent and industrious; and Chinese, superstitious.

This elegantly simple assessment technique was later replicated by several researchers (Gilbert, 1951; Karlins, Coffman, & Walters, 1969) to determine the amount of stability or change in stereotypes among later generations of Princeton students. These subsequent studies, along with Katz and Braly's original study, have been dubbed the "Princeton trilogy." In general, the Princeton trilogy revealed considerable consistency in stereotypes over three generations of students. However, some notable changes in stereotype content occurred due to U.S. involvement in prominent wars. For example, the Japanese were viewed as "intelligent" and "industrious" in 1933, but they became "sly," "imitative," and "extremely nationalistic" during the World War II years, and changed back to the earlier positive images during 1969. Similarly, the positive stereotype of Germans changed somewhat as a result of World War II.

Perhaps of most interest to researchers has been whether the stereotypes of African Americans have changed over three generations of Princeton undergraduates. From Katz and Braly's (1933) study to Karlins et al.'s (1969) study, the Black stereotype has become less negative, prompting Karlins et al. to conclude that negative stereotypes of Blacks are fading. For instance, in 1933, 84% of respondents endorsed the stereotype of Blacks as superstitious, compared to only 13% in 1969. Similarly, only 26% of respondents described Blacks as lazy in 1969, compared to 75% in 1933.

But are negative stereotypes of Blacks really fading? More recently, researchers have questioned this assumption, pointing out the flaws associated with the checklist methodology. For example, Sigall and Page (1971) argued that the apparent decrease in negative stereotyping of Blacks was due to participants' increased concerns over appearing prejudiced. Patricia Devine and Andrew Elliott (1995) suggest other problems with Katz and Braly's checklist procedure, including the use of ambiguous instructions. In the Princeton trilogy studies, for instance, it is unclear whether participants thought they were to indicate their knowledge of the cultural stereotypes (which participants may or may not personally endorse) or whether they thought they were to indicate their personal beliefs.

In an attempt to remedy the problems associated with the original checklist methodology, Devine and Elliot replicated the Katz and Braly study with some significant changes. First, University of Wisconsin-Madison undergraduates were presented the 84 original Katz and Braly adjectives, along with 9 adjectives that previous studies had indicated comprise contemporary stereotypes of Blacks (athletic, criminal, hostile, low in intelligence, poor, uneducated, sexually perverse, violent, and rhythmic). They also asked the participants to identify those adjectives that they believe represented the *cultural stereotype* of Blacks. Participants were then asked to go through the list again and indicate the adjectives that represented their *personal beliefs* about Blacks. In addition, Devine and Elliott included a measure of participants' prejudice level to determine whether high- or low-prejudiced participants differed in their trait ratings.

Their results indicated that the cultural stereotype of Blacks has indeed changed since the Princeton studies. The most frequently listed traits included only three of the original items (lazy, ignorant, musical), along with other traits not appearing on Katz and Braly's checklist (e.g., athletic, musical, criminal, poor, etc.). Contrary to the popular notion that negative stereotypes of Blacks are fading, Devine and Elliot found that the contemporary Black cultural stereotype remains highly negative. However, and importantly, high- and low-prejudiced participants differed markedly in their endorsement of the cultural stereotypes. That is, both groups of participants were equally knowledgeable about the cultural stereotype of Blacks, but only high-prejudiced participants personally endorsed the cultural stereotype.

Although the contemporary cultural stereotype of Blacks remains negative, Devine and Elliot suggest that the more promising news is that White participants' personal beliefs about Blacks are undergoing transformation. They report that participants' personal beliefs have become more positive, with low-prejudiced persons in particular using traits such as sensitive, honest, kind, and straightforward to describe Blacks.

The Katz and Braly checklist, perhaps because of its simplicity, set the stage for stereotype assessment for several decades. It was not until the 1970s that different approaches to stereotype measurement emerged.

## Percentage Technique

Researchers using Katz and Braly's checklist approach sometimes met with problems. For example, Karlins et al. (1969) found that many of the respondents were reluctant to select traits to describe groups of people, believing it to represent unwarranted generalizations or prejudice. John Brigham (1971) evaded this problem by utilizing the percentage technique, which requires respondents to estimate the percentage of group members who possess a certain attribute. The traits that receive the highest percentage ratings are considered to make up the stereotype. This type of stereotype assessment is more palatable to respondents than the Katz and Braly checklist approach. Unlike the latter approach in which respondents ascribe traits in an all-or-nothing fashion to social groups, the percentage technique allows exceptions: To say, for example, that 85% of women are family oriented is to recognize that some are not.

Using the percentage technique, Walter Stephan and colleagues (1993) asked Russian college students to indicate their stereotypes of Americans. In this study, participants were given a list of 38 traits and asked to estimate the percentage of Americans who possessed each of the traits. Their data revealed that Russians' stereotypes of Americans are positive, with the following traits receiving the highest percentage estimates: ambitious (81%), spontaneous (78%), dignified (75%), competent (75%) and energetic (75%).

The shortcomings of the percentage technique rest primarily with the relative ambiguity of what constitutes a stereotype. For example, if you think that 81% of Americans are ambitious, does this mean that ambitiousness is a strong American stereotype? We can't really say for sure until we know how ambitious you think other nationalities are. If you believe that 81% of people in general are ambitious, to say that 81% of Americans are ambitious isn't really telling us much about how you view Americans. In other words, your view of Americans is no different from your view of other nationalities. To address this issue, we have to determine which traits uniquely distinguish Americans from people in general. This is precisely the aim of the following stereotype measurement technique.

## Diagnostic Ratio Method

Using their diagnostic ratio method, McCauley and Stitt (1978) further refined the percentage technique by measuring the distinctiveness of a given attribute. First, as in the percentage method, participants indicate the percentage of members of a particular group who possess certain traits. Second, participants are to indicate the percentage of all the world's people who are likely to possess the same traits. The diagnostic ratio is then calculated by dividing the percentage of group members who possess a certain trait by the percentage of all people who possess that trait. Or, using the example above, the percentage of Americans estimated to be ambitious is divided by the percentage of ambitious people in general. Stereotypes are determined by deviations from a ratio of 1.0. For stereotypical traits, ratios should be greater than 1.0; for counterstereotypical traits, ratios should be less than 1.0.

As an example of how the diagnostic ratio measure may be used, McCauley and Stitt (1978) selected several traits demonstrated in previous research to be typical of

*Table 4.1      Diagnostic Ratio Measure of the German Stereotype*

| Characteristic | % Germans Believed to Possess (1) | % People Believed to Possess (2) | Diagnostic Ratio (1)/(2) |
| --- | --- | --- | --- |
| Efficient | 63.4 | 49.8 | 1.27 |
| Extremely nationalistic | 56.3 | 35.4 | 1.59 |
| Ignorant | 29.2 | 34.0 | 0.86 |
| Impulsive | 41.1 | 51.7 | 0.79 |
| Industrious | 68.2 | 59.8 | 1.14 |
| Scientifically minded | 43.1 | 32.6 | 1.32 |

*Adapted from: McCauley, C., & Stitt, C.L. (1978). An Individual and Quantitative Measure of Stereotypes.* Journal of Personality and Social Psychology, 36, 929–940.

Germans, along with traits that were not considered to be part of the German stereotype. Participants were asked to estimate the percentage of Germans who possessed each trait, as well as the percentage of all people who possess each trait. Table 4.1 on this page presents the diagnostic ratio measure of stereotypes for Germans. A glance at the table shows that "extremely nationalistic," "efficient," "industrious," and "scientifically minded" is part of the German stereotype, because the diagnostic ratios for those traits are above 1.0. In contrast, characteristics like "ignorant," and "impulsive" are actually counterstereotypical, because the diagnostic ratios for the traits are below 1.0.

## Free-Response Approach

An alternative technique that may be used to assess stereotype content involves using free responses, in which respondents simply write down the characteristics they believe to be typical of a social group. According to Devine (1989), the free-response technique is a more sensitive measure of stereotypes because respondents are not provided cues (e.g., a list of possible traits) that may bias stereotype content.

As an example of the free-response method, consider a recent study designed to assess stereotypes of eight groups. Yolanda Niemann and colleagues (Niemann, Jennings, Rozelle, Baxter, & Sullivan, 1994) asked University of Houston students from ethnically diverse backgrounds to list the first 10 adjectives that come to mind when considering the following ethnic/gender groups: African-American males, African-American females, Anglo-American males, Anglo-American females, Asian-American males, Asian-American females, Mexican-American males, and Mexican-American females.

Following data collection, Niemann et al. organized the free responses into a group of categories, ranging from physical descriptors to values and behaviors. Table 4.2 lists the top 20% of traits ascribed to each group. Notice the presence of within-ethnic group similarities and differences that emerged for the groups. For example, both Mexican-American males and females were described as *lower class, dark skin,* and *pleasant/friendly.* However, *hard workers, antagonistic,* and *ambitionless* was

**Table 4.2      *Free-Response Method of Stereotype Measurement***

| *Anglo-American males* | *Anglo-American females* |
|---|---|
| intelligent | attractive |
| egotistical | intelligent |
| upper class | egotistical |
| pleasant/friendly | pleasant/friendly |
| racist | blond/light hair |
| achievement oriented | sociable |

| *African-American males* | *African-American females* |
|---|---|
| athletic | speak loudly |
| antagonistic | dark skin |
| dark skin | athletic |
| muscular appearance | pleasant/friendly |
| criminal activities | unmannerly |

| *Asian-American males* | *Asian-American females* |
|---|---|
| intelligent | intelligent |
| short | speak softly |
| achievement oriented | pleasant/friendly |
| speak softly | short |

| *Mexican-American males* | *Mexican-American females* |
|---|---|
| lower class | black/brown/dark hair |
| hard workers | attractive |
| antagonistic | pleasant/friendly |
| dark skin | dark skin |
| non-college education | lower class |
| pleasant/friendly | overweight |
| black/brown/dark hair | baby makers |
| ambitionless | family oriented |

*Adapted from: Niemann et al. (1994). Use of Free Responses and Cluster Analysis to Determine Stereotypes of Eight Groups. Personality and Social Psychology Bulletin, 20, 379–390.*

used for Mexican-American males, whereas *overweight, baby makers,* and *family oriented* were used for Mexican-American females. Similar patterns appear for the other target groups.

Using the free-response method of stereotype measurement has certain advantages. This method allows researchers to capture contemporary stereotypes that do not appear on checklist methodologies. Checklist approaches typically rely upon trait descriptors, but free-response methods demonstrate greater complexity in stereotyping. For example, in Niemann et al.'s study of ethnic/gender stereotypes, stereotypes of the groups ranged from physical descriptors (dark hair, overweight, muscular appearance) to traits (intelligent, achievement oriented, athletic) to behaviors (speak loudly, baby makers, socially active).

The free-response method is not without limitations, however. One significant problem is that the data are laborious to organize in a meaningful way. Another problem concerns whether respondents are articulate enough to name the attributes they perceive in various groups. The checklist methodology, in contrast, provides the vocabulary for respondents to "recognize" their perceptions of various groups.

## Response Time Measurements

So far, our discussion of stereotype measurement techniques has been limited to the self-report variety which involves simply asking people about their beliefs about various groups in society. Although these conscious replies are useful to researchers, many question whether participants are completely forthright in their reports (Sigall & Page, 1971). Moreover, the possibility exists that stereotypes may not even be accessible to people's conscious thought (Banaji & Greenwald, 1994; Greenwald & Banaji, 1995). Thus, one method of accessing unconscious or "automatic" stereotyping is through **priming**, which involves activating particular associations in memory. Using this method, participants may classify a series of target words based on the word's evaluative meaning (e.g., "good" vs. "bad"). Immediately preceding each target word is a to-be-ignored "prime," which represents the attitude object. Primes may vary from words depicting social category labels (e.g., "Black" versus "White"; "young" vs. "old") to photographs of strangers. The critical measure of interest is the speed in which people can indicate the connotation of the target word. The rationale behind measuring people's response times is that the more closely associated two stimulus items are in memory, the faster will be the response.

As an example of how measuring reaction times may indicate stereotypic associations, consider a recent study by Anthony Greenwald and his colleagues (1998). In this study, White participants were presented with a sequence of two words, either a positive (e.g., caress, freedom, peace) or negative (e.g., abuse, death, hatred) adjective, paired with a characteristically "White" (e.g., Adam, Heather, Josh) or "Black" (e.g., Jamel, Yolanda, Tanisha) name. As the name and word appear on the computer screen, subjects were asked to make a series of simple judgments ("Is this a positive or negative word?"; "Is this a White or Black name?"). Meanwhile, the computer recorded the speed of the participants' responses.

Participants responded more quickly when they saw White names paired with pleasant words or Black names paired with unpleasant words. This alarming result apparently is due to the deep learning of negative associations to the group Black in our society. Such stereotypical associations are so overlearned that most Whites (and some Blacks, apparently) can process them more rapidly.

Russell Fazio and his colleagues (Fazio, Jackson, Dunton, & Williams) demonstrated a similar phenomenon, but with using photographs as primes rather than words. In their experiment, White participants were presented with a series of words that had positive meanings (e.g., attractive, likable, wonderful) or negative meanings (e.g., annoying, disgusting, offensive). Immediately preceding each word, participants were shown a photograph of either a White or Black person for 315 milliseconds, ostensibly as part of a facial "recognition task." Participants were instructed to learn the face while indicating their judgments of the word by pressing a key labeled *good* or a key labeled *bad* as quickly as possible. For example, a participant would see "likable" and press the key corresponding to positive meanings. Again, the critical measure of stereotyping was the speed at which participants could make their decisions. The faster the response, the more related the adjective would be to the photograph in the participant's mind.

A glance at participants' response times reveals a disturbing phenomenon: When participants saw a Black face and then a negative adjective, they responded more quickly than when a White face was paired with a negative adjective. The opposite occurred for positive adjectives.

Such unobtrusive measures of stereotyping allow researchers to "get inside people's heads" and record subtle cognitive mechanisms involved in stereotyping. These same techniques can be used to measure hidden biases about many different social groups, such as women (Blair & Banaji, 1996 ) and the elderly (Perdue & Gurtman, 1990).

As you can see, these approaches to measuring stereotypes—ranging from the traditional checklist method to the more sophisticated reaction time method—have contributed to our knowledge of stereotype content. Because of this diversity in stereotype measurement techniques, researchers now recognize that stereotypes contain more than just information about the personality traits commonly associated with group members. Stereotypes also include information about physical attributes, attitudes, preferences, and social roles typically associated with group members (Deaux & Lewis, 1983, 1984; Hamilton & Sherman, 1996; Mackie & Smith, 1998; Zebrowitz, 1996).

Given that stereotypes convey an abundance of information about social groups, one might wonder about the origins of stereotypes. In the next section, we will consider where these "pictures in our heads" come from.

➤  ## HOW ARE STEREOTYPES FORMED?

One question that has interested students and researchers alike is, How do stereotypes form, and how do such perceptions come to be a part of an individual's (or society's) beliefs? Historically, we've seen that stereotypes of social group may often reflect the prevailing economic and social relations within a country. As noted previously, stereotypes of Japanese and Germans changed dramatically during World War II, moving from positive stereotypes prior to the war to highly negative stereotypes during the war. In general, competition and conflict do have a tendency to increase negative stereotyping (Sherif et al., 1961), but competition is not the only ingredient that promotes negative stereotyping. As we shall see, several basic cognitive processes lay the foundation upon which stereotypes may then be built.

### Categorization

As Gordon Allport (1954) and Henri Tajfel (1969) remind us, categorization is a fundamental cognitive process that allows us to reduce the flow of incoming information from a complex social world. Typically we group people according to similar attributes, and attributes that are visibly identifiable (e.g., gender, age, race) and/or deviate from the norm (e.g., physical disability, sexual orientation) are likely to serve as basic categories for groupings (Brewer, 1988; Fiske & Neuberg, 1990). Once we perceive an aggregate of people as belonging to a social group, we overlook their individualities. In fact, individual members are perceived to be more alike than they really are; this process is referred to as *assimilation*. And once individuals are grouped into different social categories (e.g., heterosexuals vs. homosexuals, women vs. men), differences between the groups tend to become exaggerated; this process is referred to as *contrast*.

As an example of this process, group the following objects into meaningful categories: apple, hammer, orange, saw, pear, banana, screwdriver. If you're like most people, you probably grouped the objects into two categories: fruit and tools. Because of assimilation and contrast processes, you are likely to emphasize both the similarities among members of the two categories (within-group assimilation) and the differences between the two categories (between-group contrast). But what if you were from a culture that was not familiar with these items and had spontaneously grouped the objects into different categories, say, for example, elongated objects (hammer, saw, banana, screwdriver) vs. rounded objects (apple, orange, pear)? Because of assimilation processes, you would now perceive the banana to be more similar to a hammer and more distinctly different from an apple. The important point to be made here is that such groupings—whether of objects or people—are not made because the items in a category are in fact similar, but that perceptions of similarity are subjective and tend to reflect widespread cultural beliefs (Wittenbrink, Hilton, & Gist, 1998).

Another important point to be made about categorization is this: The mere separation of people into groups is sufficient to create stereotyping and prejudice. Utilizing what is called the "minimal group paradigm," Tajfel (1978) divided subjects into two groups, ostensibly based upon whether subjects overestimated or underestimated the number of dots on briefly presented cards. In actuality, subjects were assigned to groups randomly. Even within these artificially created groups (with no prior contact and without a history of conflict), subjects demonstrated negative stereotyping of the other group and favoritism toward their own group. Thus, categorization is the basis of stereotyping and prejudice.

## Illusory Correlation

Other research on cognitive processes suggests that we have a tendency to focus on distinctive stimuli in our environment. We notice the unusual, the atypical, the anomalous, the out of the ordinary. This does not mean, of course, that we attend only to bizarre people. We notice anyone who is distinctive within a social context, such as a man within a room full of women (Taylor, 1981).

This tendency to focus on distinctive stimuli can contribute to the development of stereotypes, as implicated in research on illusory correlation. Illusory correlation refers to an overestimation of the strength of a relationship between two variables. The variables may not be related at all, or the relationship may be weaker than assumed. Illusory correlations are especially likely to arise when members of a numerically infrequent group (i.e., "minority group") perform infrequent behaviors. For instance, many Whites in our culture have relatively little contact with Blacks. Thus, for Whites, encounters with Blacks are relatively infrequent and distinctive. In addition, undesirable behaviors occur less frequently than desirable behaviors, making any undesirable behaviors particularly attention-grabbing. When two distinctive events co-occur (such as a Black individual engaging in an undesirable behavior), people tend to perceive a relationship between Blacks and undesirable behaviors. This illusory correlation effect results from the co-occurrence of distinctive events having a disproportionate effect on judgments.

An experiment by David Hamilton and Robert Gifford (1976) demonstrates how such illusory correlations develop. In this study, participants read a series of statements describing the behavior (either desirable or undesirable) about members of two groups, the majority Group A and the minority Group B. There were twice as many statements about Group A members as about Group B members, reflecting the fact that Group B is smaller in the real world than Group A. Of the statements, two-thirds described desirable behaviors (e.g., John, a member of Group A, visited a sick friend in the hospital), and one-third described undesirable behavior (e.g., Bob, a member of Group B, always talks about himself). Even though there were more statements about Group A than about Group B, the ratio of desirable to undesirable behaviors was the same, providing the same evaluative content. Thus, Group A should have been perceived similarly to Group B. But surprisingly, participants viewed Group A (the majority group) more favorably than Group B (the minority group) because of their inclination to attend to distinctive events. Because members of Group B were infrequent and the occurrence of undesirable behaviors was infrequent also, the co-occurence of these two events was especially infrequent (Group B members behaving undesirably), producing an illusory correlation between group members and behavioral undesirability.

This illusory correlation effect has been useful in explaining the formation of negative stereotypes about minorities. As an example, male Hispanics are commonly stereotyped as aggressive or criminal (Bodenhausen, 1988; Jones, 1991; Marin, 1984). Newspaper articles about criminal behavior (a numerically infrequent behavior) performed by an individual with an Hispanic surname (a numerically infrequent ethnic group) may lead the reader to perceive erroneously a relationship between this ethnic group and criminal tendencies. Similarly, if a gay person or an ex-mental patient commits a violent crime, their homosexuality or history of mental illness invariably gets mentioned in the media because of its distinctiveness. Remember, if you will, the amount of attention the media placed on John Hinckley Jr.'s mental status following the attempted assassination of Ronald Reagan, or recall how much media attention was given to serial killer Jeffrey Dahmer's homosexuality. But if a heterosexual person or a person without a history of mental illness commits a violent crime, his or her sexual orientation or mental status is rarely reported because of its lack of "newsworthiness." Unfortunately, such reporting by the news media contributes to negative stereotypes about minority groups because of our tendency to "see" correlations between two infrequent events.

In summary, research on cognition demonstrates that intergroup conflict is not a necessary prerequisite for stereotyping and prejudice. Rather, basic cognitive processes alone can contribute to differential perceptions of groups, and ultimately lead to stereotyping and prejudice.

## Social Roles

The work of Alice Eagly and her colleagues (Eagly, 1987; Eagly & Steffen, 1984, 1986; Eagly & Wood, 1982) demonstrates the power that social roles or existing divisions of labor play in shaping stereotypic perceptions. In examining the content of stereotypes about women and men, Eagly and Steffen (1984) argue that gender stereotypes reflect people's observations of what women and men do in society. If, for instance, people consistently observe women in the "homemaker" role, they are likely to believe that the traits associated with this role are more typical of women than men. To test this hypothesis, participants read a brief description of a male or female stimulus person who was described as either a homemaker or a full-time employee. In the control condition, no occupational information was provided about the stimulus person. After reading the description, participants were asked to rate the stimulus person on a number of dimensions that reflected stereotypically masculine or "agentic" qualities (e.g., independent, aggressive, dominant, competitive) and stereotypically feminine or "communal" qualities (e.g., warm, kind, helpful, understanding).

The researchers found that participants viewed the stimulus person without the occupational information stereotypically (i.e., the woman was perceived as more communal and the man as more agentic). However, in conditions in which information about occupational role was provided, participants were more likely to base their judgments on the stimulus person's occupational role, rather than gender. In other words, homemakers, regardless of their gender, were perceived as more communal than employees. Similarly, employees, regardless of their gender, were perceived as more agentic than homemakers. These findings, then, suggest that gender stereotypes arise from our observations of women and men's differing social roles in our society.

Following Eagly and Steffen's lead, Hoffman and Hurst (1990) suggest that gender stereotypes arise not only out of observations of women and men's differing social roles, but also out of attempts to rationalize the division of labor. In a clever experiment, their participants read vignettes about two fictitious groups, "Orinthians" and "Ackmians," whose occupations were described as "child-raisers" or "city workers," respectively. Results indicated that participants spontaneously attributed agentic qualities to the city workers and communal qualities to the child-raisers. Moreover, this tendency was exaggerated when participants were first asked to explain *why* the groups occupied different roles, providing support for the notion that gender stereotypes arise largely out of an attempt to rationalize or justify the sexual division of labor.

Although evidence that social roles account for racial or ethnic stereotypes is less clear-cut, research suggests that beliefs about social class may underlie stereotypes about various ethnic groups (Jones, 1991; Smedley & Bayton, 1978). People belonging to the lower social class are commonly stereotyped as unintelligent, dirty, unreliable, and lazy (Darley & Gross, 1983; Feldman, 1972). That these unfavorable traits also are commonly ascribed to Blacks and Hispanics may reflect people's beliefs that these ethnic groups are economically disadvantaged relative to Whites. Thus, stereotypes about ethnic groups may be based in part on perceived differences in social class, and based upon Hoffman and Hurst's (1990) study, ethnic stereotypes may be used to rationalize economic disparities between dominant and subordinate groups.

## Social Transmission

Because stereotypes are deeply embedded within the cultural fabric of a society, they are often acquired "ready-made and prepackaged" (Mackie et al., 1996, p. 60) through early childhood experiences. Parents, teachers, and peers are important sources of information about other social groups. In fact, research suggests that by age 5, most children have begun to develop defined racial attitudes and show a preference for members of their own group over others (Rosenfield & Stephan, 1981). Of course, people in a child's environment are not the only contributors to stereotype acquisition. As a socialization force, the media are powerful transmitters of cultural stereotypes and play a significant role in the development of prejudice. Television, in particular, is highly accessible to children, considering that more American households have television sets than refrigerators and indoor plumbing (National Institute of Mental Health, 1983). Moreover, it is estimated that by the time a child reaches 18 years of age, she or he will have spent more time in front of a television than engaging in any other single activity besides sleep (Liebert & Sprafkin, 1988). What is important to recognize is that the mass media, television foremost among them, are central agents of socialization. Even if parents want their children to be free of stereotypes and prejudice, that outcome is improbable as long as children are allowed to watch television and films, read magazines and newspapers, and listen to the radio.

Although any form of media could be analyzed in detail, we'll restrict our discussion to television, print, and film. And our discussion of the media will also be restricted in another way. Reflecting the fact that researchers have focused primarily on the media representations of African Americans and women, much of this discussion of stereotyping in the media will reflect that bias. Whenever possible, however, the portrayal of other groups (e.g., Latinos, American Indians, gays) will be presented.

Historically, the mass media have rendered African Americans invisible. In the 1950s, for instance, African Americans rarely appeared in American television, except as singers and dancers on variety shows. And when African Americans did appear, they were often depicted in a highly stereotypical fashion. Perhaps one of the most distasteful portrayals during this period occurred on the popular show "*Amos 'n Andy*" (1951–1966), in which White actors in blackface embodied the traditional buffoonish stereotype of African Americans.

Fortunately, overtly demeaning stereotypes of the "*Amos 'n Andy*" variety no longer populate television programming today. And importantly, a recent study (Wiegel, Kim, & Frost, 1995) found that the presence of African Americans appearing in prime-time programming has increased substantially since 1978. Despite this increased visibility, however, the quality of the portrayals of African Americans remains uneven. According to Wiegel et al., African Americans are much more likely to be depicted in situation comedies, and to a lesser extent, dramas than in product advertising.

That African Americans remain heavily concentrated in situation comedies, as opposed to dramas, is perhaps no surprise given that Blacks historically have been consigned to comedic roles in primetime programming. In fact, Hacker (1992) suggests that "White America still prefers its black people to be performers who divert them as athletes and musicians and comedians" (p. 34).

Research that has focused on how Blacks are portrayed in television newscasts suggests that Blacks do not appear in as wide a range of roles as do Whites (Entman, 1994). Local newscasts, in particular, tend to portray Blacks in an unfavorable light because local television habitually covers crime and politics. According to Wilson and Gutierrez (1985), this type of coverage often depicts Blacks and other nonwhite Americans as "problem people" who either *have* problems, such as poverty and other social misfortunes (e.g., victims of fires, bad schools, or racial discrimination), or *cause* problems, such as crime. In fact, Campbell (1995) suggests that coverage of Blacks in news stories can be summed up in two stereotypes: the "positive" stereotype of Blacks as entertainers and athletes and the "negative" stereotype of Blacks as criminals.

If Blacks have fared relatively poorly in television portrayals, have their portrayals in the print media been more realistic and accurate? In general, the print media operates out of a value system that is not unlike that of television, so it is not surprising that portrayals of Blacks in newspapers and magazines carry certain racial messages. Think for a moment about newspaper comic strips. According to Barcus (1963), comic strips are unique in that they mirror American attitudes (more like a carnival mirror than a plate glass mirror, however) and offer commentary on our culture. In a recent qualitative analysis of comic strips, Lenthall (1998) notes that Blacks and other nonwhite minorities seldom appeared in mainstream comics prior to World War II, but when they did appear the images clearly conveyed subhuman status. Blacks, according to Lenthall (p. 45) were physically depicted more like apes than people and had "soft, slouching bodies . . . as though they were not yet completely used to the idea of walking erect." Immediately after World War II, Blacks disappeared from mainstream comics altogether. Lenthall argues that this invisibility of Blacks in comic strips was one way of dealing with the incongruities in the American consciousness. That is, World War II heightened democratic ideals, in which citizens touted the United States as "a land of opportunity." At the same time, however, obvious inequities based upon race continued to exist. Perhaps as an attempt to avoid dealing with the contradictions between the heightened democratic ideals resulting from World War II and the obvious inequalities in society, comic strips simply denied the presence of those treated less than equally.

Comic strips are not the only forms of print media that carry subtle (and not-so-subtle) racial messages. As an example of negative racial images contained in the print media, consider the infamous *Time* magazine cover that featured a police mug shot of O.J. Simpson. The mug shot, you may recall, was altered to make Simpson's skin pigmentation appear darker. According to critics, the magazine deliberately altered Simpson's appearance in order to reinforce White America's stereotypic image of a Black criminal (Thaler, 1997). This type of carefully crafted visual portrayal of Simpson is reminiscent of television ads in the 1988 presidential campaign that featured Willie Horton, a Black convict who raped a White woman while on a weekend furlough. The use of such visual images reinforces White America's mistaken assumption that violent crimes are disproportionately committed by Black males.

Magazine advertising, too, has been criticized for presenting an unrepresentative image of Blacks. Many investigators have noted that Blacks generally are underrepresented in advertising (Jackson & Ervin, 1991; Shepherd, 1980) and appear to be altogether absent in advertising for certain products (Kern-Foxworth, 1992). Another growing concern is that advertisers present an unrepresentative image of Blacks, particularly in terms of the physical appearance of the models. As you know, advertising tends to reflect the prevailing norms of physical beauty, and in our society what is considered "attractive" is based in Eurocentric values of physical beauty: light complexion and Caucasian-like facial characteristics (Leslie, 1995). Consequently, advertisements, particularly in mainstream media, fail to reflect the full range of complexions, hair types, and facial features among the Black population. In an analysis of advertisements, Keenan (1996) concluded that Blacks found in magazine advertisements in both predominantly "White" magazines (i.e., *Glamour* and *Fortune*) and "Black" magazines (i.e., *Essence* and *Black Enterprise*) had significantly lighter complexions and more "caucasion" features than those in editorial photographs. Assuming that editorial photographs more accurately capture the physical diversity of Blacks as a whole, this preference for lighter complexion mirrors the same color prejudices that are found in our larger society and within the African-American community itself.

Thus far, this discussion of the cultural transmission of stereotypes and prejudices has focused on the depiction of Blacks in the media, largely reflecting the focus of research within this area. But what about the depiction of other ethnic minorities? Is there any evidence that their portrayal is more realistic and accurate?

Considerably more research needs to be done with a focus on other ethnic groups. But at this time, it appears that other nonwhite ethnic groups are similarly underrepresented in the media, and when they have been depicted, there has been a notable reliance on stereotyping. Latinos, for instance, are often portrayed as violent and criminal (Omi, 1989). Asians traditionally have been depicted as cunning or inscrutable and with a tendency to pepper their speech with Chinese proverbs. And the film stereotype of American Indians is, as Trimble (1988) describes it, that of the silent Indian "staring off into space, saying nothing" (p. 188).

The portrayal of other minorities in the media has been similarly stereotypical. As you might expect, much research has focused on women's portrayal in the media. Research during the 1970s and 1980s showed that television programming seldom depicted women in occupational roles (Sternglanz & Serbin, 1974) and that women in commercials were often portrayed as subservient to men. More recent studies suggest that women are portrayed less stereotypically on television today than in the past, but that women's representation on television may differ dramatically depending upon the intended audience. A recent study (Craig, 1992) found that daytime ads, aimed at female homemakers, continue to portray women in a traditional manner. In these ads, for instance, women are typically portrayed as product users, whereas men are portrayed as product authorities. Commercials during sporting events, geared toward the male sports viewer, are heavily dominated by ads for alcohol and automotive products. Women, when they appear in these commercials, are generally depicted in subservient roles (waitress, secretary) or as sex objects. In contrast, prime-time programming tends to be oriented toward dual-career couples and single working women. Thus, women in evening commercials are increasingly depicted as successful and in positions of authority.

Even commercials on MTV, whose audience is primarily between the ages of 12 and 34, are gender stereotyped. In a recent study, Nancy Signorielli and her colleagues (Signorielli, McLeod, & Healy, 1994) found that males outnumbered females in commercials on MTV. But females, relative to males, were more physically attractive, had more beautiful bodies, and were more likely to be scantily clad. According to Signorielli et al., this emphasis on female beauty and sexuality is disturbing because it conveys the message to women that their primary purpose is to "look good."

Women's representation in print advertisements is similarly biased toward an emphasis on physical appearance. In a content analysis of women and men's fashion magazines (e.g., *Glamour, Cosmopolitan, Essence, Gentlemen's Quarterly*), S. Plous and Dominique Neptune (1997) found that female body exposure was greater than male body exposure. Additionally, Black women were shown disproportionately often wearing animal print clothing, consistent with the racial stereotype of Black women as predatory and animal-like (Collins, 1990).

Historically, lesbians and gay men have been the most invisible minority group in the media (Wolf & Kielwasser, 1991). The few gay characters that have been portrayed in films were almost always depicted as victims—of ridicule or violence—or villians. As Russo (1986, p. 32) observes, "It is not insignificant that out of 32 films with major homosexual characters from 1961 through 1976, 13 feature gays who commit suicide and 18 have the homosexual murdered by another character."

In recent years, there has been increased visibility of lesbians and gay men in the media, and even major Hollywood films have begun to depict lesbians and gay men in a more positive way. Gay people have appeared in mainstream films like *Boys on the Side, As Good as it Gets,* and *To Wong Foo, Thanks for Everything, Julie Newmar.* Television shows, too, have increasingly incorporated gay and lesbian characters in their ensemble casts. Gay and lesbian characters have appeared on shows like "Will and Grace," "Spin City," "Melrose Place," "Caroline in the City," "Roseanne," and "E.R.," to name a few. And in 1997, millions tuned in for the "coming out" episode of "Ellen," in which Ellen DeGeneres's character Ellen Morgan became the first homosexual lead character in a prime-time network show.

Overall, the media representation of various minority groups has improved in recent years. Members of minority groups appear more frequently and are depicted in a more accurate and inclusive manner than was true in the past. However, subtle stereotypical images remain present in media portrayals and can influence children and adults' beliefs about various social groups. As former Federal Communications Commissioner Nicholas Johnson once stated about television (Thompson & Zerbinos, 1995, p. 652), "All television is educational; the only question is, what is it teaching?" Research indicates that this question can be asked about other forms of media as well.

## ▶ WHAT ARE THE CONSEQUENCES OF STEREOTYPES?

So far we have seen that stereotypes are formed in diverse ways. But once stereotypes are acquired, what effect do they have on our social thoughts and actions? With the advent of the cognitive approach in psychology, many researchers moved away from cataloguing the *content* of stereotypes and instead began studying the *process* of stereotyping.

For researchers who are interested in stereotype processes, they typically have focused on how stereotypes affect our perceptions of others and our social interactions. Hamilton, Stroessner, and Driscoll (1994) provide a useful framework for examining the impact of stereotypes on our thought processes and our behavior. They focus on three issues: (a) How do stereotypes influence what we attend to and what we remember? (b) How do stereotypes influence our interpretation of events? and (c) How do stereotypes influence our social interactions? Let's examine in some detail these important issues.

## Stereotypes Influence What We Attend to and What We Remember

> *"The moment we believe in something we suddenly see all the arguments for it and become blind to all the arguments against it."*

> *George Bernard Shaw (1922)*

In the case of stereotypes, believing is seeing. Stereotypes are often activated on the basis of salient physical features, like race, sex, and age, and once activated, they influence what we attend to and what we later remember. In one study demonstrating how stereotypes might influence what we notice about others, Ellen Langer and Lois Imber (1980) asked participants to watch a videotape of a man reading aloud from the *The New York Times*. Prior to presenting the videotape, participants were given information about the man indicating that he was either distinctive in some way (e.g., an ex-mental patient, a cancer patient, a homosexual, etc.) or "normal." Following the videotape, they were asked to list any characteristics that they noticed about the person. Participants played closer attention to the man when he was labeled out of the ordinary. For example, participants who thought the man was an ex-mental patient recalled more information about his facial characteristics and physical movements than those who believed he was "normal." Moreover, applying a distinctive label to the man influenced participants' judgments of him, such that they believed him to be more different from most people than when subjects believed he was "normal." Thus, applying a label to a person often influences how others judge and evaluate that person.

Not only are we more likely to scrutinize individuals from a stereotyped group, but we are also more likely to remember information about them that is consistent with our stereotypes. Cohen (1981) asked participants to view a videotape of a woman and man having a birthday dinner. Half of the participants were told that the woman worked as a waitress, and the other half were told that she worked as a librarian. The videotaped interaction was carefully constructed so that the woman portrayed many behaviors that might be considered typical for both a waitress (e.g., likes pop music, has a bowling ball, eats hamburgers, plays guitar) and a librarian (e.g., traveled in Europe, has artwork on a wall, spent the day reading, drinks wine). Thus, all participants viewed the same videotape.

After viewing the videotape, participants immediately were asked to recall features about the woman's life. Not surprisingly, they tended to remember information that was consistent with the woman's occupational role. For instance, they more accurately remembered that the waitress "has a bowling ball" than that she "drinks wine," even though both were true. In fact, participants showed 88 percent accuracy for stereotype-consistent information, compared to 78 percent accuracy for stereotype-inconsistent information.

Although Cohen's study demonstrates that, overall, stereotype-consistent information is easier to remember than stereotype-inconsistent information, it appears that memory in general is enhanced once a stereotype is activated. Frankly, there are times that people do not always preferentially remember stereotype-consistent information. As an example, suppose you read about Agnes, a grandmother who collects social security benefits, loves to cook for family gatherings, enjoys gardening, and attends church regularly, but who also is quite skilled at rollerblading and wants to learn to surf. According to the research discussed so far, you would probably be likely to remember the information consistent with the stereotype of "grandmother"; for example, that Agnes "collects social security benefits" and "enjoys gardening." But what about the information that Agnes is an avid rollerblader or that she wants to learn to surf?

Paradoxically, the presence of a stereotype may at times improve memory for stereotype-inconsistent information, particularly if people have enough time to make sense out of the inconsistency (Hastie, 1981). Learning that Agnes also rollerblades, for instance, may surprise you, causing you to ponder that stereotype-inconsistent information in order to explain the inconsistency. Perhaps, you may reason, Agnes is a youthful grandmother who enjoys rollerblading with her grandchildren. Such extra thought about inconsistent information increases memory and may help explain why some studies show improved memory for stereotype-inconsistent information.

In summary, people tend to remember stereotype-consistent information more than they do stereotype-inconsistent information. But memory for stereotype-inconsistent information can be enhanced if people are motivated to form an accurate impression (Stangor & McMillan, 1992). When so motivated, people will attempt to reconcile the incongruent information with their stereotypes, and in the process of doing so, increase their recall for the incongruent information. Put simply, stereotypes subtly guide what we notice and remember about others.

## Stereotypes Influence Our Interpretation of Events

In addition to influencing what we notice about others, stereotypes also influence our perceptions and interpretations of events. Duncan (1976), for example, asked White college students to watch a videotape of two students having a heated discussion. At some point in the discussion, one student shoved another. The variable of interest in this experiment was the race of the students in the videotape. One version of the videotape depicted a White student shoving a Black student; another version showed a Black student shoving a White student. Alarmingly, students' interpretations of the event were affected by the race of the participants. When the Black student shoved the White student, 75 percent of students described the behavior as "violent." In contrast, when the White student shoved the Black student, only 17 percent of students perceived the behavior as "violent." Instead, students in this condition were more likely to perceive the White student's shove as "playing around" or "dramatizing." Thus, stereotypes can influence our immediate perception of ambiguous events—because of the cultural stereotype of Blacks as violent, the same shove is perceived as much more violent when performed by a Black person than a White person.

Research has also shown that stereotypes can have a biasing effect on our judgments, primarily because they guide both our information seeking and processing.

Darley and Gross (1983) describe a two-stage process in which stereotypes influence our judgments of others. First, stereotypes serve as "hypotheses" about people and form the basis of our expectations about their dispositions and behavior. But we do not necessarily apply the stereotype indiscriminately. Rather, if given the opportunity, we move to the second stage in which we test our hypotheses against reality by gathering further information about the stereotyped individual. The problem, however, is that once a stereotype is activated, we tend to seek out information that will confirm rather than refute our expectations.

A study by Darley and Gross (1983) dramatically demonstrates this biased information seeking. In this study, participants watched a videotape of a fourth-grade girl, named Hannah, with the purpose of evaluating her academic ability. The videotape depicted Hannah in her neighborhood, on a playground, and at school. Social class stereotypes were activated by environmental cues in the videotape. Half of the participants were provided information that Hannah was from a middle-class background. In this version of the videotape, Hannah was shown in an attractive surburban neighborhood, on a well-equipped playground, and in a modern school. The remaining participants were provided information that Hannah was from a lower-class background. In this videotape, Hannah's neighborhood consisted of row homes in an urban area, and the playground and school were not well maintained.

The impact of these social class stereotypes was assessed in two conditions. Half of the participants only viewed the videotape that provided information about Hannah's social class and then were asked to evaluate her academic ability. The remaining participants were also asked to predict Hannah's academic ability, but they were provided additional information that might be directly relevant to their judgments. These participants viewed another videotape in which Hannah is shown responding to achievement-test problems. Hannah's performance was purposefully ambiguous and inconsistent; that is, she answered both easy and difficult questions accurately and inaccurately.

What effect did participants' social class stereotypes have on their judgments of Hannah's academic ability? The results proved to be informative about the role that stereotypes play in social judgments. Participants who were asked to evaluate Hannah's academic performance solely on the basis of social class information did not differ in their judgments of her abilities. Apparently, they recognized that stereotypes alone are not valid bases upon which to make judgments about Hannah's academic ability. But for those participants who were able to observe Hannah's inconsistent performance on the achievement test, social class information biased their judgments. Specifically, when given the ambiguous academic performance information, they judged middle-class Hannah's academic ability to be superior to lower-class Hannah's ability.

Why would this be the case? Darley and Gross interpreted these findings in terms of the two-stage process described earlier. That is, most individuals recognize the hazards involved in arriving at conclusions based solely upon stereotypes. Thus, students in this condition recognized that stereotypes alone provide insufficient information upon which to make a judgment about Hannah. But when additional information is provided about a person, stereotypes are likely to influence how that information is interpreted. Students who observed Hannah's academic performance believed they had sufficient information upon which to draw conclusions, and they interpreted Hannah's ambiguous performance in a manner consistent with their stereotypic expectations. Ironically, more information does not necessarily lead to better judgments. In fact, people feel more entitled to judge when they have more information about a person, even if that information is ambiguous or irrelevant (Yzerbyt et al., 1998). These judgments tend to be consistent with people's stereotypic preconceptions, because stereotypes lead us to seek evidence that confirms, rather than refutes, our initial expectations.

## Stereotypes Influence Our Social Interactions

*"If we foresee evil in our fellow man, we tend to provoke it; if good, we elicit it."*

Gordon Allport (1954), The Nature of Prejudice

Thus far, we've considered stereotyping from a purely cognitive perspective, focusing on how stereotypes influence our perceptions, interpretations and memory of events. Is the impact of stereotypes limited only to our cognitive activity, or might stereotypes also guide our treatment of others?

To answer this question, consider one of the valuable functions of stereotypes—stereotypes allow us to form expectancies about others on the basis of limited information. Imagine that you are to meet Calie, a 32-year-old White woman who quit her graduate program in philosophy at UC Berkeley to work for Greenpeace. You might form an image of her as someone living in the mountains of California without a telephone, campaigning to save the seals, and driving an orange Volkswagon van that displays a "I eat tofu . . . and I vote" bumpersticker. This expectancy that you've formed most probably will serve as a guide to behavior during your interaction with her, enabling you to anticipate how she is likely to act so that you can respond accordingly. At the same time, however, your expectancies about Calie may channel the social interaction in such a way that she actually engages in behaviors that fit your stereotype. After all, *expecting* certain behaviors from people is the first step to *eliciting* those behaviors from them.

This process in which stereotyped expectations influence others' behaviors has been dubbed the "self-fulfilling prophecy" (Merton, 1948; Rosenthal & Jacobson, 1968) or the "behavioral confirmation" effect (Chen & Bargh, 1997; Snyder, 1992; Snyder & Swann, 1978). How does holding a stereotype affect another's behavior? Actually, the process of behavioral confirmation results in a complex chain of events. First, the stereotype forms the basis of the perceiver's expectancies, and the perceiver behaves toward the target as if those expectancies are true. The target, of course, responds to the perceiver's behavior in kind, thereby reaffirming the perceiver's original preconceptions. As an example, consider this scenario: Kristin tells Meg that Robert is a cool and aloof person. When Meg finally meets Robert, she unconsciously behaves toward him in a cool and aloof manner, because she expects him to be so. Not realizing that he has been stereotyped as cool and aloof, Robert responds to Meg's behavior by being—guess what—cool and aloof, thereby confirming Meg's initial expectations. Meg, of course, is unaware that she acted in line with her beliefs about Robert and doesn't realize her role in eliciting confirmatory behavior from him.

In a famous experiment, Mark Snyder and his colleagues (Snyder, Tanke, & Berscheid, 1977) demonstrated how our stereotypes can "grow legs" by actually creating and changing reality. Put yourself in the place of the typical male subject in this experiment: You have volunteered to participate in a study of "the processes by which people become acquainted with each other," and because you are in the "no non-verbal communication" condition, you will not be allowed to meet your female partner face-to-face. Instead, you will converse with her over the telephone. Before the conversation begins, the experimenter provides you with a folder that contains biographical information about your partner, along with her photograph. Half of the men received a photo of a highly attractive woman, and the remaining men received a photo of a relatively unattractive woman. In actuality, the photographs had been prepared in advance and were not really photos of the men's actual partners. Moreover, the female partners knew nothing of the photographs that the male subjects had received!

How did activation of the men's physical attractiveness stereotype influence the social interaction? As you might expect, men who anticipated chatting with either an attractive or unattractive woman formed very different impressions of her. The men who believed their partner was attractive expected her to be sociable, poised, and socially adept, whereas the men who believed their partner was unattractive expected her to be rather socially inept, awkward, and serious. Predictably, the men were more friendly and sociable if they thought the woman was attractive. What is perhaps more interesting, however, is that the women who had been labeled attractive actually behaved in a more poised, socially adept, and warm manner than did their "unattractive" counterparts. Thus, this difference in the men's interaction styles elicited differential responding by the women, providing a compelling example of how beliefs create reality.

Other studies focusing on racial stereotypes report similar findings. In a series of experiments, Word, Zanna, and Cooper (1974) had White undergraduates interview both White and Black confederates as job applicants. When the applicant was Black, the interviewer sat further away, displayed a higher rate of speech errors (i.e., stammering, hesitating), and ended the interview more quickly than when the applicant was White. If you were a job applicant, would you find the interviewer's behavior unnerving, and would your interview performance be affected? Based upon the follow-up experiment, the answer is probably yes. In the second experiment, Word et al. trained White confederates to mimic the interviewers' behaviors in the first study—either to sit farther away, make more speech errors, and end the interview quickly, or to do the opposite. When independent observers were provided with a videotape of the job interview, they judged the interviewees' performance to be poorer when they were interviewed in the style accorded initially to Black participants in the first study. In other words, the interviewees appeared more calm and self-assured when the interviewer sat closer to them and talked more fluently than when the interviewer sat at a distance and stammered.

Such confirmation effects are not restricted to the laboratory. In fact, one of the most troubling findings is that such a process may emerge within a real classroom situation. Imagine that an elementary school teacher has an ethnically diverse group of students. Imagine, also, that this teacher holds stereotypical views of academic achievement, believing that Whites and Asians are more able than Blacks and Latinos. Is it possible that this teacher's stereotypes might actually influence the students' academic performance? Most definitely, judging from the following study.

In a classic experiment, Rosenthal and Jacobson (1968) administered an achievement test to elementary school children. After the test was administered, Rosenthal and Jacobson randomly selected some students to be in the experimental group. They (falsely) told the teachers that these students were actually "late bloomers" who were expected to show tremendous gains in their learning within the academic year. At the end of the school year, Rosenthal and Jacobsen retested the children with the same achievement test and discovered that the children whom the teachers had expected to blossom intellectually did indeed show significant gains in their achievement test scores compared to the other children. Put simply, the teachers' expectancies had been fulfilled.

Naturalistic studies also provide evidence of the self-fulfilling nature of stereotypes. In an early study exploring the impact of gender stereotypes on children's academic performance, Palardy (1969) separated first-grade teachers into two groups: those who believe girls learn to read more quickly than boys, and those who believe girls and boys learn to read at comparable rates. In line with predictions based upon the self-fulfilling prophecy, girls outscored boys on a reading achievement test given at the completion of the academic year, but only in the classes in which teachers believed girls learned to read more quickly. Taken together, experimental studies and naturalistic studies support the notion that stereotypes may be self-fulfilling. Moreover, it appears that some individuals may be especially susceptible to self-fulfilling prophecies. Members of stigmatized groups, for instance, may be more likely to confirm stereotypic preconceptions, because they frequently find themselves in positions of less power relative to the perceiver. For individuals who have less power, they may inadvertently confirm others' expectations in order to smooth interpersonal interactions (Claire & Fiske, 1998; Jussim & Fleming, 1996).

Perhaps what is most disturbing about self-fulfilling prophecies is their role in maintaining erroneous stereotypes, because members of the dominant group can point to the actual behavior of stigmatized groups as "evidence" that the stereotypes are, in fact, accurate. Historically, self-fulfilling prophecies have contributed to numerous instances of stereotype maintainence. In the Middle Ages, for instance, Jews were prohibited from many professions, with one exception—they were allowed to become money lenders. (The Christian Church forbade its members to enter this profession, because charging interest was considered a sin.) As money lenders, of course, Jews naturally were concerned with being repaid, so Christians often pointed to the greedy, shrewd, and cheap nature of Jews as justification for defaulting on loans. Similarly, in the United States during the 19th century, slaves were prohibited from learning to read or receiving formal education. Slaveowners would then point to the ignorance of slaves as evidence of their innate inferiority. In these ways, self-fulfilling prophecies contribute to the perpetuation of stereotypes.

## ➤ STEREOTYPE ACCURACY?

So far, we've discussed the problems of stereotypes and their biasing effect on our perceptions of others. This approach to understanding stereotypes certainly reflects the dominant view of stereotypes as factually incorrect, illogical, and inflexible. But aren't there times, you may ask, when stereotypes contain a kernel of truth? And might stereotypes be quite useful, in the sense that they allow us to make [somewhat] accurate predictions about others?

In addressing this issue of the accuracy of stereotypes, psychologist Yueh-Ting Lee (Lee, Jussim, & McCauley, 1995) recounts an email message he received that included the following observations about the quality of life in several countries: "Heaven is a place with an American house, Chinese food, British police, a German car, and French art. Hell is a place with a Japanese house, Chinese police, British food, German art, and a French car." What gives this statement its humorous punch, Lee suggests, is that these national stereotypes contain a kernel of truth. American houses, on average, do boast more space than Japanese housing. And German cars generally have a better reputation for quality than French cars.

So are stereotypes necessarily inaccurate? In one of the earliest studies to examine stereotype accuracy, McCauley and Stitt (1978) asked White participants to estimate the percentage of Black Americans and the percentage of all Americans who possessed certain characteristics (e.g., unemployed, on welfare, completed high school). Surprisingly, the participants' stereotypes as measured by percentage estimates were quite accurate when compared to data obtained from the U.S. census. In a more recent study focusing on gender stereotypes, Janet Swim (1994) compared actual sex differences with college students' estimates of these sex differences. Although students sometimes erred in their estimations of sex differences, Swim found that students' stereotypes were fairly accurate. Moreover, students rarely got the *direction* of sex differences wrong. For example, they never erroneously believed that women are more aggressive than men.

Other researchers, however, note that stereotypes may be inaccurate in a variety of ways. Carey Ryan and her colleagues (Ryan, Park, & Judd, 1996) identified three types of potential inaccuracies: (1) *stereotypic inaccuracy*, exaggerating stereotypic attributes or underestimating counterstereotypic attributes; (2) *valence inaccuracy*, disproportionately emphasizing negative (or positive) stereotypic attributes more than the reverse; and (3) *dispersion inaccuracy*, perceiving groups to be less diverse than they actually are. To illustrate these types of inaccuracies, consider the cultural stereotypes of African Americans as poor, academically unmotivated, and athletic. Saying that the average African American is poor and on welfare represents stereotypic inaccuracy. Accentuating negative attributes (e.g., Blacks are academically unmotivated) and deemphasizing positive attributes (e.g., Blacks are athletic) represents valence inaccuracy. Dispersion inaccuracy would be saying that Blacks show less variability in their athletic ability than do Whites.

In their research, Ryan and colleagues found that group membership plays a significant role in determining the degree to which our stereotypes are accurate. In general, our stereotypes of out-group members are more likely to be inaccurate than our stereotypes of in-group members.

As you can see, this issue of whether stereotypes are accurate or not is rather complex, and consensus has not yet been reached. Although there may be ample reason to believe that stereotypes contain a component of accuracy, it's important to keep in mind that a stereotype is a stereotype—it does not reflect reality in its entirety. To view stereotypes as having a "kernel of truth" is misleading, because a partial truth is still not a truth. Moreover, *using* a stereotype, whether accurate or not, is unfair to the individual for two reasons (Stangor, 1995). First, as you know, stereotypes are never true of every group member. Second, the literature on self-fulfilling prophecies (Merton, 1948) or behavioral confirmation (Snyder, 1992) suggests that people at times will behave according to how they are expected to behave. Thus, a perceiver (e.g., a teacher) who holds a stereotype (e.g., poor children aren't academically inclined), whether accurate or not, may behave accordingly and elicit confirmatory behavior from the target (e.g., less effort, less interest, lower grades).

With this current focus on stereotype accuracy, researchers have entered into contentious debates. On the one hand, some researchers argue that the scientific study of stereotype accuracy is important to illuminate stereotyping processes and can potentially enhance sensitivity to cultural differences (Jussim, McCauley, & Lee, 1995). Other researchers (Fiske, 1999; Stangor, 1995), on the other hand, question the utility of determining the accuracy of stereotypes, largely because stereotypes are mostly about perceptions of personality trait differences that are difficult to measure objectively. Another concern is that readers of this research may conclude that stereotypes are for the most part accurate and, consequently, appropriate to use (Stangor, 1995). Regardless of one's position on the issue of stereotype accuracy, this debate is likely to continue for some time.

## ➤ WHEN ARE WE LIKELY TO STEREOTYPE?

Recognizing the importance of stereotypes in channeling simultaneously our perceptions of stereotyped group members and our behavior toward them, social psychologists have expended much effort to identify factors that influence when stereotyping may and may not occur. An important question addressed in recent research is whether stereotyping occurs spontaneously and automatically. In other words, when we encounter members of a stereotyped group, do we automatically stereotype them? And if so, does this mean that stereotyping is inevitable? In considering this topic, two issues are important. First, are stereotypes automatically activated in the presence of stereotyped group members? And second, if stereotypes are automatically activated, does this mean that people will inevitably rely upon the stereotype in making judgments about others?

To answer these questions, several social psychologists distinguish between the two "stages" of stereotyping: stereotype activation and stereotype application (Brewer, 1988; Fiske & Neuberg, 1990; Gilbert & Hixon, 1991). According to this distinction, *stereotype activation* may be triggered by a person's group or category, because we typically notice certain physical features about others, such as their race, gender, or age (Fiske, 1998; Stangor, Lynch, Dual, & Glass, 1992). But for the stereotyping process to be completed, we must use the activated stereotype in our judgments, which represents *stereotype application*. Understanding when stereotypes will be activated and when they will be applied has been an ongoing focus of recent research. Let us consider more carefully the issue of whether stereotypes activation is inevitable upon encountering a member of a stereotyped group.

### Stage One: Stereotype Activation

Whether stereotypes are automatically and inevitably activated when we encounter members of a stereotyped group is open to debate. Some researchers suggest that we may be predisposed to stereotype others automatically (Bargh, 1997; Devine, 1989; Macrae, Bodenhausen, & Milne, 1995), perhaps explaining why stereotyping and prejudice tend to be enduring phenomena. Because stereotypes are part of our cultural fabric—transmitted through explicit and implicit teachings of parents, peers, and other socializing forces—we cannot avoid learning our culture's stereotypes about various social groups. By merely watching television, for instance, we may see images of Blacks as criminals in local news footage or women as sex objects in MTV videos. The consequence is that cultural stereotypes become so overlearned that they may spontaneously and unintentionally spring to mind when we encounter members of a stereotyped group. For this reason, many argue that stereotype activation may be an automatic process, because automatic processes occur unintentionally, spontaneously, and even unconsciously (Bargh, 1997; Devine, 1989; Fiske, 1998).

Interestingly, a growing body of research suggests that stereotypes may, in fact, color our perceptions of others without our awareness or conscious intent. This automatic operation of stereotypes provides the basis for what has been termed **implicit stereotyping** (Greenwald & Banaji, 1995). Implicit stereotyping refers to unconscious or unintentional stereotyping in which the person has no conscious recollection of the triggering experience.

A recent experiment provides a good illustration of implicit stereotyping. Mahzarin Banaji and her colleague, Anthony Greenwald (1994), showed participants a list of famous and nonfamous names. The famous names belonged to actors, musicians, and writers that most undergraduates would recognize (e.g., Rod Steiger, Gladys Knight, and Doris Lessing). The nonfamous names were developed by attaching a male or female name to a common last name (e.g., Susan Walker, Peter Walker). Participants were told to read the list of 72 names (36 were famous and 36 were nonfamous, with 18 male names and 18 female names appearing in each set of famous and nonfamous names) for the ostensible purpose of judging the ease of pronunciation. The next day, they returned to the lab and were shown a new list of 144 names. This second list consisted of the previous 72 names, in addition to 72 new names that were not on the original list. Asked to identify which names were famous, participants readily recognized the Rod Steigers and the Gladys Knights, but they also mistakenly judged some of the nonfamous names from the first list as famous because of a lingering familiarity with the previously seen names.

What is particularly intriguing, though, is that incorrect judgments of fame were twice as likely to occur for male, as opposed to female, names. In other words, familiar nonfamous male names were more likely than familiar nonfamous female names to be "misremembered" as famous. Why would this be the case? According to Banaji and Greenwald, participants' stereotype of men as more important and influential biased their recall without their awareness or conscious intent.

Implicit stereotyping has also been demonstrated with different social groups, such as the elderly (Hense, Penner, & Nelson, 1995) and various ethnic groups (e.g., Devine, 1989; Dovidio, Evans, Tyler, 1986; Greenwald, McGhee, & Schwartz, 1998). In a widely cited study, Patricia Devine (1989) asked her participants to engage in a perceptual vigilance task, which involved fixating on a dot in the center of their visual field and identifying the location of various words that were presented in their peripheral visual field. They were actually participating in a priming task in which ideas or associations are activated without conscious awareness.

The words were presented very rapidly (80 milliseconds) so participants would not be able to consciously identify the words. Some of these words were related to stereotypes about Blacks (e.g., musical, ghetto, welfare, athletic, etc.) and other words were neutral (e.g., number, however, sentences, etc.). To activate subjects' racial stereotype, either 80 or 20 percent of the words were related to stereotypes about Blacks.

Following this task, participants performed a second task, ostensibly unrelated to the first. This second task involved reading a scenario describing a typical day in the life of a fictitious character named Donald, who engages in a number of ambiguously hostile behaviors. For example, Donald demands his money back after a purchase, refuses to pay his rent until his landlord repaints his apartment, and sends a dirty glass back to the kitchen at a restaurant. After reading the scenario, participants were asked to make a series of judgments about Donald, which included his level of hostility.

Because hostility and aggressiveness are part of the Black stereotype, Devine reasoned that participants who had been exposed to 80 percent stereotype-related words would perceive Donald's ambiguous behavior as significantly more hostile than those who had been exposed to only 20 percent stereotype-related words. Her results confirmed those predictions.

Devine's research is not alone in demonstrating that an activated stereotype, even when activated outside of awareness, can influence later judgments. In a similar study, Banaji and colleagues (1993) showed that priming stereotypes of men as aggressive and women as dependent can unconsciously affect participants' judgments of male and female targets. As in Devine's study, undergraduates believed they were participating in two unrelated experiments. In the "first" experiment, the students unscrambled sentences that were designed to activate either gender stereotypes of aggression (e.g., C. threatens other people, R. cuts off drivers) or dependence (e.g., G. conforms to others, T. has low self-esteem). Control subjects unscrambled sentences that were designed to be gender neutral in content.

In the "second" experiment, students read a scenario that described either a male (Donald) or female (Donna) who engaged in weakly related behaviors. For example, embedded in the scenario were sentences suggesting both dependence (e.g., "wanted to take his (her) car, so we left mine at the cafe") or aggression (e.g., "noticed his (her) mug was dirty and asked the waitress for a new one").

After reading the scenario, subjects were asked to form impressions of Donald or Donna. Compared to students who had unscrambled gender-neutral sentences, students who had been primed with aggression-related sentences perceived Donald, but not Donna, to be aggressive. Similarly, students who had been primed by the dependence-related sentences perceived Donna, but not Donald, to be dependent. This selective effect of priming on judgments of Donald and Donna reveals implicit gender stereotyping—that is, students were not aware that their underlying beliefs that men are aggressive and women are dependent influenced their judgments.

Taken as a whole, these research findings indicate that stereotyping may have some apparently automatic aspects. Such findings are intriguing, yet dismaying. If stereotyping occurs automatically, then what hope exists for eradicating stereotyping, prejudice, and discrimination? In answering this question, many researchers point out that stereotype activation is not unconditionally automatic (Gilbert & Hixon, 1991; Spencer, Fein, Wolfe, Fong, & Dunn, 1998; Kawakami, Dovidio, Moll, Hermsen, & Russin, 2000) and that many factors can inhibit it.

ARE STEREOTYPES AUTOMATICALLY AND INEVITABLY ACTIVATED?     Up until this point, it may seem as if stereotype activation is inevitable upon encountering a member of a stereotyped group. Indeed, Gordon Allport (1954, p. 21) claimed that "A person with dark brown skin will activate whatever concept of Negro is dominant in our mind." But mere exposure to a member of a stereotyped group is insufficient to activate the corresponding stereotype (Bodenhausen & Lichtenstein, 1987; Gilbert & Hixon, 1991; Locke, MacLeod, & Walker, 1994; Macrae, Milne, & Bodenhausen, 1994; Spencer et al., 1998; Wittenbrink, Judd, & Park, 1997). What, then, are the conditions under which encountering a member of a stereotyped group will activate a stereotype?

First, whether a stereotype is automatically activated may depend largely on the cultural ubiquity of that stereotype (Von Hippel, Sekaquaptewa, & Vargas, 1995). For example, gender stereotypes and African-American stereotypes may be automatically activated because of the amount of experience people in our culture have had with these stereotypes. But stereotypes of other ethnic groups or religious groups may not be automatically activated if the perceiver only has limited familiarity with the stereotype.

Second, automatic activation of a stereotype may depend upon the availability of sufficient cognitive resources. Upon encountering someone who belongs to a stereotyped group, we simply may be too preoccupied for stereotype activation to occur. After all, social interaction is a complex business which involves engaging in several activities simultaneously. As active perceivers, we often must regulate our own behavior and, at the same time, make inferences about others. According to Daniel Gilbert and Gregory Hixon (1991), such mental preoccupation or "cognitive busyness" actually decreases the likelihood that a stereotype is activated in the presence of a stereotyped group member.

To test this hypothesis, participants were asked to watch a silent videotape in which either an Asian or White female assistant turned over a series of cards bearing word fragments, such as S_Y, RI_E, and N_P. The participants' task was to make as many word completions as possible in the allotted time (e.g., SAY, SHY, SKY, etc.). The words selected could be completed in many different ways (e.g., SAY, SKY), but some words could be completed in a manner consistent with the Asian stereotype (e.g., SHY, RICE, NIP). Moreover, participants in the cognitively busy condition were instructed to rehearse an eight-digit number while making the word completions, whereas those in the not-busy condition were not asked to rehearse a number.

Gilbert and Hixon found that exposure to an Asian, rather than a White, assistant was more likely to facilitate stereotypic word completions, but only for those participants who were not cognitively busy. Apparently, cognitively busy participants lacked the cognitive resources available to activate the Asian stereotype.

Third, contextual factors that prime a perceiver's beliefs or goals can influence whether a stereotype is automatically activated. One study found that when we encounter a person who belongs to more than one stereotyped group, the target person's behavior may be a contextual factor that determines which stereotype is activated (Macrae, Bodenhausen, & Milne, 1995). Participants who observed a Chinese woman eating with chopsticks (a behavior intended to cue the Chinese stereotype) did indeed activate the Chinese stereotype and inhibit the stereotype of women. In contrast, when the same woman was observed putting on makeup (a behavior intended to cue the stereotype of women), participants activated the stereotype of women and inhibited the Chinese stereotype.

In a similar fashion, a perceiver's motivation may be a contextual factor that influences stereotype activation. Suppose you are a student whose work has been praised by a Black professor. Which stereotype is more likely to be activated, that of a professor or a Black person? Now suppose instead that your work has been harshly criticized by the same Black professor. Which stereotype is more likely to be activated in this instance? In a series of studies designed to answer questions such as these, Sinclair and Kunda (1999) hypothesized that the perceiver's self-protective motives may influence which competing stereotype is activated. Participants who had been praised by a Black medical doctor, and who were therefore motivated to hold him in esteem, activated the doctor stereotype and inhibited the Black stereotype. In contrast, participants who had been criticized by the Black doctor, and who were therefore motivated to discredit him, demonstrated the opposite pattern—they activated the Black stereotype and inhibited the doctor stereotype. Thus, motivation may influence the extent to which a stereotype is activated (or inhibited).

And finally, activation of stereotypes may be controlled by a commitment to egalitarian goals (Moskowitz, Gollwitzer, Waser, & Schaal, 1999; Moskowitz, Salomon, & Taylor, 2000). Recent research suggests that some individuals—"chronic egalitarians" who possess the motive to be fair and nonstereotypic toward members of stereotyped social groups—may not be susceptible to automatic stereotype activation. For these individuals, exposure to a member of a stereotyped group may automatically activate their egalitarian goals rather than the stereotype itself.

Thus, it appears that activation of stereotypes is not always fully automatic. In fact, social psychologists are becoming increasingly aware of factors that may inhibit stereotype activation, such as the availability of cognitive resources, the ubiquity of the cultural stereotype, contextual factors, or a commitment to egalitarianism. Nonetheless, the question of whether stereotypes are automatically activated is an important one, because stereotypes, once activated, are the lens through which we perceive others.

## Stage Two: Stereotype Application

Whereas stereotype activation is thought to be a more or less automatic process, stereotype application is believed to be a controllable process in which people may adjust their initial biased reactions. But just because stereotype application is controllable does not mean that people will exercise control: People must be both *willing* and *able* to do so (Fiske & Von Hendy, 1992). For example, a highly prejudiced person, although able to control stereotypical thinking, may be perfectly content to construe a stereotyped person in a negative manner. In contrast, a person who is low in prejudice may "make the hard choice" (Fiske, 1989) to think or act differently from what comes automatically to mind.

In their attempts to better understand the conditions under which people are most likely to apply activated stereotypes, social psychologists emphasize the importance of ability and motivation in regulating the stereotyping process. Specifically, researchers have paid particular attention to how cognitive load, mood, and power may influence one's ability and motivation to control stereotype application.

COGNITIVE LOAD    Stereotypes are assumed to be energy-saving devices, tools that "jump out of the toolbox when there is a job to be done" (Gilbert & Hixon, 1991, p. 110). Because they are energy-saving devices, we are most likely to employ stereotypes when we are short on energy (Bodenhausen, 1990), confronted with information overload (Bargh, 1994), and under time pressure (Strack, Erber, & Wicklund, 1982). In other words, we are especially inclined to rely upon stereotypes when our cognitive capacity is constrained, primarily because we are unable to engage in more thoughtful, deliberative thinking.

As an example, consider how cognitive busyness or "cognitive load" might affect the application of stereotypes. We've already seen that cognitive busyness inhibits the activation of a stereotype. But what effect does cognitive busyness have on subjects' judgments of a stereotyped group member after the stereotype is already activated? In a relevant experiment (Gilbert & Hixon, 1991, Experiment 2), college students listened to an audiotape of a woman describing a typical day in her life. Half of the students had previously viewed a silent videotape of the woman that led them to believe that she was Caucasian, whereas the remaining students had seen an Asian woman. While listening to the audiotape, some students were cognitively busy (i.e., they had to perform a visual search task), whereas others were not. Following this task, the students were asked to report their impressions of the woman.

Interestingly, cognitively busy participants were more likely to perceive the Asian woman as possessing more stereotypic traits (e.g., timid, intelligent, etc.) than the not-busy participants. Whereas cognitive busyness inhibits the *activation* of a stereotype, cognitive busyness facilitates the *application* of a stereotype. Thus, cognitively busy individuals rely on stereotypes because they lack the cognitive capacity to engage in deeper, more deliberative thinking.

Other conditions may disrupt one's ability to engage in deliberative thinking. Certain moods increase the likelihood of stereotypical thinking, partly because they either disrupt the *ability* to engage in deliberative thinking or the *willingness* to engage in deliberative thinking.

BAD MOODS AND STEREOTYPICAL THINKING    Suppose you're in a particularly angry mood because your employer passed you over for a promotion. What effect could your mood have on your judgments of a newly encountered member of a widely stereotyped group? Common sense suggests, and so does research, that anger exacerbates the tendency to engage in stereotypical thinking (Bodenhausen, 1993). Apparently, being angry can overwhelm our cognitive capacity, leading us to not think carefully about others. Consequently, we have an enhanced tendency to rely on our stereotypes when angered.

Anxiety is another mood state that appears to be quite compatible with stereotyping. Like anger, anxiety also constrains our processing capability, which facilitates stereotyping (Wilder, 1993). An interesting phenomenon related to anxiety that might contribute to stereotyping and prejudice is an awareness of one's own mortality (Schimel et al., 1999). According to **terror management theory** (Greenberg et al., 1990), being made aware of the inevitability of death is threatening to people, creating a negative mood not unlike anxiety. One way that people may defend against this "death anxiety" is by bolstering their own belief systems or conceptions of reality.

Consequently, similar people are liked because they are viewed as sharing this belief system, whereas dissimilar people are disliked because they are perceived as threatening to the belief system.

In an experiment testing these propositions, Greenberg and his colleagues (1990, p. 310) asked Christian college students in the experimental group to "write about what will happen to them as they physically die and the emotions that the thought of their own death aroused in them." Christian college students in the control group did not engage in a writing task. Following a series of questionnaires, all students were instructed to view a questionnaire ostensibly completed by another student, who was either Christian or Jewish, and to form an impression of this person. Students in the control group rated the Christian and Jewish targets equivalently. In line with the predictions based upon terror management theory, reminding students of their own mortality led to more positive evaluations of the in-group target (i.e., Christian) and more negative evaluations of the out-group target (i.e., Jewish). Thus, mortality salience increases in-group attraction and also increases bias toward those who are different.

But not all negative moods facilitate stereotyping and prejudice (Bodenhausen, Mussweiler, Gabriel, & Moreno, in press). Although anger and anxiety constrain cognitive capacity and appear to be quite compatible with stereotyping, sadness does not necessarily lead to biased judgments. In one study comparing how different types of negative moods affect stereotypical thinking, angry individuals were more likely to rely on their stereotypes, whereas individuals who were in a sad or neutral mood did not tend to think stereotypically (Bodenhausen, Sheppard, & Kramer, 1994).

GOOD MOODS AND STEREOTYPICAL THINKING    What about good moods and stereotyping? Suppose now that you encounter a person belonging to a frequently stereotyped group and you've just been told that you've received that desired promotion. Given this happy state of affairs, would you still be likely to engage in stereotypic thinking about this person? Common sense suggests that your good mood should make you less likely to stereotype, because your good mood might lead you to be charitable in your evaluations of others. Research findings suggest otherwise, however (Mackie, Queller, Stroessner, & Hamilton, 1996).

In one study of how a happy mood might enhance stereotyping (Bodenhausen et al., 1994), college students experienced a mood induction procedure designed to evoke either a happy or neutral mood. In one condition, students were asked to write about an event that made them particularly happy. In another condition, students were asked to write about the mundane events of the previous day. Immediately afterwards, students, believing they were part of a second, unrelated experiment, were asked to pretend that they were student members of the college's peer judicial review board that makes disciplinary decisions. Students read about one of two cases, involving either a physical assault (beating up a roommate) or cheating on an exam. For half of the students, the defendant fit the stereotype, whereas for the remaining students the defendant was not stereotypical. That is, for the case of assault, the defendant was given either an obviously Latino name (Juan Garcia) or an ethnically nondescript name (John Garner). For the cheating case, the defendant was either described as a "well-known track and field athlete" or was not described as an athlete. After reading the case, students were asked to rate the accused student's guilt. Results revealed that among the neutral mood participants, stereotyped targets were treated no differently than their nonstereotyped counterparts. Interestingly enough, happy participants rendered harsher judgments of the stereotyped, as opposed to nonstereotyped, targets.

Why does a positive mood contribute to stereotyping? People who are in a happy mood typically are not motivated to engage in extensive cognitive effort. It's almost as if people realize that one way to ruin a good mood is by thinking deeply about issues. Consequently, happy people prefer to coast along, relying on their initial stereotypic reactions. So does this mean that happy people are simply unable to cast aside their stereotypic preconceptions? Not at all. In fact, when happy people are motivated to think carefully, perhaps by making them accountable for their judgments, they can avoid stereotypic responses (Bodenhausen et al., 1994).

POWER AND STEREOTYPICAL THINKING   There is yet another factor that influences when people are likely to rely on stereotypes. Possessing power—defined as the ability to control others' outcomes (Fiske & Depret, 1996)—is associated with a tendency to think stereotypically. Consider for a moment the dynamics within a work or classroom setting. Secretaries know more about their bosses' preferences and habits than vice versa; students know more about their professors than vice versa. Why might this be the case? According to Susan Fiske (1993), power captures attention. She argues that powerless people must pay close attention to those who have control over their outcomes. Given the potentially high stakes for inaccuracy, powerless people do not simply rely on stereotypes in their judgments; rather, the powerless attend to more informative clues about the dispositions of the powerful in order to predict their behavior.

But what about the powerful? Do they not attend to the powerless? Fiske's research suggests that the powerful pay considerably less attention to their subordinates and are more vulnerable to stereotyping. Several factors may explain why the powerful are more likely to stereotype the powerless than vice versa. First, the powerful, by virtue of their status, do not have to think carefully about their subordinates because less is at stake for them. Second, the powerful have more demands on their attention than do the powerless. Faced with time pressure (Freund, Kruglanski, & Shpitajzen, 1985) and distraction (Gilbert, 1989) brought on by these demands, powerful people may use stereotypes simply because they are rushed.

Lest you conclude that all powerful individuals stereotype those who are beneath them in the power hierarchy, keep in mind that people can control their stereotyping, prejudice, and discrimination. The good news is that people, including the powerful, can refrain from stereotyping when properly motivated to do so. By appealing to people's desire for accuracy (Neuberg, 1989), their self-concepts as fair-minded people (Fiske & Von Hendy, 1992), and their guilt or compunctions (Devine, Monteith, Zuwerink, & Elliot, 1991), people can be motivated to view others as unique individuals, rather than members of a category.

# ➤ CONCLUSION

This chapter has presented a variety of theoretical views concerning how stereotypes are formed, maintained, and used. Stereotyping, we have learned, serves important individual and societal functions. Not only do stereotypes allow us as individuals to carve up our social world into manageable elements, but on a societal level they also allow us to justify and rationalize the exploitation of certain groups over others.

Moreover, stereotypes are self-perpetuating, in the sense that they influence what we perceive and remember about others, how we treat them, and ultimately how they respond to us. In fact, Claire and Fiske (1998) argue that stereotypes are harmful not just because they are inaccurate or usually negative in connotation, but because they guide our treatment of individuals belonging to stereotyped groups. In responding to our actions, members of stereotyped groups may unintentionally and nonconsciously confirm our initial stereotypic preconceptions, perhaps accounting for why stereotypes are so resistant to change (Bargh & Chen, 1997).

This analysis may lead us to the rather gloomy conclusion that stereotyping is inherent, inevitable, and even natural. The inevitability of stereotyping is a complex issue, and as usual, the news is both good and bad. The bad news is that stereotypes do apparently have some automatic effects, such that they are easily activated and often facilitate perception. Moreover, various moods, motivations, and cognitive constraints may exacerbate the tendency to apply stereotypes.

The good news is that people do not always engage in stereotyping. Although it might be true that people cannot fully control their spontaneous, split-second reactions upon encountering a member of a stereotyped group, people can control their ensuing responses. This distinction between stereotype activation and stereotype application is an important one, because it suggests that while stereotype activation may be more or less automatic, stereotype application is controllable.

Ultimately, the responsibility for stereotyping others lies with us. Although many factors may enhance our reliance upon stereotypes, we can refrain from stereotyping others, if we are sufficiently motivated to do so.

# 5

# Individual Differences in Prejudice

According to some estimates, there are well over 200 hate speech sites on the Internet, up from only one in 1995 (Cloud, 1999). These on-line extremists run the gamut from Holocaust denial advocates to Neo-Nazis, from "Christian Identity" followers who cite the Bible as the source of their racist views to the militia movements. With just a few keystrokes, an array of on-line hate sites can promote agendas of racism, anti-Semitism, homophobia, and terrorism. Suddenly high-tech bigots are using Web sites that have the potential to reach millions, when not too long ago organized hate groups could reach only a limited number of people with pamphlets or by marching down Main Street.

A tour of these technologically advanced Web pages reveals essays, a list of upcoming events, archival photographs of lynchings, ethnic jokes, links to similar hate groups, and even White supremacist dating services. It's all too tempting to dismiss members of these hate groups as the "lunatic fringe" that has little impact on others. But the Internet affords such hatemongers the opportunity to not only reach millions the world over, but to network easily with other like-minded individuals.

For purposes of illustration, consider a sampling of quotes that are representative of such cyberspace bigotry:

> *"The NAAWP (National Association for the Advancement of White People) does not advocate violence or bloodshed, but we will not run away from it."*
>
> *NAAWP's Web Page*

> *"Fact #18: In addition to the difference in brain weight, the Negro brain grows less after puberty than the white. Though the Negro brain and nervous system mature faster than the white brain, its development is arrested at an earlier age which limits further intellectual advancement."*
>
> *Aryan Angel's Web Page ("100 Black Facts")*

**111**

*"And lead us not into temptation, but deliver us from the JEWS. For thine is the kingdom, and the power, and the glory forever. Amen."*

*Christian Defense League's Web Page*
*("Important Bible Passages Concerning the Enemy")*

*"S.T.R.A.I.G.H.T.—Society to Remove All Immoral Godless Homosexual Trash"*

*Melchizedek Vigilance's Web Page*

Interestingly, most, if not all, of these on-line hate sites merge different forms of prejudice: anti-Black, anti-Jew, antigay, and even anti-feminist. Perhaps this is not surprising, given that many studies have shown that different forms of prejudice— towards Blacks, women, people with AIDS, gay men and lesbians, fat people, and so on—tend to dwell within the same individuals (Bierly, 1985; Crandall & Cohen, 1994; Peterson, Doty, & Winter, 1993).

Why do these differing forms of prejudice coalesce within the same individuals? Are there just certain "types" of people who are prone to be prejudiced against many different groups? Is it the case, as Gordon Allport (1950, p. 408) suggested, that prejudice "is often lockstiched into the very fabric of personality"? And if so, why?

This chapter is designed to provide some answers to these questions by taking an individual differences approach to the explanation of prejudice. In Chapter 3 we explored the importance of values in understanding prejudice, and in Chapter 4 we considered the cognitive underpinnings of prejudice. In Chapter 5 we will continue this individual-level analysis of prejudice by exploring how personality, cognitive motivations, and attitudinal orientations make individuals prone to prejudice.

We begin by examining the classic research on the authoritarian personality, one of the first comprehensive attempts to explain prejudice in terms of an individual differences orientation. Then we'll consider right-wing authoritarianism, which is a conceptual descendant of the original research. We will also explore how an intolerance for ambiguity may make individuals especially prone to prejudice, and how social ideologies—based upon religious or political beliefs—may account for individual differences in prejudice. We will also discuss an emerging line of research that calls attention to individual differences in nonprejudice. And finally, we will discuss some of the limitations of the individual differences approach to understanding prejudice. In continuing this individual level of analysis, let's start at the beginning with research developed to explain the incomprehensible horror of the Nazi Holocaust.

➤ PREJUDICE AND PERSONALITY

## Classic Research on the Authoritarian Personality

In the aftermath of World War II, several University of California, Berkeley researchers—two of whom had fled from Nazi Germany, Theodor Adorno and Else Frenkel-Brunswick—set out to understand the virulent anti-Semitism that led to the horrific slaughter of millions of Jews and other "undesirables" under Adolf Hitler's reign. The underlying goal of these "Berkeley researchers" was to explain how personality characteristics might make some people more receptive to such extreme out-group hostility.

Adorno and his colleagues argued that extreme prejudices are linked to what they called the **authoritarian personality**—a personality trait characterized by a tendency to submit to those in authority and to denigrate those who are weak or different. In their studies of more than 2,000 individuals (predominantly White and middle-class), Adorno and his colleagues set out to measure this personality style to determine whether it is associated with anti-Semitism and other forms of prejudice.

To accomplish this task, Adorno and his colleagues first developed two questionnaires: an Anti-Semitism Scale that assessed attitudes toward Jews (e.g., "I can hardly imagine myself marrying a Jew") and an Ethnocentrism Scale that assessed glorification of the in-group and hostility to a variety of out-groups (e.g., "America may not be perfect, but the American Way has brought us about as close as human beings can get to a perfect society"). Based upon their observation that the extreme prejudice in Nazi Germany was closely associated with highly conservative political and economic beliefs, they also developed a Political and Economic Conservatism Scale (e.g., "In general, full economic security is harmful; most men wouldn't work if they didn't need the money for eating and living").

Finally, the researchers developed the "F-scale" (short for *fascism*), the instrument designed to measure authoritarian tendencies. People who expressed strong agreement with items like the following were classified as having an authoritarian personality:

- Obedience and respect for authority are the most important virtues children should have.
- The wild sex life of the old Greeks and Romans were tame compared to some of the goings-on in this country, even in places where people might least expect it.
- People can be divided into two distinct classes: the weak and the strong.
- Homosexuals are hardly better than criminals and ought to be severely punished.

Adorno and his colleagues discovered that anti-Semites tended to be extremely ethnocentric (i.e., expressing hostility toward a wide range of ethnic out-groups), and to have strongly conservative political and economic beliefs. Moreover, and importantly, anti-Semites also tended to have an authoritarian personality style. As reflected in the items that compose the F-scale, this personality style includes an intolerance for weakness in others; a preoccupation with power and status; conformity to cultural values; a tendency to think rigidly or in an all-or-none fashion; preoccupation with others' sex lives; and a submissiveness to in-group authority figures.

Greatly influenced by psychodynamic theory at the time, Adorno and his colleagues argued that the development of the authoritarian personality can be traced to the family dynamics. According to this view, parents of authoritarians tended to be overly concerned with appropriate behavior and conformity to conventional moral dictates, particularly in terms of sexuality. These parents tended to be strict and use excessively harsh discipline to stifle the children's aggressive and sexual impulses. Such discipline resulted in the children repressing their own hostilities toward their parents and other authority figures and redirecting or displacing their anger onto "safe" targets who cannot retaliate. And who are these "safe" targets? Those who are smaller and weaker, of course. And as adults, the "safe" targets become those minority out-groups who are socially disadvantaged and less powerful. In other words, authoritarians submit to people who are in positions of power while simultaneously behaving aggressively to those beneath them in the status hierarchy.

Thus, Adorno et al.'s (1964) classic research explained why different forms of prejudice seem to coalesce within the authoritarian: "the political, economic, and social convictions" become "an expression of deep-lying trends in his personality" (p. 1). In other words, authoritarians' political and economic attitudes (i.e., conservatism) and social attitudes (i.e., belief in a "normal" or conventional lifestyle) account for their condemnation of ethnic minorities (e.g., Jews, Blacks, Latinos, etc.) and any other social "deviants" (e.g., homosexuals, criminals, etc.).

## Criticisms of the Research

Since the publication of Adorno et al.'s book *The Authoritarian Personality* in 1950, more than 2,000 articles have been published in four decades (Meloen, 1991). Adorno et al.'s research on the authoritarian personality initially evoked much praise, but criticisms quickly began to emerge. Subsequent researchers pointed out the methodological and measurement flaws within the original studies. According to critics, Adorno et al.'s predominantly White, middle-class sample was unrepresentative, and the questionnaires were flawed in their design. For example, all of the questionnaire items were keyed in the same "agreeing" direction, so that it was unclear whether agreement truly indicated an authoritarian response or merely a tendency to agree with any statement (Brown, 1965).

Adorno et al.'s research has been criticized on conceptual and theoretical counts as well: (a) Perhaps lack of education, low IQ, and lower social class, rather than personality, best account for prejudice (Christie, 1954; Hyman & Sheatsley, 1954); (b) The psychoanalytic perspective that guided Adorno et al.'s explanations of the authoritarian personality is itself questionable, and (c) Adorno and his colleagues, by focusing on right-wing conservatism, overlooked prejudice within the radical left (Rokeach, 1960).

For all these reasons, and perhaps because of the growing trend away from the study of personality traits in the 1960s and 1970s, the study of authoritarianism faded. However, a resurgence of interest in the "prejudiced personality" that appeared in the 1980s and 1990s has taken modern research on authoritarianism in two directions. Robert Altemeyer's (1981, 1988, 1994) research program on the Right Wing Authoritarian has, in some ways, continued the thrust of the work of the "Berkeley researchers," whereas other researchers have focused on a singular cognitive trait of authoritarians: their intolerance of ambiguity.

## Right-Wing Authoritarianism

According to Robert Altemeyer (1994), he was first introduced to the study of authoritarianism in 1965, when a professor asked him a question on his PhD candidacy exam about the methodological flaws of the F-scale. In Altemeyer's words, "I failed the question with distinction and had to write a redemptive paper" (p. 132).

Once aware of the methodological flaws of the F-scale, however, Altemeyer eventually developed a questionnaire—the Right-Wing Authoritarian (RWA) Scale—that avoided the methodological pitfalls of the original measure of authoritarianism. Altemeyer's RWA Scale taps three attitudinal clusters of the authoritarian personality: *authoritarian submission* (tendency to yield to legitimate authorities); *authoritarian aggression* (tendency to aggress against various persons); and *conventionalism* (tendency to adhere to approved social conventions).

Having developed a psychometrically adequate instrument, Altemeyer proceeded to correlate people's scores on the RWA Scale with various "worldviews." People scoring high on the RWA, relative to low scorers, tend to (a) favor conservative political parties in their countries, (b) recommend harsher punishment for lawbreakers, (c) endorse more traditional gender roles, (d) be opposed to abortion, (e) believe "gay bashing" is not that serious a crime, and (f) hold more orthodox religious beliefs (Altemeyer, 1994).

Using Altemeyer's RWA Scale, other researchers report similar relationships between authoritarianism and attitudes toward various social issues. Numerous studies have demonstrated that authoritarianism is related to gender role ideology, such that high scorers tend to endorse traditional gender roles, (Duncan, Peterson, & Winter, 1997; Walker, Rowe, & Quinsey, 1993), hold negative attitudes toward feminism (Sarup, 1976) and feminists (Haddock & Zanna, 1994), devalue political events involving women (Duncan et al., 1997), and hold extremely negative antigay attitudes (Haddock & Zanna, 1997). In terms of their attitudes toward other social and political issues, right-wing authoritarians tend to be strongly punitive in assigning sentences to criminal offenders and other violators of social norms (Christie, 1993; Feather, 1996), and not surprisingly, favored strong U.S. military action during the Persian Gulf crisis (Doty, Winter, Peterson, & Kemmelmeier, 1997). Authoritarians also were more likely to support California's Proposition 187, which passed in 1994, that restricted illegal immigrants from receiving social service benefits and free public education (Quinton, Cowan, & Watson, 1996).

Clearly, authoritarianism is linked to the values that people hold. In fact, Rohan and Zanna (1996) found that high and low authoritarians differ significantly in their value systems. High authoritarians are more likely to emphasize values related to *conformity, tradition,* and *security,* and they tend to deemphasize values concerned with *self-direction* and *universalism* (i.e., understanding and showing concern for the welfare of all human beings).

In turn, these value systems are associated with prejudice. The authoritarian's conservatism (as reflected in the high degree of importance placed on conformity, tradition, and security), combined with holding universalism in low regard, is quite compatible with prejudice toward members of other ethnic, racial, and social groups who are perceived to violate these values (Biernat et al., 1994; Zanna, 1994). Perhaps this explains why, in terms of hostility toward out-groups, RWAs have been shown to be prejudiced against so many target groups (e.g., Blacks, Latinos, Jews, aborigines, Sikhs, Japanese, Chinese, Filipinos, Africans, Arabs, feminists, homosexuals, French Canadians, the physically disabled, people with AIDS) that Altemeyer refers to RWAs as "equal opportunity bigots" (Altemeyer, 1981, 1994). In short, researchers have presented compelling evidence that right-wing authoritarianism is associated with ethnocentrism, prejudice, and hostility toward unconventional beliefs and behaviors (Peterson, Doty, & Winter, 1993).

At first glance, Altemeyer's right-wing authoritarianism appears to resemble the original formulation of authoritarianism that emerged from the "Berkeley researchers." But differences do exist between the two approaches. One important distinction between the two centers on the theoretical underpinnings of authoritarianism. Adorno et al.'s model, you will recall, invokes psychodynamic theory to explain the development of the authoritarian personality, with its emphasis on deep-lying unconscious struggles, repressed anger, and displaced hostilities. Taking a social learning perspective, Altemeyer rejects the psychodynamic explanation and instead argues that parents with harsh disciplinary styles serve as models for aggressive behavior and intolerant worldviews.

Regardless of whether researchers have adopted a psychodynamic or social learning approach to this topic, studies have consistently found that authoritarianism is a relatively stable individual difference dimension that underlies susceptibility to prejudice (Duckitt, 1992; Meloen, Van der Linden, & Witte, 1996). This is true not only for authoritarians in the United States but in other countries (e.g., Canada, South Africa, Russia) as well (Bierly, 1985; Haddock, Zanna, & Esses, 1993; Duckitt & Farre, 1994; Haddock, Zanna, & Esses, 1993; McFarland, Ageyev, Djintcharadze, 1996; Stephan, Agayev, Coates-Shrider, Stephan & Abalakina, 1994). Clearly, research on the authoritarian personality remains the most comprehensive attempt to explain prejudice in terms of personality characteristics.

## ➤ INTOLERANCE OF AMBIGUITY

In Adorno et al.'s (1950) original formulation of the authoritarian personality, they suggested that for authoritarians "there is no place for ambivalence or ambiguities. Every attempt is made to eliminate them" (p. 480). What Adorno et al. were suggesting is that authoritarians view the world in simple black-white terms, abhorring shades of gray. This belief was echoed later by Gordon Allport (1954), who argued that prejudiced persons have a tendency to think dichotomously and to have a need for "definiteness." Prejudiced individuals, Allport suggested, have a characteristic style of *thinking* that differs from that of nonprejudiced individuals. But is this necessarily true? Do authoritarians (or prejudiced people) have an overly rigid cognitive style that does not accommodate ambiguities? And if so, does this cognitive difference have any implications for susceptibility to prejudice?

Early research using various methodologies suggested that authoritarianism was indeed related to "cognitive rigidity." For example, researchers would often use the *Einstellung* paradigm to study the perseveration of mental sets. This test involves presenting participants with several paper-and-pencil problems that can be solved through the same sequence of manipulations. Once participants successfully solved a fixed number of these problems, *Einstellung* ("set") was considered to have developed. Participants were then given problems that required different manipulations in order to test whether they would indeed break their set to find the correct solution. Although numerous investigations using this paradigm found that authoritarians were more likely to perseverate or cling to past solutions in their problem-solving, other studies failed to replicate these findings (see Christie, 1993 for a review). Consequently, the research on authoritarianism and cognitive rigidity waned. A recent study (Schultz, Stone, & Christie,

1997), however, revisited the *Einstellung* issue and found greater rigidity among high authoritarians, but only when the task was important to them (i.e., they believed the task was a measure of their intelligence and could accurately predict academic performance). The reasons for this finding are not entirely clear. One speculation is that authoritarians generally are more prone to fearfulness, which disrupts their processing of information under stressful conditions (Schultz et al., 1997). Nonetheless, this research suggests that authoritarian people may be especially prone to think simplistically when anxious. And it is precisely this kind of thinking—all-or-nothing, black-and-white, us-versus-them—in which stereotypes and prejudice flourish.

Another line of research in the 1950s showed that prejudice is related to a general intolerance of ambiguity (Block & Block, 1951) and a need for definiteness (Allport, 1954). But for the most part, the search for the "dynamics of cognition in the prejudiced personality" (Allport, 1954, p. 170) lay dormant for several decades. However, interest in a cognitive style that parallels intolerance for ambiguity has resurfaced in a new concept, **the personal need for structure** (Neuberg & Newsom, 1993).

Apparently, individuals differ in the extent to which they have a strong need to simplify, order, and structure their environment. Some individuals are comfortable with ambiguities in their social environment, finding these "gray areas" captivating. Other individuals, in contrast, find such ambiguities unsettling and even threatening. These individuals are said to differ in their personal need for structure (PNS). According to Neuberg and Newsom (1993), individuals who are high in need for structure desire simple structure and clarity in situations; such persons prefer familiar social situations and consistent routines, and find the unfamiliar and the inconsistent troubling.

Stereotypes, we learned in Chapter 4, provide one way to simplify a complex world. Because of this simplifying aspect of stereotypes, individuals high in need for structure may be more likely to form stereotypes about new groups (Schaller, Boyd, Yohannes, & O'Brien, 1995) and to rely upon stereotypes in understanding others' behavior. Consider, for instance, an experiment conducted by Neuberg and Newsom (1993). Participants were informed that the purpose of the experiment was to investigate ways that people form impressions of others. They were asked to read a short scenario about an undergraduate who was having course-work and relationship difficulties and to rate the student on several dimensions. The scenario was written in such a way that it was ambiguous with respect to whether the behaviors reflected traditional male or female traits. For some participants, the student was male; for the remaining participants, the student was female. Overall, participants who were high in need for structure were more likely to use gender stereotypes when making inferences about the student's behavior. That is, high-PNS participants tended to attribute more of the "female" traits to the female student than to the male student, whereas low-PNS participants displayed no differences in their perceptions of the male and female students. These findings suggest that personal need for structure is an individual difference variable that appears to be related to whether people prefer simplistic ways of processing information. Presumably this preference for simplicity in processing information about other people accounts for the enhanced tendency to stereotype others in ambiguous situations. Emerging evidence based upon a conceptually similar construct, the need for closure (Webster & Kruglanski, 1994), also supports this notion.

According to Arie Kruglanski and his colleagues (Kruglanski & Webster, 1996), the **need for closure** refers to individuals' "desire for a firm answer to a question and an aversion toward ambiguity" (p. 264). Individuals who are motivated toward closure may "seize" and immediately "freeze" upon a judgment on the basis of inconclusive evidence, subsequently ignoring evidence to the contrary. Because individuals high in the need for closure desire quick answers to any ambiguous situation, they tend to rely upon stereotypes in making assessments of others.

In one study (Dijksterhuis, van Knippenberg, Kruglanski, & Schaper, 1996), for instance, Dutch participants varying in need for closure were presented with behavioral information about a group of soccer hooligans and were asked to form an impression of this group. Some of the behavioral descriptions were consistent with the stereotype of soccer hooligans as aggressive and unfriendly (e.g., "Hank sometimes starts a fight in a bar"), whereas other descriptions were inconsistent (e.g., "John sometimes volunteers at the local homeless shelter"). Participants were allowed to read the descriptions at their own pace and were then asked to rate the group on several dimensions related to the stereotype. It was predicted that high need for closure participants would make more stereotypical judgments about the soccer hooligans than low need for closure participants, primarily due to differences in information processing. Because stereotype inconsistent information creates ambiguity, high need for closure participants were expected to pay more attention to stereotype consistent information, as revealed by their reading latencies, and to show better recall for consistent information. The results confirmed these predictions, indicating that high need for closure participants were indeed more likely to "freeze" upon information consistent with their initial stereotypes and to ignore evidence to the contrary.

Obviously, the need for structure and the need for closure share many similar features. These two dispositional constructs are in some sense a derivative of the original formulation of authoritarianism, but they are not synonymous with authoritarianism. In other words, authoritarianism is a broader construct that encompasses several dimensions (e.g., conventionalism, aggression, and submission), whereas the personal need for structure and the need for closure measure one cognitive dimension purportedly related to authoritarianism: an intolerance of ambiguity.

These cognitive underpinnings of the "prejudiced personality" certainly suggest a link between cognitive motivations and stereotyping. But what role do these cognitive motivations play in prejudice? Although the relationship between stereotyping and prejudice is complex, we do know that stereotypes and prejudice are positively associated (Dovidio et al., 1996). At the very least, need for structure/closure is an important determinant of the way social groups are perceived and evaluated.

So far, we've seen that individual differences in personality (i.e., authoritarianism), cognitive motivations (i.e., need for structure and need for closure) contribute to prejudice and stereotyping. But prejudice, we will see in the next section, is often linked to broader social ideologies that represent what we believe to be good, just, and true.

## ➤ SOCIAL IDEOLOGIES AND PREJUDICE

In our discussion of prejudice and personality, we have hinted at basic values, beliefs, and attitudes that underlie prejudice. But an individual's values, beliefs, and attitudes often reflect social ideologies or cultural worldviews. Let's consider more closely how two such ideological orientations, religion and politics, are linked to prejudice.

## Religion and Prejudice

> *"We have just enough religion to make us hate, but not enough to make us love one another."*
>
> *Jonathan Swift*, Thoughts on Various Subjects

Most of the world's major religions espouse unconditional love and acceptance of others, without regard to race and ethnicity. Christianity in particular champions a message of universal tolerance and acceptance: "There is neither Jew nor Greek, slave nor free, male nor female for you are all one" (Galatians 3:28). Throughout history, however, prejudice and persecution have all too often rested on religious grounds. The same Jesus who preached love and acceptance of others was used to justify the Crusades and the Inquisition. And religion continues to be an ingredient in intergroup conflict today. Think of the Arab/Israeli clashes in the Middle East, Protestant/Catholic conflict in Northern Ireland, the Serb/Muslim/Croat atrocities in Bosnia, and the Sikh/Hindu dispute in India.

In Gordon Allport's (1954) words, "The role of religion is paradoxical. It makes prejudice and it unmakes prejudice. . . . Some people say the only cure for prejudice is more religion; some say the only cure is to abolish religion" (p. 444). Admittedly, religion can make us better or it can make us worse. In what ways are religion and prejudice related, and how can we explain Allport's "paradox"?

In one of the first studies of the relationship between religion and prejudice, Allport and Kramer (1946) found that Protestant and Catholic students were more prejudiced against Blacks than those without strong religious affiliations. Numerous other studies have since replicated this correlation between prejudice and religion. Despite religious teachings advocating love and acceptance, people who report being religious are also likely to be more prejudiced. This finding prompted Daniel Batson and Christopher Burris (1993) to conclude that "Among White middle-class Christians in the United States, religion is not associated with increased love and acceptance but with increased intolerance, prejudice, and bigotry" (p. 152).

To understand this puzzling finding, it's useful to recognize that there are different *ways* of being religious. Allport was the first to make this observation, suggesting that there are two forms of religiousness, and each relates differently to prejudice. Some people are *intrinsically* religious; they view their religion as central to their identity and internalize its teachings. Others are *extrinsically* religious; they view religious worship as an opportunity for social support or achieving status. Whether one views religion as a means to an end (i.e., extrinsic orientation) or an end in itself (i.e., intrinsic orientation) is relevant to understanding the link between religion and prejudice. In general, extrinsically religious people appear to be more prejudiced than intrinsically religious people (Batson & Ventis, 1982).

More recently, Batson and Burris (1993) have questioned whether intrinsically religious people are really less prejudiced than extrinsically religious people. They argue that intrinsic persons may *appear* to be less prejudiced because they are more concerned with "looking good" to others. In earlier studies, for example, prejudice was typically assessed by questionnaire, and participants may have tried to present themselves as free from prejudice. To test this hypothesis, Batson and his colleagues

(1986) investigated the actual behavior of intrinsics, rather than their self-reported attitudes. In one study, White participants were given a choice of watching a film in one of two rooms. Another person (actually a confederate) was already sitting in each of the rooms; in one room sat a White person, and in the other room sat a Black person. For half of the participants, the same film was being shown in both rooms; for the other half, a different film was being shown in each room. Choosing to sit in the room with the White person rather than the Black person represented the dependent variable. In the condition in which the same film was being shown in each of the rooms—and choice of room would clearly indicate racial prejudice—intrinsically religious participants were more likely to sit with the Black student. However, in the condition in which a different film was being shown in each of the rooms—and choice of rooms could reflect preferences in movies and not necessarily racial prejudice—intrinsically religious participants no longer preferred to sit with the Black student. Thus, intrinsically religious people, while appearing accepting, may not truly be nonprejudiced.

Fortunately, there is a third way of being religious, *religion as quest* (Batson & Ventis, 1982; Batson & Burris, 1993), which involves a questioning and self-critical approach to religion. People who are quest-oriented are open-minded, flexible, and realize the complexity in spiritual issues. They view religion as a quest for answers, accepting that they may never know the final truth about such matters. Are people with a quest orientation less likely to be prejudiced, compared to their intrinsically and extrinsically religious counterparts? The answer appears to be yes. Quest-oriented people tend to exhibit less racial prejudice in both their self-reports and actual behavior (Batson & Burris, 1993; Batson et al., 1986). Moreover, quest-oriented people are more tolerant and accepting of gay men and lesbians than those with an intrinsic or extrinsic religious orientation (Fisher et al., 1994).

Quest orientation is in many ways antithetical to fundamentalism, which *is* positively correlated with prejudice (Hunsberger, 1995). Fundamentalism, as defined by Altemeyer and Hunsberger (1992), represents "the belief that there is one set of religious teachings that clearly contains the fundamental, basic, intrinsic, essential, inerrant truth about humanity and deity" (p. 118). Fundamentalism is not a set of religious beliefs per se; rather, fundamentalism is a way of being religious that entertains no ambiguities, uncertainties, or doubts. In other words, fundamentalism is an *authoritarian* way of being religious, which incidentally is linked to right-wing authoritarianism (Altemeyer, 1996). In fact, Altemeyer argues that fundamentalism in whatever stripe (Christian, Jewish, Muslim, Hindu, etc.) is a religious manifestion of right-wing authoritarianism.

So what can we conclude about the relationship between religion and prejudice? It is not religion per se that "makes and unmakes prejudice." Rather, it is the way in which religious beliefs are held that is associated with prejudice. Only individuals who perceive religion as a quest tend to be relatively nonprejudiced.

## Political Conservatism and Prejudice

Many studies suggest that political conservatism is linked to prejudice (Dator, 1969; Eysenck, 1971; Meertens & Pettigrew, 1997; Pratto et al., 1994; Sears et al., 1997). As noted earlier, researchers investigating the authoritarian personality assumed that anti-Semitism and other forms of prejudice are associated with the political right (Adorno et al., 1950). To test this idea, they developed a political and economic conservatism scale based upon the traditional "right-left" political spectrum: conservatism advocates free enterprise, principles of self-reliance, and minimal government interference, whereas liberalism advocates greater governmental involvement (i.e., social welfare programs), limits on the power of business, and support for labor unions. In this classic research on the authoritarian personality, Adorno and his colleagues found a moderately strong correlation between political conservatism and prejudice.

More recently, Altemeyer's (1996) work on the "right-wing authoritarian" (RWA) supports the hypothesis that prejudice is associated with the political right. In their political beliefs, high RWAs tend to be conservative, opposing socialized medicine (Altemeyer, 1996) and supporting aggressive military policy (Doty et al., 1997). According to Altemeyer (1996), high RWAs show a slight tendency to support the Republican Party in the United States and the Progressive Conservative Party in Canada. This tendency to support right-wing political groups has been documented in other countries as well. In Israel, for instance, high RWA Jewish students identified with the right-wing and religious parties (Rubenstein, 1996), and Palestinian high RWAs similarly tended to support religiously fundamentalist, right-wing parties (Altemeyer, 1996).

To explore the link between political ideology and prejudice, other researchers have examined whether political conservatism is linked to opposition to government policies designed to ensure equal opportunity. In general, political conservatives are less likely than liberals to support policies such as affirmative action (Sidanius, Pratto, & Bobo, 1996) or school busing for desegregation (Kinder & Sears, 1985). But is opposition to various government programs driven by conservative political ideology or by racial hostility or by some combination of the two?

Advocates of the "principled conservatism" approach acknowledge lingering racism in American society, but argue that their opposition to governmental policies such as affirmative action is not motivated by racism (Sidanius et al., 1996). Instead conservatives maintain that their opposition is strictly grounded in a concern for establishing a truly "color-blind" society. In support of this position, Paul Sniderman and his colleagues (1991) not only failed to find evidence of greater racism among conservatives but also found that under certain circumstances conservatives may actually be more supportive of governmental assistance for Blacks.

More recently, however, this notion that people who oppose race-related policies do so because of genuine conservative ideology, as opposed to racism, has been challenged. In recent survey research, for instance, Meertens and Pettigrew (1995) assessed attitudes toward different minority out-groups and immigration policies in four Western European nations (France, the Netherlands, Great Britain, and West Germany). They showed that conservative respondents scored higher on measures of prejudice in all samples, and that both prejudice and conservatism were predictors of opposition to immigration.

A similar association between prejudice and political ideology emerged in a recent study assessing attitudes toward affirmative action. Jim Sidanius and his colleagues (1996) showed that although opposition to affirmative action was positively correlated with political conservatism, it was also correlated with racism. Thus, the argument that opposition to racial policies is based solely on conservative principles and is not a function of racism is called into question (Stoker, 1998).

That prejudice and political conservatism are associated is by now a well-established finding. A broad theory of intergroup relations, social dominance theory (Sidanius, 1993), explains this relationship between political ideology and prejudice. **Social dominance theory** proposes that (a) In almost all societies, group-based hierarchies exist in which at least one group is dominant over others and enjoys a disproportionate share of privilege (e.g., wealth, education, health), and at least one group endures a disproportionate share of disadvantage (e.g., poverty, poor health, low levels of education, low-status occupations); (b) In competing for scarce resources (e.g., wealth, social status), dominant groups seek to maintain or increase their position, and subordinate groups seek to improve their position; and (c) In this intergroup competition, groups use *ideological* strategies, such as racism, sexism, and political ideology to justify the existing social arrangement.

From this perspective, group-based inequality is sustained, in part, by *legitimizing myths*. Legitimizing myths are the specific attitudes, beliefs, and ideologies that justify the existing social hierarchy. These myths include *ethnic prejudice*, which justifies the discriminatory treatment of ethnic groups lower in the social hierarchy; *nationalism*, which is the belief that one's country is superior to other countries; *cultural elitism*, the belief that some groups in society are more "cultured" than others and are therefore more deserving of the "finer things in life"; *sexism*, the maintenance of sexual inequality, and, most relevant to our discussion here, *political conservatism*, the endorsement of continued group hierarchies based upon free enterprise and individual work ethic.

Thus, social dominance theory explains why political conservatism and racism are so consistently linked. Both conservatism and racism stem from the desire to maintain hierarchically structured group relations. However, individuals differ in the extent to which they accept ideologies that promote inequality. Some individuals endorse group-based inequality, whereas others endorse egalitarianism. Such individuals are said to differ in social dominance orientation (Pratto, Sidanius, Stallworth, & Malle, 1994).

## ➤ SOCIAL DOMINANCE ORIENTATION

While research on the authoritarian personality emphasizes the role of "personality" in the traditional sense to explain prejudice, research focusing on **social dominance orientation,** an extension of social dominance theory, explains prejudice in terms of individuals' attitudes toward intergroup relations. Social dominance orientation (SDO) refers to the extent to which a person wants his or her in-group to dominate and be superior to other groups (Pratto et al., 1994). SDO is considered to be an individual difference variable, such that people are presumed to differ in their degree of preference for inequality. For instance, individuals high in social dominance orientation are more likely to believe that hierarchical relations are necessary and natural and that some groups (usually their own) ought to be more powerful and privileged (see Table 5.1 for sample items measuring SDO).

*Table 5.1*      *Measuring Social Dominance Orientation (Sample Items)*

1. Some groups of people are just more worthy than others.
2. If certain groups of people stayed in their place, we would have fewer problems.
3. We should strive to make incomes more equal.*
4. Group equality should be our ideal.*
5. To get ahead in life, it is sometimes necessary to step on other groups.

Note. Items with an asterisk require reverse scoring.
*Adapted from: Pratto et al. (1994). Social Dominance Orientation: A Personality Variable Predicting Social and Political Attitudes. Journal of Personality and Social Psychology, 67, 741–763.*

Because people having a strong social dominance orientation are particularly likely to endorse hierarchy-enhancing legitimizing myths (e.g., political conservatism, racism, sexism), they are also more likely to hold negative stereotypes and prejudices against subordinate groups. For instance, SDO correlates positively with measures of racism, sexism, political conservatism, and belief in "law and order." SDO correlates negatively with approval of gay and lesbian rights, affirmative action, interracial marriage, and social welfare programs (Pratto et al., 1994).

As a vivid example of how numerous social attitudes are driven by the desire to maintain in-group superiority and dominance over out-groups, consider the public's reaction to the beating of Rodney King, a Black motorist, by the Los Angeles Police Department (LAPD) in the spring of 1991. Although the national media generally condemned the beating as violent and unnecessary, opinions differed as to whether the beating reflected a systemwide pattern of discrimination or an isolated event caused by the actions of a few bad police officers. Taking advantage of this unfortunate but historical event, Sidanius and Liu (1992) surveyed 154 adults in a bus terminal in Santa Monica and departure terminals in the Los Angeles International Airport about their attitudes toward the King beating. After controlling for the influence of ethnicity and education, they found that support for the LAPD's actions against King was strongly and positively correlated with social dominance orientation. As you can see, social dominance orientation is predictive of attitudes and beliefs that favor hierarchy-enhancing policies.

Interestingly, the presumed "gender gap" that exists within U.S. politics may be explained in part by sex differences in SDO. Many studies point to substantial gender differences in political attitudes. In general, more men than women support military programs, defense spending, and the death penalty. More women than men support increased governmental spending on social welfare, health, education, and enactment of gun control laws (Shapirio & Mahajan, 1986). In a recent study of U.S. college students, Pratto and her colleagues (Pratto, Stallworth, & Sidanius, 1997) found that men reported being more conservative than women, and more supportive of the Republican (versus Democratic) party. On specific policy issues, women showed greater support for gay/lesbian rights, women's policies, racial policies, and social welfare programs, whereas men showed greater support for the military.

How can we explain these sex differences in political attitudes? Sidanius and his colleagues (Pratto et al., 1997; Sidanius et al., 1994) argue that such differences can be understood as stemming from individual differences in SDO. Because SDO mainly functions to support group inequality, members of dominant groups, including men, tend to be more social dominance oriented. Other studies are consistent with this hypothesis. For example, American Whites have higher SDO levels than American Blacks and Latinos, and heterosexuals have higher SDO levels than gay men, lesbians, and bisexuals (Pratto et al., 1997).

Apparently, social dominance orientation is not a uniquely American orientation. In virtually any society, group-based hierarchies exist in which a dominant group enjoys considerable influence over groups of lesser status. Seeking to extend their work on social dominance orientation, Felicia Pratto and her colleagues (1998) measured SDO in four cultures: Canada, Taiwan, China, and Israel. They asked respondents in each of these countries about their views toward women and their country's low-status groups. The results were impressive. In all countries, men showed higher levels of SDO than women, and higher SDO was associated with greater levels of sexism. Moreover, SDO predicted ethnic prejudices in three of the four countries (excluding China). In essence, social dominance orientation operates similarly across cultures: Individuals high in social dominance are more sexist and, in most countries, harbor prejudices against lower status ethnic groups.

Although some similarity exists between the SDO construct and the "authoritarian personality," the two are conceptually distinct. Classical theory of authoritarianism postulated an aberrant personality concerned with a desire for *individual* dominance, whereas SDO concerns an orientation toward *intergroup* dominance (Pratto et al., 1994). Unlike authoritarianism, SDO is not believed to stem from deeplying unconscious impulses or to result from a concern with authority figures. Rather, SDO is an intergroup attitude that stems from childhood socialization. Because SDO arises from the desire to maintain the status of one's group in the social hierarchy, people from high status groups may act more upon this disposition and consequently perpetuate this disposition among themselves as a means of maintaining power. Consistent with this conceptual distinction, SDO correlates only modestly with Altemeyer's (1981) Right-Wing Authoritarianism Scale (Pratto et al., 1994).

Social dominance orientation and authoritarianism are not only conceptually distinct, but they appear to be empirically distinct as well. In a recent study (Whitley, 1999), right-wing authoritarianism was found to be more closely related to prejudice toward homosexuals than was SDO. In contrast, SDO appears to be more closely related to prejudice against other social groups.

## ➤ A THEORY OF NONPREJUDICE?

Up until this point, our focus on individual differences in prejudice has assumed that there are two types of people: prejudiced and low-prejudiced. This conceptualization derives in part from the use of scales designed to measure *prejudice*, rather than nonprejudice. Most measures of prejudice, for instance, identify prejudice through respondents' endorsement of prejudicial statements. Failure to endorse these statements simply indicates low-prejudice, rather than nonprejudice. Consequently, researchers' tendency to focus on individual differences in prejudice, as opposed to individual differences in acceptance, has had two effects. First, as Gordon Allport (1954) observed more than 40 years ago, "it is the pathology of bigotry and not the wholesome state of tolerance that, as a rule, interests social scientists" (pp. 425–426) and as a result, we know considerably less about tolerance than about prejudice. Second, such a focus on the problem of prejudice has led to a rather pessimistic view of interpersonal relations. Measuring prejudice, rather than acceptance and inclusivity, has contributed to the perception that prejudice is inevitable and that nonprejudice is virtually nonexistent.

Recently, Stephen Phillips and Robert Ziller (1997) have questioned this implicit assumption that prejudice is an inevitable development in personality. Following Gordon Allport's suggestion that tolerant thinking, like prejudiced thinking, is a "reflection of a total style of cognitive operation" (p. 438), Phillips and Ziller contend that nonprejudiced thought exists and that it is qualitatively different from prejudiced thought.

How might nonprejudiced thought differ from prejudiced thought? Phillips and Ziller propose that nonprejudiced thought derives from accentuating *similarities* between the self and others, whereas prejudiced thought stems from exaggerating *differences* between the self and others. Thus, the perception of similarity, or what they refer to as a universal orientation in interpersonal relations, is an essential ingredient of nonprejudice.

To measure nonprejudice, Phillips and Ziller developed the Universal Orientation Scale (UOS), which contains items that assess the degree to which individuals perceive similarities between themselves and others: "The similarities between males and females are greater than the differences"; "Older persons are very different than I am" (reverse scored); "At one level of thinking we are all of a kind." Individuals scoring low on the UOS tend to perceive differences between themselves and others, whereas individuals scoring high on the UOS tend to have a universal orientation in which they perceive commonalities between themselves and others. Unlike individuals who perceive differences between themselves and others, universally oriented people are just as accepting of ethnic minority persons as they are of nonminority persons. Moreover, universally oriented people perceive ethnic minorities and nonminorities to be equally attractive, equally similar, and equally desirable to have as potential work partners.

On the basis of this research, it appears that individuals scoring low on the UOS are more likely to use ethnicity as a basis of discrimination among people. Keep in mind, however, that people scoring low on the UOS are not necessarily prejudiced. But as you can imagine, an orientation toward perceiving differences between the self and others may indeed set the stage for prejudicial thought.

## ► LIMITATIONS OF THE INDIVIDUAL DIFFERENCES APPROACH

In this chapter, we have viewed prejudice through an individual-level lens, one which focuses on relatively stable personality, or attitudinal orientations that may predispose individuals to prejudicial thinking. But this individual-level approach has not been without its critics. Specifically, critics have argued that the personality approach: (1) underestimates the importance of situational factors in shaping people's attitudes; (2) fails to fully account for certain group phenomena; and (3) fails to distinguish description from explanation. Let us consider each of these criticisms in detail.

## Underestimation of the Importance of Situational Factors

Perhaps one of the most important criticisms of the personality approach to prejudice is that it tends to underestimate (or overlook entirely) the role of the situation in determining people's attitudes toward various social groups. According to critics, most prejudices are not the result of dysfunctional personalities or individual difference constructs. Rather, prejudice reflects conformity to norms and may be situationally specific.

The situational specificity of prejudice and discrimination is nicely demonstrated in Minard's (1952) study of a West Virginian coal-mining community where two sets of norms existed: Black/White segregation above ground and equality and integration once the workers were underground. Other studies similarly report the power of situational norms. For instance, one study of a multiracial labor union at a large steel mill in Chicago revealed that wages, promotions, and elected appointments were distributed equally among Black and White workers. Yet these same workers lived in racially segregated neighborhoods, and some White workers even belonged to a neighborhood organization that prevented Blacks from moving to the area (Reitzes, 1953). In each of these examples, the difference between the White workers' behavior at work and at home cannot easily be explained in terms of their personalities.

Closely related to situational influences on prejudice are broader social or cultural norms that affect intergroup attitudes. In a now classic study, Thomas Pettigrew (1958) measured anti-Black prejudice and authoritarianism among Whites in the United States and in South Africa. Not surprisingly, he found high levels of prejudice among Whites in South Africa and the Southern United States during that era. Although Whites in these societies were generally more prejudiced than those in the Northern United States, these groups were not necessarily higher in authoritarianism. That these entire societies were racist suggests that prejudice cannot plausibly be explained by personality dysfunction or in terms of individual difference constructs. Instead, Pettigrew argued that such high levels of prejudice can more easily be explained in terms of the existing culture of anti-Black prejudice. This conclusion is consonant with Westie's (1964, pp. 583–584) observation that "Individuals are prejudiced because they are raised in societies which have prejudice as a facet of the normative system of their culture."

In summary, critics have repeatedly argued that attempting to situate prejudice within a relatively stable aspect of an individual's personality ignores the impact that the immediate situation and broader cultural conditions have upon people's attitudes toward various social groups. As Schermerhorn (1970, p. 6) cautions us, "prejudice is a product of *situations*, historical situations, economic situations, political situations," not "a little demon that emerges in people simply because they are depraved."

## Failure to Account for Certain Group Phenomena

One of the more damaging criticisms of the personality approach to prejudice stems from the fact that this individual-level analysis fails to fully account for certain group phenomena. If prejudice simply results from stable personality characteristics, then one would expect intergroup antipathy to remain stable over time. In reality, however, levels of prejudice can change dramatically depending on the circumstances (Hogg & Abrams, 1988). To illustrate this point, consider the events that occurred during the Holocaust. In Germany, there was a long history of devaluation of Jews. But when Hitler came to power in 1933, anti-Semitism increased dramatically during the next decade or so, culminating in genocide—the ultimate expression of prejudice and discrimination (Staub, 1992; 1996).

A similar shift in prejudice toward Asian Americans occurred in the United States during World War II. Anti-Asian sentiment and discrimination certainly existed prior to the war, but when Japan attacked Pearl Harbor on December 7, 1941, attitudes toward *all* Asian Americans—not just Japanese Americans—underwent a relatively quick transformation (Ancheta, 1998). Perhaps the most vivid example of prejudice against an Asian-American community was the relocation and internment of West Coast residents of Japanese descent following the bombing. In just a matter of months, President Roosevelt issued Executive Order 9066, which authorized the Secretary of War to create military areas from which all persons may be excluded. A few weeks later, persons of Japanese descent were evacuated from an area bordering the Pacific Ocean and placed into 13 concentration camps for the remainder of the war. Over 110,000 Japanese Americans, two-thirds of whom were American citizens by birth, were treated as prisoners of war. Although Executive Order 9066 was also applicable to persons of German and Italian descent, no comparable action was taken against them (Lott, 1998).

These dramatic shifts in intergroup attitudes cannot easily be explained at the level of personality or individual difference constructs. How prejudice can be consensually shared in a society and rise and fall depending on the circumstances is clearly beyond the scope of an individual differences approach.

## Failure to Distinguish Description from Explanation

A common criticism of the "personality" or dispositional approach in psychology is that it confuses description with explanation (Skinner, 1953). The same criticism can be levied against the individual differences approach to prejudice. To say that some people are prejudiced and some aren't is merely description. According to critics, this typology appears to explain but really does *not* explain why prejudice exists.

Critics of the individual differences approach remind us that prejudice is first and foremost an intergroup phenomenon. Whatever their effect on prejudice, psychological and personality factors must be viewed in conjunction with the intergroup context. To focus only on the individual-level explanation fails to tell us how prejudice and discrimination arise in the first place.

## ➤ CONCLUSION

In this chapter, we have continued with the individual-level analysis in explaining prejudice. Many of the influences on prejudice, as we have seen, include personality (authoritarianism), cognitive motivations (intolerance of ambiguity), adherence to social ideologies (religion, political conservatism), and general attitudes toward group domination (social dominance orientation). Although these are undoubtedly important factors in explaining who within a group will be more or less prejudiced, they appear inadequate to account for prejudice on a societal level. It seems unreasonable to assume that personality factors or a singular cognitive trait can account for how prejudice becomes virtually consensual in some societies, such as in the U.S. South or South Africa during earlier decades. For example, how can an individual difference perspective explain why entire *groups* of people within a society—even the "good citizens"—harbor negative attitudes toward another group (Duckitt, 1992)?

This is not to say that personality or cognitive factors are unimportant, however. Individual difference dimensions certainly can determine the degree to which individuals accept or reject cultural norms of prejudice. Focusing on personality, cognitive, and attitudinal characteristics that make individuals susceptible to prejudice explains why individuals who are exposed to similar socialization patterns may differ in the degree to which they hold prejudicial beliefs.

Whatever their effect on prejudice and discrimination, individual differences in prejudice must be viewed in conjunction with the social conditions that create hostility. As Ervin Staub (1990) suggests, certain social conditions activate the psychological processes and motivations that lead people to devalue others. These include social and political factors such as direct competition and differential status between groups. We will move on to this level of analysis—intergroup relations—in the next chapter.

# 6

# Intergroup Relations

➤ INTRODUCTION

In 1982, Vincent Chin, a 27-year-old Chinese American, was to be married in nine days. He was celebrating his upcoming wedding at a Detroit bar when he was approached by two White automobile workers, Ronald Ebens and his step-son Michael Nitz—who had recently been laid off of work. Based upon Chin's physical appearance, the automobile workers mistakenly identified him as a Japanese, and blamed him for the loss of jobs in the automobile industry. After calling Chin a "Jap" and screaming "it's because of you we're out of work," the pair chased Chin out of the bar, eventually caught him and beat him to death with a baseball bat. Said Chin as he lost consciousness: "It isn't fair" ("It isn't fair," 1983). Four days later he died from severe head injuries. Several hundred people, originally invited to Chin's wedding, attended his funeral instead.

Ebens and Nitz pleaded guilty to manslaughter but received only three years of probation and fines of $3,780 each. As you might imagine, such light sentences for the killing sparked outrage among Asian Americans and prompted a U.S. grand jury in Detroit later to indict Ebens and Nitz on federal civil rights violations. One of the autoworkers was convicted but his conviction was later overturned on appeal. Neither Ronald Ebens nor Michael Nitz served any time in prison for the killing.

Unfortunately, this is not an isolated instance of violence toward Asian Americans. In reviewing patterns of discrimination against Asian Americans, Ancheta (1998) observes that the most virulent anti-Asian attitudes tend to peak during economic recessions and periods of intensifying labor competition. This argument is consistent with many sociological and psychological theories that trace intergroup hostilities to intergroup competition over valued, but limited resources. That is, when two groups are competing for a "piece of the pie," such as for jobs, housing, or consumer sales, one group's success comes at the expense of the other group's slice of the pie.

In this chapter, we will explore the nature of intergroup relations as they are framed not only by social competition but by one's identification with a particular group. First, we will examine how social competition engenders intergroup antagonism, and then we will turn to a discussion of how *mere membership* in a group (in the absence of real competition) may lead to in-group favoritism and out-group derogation. The chapter concludes with a discussion of how group membership forms the basis of our personal and social identity. Belonging to a group, we'll learn, gives us a sense of who we are and who we are not. The implications for prejudice will be discussed fully.

## ➤ Intergroup Conflict, Competition, and Comparison

In identifying the situational factors that give rise to prejudice, Muzafer Sherif (Sherif, 1966) argued that groups become prejudiced toward one another when they are in competition for valuable but limited resources. This view that direct competition breeds prejudice and discrimination is called **realistic conflict theory** (Levine & Campbell, 1972). In a classic field experiment, Sherif and his colleagues (Sherif et al., 1988; Sherif & Sherif, 1956) demonstrate how intergroup hostility may be caused by group competition for limited resources.

### The Robbers Cave Experiment

During the summer of 1954, Sherif and his colleagues carefully selected 22 White, Protestant, middle-class, well-adjusted, eleven-year-old boys to participate in an experiment conducted at Robbers Cave State Park in Oklahoma. The boys were from stable families, performed well academically, and did not present any behavioral problems at home or school. Unaware that they were participants in a psychology experiment, the boys—who were previously unacquainted with each other—were assigned to one of two groups. The two groups were settled on opposite sides of the camp and initially did not know about the other group's existence.

The experiment was conducted in three phases of approximately one week each. The first phase of the experiment was designed to encourage group formation and to foster in-group identity. In this stage, the boys engaged in typical camp activities, such as hiking, boating, and swimming, with members of their own group. As the week progressed, group cohesiveness increased, with each group identifying its leaders, establishing norms, and even selecting group names—the "Rattlers" and the "Eagles."

The second phase of the experiment was designed to foster intergroup competition. Now that the groups had established separate identities, the researchers introduced the Rattlers and Eagles to each other in the context of a four-day tournament between the two groups, consisting of athletic events such as baseball, tug-of-war, and touch football. For each event, the winning team received points, and at the end of the week, the team with the most points would receive a coveted trophy and each individual member would receive attractive prizes.

What initially began as a friendly competition quickly escalated into a mean-spirited, vicious rivalry. Name-calling increased ("sissy" and "coward," for example) and physical skirmishes broke out between the groups. The two groups even raided each others' cabins, overturning furniture and stealing personal belongings. In Sherif's (1966, p. 85) words, an unsuspecting observer would have characterized these well-adjusted boys from good family backgrounds as "wicked, disturbed, and vicious bunches of youngsters."

Creating intergroup hostility was easy; defusing the hostility proved to be much more difficult. The purpose of the final phase of the experiment was to uncover techniques that reduced friction between the Eagles and the Rattlers. At first the experimenters simply provided opportunities for contact between the groups, such as attending a movie together or having meals together in the same mess hall. Such "mere contact" failed to reduce the friction between the groups. In fact, insults and jeers were often exchanged between the groups during these encounters.

Quickly realizing the ineffectiveness of noncompetitive contact between the groups in reducing the hostility, the experimenters introduced several interaction situations that involved *superordinate goals*, goals that required intergroup cooperation. For example, the experimenters arranged for a truck to break down, and both groups were needed to pull the truck up a hill. In another contrived emergency, the Eagles and Rattlers had to work together to fix the camp's water supply tank. Did tasks requiring intergroup cooperation restore harmony between the groups? Most definitely, judging from the experimenters' observations. By the end of the week, many of the boys had formed friendships across group lines, exchanged addresses with members of the other group, and perhaps most revealing, members of the two groups insisted on traveling back to Oklahoma City on the same bus.

In many ways, Sherif's realistic conflict theory sheds light on the problem of prejudice and intergroup conflict. In the previous chapter, we learned that some people might be more susceptible to prejudice than others, depending on individual differences in personality or worldview. While some people are indeed more prejudiced than others, Sherif's study reminds us that no one is immune to prejudicial thought and behavior. The fact that Sherif meticulously selected his experimental participants to rule out pathology as an explanation for such intergroup hostility demonstrates that prejudice is a product of social situations. Unfortunately, the potential for extreme out-group hatred resides in all of us.

Realistic conflict theory suggests that direct competition between groups is a sufficient cause of prejudice and intergroup conflict. Put simply, pit two groups against each other in competition for limited resources and intergroup hostilities may quickly develop. Moreover, realistic conflict theory has the added advantage of being able to account for drastic changes in intergroup attitudes over time and across situations; sudden shifts in intergroup attitudes may often reflect changing political and economic relations between the groups concerned.

But actual competition between groups is not necessary to produce prejudice. What we will see in the next section is that mere *frustration* may arouse intergroup hostilities.

## Prejudice as Frustration

The opening of this chapter described how two auto workers in Detroit, Michigan, killed Vincent Chin, a Chinese American. Ironically, they assumed he was Japanese and blamed him for lost jobs in the automobile industry. Given that the auto workers were not in direct conflict with any Japanese, we see from this example that "competition" may be more imagined than real.

Why might individuals blame distressful events, such as adverse economic conditions, on an out-group member who bears no actual responsibility for the event? In a classic paper, Hovland and Sears (1940) argued that the frustration accompanying distressful events increases aggressive impulses which, in turn, are displaced onto vulnerable targets such as minority groups. To test this hypothesis, these researchers examined the relationship between the number of lynchings of Blacks in the U.S. South between 1882 and 1930 and the price of cotton, a major economic indicator. During that 49-year period there were 4,761 reported cases of lynchings, and of these, over 70 percent were lynchings of Black people. Their results revealed a negative correlation: economic decline was associated with increased numbers of lynchings. Using more sophisticated statistical techniques, Hepworth and West (1988) reanalyzed this data set and found a similar, albeit more modest, relationship between economic indicators and lynchings.

Whether a relationship exists between economic downturns and bigoted violence has recently been examined within the context of contemporary "hate crimes." Following Hovland and Sears's logic, is it possible that a similar relationship exists between economic fluctuations and aggression directed toward people on the basis of their race, religion, ethnicity, or sexual orientation? To examine this intriguing hypothesis, Donald Green and his colleagues (Green, Glaser, & Rich, 1998) tested the relationship between unemployment rates in New York City with the frequency of hate crimes directed against gay men, lesbians, Asians, Blacks, Whites, or Jews during 1987–1995. In 1987 the unemployment rate was 7.5%, dropped to 4.3% for the following year, gradually climbed to 13.0% in 1992, and thereafter fell to 7.0%. Surprisingly, their analysis of hate crime data turned up little evidence linking hate crimes to fluctuating economic conditions.

Why might this be the case? Green et al. provide two potential explanations for this absence of a relationship between economic conditions and hate crimes. First, one limiting condition to the frustration-aggression hypothesis is that aggressive impulses bred by frustration may dissipate rather quickly over time. Lynchings and contemporary hate crimes are group activities that tend to require more coordination and planning than other forms of aggression (e.g., domestic violence, child abuse). Second, the relationship between economic fluctuations and bigoted violence may depend upon the presence of political actors and organizations that redirect economic frustration onto minority groups. History is replete with examples of political figures in times of economic contraction affixing economic blame onto minority groups. Thus, the relationship between economic fluctuations and bigoted violence may depend, in large part, upon prominent political leaders who can channel this economic frustration into resentment toward minority groups. In the final analysis, the relationship between economic disadvantage and out-group violence may be mediated by many psychological and societal variables. As a result, this scapegoat theory of prejudice has declined in popularity.

## Relative Deprivation Theory

What is more critical in explaining out-group hostility is **relative deprivation**—that is, one's perceptions of being disadvantaged relative to others (Crosby, 1976; Gurr, 1970). In other words, discontent arises not just from actual disadvantage, but also from the perception (whether accurate or not) that one fares poorly compared to others.

People may experience two types of relative deprivation: "egoistic" deprivation, stemming from comparisons with in-group members, and "fraternal" deprivation, stemming from comparisons between one's own group and other groups (Runciman, 1966). This distinction is important, because it is group-based deprivation that has greater relevance to intergroup relations. As you might imagine, the perception that another group is doing better than one's in-group is likely to engender resentment toward out-group members.

A classic study demonstrates this link between relative deprivation and prejudice. Vanneman and Pettigrew (1972) surveyed more than 1,000 White voters in four U.S. cities, asking them whether they felt they were doing better or worse economically than other White workers (egoistic deprivation). They also asked these same respondents how they felt they were doing economically compared to Blacks (fraternalistic deprivation). Subjects who were either fraternally deprived or doubly deprived (egoistically and fraternalistically) exhibited the most prejudice. In terms of intergroup relations, this study demonstrates that feelings of group-based deprivation may be a more important contributor to prejudice than egoistic deprivation.

This relationship between group-based deprivation and intergroup attitudes is not limited to the United States. In one study, Guimond and Dube-Simard (1983) found that support for separatism in Quebec was greater among French-speaking respondents who felt dissatisfied when comparing salaries of francophones and anglophones (fraternalistic deprivation). However, support for separatism was unrelated to feeling deprived relative to other francophones (egoistic deprivation). In India, Muslim attitudes toward Hindus have been found to be related to feelings of group-based deprivation. Muslims are now a socially disadvantaged group, although prior to India's partition they were the ruling group. Tripathi and Srivastava (1981) found that greater feelings of deprivation based upon this change in status were associated with more hostile attitudes toward Hindus.

In accounting for prejudice, relative deprivation theory suggests that issues of *fairness and justice* shape people's attitudes toward other groups (Tyler & Smith, 1998). This might explain why some majority group members' anti-affirmative action views are related to their perceptions that affirmative action unfairly allows minority groups to achieve success more rapidly than the majority (Veilleux & Tougas, 1989).

However, intergroup attitudes are not fully explained by realistic conflict nor by issues of fairness and justice. In some cases, minority group members pose no real threat to either an individual's self-interest or group-based interest. So how can we explain prejudice under those circumstances? European social psychologist Henri Tajfel (1970) pointed out that conflicting group interests are not a necessary condition for intergroup discrimination. According to Tajfel, merely categorizing people into two groups is sufficient to foster intergroup discrimination. In other words, in the absence of competition or feelings of relative deprivation, simply belonging to a group may be a key ingredient in the development of negative bias against out-groups.

## ➤ SOCIAL CATEGORIZATION AND INTERGROUP RELATIONS

Imagine that you have volunteered to participate in an experiment with nine other people. The experimenter divides the ten people, all of whom are strangers to each other, into two groups arbitrarily by a random coin toss. The people in your group have never interacted with each other, do not have a history of antagonism with the other group, never competed against the other group for scarce resources, and are not frustrated. Will you like your group more than you like the other group? Based upon many studies, the answer is yes. Even when groups are formed randomly by the flip of a coin, participants demonstrate favoritism toward members of their own group (Billig & Tajfel, 1973: Messick & Mackie, 1989).

This startling phenomenon has been studied intensely by Henri Tajfel and his colleagues (Tajfel, 1970, 1982; Tajfel, Billig, Bundy, & Flament, 1971). In one experiment, for example, high-school boys in England were asked to participate in a study of visual perception. The boys were shown a series of 40 slides that contained a large cluster of dots, and their task was to estimate the number of dots that appeared in each slide. The experimenter informed the boys that some people are chronic "overestimators" who consistently estimate more dots than actually appeared, whereas others are "underestimators." The boys' dot estimations were then scored, and they were randomly informed whether they were over- or underestimators.

In the second phase of the experiment, the boys participated in a game that involved allocating points to each other, points that later could be cashed in for money. In this **minimal group paradigm** in which group membership is based upon trivial, even meaningless criteria, the boys consistently awarded more points to in-group members than to out-group members (Tajfel et al., 1971).

This tendency to discriminate in favor of in-group members is termed **in-group favoritism.** Such discrimination not only occurs in the distribution of valued resources, but also in terms of greater valuing of the in-group over out-groups (Brewer, 1979), increased trust of in-group members (Kramer & Brewer, 1984), and more favorable attributions for the successes and failures of in-group members than for out-group members (Weber, 1994). Interestingly, this strong preference for in-group members is also displayed unconsciously in our emotional reactions to the concepts "we" and "us." Evidence for this effect was demonstrated in an experiment by Charles Perdue and his colleagues (Perdue, Dovidio, Gurtman, & Tyler, 1990), in which 108 nonsense syllables (*xeh, vof, criw*) were presented to college students on a computer screen. Each of the syllables was randomly paired with either an in-group designating pronoun (*us, we,* or *ours*) or an out-group designating pronoun (*they, them,* or *theirs*), or, on the control trials, other pronouns (*he, she, his, hers*) that do not necessarily reflect in-group-out-group distinctions. The students' task was to decide as quickly as possible which word of the presented pair was an actual word (*us-xeh, them-vof*). Unbeknownst to the students, one nonsense syllable was always paired with in-group pronouns, and another with out-group pronouns. Following this task, the students were asked to rate each of the syllables in terms of their pleasantness-unpleasantness. The results of this experiment were revealing: nonsense syllables paired with in-group pronouns were rated more pleasant than syllables paired with out-group pronouns. This suggests that the in-group-out-group distinction carries such emotional significance that it can bias emotional responses toward neutral stimuli.

Research on minimal groups has contributed to our understanding of intergroup relations in two ways. First, this research demonstrates that intergroup bias resides, not necessarily in conflicting group-based interests, but in the in-group-out-group distinctions themselves. What we learn from minimal group research is that the categorization of people on the basis of any dimension, however trivial, can serve as the catalyst for intergroup conflict. If categorizing people into two groups on the basis of a random coin toss triggers intergroup discrimination, just imagine how much more intense these effects will be in real-life groups that share a history of antagonism.

Second, minimal group research reveals a number of in-group-out-group biases that may lead to stereotyping and prejudice. Social categorization often has several consequences for our social perception and behavior. The effect of social categorization is so robust that our intergroup perceptions, attributions, and even the language that we use reflects the importance of in-group-out-group distinctions.

## Perceptions of Out-Group Homogeneity

Sorting people into categories of "us" versus "them" affects how we perceive members of our own group, as well as the out-group. One consequence of social categorization is a phenomenon known as the **out-group homogeneity effect**, which refers to a pervasive tendency to see out-groups as more homogeneous than in-groups. In other words, we see members of the out-group as less variable ("they are all alike") than members of our own group ("we are diverse"). As an example, many Westerners are likely to lump all "Asians" together, without recognizing important cultural distinctions among the subgroups (i.e., Chinese, Japanese, Taiwanese, Korean, etc.), whereas these subgroups perceive important differences between themselves and each other.

This tendency to perceive out-group members as all alike sometimes can result in embarassing situations in which we confuse members of an out-group with each other or have difficulty differentiating between them in terms of their names or what they look like. Studies have shown that people are indeed less accurate in distinguishing and recognizing faces of racial groups other than their own (Anthony, Copper, & Mullen, 1992; Teitelbaum & Geiselman, 1997).

Support for the out-group homogeneity effect has been found in numerous laboratory studies (Judd & Park, 1988; Park & Judd, 1990; Quattrone & Jones, 1980). Judd, Ryan, and Park (1991), for example, asked business and engineering majors to make judgments about either business or engineering students as a group (in- or out-group, depending on the research participant's major). Participants rated each group on traits (e.g., extroversion) in terms of the percentage of the group who possessed those traits. Participants also estimated the variability of group members on the same set of traits. For instance, participants were asked to estimate the range of scores, from highest to lowest, that group members would have on a scale that measured extroversion. Based upon tasks such as these, Judd and his colleagues found support for the out-group homogeneity effect. That is, business majors perceived greater similarity among the engineering majors than among themselves, and the engineering majors likewise perceived greater similarity among the business majors.

Why do we tend to view out-group members as "all alike"? The most widely accepted explanation suggests that differences in *familiarity* explain the degree to which out-group members seem to be so homogeneous (Linville, Fischer, & Saloven, 1989). We typically spend considerably more time with in-group members than with out-group members. Because of this greater contact and familiarity, we notice subtle differences among in-group members. By contrast, our lack of interaction with out-group members may explain why we are unlikely to view them as individuals with varying opinions, attitudes, values, and traits.

Before leaving this discussion of out-group homogeneity, it is important to note that the perception of out-group homogeneity is far from universal. Sometimes the reverse has been found: the in-group is judged to be more homogeneous than the out-group. Interestingly, this "in-group homogeneity effect" has been found primarily with minority groups. Using the minimal group paradigm, Simon and Brown (1987) manipulated the numerical size of the in-groups and out-groups, such that in some conditions, participants thought their group was a minority group while in other conditions participants thought they were in the majority. Their results indicated that the minority group showed an in-group homogeneity effect, while the majority group showed the typical out-group homogeneity effect.

Why might belonging to a minority group prompt perceptions of greater in-group similarity? Two factors may account for this phenomenon. First, differences in group size itself may have contributed to an in-group homogeneity effect, because it is reasonable to assume that the group with the greatest number of members (i.e., the majority group) should be more variable. Second, belonging to a minority group may prompt the members to emphasize their similarities with each other. When members belong to an embattled minority, for instance, they may be motivated to emphasize their similarities with each other in order to mobilize against the majority.

## Attributional Effects

In-group-out-group distinctions not only affect social perception, but **attribution** as well—that is, the explanations used to interpret people's behavior. When we observe someone's actions, we typically explain the person's behavior either in terms of a situational factor (external attribution) or a personal factor (internal attribution). For example, suppose your friend Rick informs you that he is failing his history class. How do you explain this event? If you explain Rick's misfortune in terms of personal qualities—that is, he's not very bright, he doesn't exert much effort, etc.—then you've used an internal attribution. If, on the other hand, you explain Rick's failure in terms of situational factors—the professor is unfair and highly subjective in grading—then you've used an external attribution.

Many factors influence whether we make an internal or external attribution for people's behavior. Most relevant to our discussion here, our attributions will often differ in terms of whether we are explaining an in-group member's behavior or an out-group member's behavior. Specifically, we tend to attribute an in-group member's desirable behavior (e.g., community volunteerism) to internal factors (e.g., their admirable qualities), whereas we may attribute the same desirable behavior by out-group members to external causes (e.g., "resumé padding"). The opposite occurs in explaining undesirable behavior. We tend to attribute an in-group member's undesirable behavior (e.g., unemployment) to external factors (e.g., tight job market), whereas we may attribute the same undesirable behavior by out-group members to internal factors (e.g., laziness). This tendency to make more complimentary attributions about in-group members than about out-group members has been dubbed the **ultimate**

**attribution error** (Pettigrew, 1979) because of its potentially harmful consequences for intergroup relations.

The ultimate attribution error has been demonstrated in numerous studies, ranging from the attributions made by members of different sports teams to different ethnic groups (Hewstone, 1990). An early study that focused on attributions made for different ethnic groups clearly demonstrates this systematic bias. Taylor and Jaggi (1974) compared the attributions made by Hindus to either positive or negative actions performed by an in-group member or by an out-group member. When Hindu participants read a story about positive behavior on the part of an in-group (Hindu) actor, they made internal attributions, whereas negative behaviors were not credited to internal dispositions. The opposite process occurred when explaining behavior on the part of an out-group (Muslim) actor: internal attributions were made for negative behavior, and external attributions were made for positive behavior.

The role of attribution, while present in the *explanations* that we use for others' behavior, is also present in the language that we use to *describe* behavior. As we will see in the next section, subtle variations in language occur, perhaps without our conscious awareness, in describing the behaviors of in-group and out-group members.

## Linguistic Intergroup Bias

*"Language exerts hidden power, like the moon on the tides."*

Rita Mae Brown

Language plays an important role in the transmission of cultural stereotypes from person to person and from generation to generation. Sometimes the role of language is blatantly obvious, reflected in the labels used to refer to social groups. For example, Americans of African descent may be referred to as "niggers," "Negroes," "Blacks," and "African Americans," and people with preference for same-sex partners may be labeled "queers," "fags," "homosexuals," or "gays"—terms that refer to the same categories, but convey very different sentiments.

Language can convey stereotypes in a much less obvious way, however. Anne Maass and her colleagues (Maass, 1999; Maass & Arcuri, 1996; Maass, Milesi, Zabbini, & Stahlberg, 1995) found that one aspect of language, the level of abstraction, differs depending upon whether one describes an in-group member's behavior or an out-group member's behavior. When spontaneously describing the positive behaviors of an in-group member, people are more likely to use abstract, trait-like terms to describe behavior. For example, an in-group member who donates to Toys for Tots is more likely to be described as "thoughtful," or "altruistic," whereas an out-group member displaying the same behavior may be described in more concrete terms, such as "helping." The use of a concrete description ("helping") when describing an out-group member's positive behavior suggests that the behavior is an isolated event, rather than an enduring characteristic of the actor. Conversely, negative in-group behaviors are more likely to be described in terms of specific, concrete behaviors, whereas negative out-group behaviors are described in abstract generalities. For instance, an out-group member who displays aggressive behavior is more likely to be described as "violent," whereas an in-group member who displays the identical behavior may be described as "hitting someone." This systematic bias in language use, in which positive in-group behavior and negative out-group behavior is described in abstract terms, and negative in-group behavior and positive out-group behavior is described in concrete terms, is called the **linguistic intergroup bias** (LIB) and plays a crucial role in the interpersonal transmission of stereotypes (Wigboldus, Semin, & Spears, 2000).

Over the last ten years or so, the LIB has been tested in more than 30 experiments in a wide range of intergroup and cultural contexts (Maass, 1999). Biases in the level of language abstraction consistent with the LIB have been obtained in a variety of experimental studies, focusing on competing sports teams (Franco & Maass, 1996), Southern versus Northern Italians (Maass, Ceccerelli, & Rudin, 1996; Maass et al., 1995), political party affiliation (Karpinski & von Hippel, 1996), Black-White relations in the United States (Von Hippel, Sekaquaptewa, & Vargas, 1997), and even competing interest groups such as hunters and environmentalists (Maass et al., 1996).

Importantly, the LIB has not been confined to experimental settings: Naturalistic studies have also confirmed the LIB. One study of broadcast journalism analyzed the eight o'clock news by Italian public television during the first week of the Gulf War in 1991 as well as during the first week after the war (Maass et al., 1994, Exp. 3). Although no language bias emerged in statements about the in-group (allied forces or leaders), a strong language bias emerged against the out-group (Iraqi forces or leaders): The more negative the statements about Iraqi forces or leaders, the more abstract they tended to be. Interestingly, this language bias quickly disappeared in the week following the war.

In another study, Maass and her colleagues (Maass et al., 1994, Exp. 2) analyzed newspaper reports of an anti-Semitic episode in which neo-fascist groups had exposed banners depicting swastikas and anti-Semitic slogans during a basketball game between an Italian and Israeli team. Although both Jewish and non-Jewish newspaper journalists harshly criticized the neo-fascist groups, they differed in language abstraction. Compared to Jewish journalists, non-Jewish journalists used much more concrete language to describe the anti-Semitic behaviors. Jewish journalists, on the other hand, described the episode in more abstract terms, generalizing beyond the specific event. Similar reporting biases have also been observed in sports journalism (Maass et al., 1994; Ng & Tait, 1994).

The presence of the LIB has been well established. But what are the mechanisms that sustain differential language use in intergroup contexts? Two competing explanations for the LIB have been suggested, one cognitive, the other motivational in nature. According to the cognitive explanation, the LIB derives from *differential expectancies,* such that people use abstract language when describing behaviors that fit their expectancies (or stereotypes), because abstract language implies a stable, enduring characteristic of the actor. In contrast, unexpected (or counterstereotypical) behavior is more likely to be described in concrete terms, implying that the behavior is atypical. As an example, if an Asian-American woman were seen hitting someone, people would describe her behavior in concrete terms ("Vivian Fong hit someone"). In contrast, if an African-American male displayed the same behavior, people would describe the event in abstract, trait-like terms ("Rasheed Brown is violent"). Thus, the cognitive account of the LIB suggests that expectancy-congruent behaviors are described at a higher level of abstraction than expectancy-incongruent behaviors (Karpinski & von Hippel, 1996; von Hippel, Sekaquaptewa, & Vargas, 1997).

Evidence for the role of expectancies in the LIB comes from many studies (Karpinski & von Hippel, 1996; Maass et al., 1995). In one study, Maass and her colleagues (Maass et al., 1995) presented people with a series of behaviors exhibited by a target who was described as intelligent (or sociable). Subsequently, participants were presented with a cartoon showing the target person behaving in a way that either confirmed or disconfirmed the expectancy. The participants' task was to select one of four descriptions of the target's behavior, ranging in degree of abstraction. Consistent with the expectancy interpretation of the LIB, participants described expectancy-congruent behaviors at a higher level of abstraction than expectancy-incongruent behaviors.

Notice that the cognitive account of the LIB does not necessarily require an intergroup context. In the experiment cited above, a sense of group membership was not invoked in participants. This suggests that it is not necessary for an in-group or an out-group to be present for people to exhibit the LIB. The fact that the LIB can be produced by expectancies alone suggests a purely cognitive underpinning to the LIB.

Another equally plausible explanation for the LIB is rooted in motivational principles. According to this perspective, the LIB is driven by *in-group-protective motives*, in which the linguistic bias serves to protect or enhance one's social identity. As we will discuss in greater detail later in this chapter, people have both a personal identity and a "collective" or social identity (Brewer, 1991; Tajfel & Turner, 1986). One's personal identity involves unique, individual characteristics, whereas one's social identity is the reputation gained from membership in a social group. By using concrete descriptors of negative in-group behaviors and positive out-group behaviors, and by using abstract descriptors of positive in-group behaviors and negative out-group behaviors, people are able to maintain a positive image of their own group. In other words, people tend to use language that clearly favors the in-group, and this bias serves to enhance one's social identity or collective self-esteem.

Studies confirm that the LIB is indeed sensitive to motivational needs. The previously cited analysis of broadcasting reports during the Gulf War showed a clear language bias against Iraq during the first week of the war, when conflict was intense, but the language bias quickly disappeared in the week following the war. In a more controlled test of the motivational underpinnings of the LIB, Maass et al. (1996, Exp. 1) demonstrated that the LIB is exacerbated under threat. In this study of competing interest groups, hunters and environmentalists, Maass et al. either reinforced or reduced the antagonism between the two groups. In some conditions, participants received information that the opposing group was taking an antagonistic stance, whereas in other conditions, they believed the opposing group was displaying a cooperative attitude. As in other studies, participants were shown cartoons in which hunters or environmentalists displayed positive or negative behaviors and were asked to describe the behaviors. The analysis of language abstraction confirmed that the LIB was significantly greater under competition than under cooperation.

So to go back to our original question, which explanation of the LIB is correct—the cognitive explanation based upon differential expectancies or the motivational explanation rooted in in-group protective motives? Both explanations are correct. Clearly, differential expectancies are sufficient to produce the LIB, but intergroup competition enhances this effect in much the same way it enhances in-group favoritism or out-group derogation.

Before leaving the topic of linguistic intergroup bias, let us consider the issue of whether the LIB operates outside of awareness. That is, are people using a greater or lesser degree of abstraction without being fully aware of it? A number of researchers suggest that the LIB operates in an unconscious fashion (Franco & Maass, 1996; Maass & Arcuri, 1996; von Hippel et al., 1994; von Hippel et al., 1995, 1997), and may even be an implicit indicator of prejudice. In one study, William von Hippel and his colleagues (1997) presented White students a series of fictitious newspaper articles about Blacks and Whites involved in activities that varied in stereotypicality. For example, each student read one stereotype-congruent article (about an African-American slam-dunk contest winner or European-American spelling bee winner) and one stereotype-incongruent article (about a European-American jewelry thief or an African-American embezzler). The students' task was to rate, for each article, the appropriateness of different descriptions ranging from the most concrete ("Johnson performs 360-degree slam-dunk") to the most abstract ("Johnson is athletic"). This measure of LIB was then used as a predictor of prejudiced responses to an individual African American or European American. The results showed the LIB-based measure was a better predictor of prejudicial reactions to an out-group member than explicit measures of prejudice that simply ask people what they think or feel about various social groups.

At this time, it may be premature to say definitively that the LIB is an unintentional and unconscious phenonenon, such that people are largely unaware of the subtleties of linguistic abstraction in their speech (Maass, 1999). As more studies demonstrate that the LIB escapes intentional control, then the LIB may emerge as a useful and unobtrusive marker of people's "true" feelings toward various minority groups.

➤ THEORIES OF IN-GROUP IDENTIFICATION

So far, we've considered the behavioral consequences of social categorization, ranging from attributional biases that favor the in-group to in-group favoritism, or discrimination that favors the in-group. But what is it, *exactly*, that causes us to identify so strongly with our in-group, to show favoritism to our in-group, and, at times, to discriminate against the out-group? Several theories attempt to explain this relationship between the self and the group: (a) **social identity theory,** which suggests that people use group membership as a source of pride, (b) **self-categorization theory,** which identifies the cognitive mechanisms that underlie social identity, and (c) **optimal-distinctiveness theory,** which attempts to specify when we are likely to be group-identified as opposed to self-identified. Let's consider each of these theories in greater detail.

### Social Identity Theory

Social identity theory (SIT), developed by Henri Tajfel and John Turner (1985), originated as an explanation of the in-group favoritism effect obtained in the minimal group paradigm. In the minimal group paradigm, you'll recall, members of two arbitrarily defined groups are provided the opportunity to allocate valued resources to anonymous in-group and out-group members. Group members typically act in a way that clearly represents in-group favoritism, allocating a greater share of the resources to their own group members.

This discrimination effect is difficult to explain on the basis of realistic conflict theory (Sherif, 1966), which was the dominant theory of intergroup behavior at that time. The major premise of realistic conflict theory is that intergroup conflict is rooted in competition between *real* groups over scarce resources. In the minimal groups paradigm, the groups formed do not necessarily conform to the characteristics normally associated with "real" groups: No social interaction takes place between the groups; no real conflict of interest exists; and a prior history of relations between the groups is lacking. In Tajfel and Turner's words (1985), "these groups are purely cognitive and can be referred to as *minimal*" (p. 14), yet group members acted as though the groups were real for them.

To explain this intergroup discrimination effect, Tajfel and his associates (Tajfel & Turner, 1986; Turner, 1981, 1982) developed social identity theory (SIT). Social identity theory contains three main arguments: (1) people are motivated to maintain a positive self-concept; (2) a significant part of the self-concept derives from identifying with social groups; and (3) people sustain their own positive social identity by comparing the in-group favorably to out-groups. Thus, SIT assumes that in many social situations people's self-concepts are derived from the groups to which they belong. Because people are generally motivated to think well of themselves, they are likely to ascribe positive characteristics to the groups to which they belong and to belittle groups to which they do not belong. In other words, "social identity" represents a way to feel good about the groups to which one belongs, and ultimately, to feel good about oneself.

Although SIT has undergone many revisions, the theory remains based upon three core ideas: categorization, identification, and comparison. Let's consider each of these ideas in greater detail, with an emphasis on explaining the results of the minimal group studies.

*Categorization*     Tajfel (1982) assumes that a fundamental tendency of the human mind is to simplify and make more manageable the complex social world, leading people to categorize themselves and others. We categorize people in much the same way as we categorize objects, and these categorizations—Christians, Muslims, conservatives, liberals, Northerners, Southerners, for instance—magnify similarities among members of a particular social group and heighten distinctions between social groups.

Although some studies suggest that mere categorization alone is sufficient to trigger intergroup discrimination favoring the in-group (Bourhis, Sachdev, & Gagnon, 1994; Brewer, 1979), SIT suggests that another ingredient, identification, contributes to the discrimination effect. In other words, social categorization, assumed to be a universal cognitive process, leads to the most basic distinction between "us" (in-group) and "them" (out-group).

*Identification*     Social identity theorists typically acknowledge multiple identifications, distinguishing between *personal identity* and *social identity*. Personal identity is usually rooted in traits or idiosyncratic attributes (e.g., athletic, musically talented, artistic, etc.) that comprise a portion of one's self-concept. Social identity, in contrast, is that part of one's self-concept that derives from membership in a social group (or groups). From the perspective of social identity theorists, membership in a group not only provides a sense of "we-ness," but also a sense of "me-ness."

Social identification begins with the application of a label to oneself—"I am Catholic," "I am a psychology major," or "I am a Republican"—with the recognition that some other people share this characteristic. Because people generally want to think highly of themselves and their group, they strive to differentiate their group from the other group and to elevate the position of their group. One way to do so is through making favorable social comparisons between the in-group and the out-group.

*Comparison*   Despite John Donne's caution that "comparisons are odious," it is human nature to want to evaluate our abilities and opinions (e.g., "Am I good in math?"; "How well am I doing financially?"; "Do I have a good sense of humor?"), and the way that we do this is through comparing ourselves with relevant others (Festinger, 1954). At the individual level, comparisons with others shape our personal identity as mathmatically gifted or inept, rich or poor, witty or dour. Comparing favorably to others enhances our personal self-esteem.

Just as we strive to enhance our personal self-esteem through comparisons with others, we want to enhance our social identities through comparisons with other groups. Regardless of the group to which we belong, there are some dimensions on which our group fares well. Tajfel and Turner (1986) argue that it is precisely these favorable dimensions that we use in making comparisons with other groups, resulting in a boost to our self-esteem through our affiliation with a successful group.

EXPLAINING THE MINIMAL GROUP EXPERIMENTS   How might the assumptions of SIT explain the minimal group effects? In the minimal group paradigm, the experimenter arbitrarily imposes two basic categories: underestimators and overestimators (or Group X and Group Y, depending upon the experimental procedure). These categories are essentially meaningless. So why does categorization in the minimal group paradigm lead to intergroup discrimination? According to SIT, the participants recognize their group membership ("I am an overestimator"; "I am a member of Group Y") within the minimal group paradigm. They are also motivated to enhance their social identity. In the minimal group paradigm, individuals can achieve positive social identity through making comparisons between the in-group and the out-group on the only dimension available to them, namely resource distribution. Thus, by discriminating in the distribution of resources, participants achieve positive social identity and a corresponding boost in their self-esteem (Abrams & Hogg, 1988; Hogg & Abrams, 1990; Tajfel & Turner, 1979).

Intergroup discrimination in the minimal group paradigm has proven to be a remarkably robust phenomenon. Studies using the minimal group paradigm with children and adults in a variety of countries (e.g., United States, Great Britain, Japan, Switzerland) have yielded highly similar results: Categorization into groups elicits favoritism toward the in-group (Mullen, Brown, & Smith, 1992).

Of course, the use of the minimal group paradigm to study prejudice has not been without its critics. Researchers have questioned whether the results can be extended to real groups, noting the high degree of artificiality within this laboratory paradigm (Aschenbrenner & Schaefer, 1980). Others (Billig, 1973; Gerard & Hoyt, 1974; Tajfel & Billig, 1974) have suggested that the in-group favoritism effect within the minimal group paradigm stems from demand characteristics; that is, that the participants merely acted in the way they thought the experimenter wanted. However, even when using a broader range of approaches and real-world groups, researchers continue to find that people evaluate their own group more favorably than an out-group.

INFLUENCES ON SOCIAL IDENTITY    According to SIT, the desire to achieve or maintain a positive social identity motivates in-group favoritism and out-group derogation (Tajfel, 1982). But are some factors particularly likely to activate social identity motives? The answer appears to be yes—numerous situational and individual factors influence whether social identity motives are aroused, which may ultimately lead to intergroup discrimination and out-group derogation.

First, the relative size of the in-group may be an important situational factor that influences whether one is likely to engage in intergroup discrimination or out-group derogation. Numerous studies have demonstrated that in-group favoritism and in-group loyalty is greater for members of numerical minority groups than among majority group members (see Mullen, Brown, & Smith, 1992, for a review).

Second, individual differences in the extent to which people identify with a particular social group have been demonstrated to lead to greater discrimination (Gagnon & Bourhis, 1996; Perreault & Bourhis, 1999) and out-group derogation (Wann & Branscombe, 1990). In one study of sports fans, for example, Nyla Branscombe and Daniel Wann (1992b) found that persons highly identified with a sports team are more likely to engage in out-group derogation following a threat to social identity (i.e., a defeat) than those low in indentification.

Strong identification with a group is also implicated in the desire to maintain clear distinctions between one's own group and out-groups. Jim Blascovich and his colleagues (Blascovich, Wyer, Swart, & Kibler, 1997) reasoned that racially prejudiced people, who are assumed to identify strongly with their racial in-group, would be more concerned with accurately distinguishing between their own racial group and other groups. To test this idea, the researchers devised an experiment to determine how long individuals differing in levels of prejudice would take to categorize people by race.

In this experiment, high- and low-prejudiced undergraduates viewed photographs of a variety of human faces and control targets (black, white, and gray ovals) on a video monitor. Of the 36 facial photographs presented, 14 had been determined through pretesting to be easily identified as White, 12 were easily identified as Black, and the remainder were racially ambiguous. The participants' task was to identify verbally as quickly as possible the race of each individual and the color of the control targets. Consistent with the hypothesis that racially prejudiced people would be more concerned with accurate racial categorizations, the amount of time taken to identify the racially ambiguous faces varied according to prejudice level. That is, high-prejudiced individuals deliberated longer when making judgments of ambiguous faces than did low-prejudiced individuals. Interestingly, high-prejudiced individuals also made more nonverbal vocalizations than low-prejudiced individuals when presented with ambiguous faces, suggesting they were hesitant to make a decision. For people who are strongly identified with an in-group, such as racially prejudiced individuals, carefully distinguishing between "us" and "them" may be the first step toward in-group favoritism and out-group derogation.

Finally, differences among in-group members in terms of their status within the group may also contribute to the likelihood of out-group derogation. According to Jeffrey Noel and his colleagues (1995), marginal members of an in-group are more likely to engage in out-group derogation than members with higher status. To test this hypothesis, Noel et al. took advantage of naturally occurring groups on a university campus—active and pledge members of fraternities and sororities—and assessed either privately or publicly their views of members of other same-sexed Greek organizations. They reasoned that pledges, who are in the process of being initiated in a group but who are not fully accepted members, should be more concerned with enhancing their status within the group. One way to do this is to publicly derogate out-group members in an attempt to win the favor of in-group members. The results supported these predictions. To gain acceptance by active members, pledges, uncertain of their status within the group, were more likely than active members to publicly derogate out-groups.

THE DILEMMA OF BELONGING TO LOW-STATUS GROUPS   A principle assumption of SIT is that people derive a sense of self-worth from the groups to which they belong. But what happens if individuals belong to a group that is deemed undesirable in a society or to a group that has relatively low status? How do group members cope with this awareness that their social identity is devalued in the eyes of others?

Although belonging to a negatively evaluated group may pose a threat to one's social identity, it does not lead inevitably to low personal or collective self-esteem (Crocker & Major, 1989; Tajfel, 1982; Tajfel & Turner, 1986). In fact, comparisons of average levels of self-esteem among stigmatized and nonstigmatized groups generally have yielded few differences. For example, studies comparing the self-esteem of African Americans to that of European Americans typically find no difference or higher self-esteem in African Americans (see Crocker & Major, 1989, for a review). Moreover, Jennifer Crocker and her associates (Crocker, Luhtanen, Blaine, & Broadnax, 1994) report that African-American and Asian-American college students regard their racial group as positively as European Americans regarded their own. Thus, these findings suggest that individuals who belong to stigmatized groups may cope with their plight in ways that serve to protect their self-esteem.

Most versions of SIT (Tajfel & Turner, 1986; Hogg & Abrams, 1988) outline three tactics that members of devalued groups can employ to achieve positive social identities: **individual mobility, social competition,** and **social creativity.** The underlying goals of these tactics differ in terms of whether they are employed to enhance personal identity or social identity (Branscombe & Ellemers, 1998; Ellemers, Wilke, & von Knippenberg, 1993; Hogg & Abrams, 1988; Jackson, Sullivan, Harnish, & Hodge, 1996). Those tactics designed to enhance personal identity are basically *individual-level strategies*, which maintain a positive identity for the individual without necessarily improving that of the in-group. Tactics aimed at enhancing social identity are *group-level strategies*, because they achieve a positive identity for the in-group as a whole, rather than only for the individual person. Let's consider each of these broad strategies in greater detail.

*Individual-Level Strategies*   Individual mobility can be conceptualized as an individual-level strategy, because the goal is to achieve a positive personal identity. This strategy may involve an actual attempt to leave the low-status group and join a more positively valued group. For example, individuals who attempt to improve their lot in life through hard work or education are often attempting to pass from a lower to higher social position. This approach works only if entry into the dominant group is possible, however. In some cases, entry into the dominant group is not possible, as in cases in which group distinctions are based upon sex or race.

If individuals cannot redefine themselves as members of the dominant group, some individuals may psychologically leave their group by dissociating from the in-group. Attempting to "pass" as a member of the dominant group or distancing oneself from the in-group are other examples of individual mobility. The important feature of individual mobility is that it does not facilitate a positive view of the in-group as a whole, but it does achieve a personal solution to an unfavorable social identity.

*Group-Level Strategies*   When circumstances will not support individual mobility, Tajfel (1978) proposed that individuals may use other strategies, such as social competition or social creativity, to maintain a positive social identity. Social competition involves direct competition between the subordinate and dominant groups on dimensions consensually valued by both groups, and clearly represents a group-level strategy because the intent is to improve the actual standing of the devalued group. According to SIT, social competition is likely to occur if intergroup relations are unstable—that is, the subordinate group perceives that the existing state of affairs is illegitimate *and can be changed* (Tajfel & Turner, 1986).

If direct competition with the out-group is impossible or very difficult, then members of low-status groups may engage in indirect responses. SIT groups these indirect responses under the umbrella term "social creativity" and includes three approaches.

First, lower status group members may *identify new dimensions* on which to compare themselves with the out-group. By introducing a new comparison dimension on which the in-group fares favorably, a more positive identity for the in-group as a whole can be achieved. Thus, for example, gay people may claim as a group, "we are more inclusive and tolerant than most in the heterosexual community."

Second, lower status group members may attempt to *change the desirability of group attributes* so that comparisons that were previously negative are now evaluated positively. In other words, members of the low-status group may redefine the stigma by making the devalued characteristic a source of pride. During the 1960s in the United States, for instance, the term "Black" had a negative connotation, and the slogan "Black is beautiful" was an attempt to reaffirm Black identity. Similarly, during the 1960s Mexican Americans reclaimed with a sense of pride "Chicano," originally a pejorative term used to describe Mexican Americans. And, more recently, the gay rights movement in the United States has promoted "gay pride" as a means of enhancing social identity. These examples illustrate a group-level strategy intended to achieve a positive identity for the in-group as a whole, rather than only for the individual.

Finally, members of low-status groups may *select new out-groups* for intergroup comparisons. This tactic may include a comparison with a group of equal or lesser status. Alternatively, members of low-status groups may choose to make intragroup comparisons, in which they restrict their comparisons to *other* in-group members. To salvage their self-esteem, for instance, disadvantaged group members may choose to compare their income to other in-group members, rather than compare with a higher status group. However, this form of social creativity may be conceptualized as a more individualistic method of coping with disadvantaged status, because it will not improve the status of the in-group as a whole (Branscombe & Ellemers, 1998).

Overall, SIT identifies a variety of responses available to disadvantaged group members when confronted with rejection or discrimination that serve to protect their personal and social identity. At this time, however, SIT does not predict the specific response that a disadvantaged group may make to an unfavorable social identity, and this is certainly a theoretical shortcoming (Hinkle, Taylor, Fox-Cardamone, & Ely, 1998).

TESTS OF THE MOTIVATIONAL PROPERTIES OF SIT   Social identity theory, as you can see, emphasizes both cognitive and motivational factors. First, individuals must cognitively carve the social world into at least two different categories that distinguish the self from others ("us" and "them"). Second, the desire to maintain or enhance positive self-esteem, which is derived in part from group membership, motivates people to engage in discriminatory behavior and to view the in-group as superior to the out-group. This motivational aspect of SIT has received considerable attention from researchers (Abrams & Hogg, 1988; Hogg & Abrams, 1990).

The major assumption of SIT is that people favor their in-group over other groups in an effort to boost their group's status, which in turn boosts their own self-esteem. Hogg and Abrams (1990) derived two basic corollaries from this assumption, which have come to be known as the "self-esteem hypothesis": (1) intergroup discrimination enhances social identity and, thus, self-esteem, and (2) threats to social identity motivate intergroup discrimination to restore self-esteem.

Given that self-esteem motivation is so critical to SIT, does research support these predictions? Unfortunately, the empirical evidence supporting the "self-esteem hypothesis" is mixed at best. In a recent review of over 40 studies concerning the self-esteem hypothesis, Rubin and Hewstone (1998) concluded that there seems to be greater support for Corollary 1 than Corollary 2. In other words, the idea that intergroup discrimination enhances self-esteem is supported by more evidence than the idea that individuals with low self-esteem are more prone to discriminate than individuals with high self-esteem.

Rubin and Hewstone (1998) suggest that the murky findings surrounding the self-esteem hypothesis may be due to two reasons. First, the conflicting research findings may reflect the vast array of methodologies employed to investigate the role of self-esteem in intergroup discrimination, with some studies employing the minimal group paradigm while others rely upon "real" groups (rather than groups created in the laboratory) that have a history of conflict.

Second, the unclear results may stem from the different ways in which investigators have measured self-esteem. Some researchers, for instance, have used measures of *personal* self-esteem to test hypotheses of social identity theory, whereas others have more appropriately used measures of *collective* self-esteem. How self-esteem is conceptualized may have important implications for linking self-esteem to intergroup discrimination.

Because the role of self-esteem in social identity is so complex and still not fully understood, some researchers have questioned whether it is a primary motivational force (Deaux, 1996). Indeed, recent derivations of social identity theory deemphasize self-esteem motivation (Brewer, 1991; Turner, Hogg, Oakes, Reicher, & Wetherell, 1987). Self-categorization theory (Turner et al., 1987), which we will turn to next, omits the motivational aspects of SIT and instead emphasizes the cognitive underpinnings of social identity processes.

## Self-Categorization Theory

Self-categorization theory (Turner, 1978, 1982, 1984) emerged as a direct outgrowth of social identity theory, stressing the cognitive rather than motivational aspects of social identity. Similar to SIT, self-categorization theory (SCT) acknowledges that people sometimes perceive themselves as unique individuals (personal identity), whereas at other times, they may perceive themselves in terms of their group membership (social identity). From the perspective of SCT theorists, social identity and personal identity are not different forms of identity per se, but rather different levels of self-categorization.

Self-categories vary in their level of inclusiveness. Persons may self-categorize at the superordinate level (for example, defining self as part of humanity); an intermediate level (for example, defining self on the basis of a group membership); or they may self-categorize at a subordinate level (for example, defining self as a unique individual different from in-group members). Although these self-categories vary in levels of abstraction, each are equally "real" and accurately reflect the self.

Thus, SCT assumes that people have multiple identities and often make choices among these identities as they move from one situation to another. For instance, each of us is a member of many different groups or social categories. We are Canadian, Vietnamese, German, Nigerian, or some other nationality. We may categorize ourselves in terms of our race, ethnic group, gender, or sexual orientation. Many of us may also belong to various community organizations, religious groups, or political parties. The self-categorization (or identity) that we select at any given moment depends upon the social context. Penelope Oakes (1987) has described the choice of an identity in terms of an "accessibility x fit hypothesis." Accessibility refers to the readiness of a perceiver to use a particular categorization, which may be influenced by a person's past experiences or the extent to which the person identifies with a group. Some people have *chronic* group identifications that are almost always accessible. For African Americans, their "blackness" is a central element of their self-definition in most contexts; for many people, their professional identification is accessible in many situations.

Fit is a more complex notion, referring to the degree that a social categorization matches reality. For a social categorization to "fit," it must make sense in the current social context. When we are abroad, for example, we are more likely to define ourselves in terms of our nationality, perceiving a great deal of similarity between ourselves and others from our country. On the other hand, if we happen to be at a political rally, we may be more likely to construe ourselves in terms of our political membership. As these examples demonstrate, self-categorization is not static, but instead is a fluid process that can be activated contextually.

When self-categorization is applied at the group level, people perceive themselves less as unique people and more similar to in-group members. In the language of SCT theorists, *depersonalization* occurs, whereby individuals view themselves as interchangeable with other group members and "it is this process that transforms individual into collective behavior as people perceive and act in terms of a shared, collective conception of self" (Turner, 1999, p. 11). The process of depersonalization does not represent a loss of identity, but rather a shift from the personal to a collective identity.

Once we define ourselves in terms of others, perceiving ourselves as "we" and "us" as opposed to "I" and "me," cognitive processes exacerbate group distinctions. When group boundaries are formed, we tend to minimize intragroup differences and maximize intergroup differences. Imagine, for example, a discussion between men and women in which all women agree with each other but disagree with the men. In this context, a woman's social self-category "female" is likely to become salient, and she will perceive the other females as more similar to each other (and her) and more different from the males. Such basic cognitive processes set the stage for stereotyping, prejudice, and intergroup conflict.

As you can see, SCT is heavily cognitive, emphasizing categorization processes to the exclusion of motivational processes. Although SCT is an extension of social identity theory, the two are separate, yet complementary theories (Turner, 1999). Both theories invoke the same concept of social identity, but SCT stresses cognitive principles to predict when and how people are likely to self-categorize.

## Optimal-Distinctiveness Theory

Optimal-distinctiveness theory (Brewer, 1991) is a close relative to SCT, sharing many of the same assumptions that provide a framework for understanding short-term fluctuations in identity. Whereas SCT offers a *cognitive* explanation for social identity choice, optimal-distinctiveness theory introduces a *motivational* component that predicts when we are more likely to be group-identified or individual-identified. According to Marilyn Brewer (1991), two core human motives influence our choice of social identifications: the need to be unique and the need to belong. Optimal-distinctiveness theory conceptualizes identity as a tension between inclusiveness (the need to belong) and distinctiveness (the need to be unique). In other words, we want very much to fit in, to belong, and to derive enjoyment from group memberships, but at the same time, we want to be our own person and to be recognized for own unique qualities.

The optimal-distinctiveness model predicts that our identities are selected and activated to the extent that they help us to achieve a balance between feelings of inclusion and distinctiveness. If a group becomes too large, for instance, feelings of depersonalization may prompt us to deal with our need for distinctiveness by seeking out identification with a smaller group. On the other hand, if we are alone and isolated in our uniqueness, we may seek membership in a group that allows us to feel a sense of connectedness with others. Belonging to groups that are small enough for us to feel unique provides what Brewer calls "optimal distinctiveness" or, in other words, the maximum satisfaction of the competing needs for inclusion and distinctiveness.

Consistent with these predictions, Brewer and Weber (1994) found that, when people were assigned to a distinctive minority (said to comprise only 20 percent of the population), they showed greater identification with their in-group. On the other hand, when assigned to a majority group (said to comprise 80 percent of the population), people exhibited a need to differentiate themselves from this in-group. In another study, Brewer and her colleagues (Brewer, Manzi, & Shaw, 1993) enhanced participants' degree of depersonalization by providing instructions worded in such a way as to increase their inclusion in the group "college student." Increasing the need for differentiation in this manner led students to identify more with another available group when this group was a distinctive minority (representing 20 percent of the population) than when it was a majority (80 percent of the population).

In summary, Brewer argues that it is the motivation for optimal distinctiveness, rather than the desire for positive social identity as postulated by SIT, that influences the choice of identity at any given point in time. In fact, she maintains that the need for distinctiveness is independent of the need for a positive social identity, such that identification with stigmatized groups can allow a person to achieve the optimal balance between the competing needs for inclusion and differentiation (Brewer, 1991).

## Summary

These three theories of in-group identification—social identity theory, self-categorization theory, and optimal-distinctiveness theory—link the individual to society. These theories share the core assumption that our group memberships are an important part of our self-concept, and that they help us to define who we are, what we are like, and how we are similar to and different from others. The theories differ, however, in their explanations for *why* we identify with a social category (Sherman, Hamilton, & Lewis, 1999).

Social identity theory suggests that we identify with groups because they serve as a source of self-esteem; self-categorization theory proposes that we identify with groups in order to clarify our perception of the social world and to identify our place within it; and optimal-distinctiveness theory explains social identification as a search for balance between the countervailing needs for distinctiveness and inclusion.

Each of these explanations for social identification has received empirical support, suggesting that one single motive is probably insufficient to explain every facet of social identification. More likely, multiple motives lie behind social identification processes. The challenge that lies ahead for researchers, in the words of Kay Deaux (1996, p. 792), "is to determine which motives are important to whom on what occasions."

## ➤ CONCLUSION

In this chapter, we have explored the origins of prejudice and discrimination in terms of the nature of intergroup relations. Several theories of intergroup relations have been presented, and each falls into one of two broad frameworks for understanding how intergroup relations evolve into prejudice and/or discrimination.

One framework emphasizes "social competition" as the root of intergroup antagonism, with perhaps Sherif's (1966) realistic conflict theory best exemplifying this approach. Relative deprivation theory also falls into this framework, not necessarily because of *actual* conflict of interests, but rather the *perception* of being disadvantaged relative to others.

The alternative framework for explaining how group relations can evolve into conflict and hostility emphasizes the cognitive and motivational underpinnings of "social categorization." From this perspective, categorizing oneself and others into social groups can lead to prejudice, in the form of favoring one's in-group over out-groups. The many cognitive consequences of social categorization (e.g., the out-group homogeneity effect, attributional biases, etc.) set the stage for intergroup antipathy. Within this framework, social identity theory and its derivatives (e.g., self-categorization theory and optimal-distinctiveness theory) attempt to explain why we identify so strongly with our in-group.

Although it is tempting to view these two broad frameworks in an either/or fashion, it is more likely that both frameworks provide an accurate snapshot of how group interactions evolve into intergroup conflict. While social categorization alone is sufficient to lead to intergroup bias, social and political factors such as resource scarcity, competition, and power can certainly fuel intergroup hatred. To attain a more complete understanding of prejudice, we must understand both the social categorization process and the nature and consequences of competition.

# 7

# *Stigma and Identity*

Until recent years, virtually all social psychological research has focused on the perpetrators of prejudice, identifying the cognitive and motivational processes that give rise to their prejudicial views. Implicitly, this approach to the study of prejudice represents the psychology of the relatively powerful—those members of dominant and advantaged groups who hold power over disadvantaged group members.

What has been missing from such discussions of prejudice is the psychology of the relatively powerless—that is, how targets of prejudice react to and cope with their plight. Admittedly, some classic discussions of prejudice included the perspective of stigmatized groups, but the general assumption was that the stigmatized internalize the negative stereotypes and images about them that permeate a culture. In his classic book *The Nature of Prejudice*, Gordon Allport (1954) implied that the experience of being stigmatized has negative consequences for one's identity and psychological adjustment: "One's reputation, whether false or true, cannot be hammered, hammered, hammered into one's head without doing something to one's character" (p. 142). And in 1956, Erik Erikson claimed that "there is ample evidence of inferiority feelings and/or morbid self-hate in all minority groups" (p. 55). But are victims of prejudice necessarily filled with self-loathing, as classic research suggests?

Over the past decade, social psychologists have begun concentrating on the psychological experiences of devalued groups, and a more complete picture of how the stigmatized perceive and respond to prejudice is rapidly emerging. In this chapter, we will examine prejudice more closely from the targeted person's perspective.

To understand the predicaments of the stigmatized, we must first consider what it means to be stigmatized. This discussion is structured around Goffman's (1963) analysis of social stigma and how individuals with a "master status" process their interactions with others. After exploring these issues, we will consider how prejudice affects one's sense of identity and self-worth. What effect, for example, does prejudice have on the stigmatized's self-esteem and self-image? What consequences do prejudice and discrimination have on the lives of disadvantaged group members? Finally, we'll consider how individuals attempt to cope with their devalued identity.

> ## STIGMA AND PREJUDICE

In Chapter 1, we introduced the concept of **stigma**, which is an attribute that is deeply *discrediting* in a particular social context. Thus, a person who is stigmatized is a person who possesses a devalued social identity, or membership in some social category, that serves to discredit the person in the eyes of others (Crocker, Major, Steele, 1998).

This view of stigma stems from the classic analysis of sociologist Erving Goffman, who suggested that there are three types of stigmatizing conditions: (a) *tribal stigmas*, which are familial and passed from generation to generation, and include membership in devalued racial, ethnic, or religious groups; (b) *abominations of the body*, which include physical handicaps and deformities, disfiguring conditions, and obesity; and (c) *blemishes of individual character*, which are devalued social identities related to one's personality or behavior, such as addiction, homosexuality, and imprisonment.

Goffman's typology reveals a wide variety of stigmatizing attributes, and it acknowledges important dimensions along which stigmatizing conditions differ. Tribal stigmas and many abominations of the body are "ascribed" categories of stigma, because in most cases people have no choice in assuming them. Blemishes of individual character, on the other hand, represent "achieved" categories of stigma, because these stigmas are perceived as having a volitional component. However, Goffman's analysis of stigma is problematic in the sense that some stigmas arguably may belong to two categories. Obesity is one such stigma, because it is commonly viewed as both an abomination of the body and a blemish of individual character (Allon, 1982).

Rather than identify *types* of stigmas, other theorists conceptualize stigmatizing conditions along *dimensions* in which they differ. Jones and his colleagues (Jones et al., 1984) suggest six crucial dimensions: (a) the *visibility* of the stigmatizing condition (Is the condition obvious or hidden?); (b) the *controllability* of the condition (Is the person responsible for the condition?); (c) the *aesthetic qualities* of the stigma (Is the condition ugly or repulsive?); (d) the *prognosis* of the stigmatized condition (What is the ultimate outcome of the condition?); (e) the *danger* posed by the person (Is the condition threatening to others?); and (f) the degree of *social disruptiveness* (Does the condition hamper social interaction?).

These dimensions are useful in allowing us to understand the complexities that define any stigmatizing attribute. For example, physically disabled or disfigured individuals may be stigmatized primarily because of the aesthetic qualities of their condition. Similarly, the prognosis dimension suggests that conditions that are degenerative (e.g., terminal illness, old age) are likely to be stigmatized. And other conditions may be stigmatized because they disrupt social interaction (e.g., schizophrenia, Tourette's syndrome).

In general, highly negative stigmas are those that are visible, aesthetically displeasing, dangerous to others, and disruptive of social interaction due to avoidance or awkwardness. Although comparing any two stigmatizing conditions is fraught with difficulty, consider the complexities associated with acne and AIDS. Having acne is clearly less stigmatizing than having AIDS, because AIDS is perceived as an unattractive (at least in the advanced stages), deteriorating condition that is potentially dangerous to others, and perhaps even "freely chosen" in the sense that the person might be perceived as responsible for the condition (Crandall, Glor, & Britt, 1997; Herek, 1999). On the other hand, acne is visible and aesthetically displeasing which may cause social rejection that the AIDS patient (in the early stages) can escape through withholding medical information.

Although each of these six dimensions has implications for people's reactions to the stigmatized, two dimensions are especially important in understanding the phenomenology of the stigmatized: visibility and controllability. Let us consider these two dimensions in greater detail.

## Visibility

Stigmatizing conditions that are immediately visible, such as race, gender, obesity, physical disabilities, or disfiguring conditions, may be especially likely to assume a "master status" (Frable, Blackstone, & Scherbaum, 1990) in the sense that these attributes may overwhelm judgments made about a person. Because a visibly stigmatizing attribute discredits a person before an encounter even begins, visibly stigmatized persons must, of course, think and worry about how others will react to the stigma.

As an example of the mental life of the visibly stigmatized, consider the following experiment. Kleck and Strenta (1980) recruited college women to play the role of a disfigured person in an interaction with another participant. These women were led to believe that the purpose of the experiment was to determine how others reacted to a facial scar created with theatrical makeup. In reality, the purpose of the experiment was to see how the women themselves, when made to feel stigmatized, would perceive others' behavior toward them. How was this ruse accomplished? After applying the makeup, the experimenter provided each woman a hand-held mirror so she could see the authentic-looking scar. Once she put the mirror down, the experimenter applied moisturizer to "keep the makeup from cracking." Unbeknownst to the women, the moisturizer removed the scar.

These women, believing that their interaction partner thought they possessed a conspicuous facial scar, felt and behaved more negatively during the interaction, even though the scar was never in fact visible. This study suggests that the self-consciousness created by a visible stigma may disrupt social interactions in part because of the stigmatized person's awareness of how others may react to them.

People who have a stigma that can be hidden—a *concealable stigma*, such as homosexuality, a prison record, or many physical illnesses—have a different set of concerns. Unlike their visibly stigmatized peers, those with concealable stigmas cannot simply scan the environment and identify others who share the same stigmatizing condition. As a consequence, people with concealable stigmas may be particularly vulnerable to social isolation. In fact, one study (Frable, Platt, & Hoey, 1998) of college students with concealable stigmas (students who indicated that they were gay, bisexual, or lesbian; bulimic; or that their family earned less than $20,000 each year) found that these students led lives that were "more academic and less social" (p. 915) than their visibly stigmatized peers. Moreover, these students with concealable stigmas reported lower self-esteem and more negative affect than both visibly stigmatized and nonstigmatized students.

Concealment can have other costs. Concealing a stigma has been related to poorer physical health or increased psychological problems. HIV infection, for instance, progresses more rapidly among HIV-positive gay men who conceal their homosexual identity than it does among those who are "out" (Cole, Kemeny, Taylor, Visscher, & Fahey, 1996). Similarly, concealment of a stigma like abortion is associated with greater psychological distress (Major & Gramzow, 1999).

Because their stigma is not visible, people with concealable stigmas may engage in a deliberate effort to conceal the stigma. Convicted criminals, for instance, can refuse to divulge their past offenses, gay people can camouflage their sexual orientation, bulimics can hide their disordered eating behaviors, cancer-striken people can conceal their illness, and in some cases, light-skinned Blacks can adopt a White racial identity. These attempts at "passing," as Goffman (1963) labels it, may smooth interactions with nonstigmatized others, but they come with their own set of problems.

People who choose to conceal their stigma must carefully process their interactions with nonstigmatized others to determine their attitudes toward the stigmatizing condition, and they must consider in every new situation how much about themselves they wish to reveal (Goffman, 1963; Frable et al., 1990). Maintaining a concealable stigma in social interactions requires a great deal of mental control, and a recent study suggests that attempts to conceal a stigma result in a preoccupation with the stigma (Smart & Wegner, 1999). Concealing a stigma is, in many ways, akin to keeping a secret, which typically involves pushing the secret out of one's mind. Such mental control of an unwanted thought, as we learned in Chapter 4, has the ironic effect of making it even more accessible (Wegner, 1994).

Of course, individuals with concealable stigmas can avoid these concerns by choosing to become visible. Many individuals with concealable stigmas may literally "wear their stigma on their sleeve." For instance, they may use symbols and clothing to announce their group membership (e.g., a pink triangle, a rainbow flag, a Star of David).

## Controllability

Stigmatizing conditions are viewed as controllable to the extent that a person is viewed as responsible for the onset of the condition. In general, people whose stigmas are perceived as a consequence of their own behavior (e.g., alcoholics, addicts, convicts, people with AIDS, etc.) are evaluated more negatively than those whose stigmatizing conditions are not viewed as under volitional control, such as the disabled or cancer patients (Jones et al., 1984; Weiner, Perry, & Magnusson, 1988).

For many stigmatizing conditions, however, considerable disagreement exists about who or what is to blame for the stigma. Some people, for instance, may consider obesity to be due either to biological factors over which one may have little control, or a lack of willpower (a blemish of character, in Goffman's analysis), which is under one's control. Similarly, the origins of sexual orientation are hotly debated, with recent surveys indicating that people in the United States are about evenly split over whether sexual orientation is biologically determined or just simply a "lifestyle choice"(Whitley, 1990). Perceptions of responsibility for these two stigmatizing conditions have important implications: both antifat attitudes and antigay attitudes are strongly related to beliefs about controllability (Crandall, 1994, 1995; Herek & Capitanio, 1995; Quinn & Crocker, 1998; Whitley, 1990).

Interestingly, perceptions of responsibility may apply not only to the onset of a stigmatizing condition, but also to the elimination of it (Brickman et al., 1982). In some cases, people may not be held responsible for the onset of a stigmatizing condition, but they made be held accountable for eliminating it (as in some views of poverty).

But for those who do successfully remediate a stigma, such as recovered alcoholics, formerly obese people, or rehabilitated criminals, are they granted credit for self-improvement? Apparently, the answer is no: Overcoming a stigma does not necessarily lead to more favorable evaluations. This paradoxical finding was demonstrated in a study by Rodin and Price (1995), in which they presented participants with information about an individual who had remediated a stigma (obesity by dieting, unattractiveness by having plastic surgery, social ineptness by learning social skills, etc.). Despite successfully removing the stigma, a person with a history of stigma was still viewed as less favorable than a person without a history of stigma. Thus, individuals who have successfully remediated a stigma must still contend with others' lingering perception of them as "damaged goods" (Rodin & Price, 1995). The implication is that a person who wants to make a favorable impression would do better *not* to reveal any past stigmatizing conditions.

Why might a person with a history of stigma be judged less favorably than a person with no such history? Rodin and Price (1995) offer two possible explanations. One reason may be that one can never be certain of the permanency of remediation. In other words, recovering from an addiction or losing a significant amount of weight may be perceived as a temporary condition, with the formerly stigmatized person always remaining vulnerable to the stigmatizing condition in the future. Perhaps perceivers anticipate that the formerly obese will not be able to maintain their new bodyweight or that the recovered alcoholic will not remain sober. Blemishes of character especially might be viewed as difficult, if not impossible, to overcome.

Another possibility is that the formerly stigmatized remains contaminated, similar to the type of magical thinking exemplified by the law of contagion (Rozin & Nemeroff, 1990). The law of contagion holds that when two objects touch, they continue to influence each other via transmission of an "essence." For example, a sweatshirt worn by someone with AIDS would be viewed as less desirable than had the shirt been worn by someone else. Similar reasoning may explain why the once stigmatized are still viewed as "tainted."

## Stigma by Association

This discussion of the "contagion effect" brings us to an interesting phenomenon—people who are merely associated with those unfavorably "marked" are also likely to be denigrated. This phenomenon, termed "courtesy stigma" by Goffman (1963), or more recently "stigma by association" (Neuberg, Smith, Hoffman, & Russell, 1994) has been examined in numerous studies. For example, families with retarded children (Birenbaum, 1970), wives of incarcerated husbands (Sack, Seidler, & Thomas, 1976), or dating partners of disabled persons (Goldstein & Johnson, 1997) are themselves stigmatized because of these associations.

In one study designed to explore this stigmatization process, Neuberg and his colleagues (1994) had male participants watch a videotaped conversation between two male friends, but prior to observing the film participants were given information about each target's sexual orientation. In some conditions both men were described as gay or both were identified as heterosexual. In other conditions, only one of the men was identified as gay, whereas the other was identified as heterosexual. After participants observed the videotaped interaction, they rendered judgments about each target's personality. Not surprisingly, Neuberg et al. found that the gay target was viewed negatively, but they also found evidence of stigma by association. That is, the heterosexual actor was denigrated if he was viewed with a homosexual rather than heterosexual friend.

Apparently, this contagion of stigma extends to those who merely associate with the stigmatized. Perhaps one of the most bizarre examples of stigma by association occurs in the area of occupations, in which individuals who merely work with the stigmatized (e.g., psychiatrists who work with the mentally ill or those who work with the dying or dead, such as morgue attendants) are often held in low regard (Posner, 1976). Similarly, ethnographic researchers who study "deviant subcultures" (i.e., gay or S&M subcultures, prostitution) are themselves considered sexually suspect (Kirby & Corzine, 1981).

## ➤ PREJUDICE: THE TARGET'S PERSPECTIVE

At some time or another, each of us, however temporarily, has experienced the shame of stigma. Perhaps we were chubby as children, or had acne as teenagers. Or maybe we were ashamed of our gay sibling or our alcoholic parent. Maybe we were even teased as children, called "four-eyes," "pizza-face," "fatso," or "metal-mouth." In these instances we became acquainted with stigma and its effect on our identity.

But what happens to people who are frequent targets or potential targets of prejudice? What is it like to grow up in a society in which prejudice and discrimination are targeted toward you and members of your social group? How do prejudice and discrimination affect the lives of those with devalued social identities?

We know that prejudice and discrimination have tangible costs to stigmatized individuals. Belonging to a stigmatized group affects one's life outcomes in obvious ways by creating barriers to employment, housing, and education. Numerous studies, for instance, have shown that members of stigmatized groups experience difficulty finding adequate housing. In one experiment (Yinger, 1995), White, Black, and Latino actors contacted realty and leasing agents to inquire about homes and apartments. Even when the actors were identical in every respect except ethnicity, the real estate agents favored the White clients: They made more follow-up calls to White clients and provided them with more housing options, while steering Black and Latino actors to minority neighborhoods.

People with AIDS experience similar housing discrimination. In one study, landlords who advertised rental properties in newspapers were more likely to describe their property as unavailable when prospective tenants identified themselves as having AIDS (Page, 1999).

Other types of discrimination abound for stigmatized individuals. On virtually all socioeconomic indices, members of racial minorities fare poorly compared to Whites, and women are disadvantaged relative to men (Phillips, 1990; Stroh, Brett, & Reilly, 1992). Ayres and Siegelman (1995) report that White men are offered better deals on automobiles than White women (who pay $109 more), who in turn are offered better deals than Black women ($318 more) and Black men ($935 more).

Overweight people are not immune from the effects of prejudice and discrimination. They face discrimination in hiring and in the workplace (Allon, 1982) and overweight women receive less financial support from their parents to attend college than thinner women (Crandall, 1995).

Undoubtedly being the target of prejudice has real economic costs. But fully understanding prejudice from the target's perspective requires that we consider the target's perceptions and responses to prejudice. Following Swim and Stangor's (1998) lead, we will discuss the target's perspective in terms of (a) encountering prejudice, (b) the consequences of prejudice, and (c) coping with prejudice.

## Encountering Prejudice and Discrimination

Suppose you belong to a visibly stigmatized group—perhaps you are a woman, African American, disabled, or obese—and after interviewing for a job, you're told that the firm has hired another candidate. You might wonder, "Was I not hired because I am a woman [African American, disabled, or obese] or because someone else was simply more qualified?"

Members of many groups in society frequently face this sort of predicament. In some cases, it may be apparent to them that the negative outcomes or evaluations they receive reflect discrimination. More often, however, members of stigmatized groups may be uncertain whether they have, in fact, been discriminated against. Part of the experience of being a stigmatized group member is deciding whether particular events are indicative of prejudice or discrimination. Two avenues of research focus on how the stigmatized perceive the discrimination that confronts them.

ATTRIBUTIONAL AMBIGUITY   People in general tend to ask "why?" when they receive negative feedback from others, or when they are insulted or otherwise treated badly. Determining the causes of these events is difficult for anyone, but Crocker and Major (1989; Crocker, Voelkl, Testa, & Major, 1991) suggest that the causes of negative events are likely to be particularly ambiguous for stigmatized individuals. If a stigmatized person receives negative evaluative feedback, it could be that the person performed poorly and deserves the criticism. On the other hand, the possibility exists that the evaluator's feedback may be biased by his or her own personal prejudices.

Stigmatized persons face a similar attributional predicament when confronted with positive feedback as well. Positive outcomes from others may reflect one's merit, *or* it could be that the evaluator is judging their work positively out of sympathy or fear of appearing prejudiced. Such suspicions for the stigmatized can be deeply frustrating and can have both positive and negative consequences for the stigmatized individual's self-esteem.

Studies by Jennifer Crocker and her colleagues (Crocker et al., 1991; Crocker, Cornwell, & Major, 1993) have examined this attributional ambiguity for several stigmatized groups, including women, African Americans, and obese individuals. In one study (Crocker et al., 1991, Study 2), African-American and White students received either a positive or negative evaluation from a White student in a nearby room. Half of the participants believed that the White student could see them through a one-way mirror in which the blinds in front were up (the *seen* condition), whereas the other half believed that the White student was unaware of their racial status because the blinds were down (the *unseen* condition). Crocker and her colleagues reasoned that when the blinds were up, students in the seen condition would be in a state of attributional ambiguity. That is, any evaluations they received (whether positive or negative) from the White student could potentially be due to the student's awareness of their race.

The results showed that leaving the blinds up on the one-way mirror did indeed create a state of attributional ambiguity: African-American students were more likely to attribute the other student's evaluations, whether positive or negative, to race or prejudice. Moreover, and importantly, attributions to prejudice had both benefits and drawbacks for the African-American students. When the participants thought that the White evaluator could *not* see them, their self-esteem scores predictably increased following positive feedback and decreased following negative feedback. However, when the participants thought that the White evaluator *could* see them, negative feedback did not lower their self-esteem scores, because they attributed the negative feedback to prejudice. In this case, attributions to prejudice served an important self-protective function for the African-American students.

What may be more surprising is what occurred following positive feedback when participants believed that the evaluator was aware of their race. Participants in the unseen condition, you'll recall, showed an increase in their self-esteem in response to positive feedback. But for participants in the seen condition, their self-esteem actually dropped following positive feedback! Why? Apparently, the participants tended to discount the positive feedback if they believed that the White evaluator was aware of their race. Thus, suspecting that positive feedback from Whites is not genuine made it difficult for the African-American students to take credit for positive outcomes.

Do members of other stigmatized groups (e.g., women, the obese) respond in a similar fashion following positive or negative feedback? Crocker and her colleagues (Crocker et al., 1991) have found that although women may attribute negative feedback from men to prejudice, they are less likely to be mistrustful of positive feedback. Other studies that have used obesity as the stigma criterion have found important differences, however. For example, Crocker et al. (1993) found that overweight women who experienced rejection from men attributed the negative feedback to their weight, rather than to the men's prejudices. In other words, the overweight women perceived rejection based on weight as legitimate, suggesting that they believed themselves to be deserving of negative treatment.

At this point, it's important to recognize how subtle differences among stigmatizing conditions may influence attributions to prejudice. Although race, gender, and obesity are visibly stigmatizing attributes, these stigmas differ on one important dimension: their perceived controllability. Whereas a person's skin color or sex is uncontrollable, weight is perceived in our culture as under a person's control. That may explain why overweight women are less likely than Blacks or women in general to attribute negative feedback to prejudice.

Attributing negative outcomes to prejudice protects the self-esteem of stigmatized group members. But we will learn in the next section that attributions to prejudice can have its costs as well.

PERSONAL-GROUP DISCRIMINATION DISCREPANCY    Another interesting finding in social psychological research is that disadvantaged group members believe that discrimination may be directed toward "them, but not me." That is, disadvantaged group members are more likely to recognize higher levels of discrimination against their group in general than against themselves, personally, as members of that group. This tendency to report group but not personal discrimination is known as the **personal-group discrimination discrepancy** (PGDD) (Taylor, Wright, Moghaddam, & Lalonde, 1990), and it has been observed in a number of devalued groups: women in the United States and Canada (Crosby, 1982, 1984; Olson, Roese, Meen & Robertson, 1995); Black and Asian university students in the United States and Canada (Ruggiero & Major, 1998; Ruggiero & Taylor, 1997); Canadian immigrants (Taylor et al., 1990); lesbians and gay men (Birt & Dion, 1987; Crosby, Pufall, Snyder, O'Connell, & Whalen, 1989); and the Inuit of Arctic Quebec (Taylor et al., 1994).

What are the psychological mechanisms that underlie the PGDD? Two explanations have been offered, one cognitive, the other motivational in nature. The cognitive explanation suggests a bias in the way that people generally process information, such that information about the group may be processed more simplistically than information based on personal experience (Quinn, Roese, Pennington, & Olson, 1999). Media reports of discrimination, for example, may lead people to exaggerate the prevalence of discrimination against the minority group as a whole, whereas estimates of personal discrimination may be more accurate.

The second, and perhaps more compelling, explanation for the PGDD focuses on motivational processes. According to this explanation, individuals deny, or at least minimize, their personal experience with discrimination because it is psychologically beneficial to do so. Perceiving oneself as a victim is aversive (Crosby, 1982; Crosby et al., 1989), and a pattern of making attributions to prejudice appears to harm the psychological well-being of disadvantaged group members (Branscombe, Schmitt, & Harvey, 1999). In fact, a recent study has shown that perceiving oneself as a victim of gender discrimination is predicted by high levels of depression in women (Kobrynowicz & Branscombe, in press).

To test the idea that minimizing personal discrimination has psychological benefits, Ruggiero and Taylor (1997) asked two disadvantaged groups, Asians and Blacks, to react to a failing test grade after receiving information about the probability that they had been discriminated against by an out-group evaluator. In this experiment, participants were given a test that ostensibly measured their future career success. Immediately after completing the test, the experimenter explained to the participants that eight evaluators were being paid to grade the tests and that one of the judges would grade their answers. The experimenter confided that all of the evaluators were male and that either all (100%), six (75%), four (50%), two (25%), or none (0%) discriminated against the participants' racial group. Thus, the participants were given information about the particular chance that a biased evaluator would grade them.

After a delay, during which the evaluator presumably graded the test, the test was returned to the participants with the grade "F" marked on the paper. The participants then were asked to rate the extent to which their failing grade was due to the quality of their answers or to discrimination. Interestingly, the results showed that both Asians, and to a lesser extent, Blacks were rather reluctant to attribute their failing grade to discrimination; in fact, unless participants were informed that discrimination was a certainty (100% condition), they preferred to blame their failure on the quality of their answers instead of discrimination. Other studies using women or experimentally created low-status groups show the same pattern: disadvantaged group members are more likely than advantaged group members to attribute failure to their own shortcomings rather than to prejudice (Ruggiero & Major, 1998; Ruggiero & Marx, 1999).

Did minimizing discrimination have any psychological benefits for the participants in Ruggiero and Taylor's (1997) study? Apparently, the answer is yes. Compared to those who minimized discrimination, participants who attributed negative feedback to discrimination experienced lower levels of social self-esteem and a greater loss of perceived control over personal events in their lives. Thus, by minimizing the discrimination that confronts them, disadvantaged group members accrue two major psychological benefits: They are able to maintain perceptions of control over personal events in their lives, which is a major marker for emotional health (Lachman & Weaver, 1998), and they protect their social self-esteem (Ruggiero & Taylor, 1997).

At first glance, this tendency to readily perceive group discrimination but not personal discrimination may appear to be at odds with the research on attributional ambiguity. After all, Crocker and her colleagues demonstrated that members of some stigmatized groups are quite willing to make attributions to prejudice and discrimination. But if we look closely at the procedures used by Crocker and her colleagues (e.g., leaving the blinds up or down in front of the one-way mirror), we'll notice that, for the participants, there was no ambiguity about whether they were discriminated against. In other words, African-American participants made attributions to prejudice only when they knew the White evaluator could see them. Attributions to prejudice in this experimental condition are analogous to Ruggiero and Taylor's (1995) participants attributing their failing grade to discrimination only in the 100% condition, in which they were told that discrimination was a virtual certainty.

Thus, disadvantaged group members, in most cases, minimize the discrimination that confronts them. The social implications of this "minimization of personal discrimination" findings are disturbing. If disadvantaged group members do not perceive themselves as being discriminated against, and instead attribute negative outcomes to their own personal inadequacies, they may not be inclined to take collective action to remove barriers to their advancement. Put simply, the reluctance of disadvantaged group members to perceive discrimination may lead to the erroneous conclusion that discrimination is no longer a problem.

## Consequences of Prejudice

Thus far, we have considered how individuals who are targets of negative stereotypes understand and interpret their experiences as members of devalued groups. We turn now to the consequences of prejudice for stigmatized individuals, with a focus on how being a target of stereotyping and prejudice may disrupt academic performance and make one vulnerable to distress.

STEREOTYPE THREAT AND ACADEMIC UNDERPERFORMANCE    That certain minority groups face negative stereotypes about their academic ability is well documented. Non-Asian minorities, particularly African Americans, American Indians, and Latinos, must contend with negative stereotypes about their ability in every domain of academic achievement, whereas women must do so primarily in the areas of math and the physical sciences. Are these negative stereotypes reflective of actual differences in academic performance among various groups in the United States?

Unfortunately, the answer is yes. Nearly every indicator of academic achievement from grade school to college points to a gap between the achievement of non-Asian minorities and their European-American and Asian-American counterparts. In elementary school and high school, African-American and Latino students receive lower grades, have higher dropout rates, and obtain lower scores on standardized tests (Romo & Falbo, 1995). African-American and Latino students are also less likely to apply to college and are much more likely to drop out after entering (American Council on Education, 1995–1996).

Statistics also suggest similar discrepancies in academic outcomes between males and females in domains that require advanced quantitative skills. From elementary school to middle school, no differences between boys and girls are apparent on standardized math scores, but beginning in junior high girls begin to lag behind boys on standardized tests of math ability (Hyde, Fennema & Lamon, 1990).

How can we explain this academic underachievement of women and non-Asian minorities? Explanations abound, citing factors such as socioeconomic disadvantage (White, 1982), cultural orientations (Ogbu, 1986), low teacher expectations (Sadker & Sadker, 1994), and genetic differences in intelligence (Benbow & Stanley, 1980; Hernstein & Murray, 1994).

Although some of these explanations may hold intuitive appeal, social psychologist Claude Steele (1997) argues that another factor—what he has termed **stereotype threat**—is a major contributor to the academic underperformance of women and non-Asian minorities. Stereotype threat refers to the apprehension experienced by members of stigmatized groups in situations in which they fear that they may inadvertently confirm a negative stereotype about their social group. One consequence is that situations that remind the stigmatized about the negative stereotypes about their academic ability (e.g., "girls can't do math"; "black people are intellectually inferior") arouse enough anxiety to be distracting and upsetting, disrupting performance on standardized tests such as the SAT or GRE.

In one of the first experiments to test the idea that stereotype threat affects academic performance, Steele and Aronson (1995) administered a difficult verbal test, the GRE, to Black and White students at Stanford University. Because most of these students were sophomores, the test was particularly challenging for them. Half of the students were told that the test was "diagnostic" of their intellectual ability—that is, that the test was "a measure of verbal abilities and limitations" (p. 799). The other half were led to believe that the test was not a measure of a person's level of intellectual ability; rather, the test was described as a study of the "psychological factors involved in solving verbal problems" (p. 799). This condition was the "nondiagnostic" condition and was not expected to arouse stereotype threat.

What effect did this difference in instructions have on the students' performance? White students performed equally well regardless of whether or not they believed the test was diagnostic of intellectual ability. But for the Black students, this simple difference in instruction had a profound effect on their performance. Consistent with the notion of stereotype threat, Black students who believed the test was nondiagnostic of their intellectual ability performed as well as White students, whereas those who thought the test was a measure of their intellectual ability performed worse than the White students.

Seeking evidence of the *subjective experience* of stereotype threat, Steele and Aronson (1995) conducted a follow-up experiment to determine whether merely taking a difficult test made Black students mindful of their race and the corresponding stereotype of intellectual inferiority. Again, Black and White students were given a difficult verbal test in which they were told the test was either diagnostic or nondiagnostic of their intellectual ability. Just before taking the test and after receiving the experimental instructions, however, participants completed two tasks: a measure of stereotype activation and a measure of stereotype avoidance.

The measure of stereotype activation required completing 80 word fragments, some of which could be completed with words symbolic of African-American stereotypes (e.g., _ _ ce [race], _ _ or [poor], or la_ _ [lazy]). Nonstereotypic completions of these words, for example, could include "face" or "rice," instead of race, or "late" or "lace," rather than "lazy." Other words could be completed in such a way as to be symbolic of self-doubt (e.g., lo_ _ _ [loser], du_ _ [dumb], or fl_ _ _ [flunk]).

If merely anticipating a diagnostic test of their intellectual abilities is enough to activate stereotype threat among Black students, then these students should complete more word fragments with stereotype-related words. This is precisely what happened. Black students who believed the test was a measure of intellectual ability were more likely to complete the words in a stereotype-related fashion than those who were not told the test was diagnostic of intellectual ability. White students in either condition made few stereotype-related completions. Thus, the racial stereotype and the self-doubts associated with it were highly accessible to those Black students experiencing stereotype threat.

Interestingly, in this same experiment, Steele and Aronson found evidence that the Black students under stereotype threat also exhibited greater motivation to dissociate themselves from the stereotype. As a measure of stereotype avoidance, students were asked to rate their preferences for various activities, some of which are associated with African-American images (e.g., basketball, hip-hop), whereas others are not (e.g., tennis, classical music). A striking difference emerged on this measure: Black students who expected to take a test of their ability rebuffed activities associated with African Americans, reporting less interest in, for example, basketball and hip-hop, than did Whites. Black students assigned to the nondiagnostic condition, in contrast, did not show this tendency to avoid racially stereotypic preferences.

Clearly, this line of research demonstrates African-American students' susceptibility to racial stereotyping in academic domains. A recent study suggests that stereotype threat is also applicable to women in the domain of mathematics. Using a paradigm similar to that used to assess vulnerability to racial stereotyping, Spencer and his colleagues (Spencer, Steele, & Quinn, 1999) recruited male and female students at the University of Michigan who were equally prepared at math (e.g., who had scored above the 85th percentile on the math section of the SAT or ACT) to take a math test. The items were taken from the advanced GRE tests in math, so the test was challenging for the students. To evoke the common stereotype about women's math ability, half of the participants were told that the test they were about to take had shown gender differences in the past. The remaining participants, in contrast, were not led to believe that there were any gender differences in performance on the test. The researchers reasoned that women who were told that the test had shown gender differences should experience stereotype threat, which, in turn, should disrupt their performance on the test. The results confirmed this prediction. When the participants believed that the stereotype was not applicable, in the "low stereotype threat condition," women and men performed equally well on the test. However, when the stereotype was made applicable, in the "high stereotype threat condition," women performed significantly worse than equally qualified men did.

The phenomenon of stereotype threat is not limited to African Americans and women. In fact, Steele (1997) reminds us that stereotype threat is applicable to *any* group to which a negative stereotype impugns their abilities. Individuals from lower socioeconomic classes, for instance, must often contend with a negative stereotype about their group's intellectual ability and competence. Working in France, Jean-Claude Croizet and Theresa Claire (1998) found that college students of a lower socioeconomic class performed less well than upper-class college students under the threat of a stereotype-relevant test.

And interestingly, stereotype threat does not uniquely affect members of subordinate groups. Even White males—a group that has not experienced a history of stigmatization nor internalized any feelings of group inferiority—may be capable of feeling stereotype threatened in some cases (Stone, Lynch, Sjomeling, & Darley, 1999). A recent study by Aronson and his colleagues (Aronson, Lustina, Good, & Keough, 1999) demonstrated that White males with high ability in math who were exposed to the stereotype of Asian superiority in math underperformed on a challenging math test, compared to a similar group of nonstereotype-threatened White males.

The conclusions to be drawn from this research is that stereotype threat in its general form is potentially applicable to any group member in a variety of domains—from academics to sports (Stone et al., 1999)—because we are all members of one group or another that is negatively stereotyped in society. However, not everyone is equally threatened and disrupted by a negative stereotype. Poignantly, individuals who are most invested in a domain—for instance, serious students who want to do well, who think of themselves as good students, and for whom doing well is very important—are the ones most impaired by stereotype threat (Steele, 1997).

REDUCING STEREOTYPE THREAT   Can stereotype threat be reduced within academic domains? It is possible, according to Steele (1997). He advocates a type of learning environment that he terms "wise schooling," which suggests to minority students that they are not viewed through the lens of a stereotype and that they are being held to high standards because of a belief in their intellectual potential. Among his suggestions, Steele proposes particular strategies: (a) eliminating remediation classes that often reinforce self-doubts about academic ability, (b) stressing intelligence's expandability, (c) nonjudgmental responsiveness, (d) imputing ability, (e) group study, and (f) fostering trust in the schooling environment.

As an example of how trust can be fostered within the learning environment, Geoffrey Cohen and his colleagues (Cohen, Steele, & Ross, 1999) examined how a mentor or teacher could give critical feedback across the "racial divide" and still have that feedback trusted. Consider, for instance, how a Black student may react to critical feedback from a White professor. Critical feedback, as we learned in our discussion of "attributional ambiguity" may be threatening because the student may suspect that he or she has been judged in light of a negative stereotype. Can different ways of providing feedback engender trust in this situation? Should the mentor give feedback unalloyed, without softening it? Or should the mentor buffer criticism with high praise?

To answer these questions, Cohen et al. asked Black and White students at Stanford University to write essays about their favorite teachers, for possible publication in an education journal. The experimenter snapped a Polaroid picture of each student before he or she left the first experimental session and placed it on top of the essay. The ostensible purpose of the photo was to accompany the essay if it was selected for publication. The real purpose, however, was to let the students know that the evaluator would be aware of their racial identity.

When students returned to the laboratory a few days later, they were given written feedback regarding their essay from "Dr. Gardiner Lindsay" (a name that pretesting had shown to be recognizably Caucasian) and were asked to review his comments. The written review was essentially the same for all students, except students received (a) unbuffered criticism, (b) criticism buffered by general praise of their performance, or (c) "wise criticism" (i.e., criticism invoking high standards and affirmation of the student's potential to meet those standards).

Cohen and his colleagues found that Black students did in fact respond differently than White students to these different ways of giving feedback. Black students perceived unbuffered criticism and criticism buffered by praise less favorably than Whites; in general, they perceived these criticisms as probably biased and they were less motivated than Whites to improve their essays. However, Black students responded as positively as White students to "wise criticism," demonstrating that this combination of high standards and assurance elicited greater trust of the criticism.

Other aspects of the learning environment influence the level of stereotype threat and the degree to which it affects minority students. The presence of a stereotype-disconfirming role model—in the form of an educator—may alleviate minority students' concern about negative stereotypes. In fact, David Marx and his colleagues (Marx, Brown, & Steele, 1999) report a study in which women math students were less vulnerable to stereotype threat in the presence of a female experimenter whom they presumed to be highly competent in math.

Such studies as these point to the importance of changing features of the learning environment to reduce the negative effects of stereotype threat. Apparently, stereotype threat can be reduced when people think they are in an environment where they will not be treated stereotypically.

STIGMA AND VULNERABILITY TO DISTRESS    Members of socially stigmatized groups are frequently targets of negative stereotypes, prejudice, and discrimination. Earlier in this chapter, we discussed briefly the tangible costs of prejudice to stigmatized group members, in terms of access to employment, education, and housing. On a less obvious level, what effect does prejudice and discrimination have on the well-being of stigmatized individuals?

Some evidence suggests that prejudice and discrimination exact a toll on the psychological well-being of stigmatized individuals (Allison, 1998). Depression, for instance, is more common among women than men (Nolen-Hoeksema & Girgus, 1994). Similarly, African Americans (Aneshensel, Clark, & Frerichs, 1983) and Asian Americans (Abe & Zane, 1990) experience higher levels of depression than European Americans, and gay adolescents are particularly vulnerable to depression (Bell, Weinberg, & Hammersmith, 1981). Some studies have linked the stigma of being overweight with higher rates of depression, whereas other studies do not find any differences between the overweight and those who are not (Friedman & Brownell, 1995). However, recent research suggests that overweight individuals who endorse a Protestant ethic ideology (i.e., belief in hard work, self-reliance, and self-discipline) are particularly susceptible to psychological distress, largely because they are more likely to view themselves as moral failures (Quinn & Crocker, 1999).

Moreover, the stress of prejudice could potentially lead to negative health outcomes among some members of oppressed groups. In an article published in the *American Journal of Public Health*, for instance, Harvard epidemiologist Nancy Krieger and physician Stephen Sidney (1996) argue that one of the reasons Blacks are much more likely than Whites to suffer from high blood pressure is because of racial discrimination. In their study of 4,100 Black and White men and women, all between the ages of 25 and 37, reports of discrimination and unfair treatment were correlated with higher blood pressure readings.

In a related vein, Sherman James (James, Hartnet, & Kalsbeek, 1984; James, 1994) argues that the tale of John Henry provides a metaphor for the stress African Americans experience in their daily competition to succeed in society. In the old song about the "steel-drivin' man," the Black-American folk hero John Henry competes against a steam drill to see who can lay rail faster. Seconds after being declared the victor, John Henry dies of exhaustion. James coined the term "John Henryism" to describe a psychological syndrome associated with hypertension: a strong predisposition to cope actively in the face of adversity. In his research, James documented that Black Americans who score highest on a 12-item scale that measures high-effort coping are at risk for hypertension. These individuals embrace core American values—hard work, self-reliance, and determination—but taken to extremes, James argues that it can lead to poor health for those who find it difficult to attain cultural ideals of achievement and economic success.

All this seems to paint a rather bleak picture for stigmatized individuals. But on a more optimistic note, not all stigmatized individuals are vulnerable to psychological or physical distress. In fact, although some stigmatized individuals are vulnerable to depression or stress-related diseases, the vast majority are able to maintain positive views of themselves and their lives. As an example, let's look for a moment at the relationship between being a member of a stigmatized group and self-esteem.

STIGMA AND SELF-ESTEEM   As mentioned earlier, most classic discussions of the effects of prejudice on one's identity and self-worth typically assumed that the stigmatized internalize the broader society's negative views of them. This "self-hatred" thesis is based upon the **looking-glass self** hypothesis (Cooley, 1992; Mead, 1934), which suggests that one's self-image derives in large part from how one is viewed by others. The implication of this analysis for the stigmatized is obvious: Stigmatized individuals should have an unhealthy, negative self-concept.

Among the most widely cited studies that support the view that prejudice seriously harms the self-image of the stigmatized is the classic doll study by Kenneth and Mamie Clark (1947). In this study, 253 Black children aged 3 to 7 from Arkansas and Massachusetts were given a choice of dolls that were identical in every respect, except for skin and hair color. Two dolls were brown with black hair, and two were white with blond hair. Each child was asked a series of questions that centered on two issues: racial identification and racial preference. To assess racial identification, the experimenters asked the children to select the doll that "is a white child"; "is a colored child"; and "looks like you." Racial preference was assessed by asking the children to select the doll that "you like best"; "is a nice doll"; "looks bad"; "is a nice color."

Clark and Clark found that even at the youngest age children could correctly identify the racial categories: 94 percent made the correct choice when asked which doll "looks white," and 93 percent when asked which doll looks "colored."

The more troubling results, however, involved the children's response to the questions that assessed racial preferences. The majority of children (67 percent) selected the white doll as the one that they liked best, and 60 percent said it was the doll that had a nice color. On the other hand, when asked which doll "looks bad," 59 percent of the children chose the brown doll. These results suggested that the negative consequences of prejudice and discrimination appear early in African-American children, and that the effects of belonging to a stigmatized group are a negative view of themselves and their group.

Fortunately, later replications of the doll study (Brand, Ruiz, & Padilla, 1974; Katz & Zalk, 1974) found that the preference among Black children for the white doll no longer exists. But for several decades following the Clarks' study, social psychologists took for granted that negative stereotypes about one's group ultimately become internalized and cause rejection of one's own group, even of oneself.

More recently, the validity of this assumption has been called into question on two important grounds. First, studies have shown that having a devalued social identity does not necessarily lead to negative evaluations of one's social group. One study, for example, found that both Black and Asian college students evaluated their own racial group as positively as Euro-American students regarded their own (Crocker et al., 1994). Second, empirical studies have failed to find a consistent link between belonging to a stigmatized group and lower personal self-esteem. For instance, a recent quantitative review of research that involved more than half a million respondents spanning a period between 1960 and June 1998 found that Black children, adolescents, and young adults have higher average self-esteem than their White counterparts (Gray-Little & Hafdahl, 2000). Similarly, in another review of studies comparing the self-esteem of a variety of stigmatized groups, Crocker and Major (1989) point out that Blacks and Latinos have self-esteem scores that are equal to or higher than scores for Whites. Studies comparing self-esteem in males and females typically find little if any differences between the two groups, but when gender differences are found, they are usually small and favor males (Kling, Hyde, Showers, & Buswell, 1999). Similarly, obese and non-obese populations do not reliably differ in levels of self-esteem (Friedman & Brownell, 1995; Quinn & Crocker, 1999). In their review, Crocker and Major (1989) concluded that "In short, this research, conducted over a time span of more than 20 years, leads to the surprising conclusion that prejudice against members of stigmatized or oppressed groups generally does not result in lowered self-esteem for members of those groups" (p. 611).

## Coping with Prejudice

So how do targets of prejudice maintain their self-worth in the face of constant devaluation? In Chapter 6, if you recall, we discussed the "dilemma" of belonging to low status groups within the context of social identity theory, and how disadvantaged group members may protect their self-worth by (a) devaluing those areas in which their group is disadvantaged, or (b) comparing their outcomes to in-group members rather than relatively advantaged out-group members. These strategies have received considerable support as methods of protecting the self-esteem of disadvantaged group members (Ellemers, 1993). In this section, we will focus on two self-protective strategies—one psychological, the other behavioral, that stigmatized individuals may use to protect themselves from the consequences of prejudice.

PSYCHOLOGICAL DISENGAGEMENT AND DISIDENTIFICATION    Individuals who are targets of stereotypes in a certain domain may cope with their plight by psychologically disengaging their self-esteem from that domain. **Psychological disengagement** refers to the initial detachment of one's self-esteem from outcomes in a particular domain, such that feelings of self-worth are not dependent upon successes or failures in that domain. For example, stigmatized individuals may anticipate poor outcomes in contexts in which negative stereotypes are salient, or in situations in which feedback is expected to be biased or unfair. The experience of stereotype threat may lead stigmatized individuals to disengage their self-esteem from these contexts. Furthermore, over time, repeated exposure to negative stereotypes may lead stigmatized individuals to chronically disengage their self-esteem from those domains, a process Claude Steele (1992, 1997) refers to as **disidentification**. Disidentification occurs when one defines or redefines the self-concept in such a way that a particular domain (e.g., academics, sports, etc.) is not used as a basis of self-regard.

As an example of this chronic disengagement of one's self-esteem from a particular domain, consider Steele's (1995) personal account:

> I did this with the baritone horn in the eighth grade. After the band instructor told me, as I was going on stage with the band, that I could hold the horn but that I didn't have to play [it], I began to realign my self-view so that competence on the horn would not be an important basis of my self-esteem. I looked for other identities. . . . This normal process of identity formation and change can be pushed into use as a defense against the glare of stereotype threat. It is, of course a costly defense . . . [which may] undermine the capacity for self-motivation that is part of having an identified relation to a domain (p. 4).

In our society, African Americans confront devaluation in academic domains and, as a consequence, they may come to expect unfair treatment in academic settings. These expectations may lead African Americans to disengage their self-esteem from performance outcomes in academic settings, and over the long run, to divest themselves from that domain. In fact, a recent study (Major, Spencer, Schmader, Wolfe, & Crocker, 1998) found that the self-esteem of Black students, compared to White students, was less responsive to performance feedback on an intellectual test. Specifically, White students had higher self-esteem after success than after failure, whereas Black students' self-esteem was unaffected by success or failure feedback, suggesting that Black students were psychologically disengaged in this domain.

It is important to stress that psychological disengagement and disidentification may happen to any members of a stigmatized group who must contend with negative stereotypes about their abilities. For example, when a female student in a math class experiences stereotype threat, she may learn to care less about math, to realign her self-worth so that it is not dependent upon her math performance—in short, to disidentify with math achievement.

For targets of negative stereotypes, disidentification with a domain is a coping strategy that has positive implications for self-esteem. But it is a coping strategy that can be quite costly, particularly in important domains of life like academic achievement.

BEHAVIORAL COMPENSATION   As we have seen, disengagement and disidentification serve to mitigate the psychological damage that negative stereotypes have on stigmatized individuals' self-esteem. These forms of coping represent attempts to change the way the stigmatized think and feel about negative outcomes once they have already occurred. A second coping strategy that stigmatized individuals may use has a different goal: to prevent the occurrence of negative outcomes altogether. This strategy, referred to as **behavioral compensation** (Miller & Myers, 1999), involves attempting to overcome prejudice or disprove stereotypes by behaving in positive ways. For example, a stigmatized person might be particularly warm and friendly or use humor to "head off" people who might be prejudiced against them.

According to Carol Miller and Anna Myers (1999) stigmatized individuals experience similar barriers to achieving goals as do people faced with psychological or physical impairments. Just as a person learns to compensate for a physical or psychological impairment, so too might stigmatized individuals compensate for prejudice.

Miller and her colleagues' research focuses on the stigma of being heavyweight and how heavyweight women attempt to control outcomes despite the prejudice of others. In one study of the impressions that heavyweight women make on others (Miller, Rothblum, Felicio, & Brand, 1995), they found that obese women who thought they might be interacting with someone who was prejudiced against them effectively deployed their social skills to create as positive an impression as their non-heavyweight counterparts.

We should note, by the way, that adopting compensatory strategies such as trying harder or being warm and friendly places an undue burden upon stigmatized individuals. Nonetheless, stigmatized individuals may hone these skills to prevent or reduce the impact of prejudice on their lives.

➤ CONCLUSION

> *"At certain times I have no race, I am* me. *When I set my hat at a certain angle and saunter down Seventh Avenue, Harlem City, feeling as snooty as the lions in front of Forty-Second Street Library, for instance . . . The cosmic Zora emerges. I belong to no race nor time. I am the eternal feminine with its string of beads."*
>
> Zora Neale Hurston

> *"I feel most colored when I am thrown against a sharp white background."*
>
> Zora Neale Hurston

Social psychological theorizing traditionally has assumed that the experience of being devalued has enormously damaging effects on a person's sense of identity and self-worth. What we've learned in this chapter is that targets of prejudice do not inevitably internalize negative views of themselves, nor are they necessarily plagued with low self-esteem. Rather, the experience of stigma depends upon what social context one is in and the meaning that one's social identity has in that context (Crocker, 1999). The research on stereotype threat, in which self-doubt among highly capable African-American students or women math students is evoked only when they risk being judged by a negative stereotype, clearly demonstrates how stigma may be experienced in some contexts, but not others.

Certain contexts in which stigmatized individuals find themselves can be deeply affirming. The mere presence of similarly stigmatized others, for instance, has an affirming effect on gay, bisexual, lesbian, and bulimic individuals (Frable et al., 1998). In a similar way, African-American students at predominately Black colleges possess positive self-views within an academic context (Allen, 1992), and students of color view themselves more positively when their instructor shares the same ethnicity (Brown, 1998).

In the last decade, social psychologists have begun to develop a greater understanding of the psychology of stigmatized individuals. To fully understand prejudice and its impact, we must not focus exclusively on the perpetrators of prejudice. By including the perspective of the stigmatized—their encounters with and responses to prejudice, how they interpret their experience as members of devalued groups, and how they cope with this experience—we develop further insights into the psychology of prejudice.

# 8

# Reducing Prejudice

What causes prejudice? In our attempt to determine the origins of prejudice, we have examined the roots of this complex phenomenon. What we have learned is that social psychology does not provide a generic, comprehensive theory of prejudice (Duckitt, 1992; Pettigrew, 1986). At best, there are many theories, each with its own level of analysis.

To understand the origins of prejudice, we have taken a sociopolitical and historical perspective to explain how certain characteristics—race, gender, and sexual orientation, for instance—have come to be important for distinguishing among various groups in society. We have also considered how group-level factors, such as competition between groups for scarce resources, contribute to prejudice (Sherif & Sherif, 1953). And we have realized that actual competition between groups is not a necessary prerequisite for intergroup conflict. In fact, the mere act of categorizing individuals into groups is sufficient to arouse in-group bias, prejudice, and discrimination (Tajfel, 1969, 1978).

We have also examined in great detail how individual-level factors contribute to prejudice. Compelling evidence indicates that although blatant racism is on the wane, a "newer" form of racial prejudice exists in which people express racial bias in more disguised ways. The theories of modern racism, aversive racism, and symbolic racism (Gaertner & Dovidio, 1986; McConahay, 1986; Sears, 1988) describe this contemporary form of racism. More recently, the basic ideas underlying contemporary forms of racism have been imported to the study of sexism, where it is assumed that sexist attitudes too have moved from blatant expressions to more subtle, covert forms.

Continuing with an individual-level analysis of prejudice, we considered how personality (authoritarianism), cognitive motivations (intolerance of ambiguity), adherence to social ideologies (religion, political conservatism), and general attitudes toward group domination (social dominance orientation) might make individuals susceptible to prejudice. And finally, we have gained an understanding of how stereotyping relates to prejudice. Stereotypes can operate outside of our awareness and color our perceptions of others without our conscious intent. Stereotypes are easily activated and, once activated, may influence our reactions to social groups. At a societal level, stereotypes serve the important function of allowing us to justify and rationalize the exploitation of certain groups over others.

Although it may seem that social psychological research has been more successful in identifying the causes of prejudice than proposing solutions, social psychologists have attempted to apply principles that underlie each of these levels of analyses to eliminate prejudice. In this final chapter, we will consider prejudice reduction techniques based upon each of these levels of analyses. First, we will consider individual-level interventions with an emphasis placed on the motivation to control stereotypical thinking. Next, we will consider group-based interventions to prejudice, with a primary focus on the contact hypothesis and its applications within the school system. We will then turn our attention to societal-level interventions to reduce prejudice. Finally, we'll revisit the issue of whether prejudice is inevitable that was addressed in Chapter 1.

## ➤ INDIVIDUAL-LEVEL INTERVENTIONS

Individual-level analyses of prejudice begin with the assumption that prejudice is rooted in how individuals think, feel, and behave toward members of certain groups. This "micro-level" analysis, then, considers how an individual's values, personality, and propensity to stereotype make people susceptible to prejudice.

Based upon this perspective, individual-level interventions primarily rely on strategies that decrease the likelihood that one will use stereotypes in making judgments about others. Let us consider in greater detail how controlling stereotypic thoughts may be a key to prejudice reduction. We'll begin this discussion by considering whether well-intentioned individuals who wish to avoid the use of stereotypes can possibly do so.

### Stereotype Suppression

> *"The highest possible stage in moral culture is when we recognize that we ought to control our thoughts."*
>
> *Charles Darwin (1871),* The Descent of Man

We spend a great deal of time trying to banish unwanted thoughts from our consciousness. When we try to avoid thinking about depressing events, former lovers, or the desire to consume yet another chocolate bar, we are exercising mental control (Wegner & Wenzlaff, 1998). Yet anyone who has attempted to suppress such unwanted thoughts realizes the surprising cost: Banished thoughts ironically return with a vengeance. As a simple example of how thought suppression has this paradoxical effect, take a few moments and try not to think about a white bear. If you're like Daniel Wegner's (1987) research participants, you now have a bizarre mental preoccupation with white bears! 

Why might suppressing thoughts of white bears, old flames, and food cravings result in the ironic return of those unwanted thoughts later? Wegner (1994) explains this "rebound" effect in terms of two processes that are instigated once people desire to avoid a particular thought. The first process is a monitoring process, believed to be automatic or effortless, that scans the mental environment to detect any signs of the unwanted thought. If the unwanted thought is detected, a second process is initiated. This second process, termed the operating process, replaces the unwanted thought with suitable distractor thoughts. This cycle of mental control (i.e., detection, then distraction) has the ironic effect of making the unwanted thought even more accessible. Because the monitoring process continuously checks for the unwanted thought, this thought is repeatedly primed and actually becomes more and more accessible. As long as the operating process is being exercised, however, attention will be directed away from the unwanted thought. But if the intention to avoid the unwanted thought is relaxed, the unwanted thought may *rebound*. The paradoxical consequence is that the more we try to avoid a particular thought, the more we may fail to do so.

Many have argued that the key to prejudice reduction lies in controlling stereotypic thoughts (Devine, 1989; Fiske, 1989). For a variety of reasons ranging from personal convictions to social norms, individuals may be motivated to avoid thinking about others in stereotypic terms. But what happens when these individuals "just say no" to stereotypic thinking? Does consciously suppressing such undesirable thoughts have the intended effects?

Wegner's research on the unintended effects of thought suppression suggests that efforts to suppress stereotypic thought may actually make it stronger. In a study of stereotype rebound effects (Macrae, Bodenhausen, Milne, & Jetten, 1994), college students were shown a photograph of a "skinhead" and were asked to spend five minutes writing a description of a typical day in his life. Participants were either explicitly instructed to avoid thinking in a stereotypic fashion while writing their descriptions (suppression group) or were given no such instructions (control group). After the passage was written, the experimenter showed the participants a photograph of a different skinhead, and asked them to write a second passage describing him. This time, though, participants were not given any special instructions to avoid stereotypical thinking.

Later, independent judges rated each passage in terms of its stereotypicality. Relative to the control group, participants who were asked to suppress their stereotypical thoughts while writing the first passage did so. But for the second writing task in which the admonishment to avoid stereotypes was lifted, participants in the suppression condition actually constructed passages that were even more stereotypic than passages written by participants who had never suppressed stereotypes in the first place. Consistent with Wegner's (1994) model of thought suppression, attempts to consciously control stereotypes led to stereotypes "flooding" participants' minds once temporary inhibitions became relaxed. Moreover, in a follow-up study, Macrae and his colleagues (1994) found that attempts to inhibit stereotypical thoughts had an effect on subsequent overt behavior. Participants who suppressed the stereotype of skinheads in their initial passages later chose to sit further away from a skinhead than participants in a control condition.

Since this initial study, a growing body of research has documented many paradoxical effects of stereotype suppression. For example, efforts to suppress stereotypes actually make the stereotype more accessible (Macrae et al., 1994) and memorable (Macrae, Bodenhausen, Milne, & Wheeler, 1996). Moreover, stereotype rebound also occurs when individuals spontaneously suppress stereotypes, rather than in response to an experimenter's explicit instruction to do so (Macrae, Bodenhausen, & Milne, 1998; Wyer, Sherman, & Stroesser, 1998). For these reasons, a number of researchers question whether stereotype suppression is a viable route to controlling stereotypical thinking (Bodenhausen & Macrae, 1996; Bodenhausen, Macrae, & Garst, 1998).

Other researchers are more optimistic about the efficacy of stereotype suppression as a stereotype control technique, and they suggest that stereotype suppression can succeed under certain circumstances (Monteith, Sherman, & Devine, 1998; Monteith, Spicer, & Tooman, 1998). Monteith and her colleagues point out that most studies of stereotype suppression to date have investigated stereotypes that most people are not motivated to control (e.g., skinheads, child molesters, and supermodels). Applying stereotypes to these groups, they argue, is fundamentally different from stereotyping other social groups that historically have been targets of prejudice and discrimination. Because many college students hold strong personal beliefs against stereotyping African Americans, women, and gays, suppressing stereotypes about these groups may not necessarily lead to the typical rebound effect.

Related to this issue of which group is being stereotyped, Monteith and her colleagues (1998) suggest that the most important factor in determining whether stereotype suppression will lead to a subsequent rebound of stereotypes is the personal attitude of the suppressor. If individuals have well-internalized personal beliefs against stereotyping (i.e., low-prejudiced individuals), then attempts at stereotype suppression may not have negative, unintended consequences. To test this hypothesis, Monteith and her colleagues replicated Macrae et al.'s (1994) experiment, except this time using gay males as the target stereotyped group. In this study, participants were given a photo of a gay, male couple and were asked to write a passage about a typical day in their life. Some participants were explicitly instructed to avoid stereotypical preconceptions in their description, whereas others were not. Results indicated that high- and low-prejudiced persons do, in fact, differ in susceptibility to the stereotype rebound effect. Contrary to Macrae et al.'s (1994) findings, low-prejudiced individuals did not show evidence of stereotype rebound or heightened accessibility following suppression. However, for individuals who held negative attitudes toward gays, suppressing stereotypic thoughts increased the accessibility of the stereotype.

In summary, it seems that stereotype suppression may be a means of controlling stereotypic thoughts. Although banishing stereotypic thoughts potentially may lead to greater mental preoccupation with the unwanted thoughts, rebound effects do not always occur. Suppressing stereotypes may be an effective strategy for social groups for which there are strong social norms prohibiting the use of stereotypes. Likewise, low-prejudiced individuals, who possess strong personal beliefs against stereotyping, are less susceptible to the rebound effect.

## Self-Regulation of Prejudiced Responses

Research on stereotype suppression suggests that control over stereotyping is possible. This is an important point, because it suggests that well-intentioned people can potentially reduce prejudicial responding (Kawakami, Dovidio, Moll, Hermsen, & Russen, 2000). An extensive program of research by Patricia Devine and Margo

Monteith (Devine, Monteith, Zuwerink, & Elliott, 1991; Devine & Monteith, 1993; Monteith, 1993) reveals that many individuals can avoid prejudicial responding, if they have the motivation and the ability to do so.

If you recall from our discussion of stereotype activation and application in Chapter 4, Patricia Devine (1989) argues that stereotypes are often highly accessible and easily used due to our socialization in a highly prejudiced society. That's the bad news. But another aspect of Devine's research provides considerable optimism for the reduction of prejudice. Many people strongly endorse egalitarian values that conflict with initial stereotypical thinking. Put simply, many people want to do and say the right thing, and the discrepancy between their spontaneous stereotypical thinking and their nonprejudiced standards leads to feelings of compunction. As a result, these individuals will be motivated to avoid subsequent stereotyping. Thus, guilt appears to be a key factor in reducing prejudice.

Thus far, we have discussed the self-regulation of prejudice in well-intentioned people who are motivated to avoid prejudiced responses. The challenge is to devise ways to motivate high-prejudiced individuals to similarly regulate their prejudiced responses. This may be difficult, because high-prejudiced individuals tend not to experience as strong a moral obligation to curb their prejudiced responses as do low-prejudiced individuals. Nonetheless, as Monteith and Walters (1998) point out, many high-prejudiced individuals possess an egalitarian self-image that defines egalitarianism in terms of equality of opportunity (as opposed to construing egalitarianism in terms of individualism). Perhaps the key to reducing prejudice in these individuals is to challenge them to regulate their behavior to achieve consistency with this value.

Devine and her colleagues caution us that self-regulation of prejudiced responses is not an all-or-nothing event. Rather, prejudice reduction is a *process* that involves motivation and ability, much like breaking a bad habit (Devine, Evett, & Vasquez-Suson, 1996). As in the breaking of any habit, one must first resolve to overcome the habit (i.e., motivation), and then develop the necessary skills (i.e., ability).

## ▶ GROUP-BASED INTERVENTIONS

According to group-level theories of prejudice, intergroup conflict often arises out of "social categorization," the tendency to categorize oneself and others into social groups. This categorization process can lead to prejudice, in the form of favoring one's in-group over out-groups. Prejudice reduction techniques based upon group-based theories of prejudice tend to emphasize how members of different groups can be brought together to work cooperatively and interdependently toward a common goal.

### The Contact Hypothesis

> See that man over there?
> Yes.
> Well, I hate him.
> But you don't know him.
> That's why I hate him.

Gordon Allport (1954, p. 265) cites this parable to illustrate the popular belief that prejudice grows out of ignorance and that if people only knew what members of other groups are really like, they would not stereotype, be prejudiced, or discriminate against them. This line of reasoning leads to a principle known as the **contact hypothesis,** which in its simplest form states that contact between members of different groups will improve relations between them.

Of course, Allport was not so naive as to believe that contact alone is sufficient to promote positive relations between members of different groups. Recognizing that contact can also heighten conflict between groups, Allport identified necessary conditions for contact to have the intended effect of reducing prejudice. Subsequent researchers have distilled Allport's original formulation to the four main conditions necessary to promote positive intergroup relations (Amir, 1969; Cook, 1962, 1985). Let's consider the four most significant conditions.

**COOPERATION**  Numerous studies have shown that cooperation between members of different social groups reduces both in-group favoritism and animosity toward out-group members (Desforges et al., 1991; Gaertner, Mann, Dovidio, Murrell, & Pomare, 1990; Rabbie, Benoise, Oosterbann, & Vissner, 1974; Worchel, 1986). The importance of working toward mutual goals can best be illustrated if we return to Muzafer Sherif's "Robbers Cave" experiment (discussed in Chapter 6). After creating a vicious rivalry between the Eagles and Rattlers, Sherif initially tried to reduce intergroup conflict by providing opportunities for contact between the groups, such as sitting together at movies or having meals together in the same building. Not only did this "mere contact" fail to reduce conflict, it actually intensified the conflict between the two groups. The contact in the dining hall, for instance, resulted in a food fight between the two groups.

After trying several other approaches to reduce the hostility, Sherif introduced several contrived "emergencies" that required both groups to work together to solve the problem. The plan worked beautifully. After several such incidents in which the boys had to cooperate to achieve desired goals, intergroup conflict was reduced sharply.

To maximize the effectiveness of cooperative interaction in reducing prejudice, the cooperative endeavor should result in a successful solution to the problem at hand. Indeed, Stephen Worchel and his colleagues (Worchel, Andreoli, & Folger, 1977) found that when a cooperative endeavor between experimentally created groups with a history of conflict ends in failure, dislike for out-group members was actually increased. What may happen in these circumstances is that the out-group serves as a ready-made scapegoat on which to blame the failure.

**EQUAL STATUS**  Another important factor associated with contact that has received wide attention is the principle of equal status. In many racially or ethnically mixed group settings, this is not easily achieved because individuals often come into the situation with status differences based upon group memberships. However, if group members are roughly equal in social or economic status, contact has positive effects on attitudes. White people, for instance, have more positive attitudes toward Blacks in general if they have friendships with African Americans of an equal or higher status (Jackman & Crane, 1986).

If equal status between groups cannot be achieved on socioeconomic dimensions, then at least the groups should be of equal status within the contact setting (Aronson, Blaney, Stephan, Sikes, & Snapp, 1978; Weigel, Wiser, & Cook, 1975). If, for example, a teacher treats White children better than Black children, no amount of intergroup contact will be helpful in reducing either group's prejudice.

ACQUAINTANCE POTENTIAL    A third condition necessary for successful contact involves close, personal contact that has "acquaintance potential" (Cook, 1978). Simply waiting in line next to someone from a different social group will not ensure a reduction in prejudice. Rather, contact over an extended period of time is necessary for people to get to know each other as individuals. Such repeated contact allows the opportunity to form friendships, and people with friends from other groups are more likely to have favorable attitudes toward those groups (Pettigrew, 1997).

Establishing friendships with someone from a different social group allows us to dispel negative stereotypes about the group. Moreover, the psychological intimacy associated with friendship allows us to empathize and identify with members of the other group.

INSTITUTIONAL SUPPORT    Finally, intergroup contact works best in eliminating intergroup hostility when contact occurs in a setting in which existing norms favor group equality. When those in authority, such as politicians, school principals, and other leaders unambiguously endorse egalitarian norms, intergroup contact is more successful.

## Applications of Contact Theory

SCHOOL DESEGREGATION    Among the documents considered by the U.S. Supreme Court in the *Brown v. Board of Education* case (1954) was a paper entitled "The Effect of Segregation and the Consequences of Desegregation: A Social Science Statement." In this Social Science Statement, 32 experts in race relations—anthropologists, psychologists, psychiatrists, and sociologists—argued that segregation has negative effects on the self-esteem of Black children and that *under certain conditions* desegregation could promote positive race relations. What were those conditions specified in the Social Science Statement?

> The available evidence also suggests the importance of consistent and firm enforcement of the new policy by those in authority. It indicates also the importance of such factors as: the absence of competition for a limited number of facilities or benefits; the possibility of contacts which permit individuals to learn about one another as individuals; and the possibility of equivalence of positions and functions among all of the participants within the unsegregated situation. (The Effect of Segregation, 1953, p. 437).

So did school desegregation actually reduce prejudice? The evidence is mixed (Cook, 1984; Miller & Brewer, 1984). In a review of 18 studies conducted during and after desegregation, Stephan (1978) concluded that about half of the studies (48%) showed that desegregation actually *increased* Whites' prejudice towards Blacks, and in only a few instances (16%) was desegregation associated with a reduction in prejudice. For Black Americans, desegregation tended to have the opposite effect: Desegregation reduced Blacks' prejudices toward Whites more frequently than it increased them.

School desegregation, then, has not always been successful in reducing prejudice. But does this finding mean that the contact hypothesis is flawed? Not at all, according to Stuart Cook (1984, 1985), one of the original writers of the Social Science Statement. Cook argues that desegregation did not have the intended effects on racial attitudes, largely because desegregation was seldom implemented in the manner specified by the contact hypothesis (and also recommended in the Social Science Statement). Desegregation was often implemented by reluctant authorities, and sometimes under the threat of legal sanction (violating the "institutional support" requirement for effective intergroup contact); children from different backgrounds came into the situation with preexisting differences in status based upon group membership; and typical classroom activities foster competitive, rather than cooperative, experiences.

Thus, desegregation has rarely been implemented in ways consistent with the major conditions specified in the contact hypothesis. In the next section, we consider a classroom intervention deliberately designed to take advantage of the principles of effective contact.

COOPERATIVE LEARNING    Cooperative learning programs, developed by social psychologists to improve intergroup relations within classrooms (Hertz-Lazarowitz & Miller, 1992; Johnson & Johnson, 1992; Slavin, 1978; Weigel, Wiser, & Cook, 1975) require that students work together to achieve common goals. Consider, for example, the *jigsaw method* developed by Elliot Aronson (Aronson et al., 1978; Aronson & Thibodeau, 1992). Just as in a jigsaw puzzle, each piece—each student's contribution—is essential for completion of the final project. Here's how it works: The teacher assigns each student to a heterogeneous six-member group. Not coincidentally, the teacher also divides the lesson into six parts and gives each child an opportunity to become an "expert" on one part of the lesson. The students learn their own part of the lesson and then have the responsibility to teach what they've learned to the other group members so they can all do well on the test. In essence, the students in each group are dependent on one another to learn the material effectively.

What is the benefit of such cooperative learning techniques? First and foremost, cooperative learning has been shown to improve children's academic performance. But even more important, cooperative learning boosts children's conflict-management skills and helps them appreciate individual and cultural differences. Three decades of research have shown that cooperative learning techniques like the jigsaw method significantly improve intergroup relations. Cross-ethnic friendships and liking for other students are increased by this technique (Johnson & Johnson, 1992; Slavin, 1985; Weigel et al., 1975), and the self-esteem of minority group children is enhanced as well (Blaney et al., 1977; Johnson & Johnson, 1992).

Cooperative learning techniques work because all of the necessary conditions for effective contact are fulfilled: The students must cooperate to achieve their goals, the students are accorded equal status in the learning situation, the students have ample opportunity to interact with each other and develop friendships, and the intergroup contact has the clear approval and support of an authority, the class-room teacher.

## How Does Contact Change Intergroup Attitudes?

In his review of evidence relating to the contact hypothesis, Thomas Pettigrew (1998) notes that the original formulation of the contact hypothesis specifies *when* contact is likely to change intergroup attitudes, but it fails to explain *how* and *why* the change occurs. According to Pettigrew, four explanations are commonly offered to explain how contact leads to positive attitude change. First, intergroup contact may change attitudes because it provides participants an opportunity to acquire new and more accurate information about the out-group. Repeated contact with out-group members can lay the ground for disconfirmation of negative stereotypes (Rothbart & John, 1985) and also lead to the discovery of similarities between the in-group and the out-group, which may lead to greater liking for the out-group (Stephan & Stephan, 1984).

Second, contact may change attitudes through a process of dissonance reduction. Dissonance theory (Festinger, 1957) suggests that one way to change people's attitudes is first to change their behavior. If contact situations provide an opportunity to engage in positive social interactions with members of a disliked group, then this behavior is inconsistent with prejudiced attitudes. Consequently, people may resolve the inconsistency between the new behavior and prejudiced attitudes by changing their attitudes toward the out-group.

Third, repeated contact generates affectional ties. Contact with out-group members under optimal conditions can be positively rewarding and lead to intergroup friendships. Positive emotions generated by friendships may "spill over" to the out-group as a whole (Cook, 1962).

Finally, intergroup contact provides insight into in-groups as well as out-groups. Interacting with out-group members leads to a reappraisal of in-group norms and customs as the "only" way to manage the social world. In fact, increased contact with diverse groups facilitates a broadening acceptance of others, which is associated with a reduction in prejudice (Pettigrew, 1996).

## Models of Intergroup Contact

Although successful contact experiences may improve intergroup relations in the immediate situation, contact does not always generalize beyond the immediate situation to beliefs about the out-group as a whole. As an example, Jennifer, a White fourth-grade student, may emerge from a jigsaw exercise with Jamal convinced that he is a great person, but she still may retain a negative attitude toward African Americans in general. Jennifer may decide that Jamal is terrific because he is "different" from other African Americans, allowing her to keep her stereotypic beliefs intact.

This example demonstrates that generalization from the individual to the out-group is not an automatic process. What type of contact will successfully generalize beyond the immediate situation? How should contact be optimally structured in order to change the way that we cognitively represent groups? We learned in Chapter 6

(Intergroup Relations) that once we place people in separate groups, we treat them differently. How do different factors of intergroup contact (e.g., cooperation, personal interaction) operate to reduce the way we categorize others?

Several different models of intergroup contact have been developed that address these issues. Each of these models has its origins in social identity theory (SIT) and acknowledges the central role of social categorization (i.e., making "us" versus "them" distinctions) in creating intergroup bias. Moreover, these models assume that when group boundaries are salient, individuals will respond to each other in terms of their corresponding group memberships rather than their personal identities. Despite this common theoretical base, each model makes somewhat different predictions.

**THE PERSONALIZATION MODEL: DECATEGORIZATION** Brewer and Miller (1984) argue that intergroup contact is more effective when in-group-out-group distinctions are not salient. In other words, the ideal contact experience is person-to-person, allowing participants to get to know each other *as individuals*. A lack of personalized contact—as when individuals interact with each other as representatives of different social categories—makes it more difficult to reduce prejudice. Thus, the **personalization model** posits that contact will be effective if it consists of highly personalized rather than category-based interactions. According to Brewer and Miller, personalized interactions reduce prejudice by encouraging people to view out-group members in individuated ways, which may lead to "decategorization" or a decreased tendency to use social category membership as a basis for future interactions.

Support for the effectiveness of personalized contact with out-group members comes from experimental studies with artificially created groups (Bettencourt, Brewer, Rogers-Croak, & Miller, 1992; Miller, Brewer, & Edwards, 1985). In the typical paradigm, participants are arbitrarily assigned to one of two groups ("overestimators" or "underestimators") ostensibly on the basis of their performance in a dot estimation task. To increase identification with their group, members first spend time working together on a project. Then four-person teams are created, comprised of two overestimators and two underestimators. At this point, the independent variable is introduced. Some teams are encouraged to socialize and get to know each other (i.e., a "personalized" approach), whereas other teams are instructed to be highly task oriented (i.e., a "depersonalized" approach). Consistent with Brewer and Miller's decategorization model, the teams that adopted a "personalized" approach exhibited less in-group bias than those who adopted a more "depersonalized" model of interaction.

Critics of the personalization model point out that while personalization may make for a positive interaction experience, the effects may not generalize to attitudes toward the group as a whole (Hewstone, 1996; Rothbart & John, 1985). This is particularly true if the out-group member is not viewed as a "typical" member of the out-group. For instance, if participants become so personally acquainted with each other that they lose sight of group memberships, then they have no reason to generalize beyond the individual to the out-group category.

**MUTUAL INTERGROUP DIFFERENTIATION MODEL: MAINTAINING A DISTINCT SOCIAL IDENTITY** Taking an approach that diverges sharply from the personalization model, Hewstone and Brown (1986) argue that contact should be experienced as an *intergroup* interaction rather than an *interpersonal* one. Their **mutual intergroup differentiation model** recommends positive intergroup contact in which group membership remains salient, and the groups are given distinct but complementary roles to play in achieving a common goal. Hewstone and Brown argue that mutual intergroup differentiation reduces bias in two ways. First, making group affiliations salient ensures that the participants "see each other as representatives of their groups and not merely as 'exceptions to the rule'" (Hewstone & Brown, 1986, p. 18). Second, recognizing each group's experience and area of expertise encourages both groups to respect and value the other's contribution (Dovidio, Gaertner, & Validzic, 1998).

At first blush, it may seem that the distinct social identity model recommends a paradoxical strategy to reducing prejudice—that to successfully generalize beyond the contact situation, in-group-out-group distinctions must be maintained. However, this model recommends maintaining group distinctions while simultaneously optimizing the recommended conditions (i.e., cooperation to achieve superordinate goals) for a successful contact experience.

This model, of course, is not without its critics. Such intergroup contact may reinforce perceptions that the groups are distinctly different and unwittingly perpetuate in-group-out-group categorization (Brewer & Brown, 1998). Moreover, intergroup encounters may provoke greater anxiety than interpersonal ones, thereby having a negative effect on intergroup relations (Brewer & Brown, 1998; Hewstone, 1996). Thus, the effectiveness of the cooperative contact between the groups is the critical ingredient ensuring the success of this approach.

Common In-Group Identity Model: Recategorization    A third model of successful intergroup contact shares the same premise as Brewer and Miller's (1985) personalization model that intergroup conflict may be influenced by the ways that group members view group boundaries. Rather than decreasing the salience of group boundaries, however, this model alters the nature of them.

The **common in-group identity model** (Gaertner et al., 1989, 1993, 1994, 1999) posits that contact will be effective when members' perceptions of two separate groups ("us" and "them") become one inclusive category ("we"). According to this model, one reason that superordinate goals are a key element in successful contact experiences is that participants' representations of the groups are "recategorized" by creating a superordinate identity as "one group." Thus, redefining out-group members as in-group members exploits the in-group bias effect, increasing attraction to those former out-group members. It is further assumed that this common in-group identity may generalize to other members of the out-group who may not be involved in the immediate situation.

Empirical support for the common in-group identity model comes from both laboratory and field studies. Environmental factors that influence the salience of group boundaries, such as proximity based upon seating arrangements (Gaertner, Mann, Murrell, & Dovidio, 1989), shared positive mood (Dovidio, Gaertner, Isen, Rust, & Guerra, 1998), or similar style of dress (Dovidio, Gaertner, Isen, & Lowrance, 1995) can reduce intergroup bias by inducing members of different groups to perceive themselves as one group. And, of course, different factors of the contact experience itself, such as cooperating to achieve a common goal, have a similar effect on perceptions of group boundaries (Gaertner, Mann, Dovidio, Murrell, & Pomare, 1990).

"Recategorization" appears to be a very promising approach to the reduction of prejudice. But as Hewstone (1996) warned, it is unclear at this time whether it can overcome antagonism between groups with a history of conflict (i.e., non-laboratory groups). Tests of the common in-group identity model in field settings have yielded support for the model, however. In one such study, Gaertner and his colleagues (Gaertner, Rust, Dovidio, Bachman, & Anastasio, 1994) surveyed more than 1,300 students in a multi-ethnic high school to determine whether their perceptions of the student body as "one group" or "separate groups" was correlated with their feelings toward both their in-group and various out-groups. Consistent with the common in-group identity model, the more that students felt that they belonged to one group, the lower the intergroup bias.

## An Integration

Social psychological research demonstrates that all three models of contact can, under appropriate conditions, successfully reduce prejudice and discrimination. Although each of the models has roots in social identity theory, the models make different assumptions about what constitutes optimal intergroup contact. How might we resolve these seemingly contradictory models of contact?

In an answer to this question, Pettigrew (1998) advocates viewing the models in a sequential fashion to resolve the apparent contradictions between them. He conceptualizes intergroup contact as occurring in three stages. In the early stages of contact, reducing the saliency of group boundaries ("decategorization") is advantageous because personalized contact overcomes the initial anxiety associated with contact and leads to increased attraction for individual out-group members. Later, under conditions of repeated contact, group membership must be made salient ("mutual intergroup differentiation") to maximize the generalization of contact effects to out-group members not in the immediate situation. In the final stages of contact, "recategorization" becomes possible in which the "we" and "they" boundaries become blurred. Pettigrew, however, acknowledges that many interacting groups never reach this final stage of an all-encompassing group identification. We'll return briefly to these models of intergroup contact in the following section as we discuss societal-level interventions to reduce group conflict.

## ➤ SOCIETAL-LEVEL INTERVENTIONS

So far, we have examined prejudice reduction efforts that are directed at the individual or the intergroup context. Because prejudice and discrimination are embedded within a larger sociopolitical context in which groups differ in access to economic and political power, it is necessary to consider macro-level approaches to reducing prejudice and discrimination. In this section, we will consider two issues at the center of the debate about intergroup relations: the desirability of different models of intergroup relations and the controversy over affirmative action.

## Promoting Social Harmony: Assimilation or Multiculturalism?

The United States has always been a nation of immigrants, both voluntary and forced. As a result, its inhabitants have had to confront complex and deeply ingrained ethnic divisions. Moreover, in recent years we have witnessed a heightened awareness of the increasing ethnic diversity within the United States. According to the U.S. Census Bureau, non-Hispanic Whites currently account for 72 percent of the population, Blacks 12 percent, Hispanics 11 percent, Asians 4 percent, and the remaining 1 percent consists of American Indians. By the year 2050, the Census predicts that Hispanics will account for about 25 percent of the population, Blacks 14 percent, Asians 9 percent, American Indians 1 percent, with the non-Hispanic White population declining to 51 percent (U.S. Census Bureau, 1996).

Not only are the demographics of the United States changing in profound ways, but so too are the notions of what best constitutes the ideal model of intergroup relations. The traditionally popular approach to intergroup relations has been to encourage people of every color and background to adopt a superordinate identity as "one America." This philosophy is reflected in our national motto, *e. pluribus unum* (from many, one). Today, however, there no longer seems to be a consensus about what that should mean.

Traditionally, assimilation has been seen as the goal, or ideal, in American society. Assimilation typically has been conceptualized in two ways. Great emphasis has been placed on the idea of America as a "melting pot," in which all new immigrants can be transformed into Americans. In this type of *melting-pot assimilation*, citizens cease to think of themselves in terms of their ethnicity and regard themselves instead as Americans. In essence, the concept of the melting pot assumes that diverse ethnic groups will forsake their cultural traditions to form a new creation, an entirely new ethnicity called "Americans." *Minority group assimilation* involves nondominant groups adopting the language, customs, and values of the dominant group. In this form of assimilation, groups are expected to shed their cultural uniqueness quickly and as completely as possible and take on the core values of the dominant group.

Critics scoff at the concept of assimilation, arguing that assimilation simply means little more than "Anglo conformity"—a demand that all minority groups conform to the expectations of the dominant, White group (Gordon, 1964). Moreover, critics contend, people are motivated to retain their cultural heritage, which is important to the individual's self-concept. Asking people to deny their cultural heritage is like asking them to deny their identity. As a result, proponents of **multiculturalism** argue that the best way to achieve social harmony is to recognize and appreciate our diversity. Multiculturalism implies that various groups in society have mutual respect for one another's culture, and that each group in society retains distinct cultural characteristics. Whereas the assimilationist approach seeks the elimination of ethnic boundaries, the multiculturalist approach seeks to preserve them.

Critics of multiculturalism worry that preserving ethnic boundaries promotes separatism and division and may possibly lead to a cultural "Balkanization" of the United States. Maintaining group boundaries, they argue, will inevitably provoke conflict and discrimination.

This debate concerning the relative merits of assimilationist and multicultural approaches to achieving social harmony has largely involved political scientists, economists, and sociologists. Only very recently, however, have social psychologists begun to explicitly address this issue (Hornsey & Hogg, 2000a; Hornsey & Hogg, 2000b; Wolsko, Park, Judd, & Wittenbrink, 2000). In many ways, the tension between the assimilationist and multicultural approaches reflects the debate among social psychologists about how best to structure intergroup contact to reduce prejudice and discrimination.

In arguing that the best way to improve group relations is to bring separate groups ("we" and "they") into an integrated whole by encouraging group members to categorize at a superordinate level ("us"), the common in-group identity model (Gaertner et al., 1989) of intergroup contact bears a striking resemblance to the assimilationist model. The assimilationist model, which encourages ethnic groups to minimize their ethnic distinctions in favor of a common group identity, advocates recategorization of different groups into one group. In fact, the dominant social psychological approach to prejudice reduction has operated under the similar assumption that rigid in-group-out-group distinctions perpetuate prejudice, and therefore, that the reduction of prejudice can be achieved through techniques that reduce the saliency of group boundaries (Wolsko et al., 2000).

Other social psychologists argue that reducing the saliency of group boundaries can be an impossible task if group members do not want to relinquish their ethnic identity, and that to attempt to do so may very well destroy important differences between groups. Malcolm X encapsulated this notion in stating, "Black will never be white. White will never be black. And that is as it should be." The mutual intergroup differentiation model of contact (Hewstone & Brown, 1986)—similar to the multiculturalism approach—advocates maintaining group distinctions and appreciating the similarities and differences between groups.

Which approach works best to promote social harmony between groups, the assimilationist (i.e., nurturing a common group identity) or multicultural approach (i.e., striving to maintain as much of our group identities as possible)? It seems likely that a "middle ground" is necessary in which ethnic identities are nourished within the context of a superordinate identity (Hornsey & Hogg, 2000a; Hornsey & Hogg, 2000c). This approach, dubbed *integration* by John Berry (1984), assumes that identification with both the subgroup and the superordinate group can exist simultanously. Undoubtedly, harmonious intergroup relations depend upon both the appreciation of group differences and the acknowledgement of a common superordinate identity as members of humanity.

## Legislating Against Discrimination

> *"Not only are we using the tools of persuasion, but we've got to use tools of coercion. Not only is this thing a process of education, but it is also a process of legislation."*
>
> Martin Luther King, Jr.

In Gordon Allport's classic book *The Nature of Prejudice* (1954), he titled one chapter "Ought There to Be a Law?" This considered the role of legislation in reducing discrimination and prejudice. Legislation, Allport argued, may be "one of the major methods of reducing, not only public discrimination, but private prejudice as well"

(p. 477). Is this legal approach to reducing prejudice and discrimination a good idea? Yes, for several reasons.

First, laws against discrimination help to ease the plight of minority group members by reducing the impact of prejudice on their lives. Legislation is not aimed at reducing prejudice directly. As you know, it is impossible to legislate against prejudice—we simply cannot tell people how they *should* think or feel. But through legislation we can lessen discriminatory *behavior*, which impacts the everyday lives of minority group members.

Second, laws establish *norms* for appropriate behavior. Laws are essentially legal norms that create a standard for the expected behavior. As a result of civil rights laws that have equalized the treatment of Blacks and Whites in the United States, people have reevaluated their beliefs about what is right and wrong. Even if we disapprove of a particular law, the law still reminds us what our conduct should be.

Finally, social psychologists have long known that behaving differently often precedes thinking differently. Through the process of dissonance reduction, people will often change their attitudes to correspond to their behavior (Leippe & Eisenstadt, 1994). Thus, legislation against discriminatory behaviors indirectly decreases prejudice.

## The Case of Affirmative Action

Since Allport's (1954) writing, the Civil Rights Act, with its sweeping antidiscrimination provisions, was signed into law in July of 1964. However, this legislation did not create true equality of conditions immediately because, as recognized by President Lyndon B. Johnson, "You do not take a person who for years has been hobbled by chains, and liberate him, bring him up to the starting line, and then say, 'You are free to compete with all the others'" (quoted by Hacker, 1992, p. 119).

In 1965 President Johnson signed Executive Order 11246 that directed all federal contractors to take "affirmative action to ensure that minority applicants are employed, and that employees are treated during employment, without regard to their race, color, religion, sex, or national origin." In subsequent orders, affirmative action has been expanded to include requirements that contractors must (a) make an active effort to recruit women and minorities where they are underrepresented and (b) develop a specific set of goals and timetables for achieving greater representation of minority group members and women in jobs.

Affirmative action, designed to remedy the effects of past and present institutional discrimination, has become an increasingly controversial issue. Part of the controversy stems from the American public's lack of knowledge about what affirmative action comprises, contributing to confusion about this complex policy. Let's begin our discussion of affirmative action by first defining the term.

WHAT IS AFFIRMATIVE ACTION?    **Affirmative action** occurs whenever an organization "expends energy to make sure there is no discrimination in employment or education" (American Psychological Association, 1996, p. 5). Affirmative action employers go out of their way (take positive action) to achieve a balanced representation of workers. Affirmative action differs from *equal employment opportunity* (EEO) policies. Equal employment opportunity policies simply prohibit intentional discrimination, but do not take corrective action to ensure fairness in hiring and promotion. Compared to affirmative action policies, EEO policies may be viewed as passive.

In considering affirmative action policies, a distinction can be made between two types, classical affirmative action and new (more recent) affirmative action. (Crosby & Cordova, 1996). *Classical affirmative action* was instituted in 1967 by Lyndon Johnson's Executive Order 11246, which mandated that employers monitor their utilization of individuals from target groups (e.g., women) to determine whether it reflects the availability of talent in a community. If an affirmative action employer determines that it is underutilizing people from one of the designated categories (e.g., a university employs few women in the humanities despite a large available pool of women with Ph.D.s in the humanities), the employer must devise a plan to correct the imbalance. The plan might include developing strategies to improve recruitment and increase retention of individuals from underrepresented groups or allocating resources to dispel images of the organization as hostile to women and/or minorities. Thus, classical affirmative action is a monitoring system in which the organization expends energy to make sure that equal opportunity exists for members of traditionally disadvantaged groups.

More recently, *new affirmative action* policies have involved preferential treatment or "set-asides" in which a certain percentage of jobs or other opportunities go to minorities or women without regard to their qualifications. This approach to affirmative action is not very common (Crosby & Cordova, 1996), because from a legal standpoint it is much more difficult to justify than classical affirmative action. Nonetheless, it is these newer affirmative action policies that have received a disproportionate amount of attention from critics.

THE AFFIRMATIVE ACTION DEBATE  Critics of affirmative action believe that people should be selected for positions based on merit alone and that preferential treatment for minority and female applicants moves the United States away from the goal of achieving a truly "color-blind" and "gender-blind" society. Preference for minority or female applicants is simply another form of discrimination, reverse discrimination, which forces many Whites (or males) to unfairly pay the price for past discrimination.

According to proponents of affirmative action, past discrimination has left minorities in a disadvantaged position, so that "color-blind" or "gender-blind" admission or hiring is *not* really fair: Minorities and women, after generations of discrimination, do not have all the advantages that White males have. To achieve even a semblance of racial or gender equality today, some kind of racial or gender preferences must be made in hiring and admission procedures.

Another line of argument presented by critics of affirmative action maintains that affirmative action was not meant to be permanent, but was instead intended as a temporary measure to level the playing field. Although some critics might concede that affirmative action may have been necessary 30 years ago, they argue that the playing field is fairly level today. Proponents of affirmative action, in contrast, say that the playing field is far from level and that affirmative action is necessary until equality is attained.

These debates cannot be resolved here. However, psychological research on affirmative action has dealt with two other criticisms of affirmative action. One criticism is that affirmative action has had the unintentional effect of increasing prejudice toward minorities and women. The other criticism is that affirmative action undermines the self-esteem of women and minorities. Let's consider these issues in detail.

**DOES AFFIRMATIVE ACTION STIGMATIZE BENEFICIARY GROUP MEMBERS?** In recent years, affirmative action has come under attack from some African-American conservatives who argue that such policies have the unintended effect of reinforcing negative stereotypes about beneficiary groups among the dominant group. Shelby Steele (1990) contends that the very presence of affirmative action reinforces the perception that minority groups are inferior and thus require special assistance to succeed in the workplace. Thus, from his perspective, affirmative action creates majority group resentment, which can be damaging to African Americans and other minorities in the long run.

Has affirmative action served to enhance or worsen attitudes held by dominant group members toward beneficiary groups? Much of the relevant research on this issue has focused on how dominant group members evaluate the competence of individuals who are direct beneficiaries of preferential selection procedures (Esses & Seligman, 1996). Laboratory studies by Heilman and her colleagues (Heilman, Block, & Lucas, 1992) show that both males and females tend to assume that females hired under affirmative action programs are less competent than those selected without affirmative action. Other studies that ask respondents to evaluate Blacks and other minorities report similar findings (Garcia, Erskine, Hawn, & Casmay, 1981; Summers, 1991). In one study (Garcia et al., 1981), researchers had White male and female undergraduates evaluate minority applicants to graduate school in psychology. The applicant was either accepted or rejected, and there either was or was not an affirmative action policy statement. Results indicated that the minority applicant was evaluated less favorably when commitment to affirmative action was emphasized than when it was not mentioned.

These studies dealt with reactions to individual group members who benefited from affirmative action programs. Does this stigmatization generalize to evaluations of the beneficiary group as a whole, as S. Steele (1990) claims? Unfortunately, the answer may be yes. Maio and Esses (1998) provided 51 Canadian undergraduates with information about a new, relatively unfamiliar immigrant group, Surinamers. The information they disseminated was always positive, stating that the group would contribute to the Canadian economy. Information in the experimental condition also mentioned that the Surinamers would be eligible for affirmative action. Their results showed that the group was perceived as less competent and less skilled when affirmative action was mentioned than when it was not.

Thus, dominant group members typically view individual beneficiaries of affirmative action programs as less competent and qualified than those selected without affirmative action, and this effect may indeed generalize to evaluations of the beneficiary group as a whole. To mitigate these stigmatizing effects, the woman or minority member's accomplishments and contributions to the organization should be emphasized to others in the workplace.

**DOES AFFIRMATIVE ACTION UNDERMINE THE SELF-ESTEEM OF WOMEN AND RACIAL MINORITIES?** In his book *The Content of Our Character*, Shelby Steele (1990) echoes Martin Luther King, Jr. when he asks that people judge African Americans by "the content of our character" and not "the color of our skin." His opposition to affirmative action partly stems from his belief that the policy serves to undermine the self-esteem of the very individuals who are intended to benefit from the program. For example, women and members of racial minorities may commonly encounter the view from others that "you're only here to fill a quota—you're not really qualified." This may prompt women and minorities to discount their own qualifications, leading to self-doubt about their own abilities. What is the evidence to support this claim?

There is some indication that minority group members may have to contend with a cloud of suspicion regarding their competence. In one survey study of African-American, Hispanic-American, and American-Indian students at two elite colleges (Traux, Cordova, Wood, Wright, & Crosby, 1998), nearly three-quarters (73%) of the students acknowledged that they had wondered whether their peers questioned their intellectual abilities because of affirmative action. About half (47%) of the students believed that their *professors* were suspicious about the reasons for their admittance. Thus, these students clearly acknowledged the stigmatizing effects of affirmative action. However, this study did not examine whether this cloud of suspicion led the students to second-guess their own abilities.

Although many experimental studies have explored the question of whether affirmative action has adverse effects on beneficiaries in terms of their self-evaluations of ability, virtually all the evidence regarding the negative consequences for self-esteem is based on the reactions of women as beneficiaries. In a series of laboratory studies, Heilman (1994) has shown that women felt more insecure about their leadership ability and task performance when they were told they were selected for a leadership role on the basis of sex rather than merit. But the selection procedure in this study differs importantly from the procedures employed in actual affirmative action programs, where organizations attempt to hire on the basis of *both* group status and qualifications. In one study in which women were told that selection procedures considered both merit and sex (Major, Feinstein, & Crocker, 1994), for instance, women's self-evaluations did not suffer negative consequences.

Few experimental studies have examined racial minorities' psychological reactions to race-based preferential selection. However, one study (Stanus, Winfred, & Doverspike, 1996) suggests that the negative consequences of being preferentially selected are muted as long as Hispanic and African Americans do not feel that they are less qualified than other applicants.

Taken together, these studies suggest that affirmative action programs are more likely to have negative consequences for the self-esteem of women and minorities when the selection procedures provide no information about qualifications. In everyday situations outside the laboratory, members of beneficiary groups typically do not perceive affirmative action to be based only on group status (Taylor, 1994). This may explain why many survey and interview studies have found no adverse effects in such areas as job satisfaction, motivation, and life satisfaction for women and minorities who work for affirmative action employers (Ayers, 1992; Taylor, 1994).

## Summary

The societal debate about affirmative action policies has become increasingly polarized. According to the American Psychological Association (1998), affirmative action is "a policy that suffers an identity crisis" because there is great variability in what the public thinks affirmative action entails. Many people think affirmative action is a "numbers game" synonymous with quotas, "set-asides," and the hiring and/or promotion of less qualified women and minorities at the expense of White males. Evidence suggests that public reactions to various affirmative action programs differ dramatically depending upon how affirmative action is defined and implemented (Bobocel, Son Hing, Davey, Stanley, & Zanna, 1998; Pratkanis & Turner, 1996).

When considering the impact of affirmative action programs in reducing prejudice and discrimination, it is important to consider outcomes for both individuals and for a group as a whole (Esses & Seligman, 1996). Social psychological research that has focused on perceptions of individual beneficiaries of affirmative action programs suggest that their qualifications are often discounted by out-group members. Moreover, some studies suggest that affirmative action beneficiaries may doubt their own qualifications, but only when they have been led to believe that they succeeded because of their group membership alone. When affirmative action policies are based on both qualifications and group membership, beneficiaries do not question their abilities and qualifications.

At the group level, the existence of affirmative action programs may exacerbate negative perceptions of beneficiary groups. However, it is important to keep in mind that affirmative action programs have created important opportunities for individuals who experience societal discrimination. Data on the employment, income, and occupational attainment of women and minorities before and after the enactment of affirmative action indicate that, in general, gains have been made (Burnstein, 1978; Konrad & Linnehan, 1995; Murrell & Jones, 1996; Smith & Welch, 1984). Although the existence of affirmative action can cause less favorable perceptions of beneficiary groups in the short term, improvements in group status might lead to more favorable perceptions of minority groups in the long term.

Although affirmative action may have unintended negative consequences at both the individual and group levels, affirmative action remains one of the more effective ways to address racism and sexism in our society. By removing discriminatory barriers, affirmative action may ultimately be "a cure for prejudice" (Pratkanis & Turner, 1996, p. 128).

## ➤ Is Prejudice Inevitable?

> *"Racism is like the local creeping kudzu vine that swallows whole forests and abandoned houses; if you don't keep pulling up the roots it will grow back faster than you can destroy it."*
>
> Alice Walker, In Search of Our Mother's Gardens, *1983*

This statement made by Alice Walker, although referring specifically to racism, is applicable to prejudice in general. For those of you who do not live in the American South and may be unfamiliar with kudzu, it is a seemingly unstoppable vine that can grow over a foot a day in the summer. In many ways, prejudice may seem similarly unstoppable because so many forces conspire against harmonious intergroup relations.

In Chapter 1, we posed the question of whether prejudice is inevitable. After considering the many ways that prejudice is fostered—at the individual, intergroup, and societal levels—you may be tempted to conclude that it is. It does seem that certain psychological processes, such as the tendency to categorize in order to simplify our social world, may be inevitable. Intergroup processes, in which we perceive ourselves and others in terms of group membership, lead us to exaggerate differences between and among groups, significantly adding to the potential for conflict. And finally, prejudice and discrimination are embedded within the larger sociocultural system. Institutionalized discrimination, for instance, serves to restrict the choices, opportunities, and rights of groups of individuals. Stereotypes about disadvantaged groups then emerge to justify the existing social arrangements.

Admittedly, all this paints a pessimistic picture for promoting nonprejudice. Ironically, though, the fact that prejudice stems from so many causes suggests many promising paths to reduce, if not eliminate, it. Group-level interventions that encourage cooperation, the appreciation of group differences, and the acknowledgement of a common identity can help to reduce conflict between groups. Societal-level interventions, such as legislating against discrimination to blunt institutional discrimination, serve to create positive, widespread change.

Unlike societal strategies or even group-level strategies, individual strategies to reduce prejudice have less widespread impact. But we must not forget individual responsibility in promoting greater social tolerance and harmony. Prejudice reduction at the individual level is a continual process, one that involves monitoring not only our tendency to think stereotypically but our outward expressions of prejudice as well. But for those of us motivated to do so, it is an achievable goal.

It is clear that the way to eradicate prejudice is by pulling up the roots—roots that are firmly planted in the individual, in group dynamics, and in the larger society. And this may be, as Alice Walker suggests, an unceasing process—one that is not achievable in our lifetimes. But working toward eliminating centuries of bias based upon race, gender, sexual orientation, and other factors is a worthy challenge that we must undertake.

# REFERENCES

Abe, J.S., & Zane, N.W.S. (1990). Psychological maladjustment among Asian and White American college students: Controlling for confounds. *Journal of Consulting and Clinical Psychology, 37,* 437–444.

Abramowitz, A.I. (1994). Issue evolution reconsidered: Racial attitudes and partisanship in the U.S. electorate. *American Journal of Political Science, 38,* 1–24.

Abrams, D., & Hogg, M. (1988). Comments on the motivational status of self-esteem in social identity and intergroup discrimination. *European Journal of Social Psychology, 18,* 317–334.

Adams, H.E., Wright, L.W., & Lohr, B.A. (1996). Is homophobia associated with homosexual arousal? *Journal of Abnormal Psychology, 105,* 440–445.

Adorno, T.W., Frenkel-Brunswik, E., Levinson, D.J., Sanford, R.N. (1950). *The authoritarian personality.* New York: Harper Row.

Agnew, C.R., Thompson, V.D., Smith, V.A., Gramzow, R.H., & Curey, D.P. (1993). Proximal and distal predictors of homophobia: Framing the multivariate roots of out-group rejection. *Journal of Applied Social Psychology, 23,* 2013–2042.

Alien, W.R. (1992). The color of success: African American college outcomes at predominantly White and historically Black public colleges and universities. *Harvard Educational Review, 62,* 25–44.

Allison, K.W. (1998). Stress and oppressed category membership. In J.T. Swim and C. Stangor (Eds.), *Prejudice: The target's perspective.* New York: Academic Press.

Allon, N. (1982). The stigma of overweight in everyday life. In B. Wolman (Ed.), *Psychological aspects of obesity: A handbook* (pp. 130–174). New York: Van Nostrand-Reinhold.

Allport, G.W. (1950). Prejudice: A problem in psychological and social causation. *Journal of Social Issues, Supplement Series, Number 4.*

Allport, G.W. (1954). *The nature of prejudice.* Reading, MA: Addison-Wesley.

Allport, G., & Kramer, B.M. (1946). Some roots of prejudice. *Journal of Psychology, 22,* 9–39.

Altemeyer, B. (1981). *Right-wing authoritarianism.* Winnipeg: University of Manitoba Press.

Altemeyer, B. (1988). *Enemies of freedom: Understanding right-wing authoritarianism.* San Francisco: Jossey-Bass.

Altemeyer, B. (1994). Reducing prejudice in right-wing authoritarians. In M.P. Zanna & J.M. Olson (Eds.), *The psychology of prejudice: The Ontario symposium, Vol. 7* (pp. 131–148). Hillsdale, NJ: Erlbaum.

Altemeyer, B. (1996). *The authoritarian specter.* Cambridge, MA: Harvard University Press.

Altemeyer, B., & Hunsberger, B. (1992). Authoritarianism, religious fundamentalism, quest, and prejudice. *The International Journal for the Psychology of Religion, 2,* 113–133.

**American Council on Education** (1995–1996). *Minorities in higher education.* Washington, DC: Office of Minority Concerns.

**American Psychiatric Association** (1952). *Diagnostic and statistical manual of mental disorder (DSM-I).* Washington, DC: Author.

**American Psychiatric Association** (1968). *Diagnostic and statistical manual of mental disorder (DSM-II).* Washington, DC: Author.

**American Psychological Association** (1996). *Affirmative action: Who benefits?* Washington, DC: Author.

**Amir, Y.** (1969). Contact hypothesis in ethnic relations. *Psychological Bulletin, 71,* 319–342.

**Ancheta, A.N.** (1998). *Race, rights, and the Asian American experience.* New Brunswick, NJ: Rutgers University Press.

**Aneshensel, C.S., Clark, V.A., & Frerichs, R.R.** (1983).Race, ethnicity, and depression: A confirmatory analysis. *Journal of Personality and Social Psychology, 44,* 385–398.

**Anthony, T., Copper, C., & Mullen, B.** (1992). Cross-racial facial identification: A social cognitive integration. *Personality and Social Psychology Bulletin, 18,* 296–301.

**Aronson, E., Blaney, N., Stephan, C., Sikes, J., & Snapp, M.** (1978). *The jigsaw classroom.* Beverly Hills, CA: Sage.

**Aronson, E., & Thibodeaux, R.** (1992). The jigsaw classroom: A cooperative strategy for reducing prejudice. In J. Lynch, C. Modgil, & S. Modgil (Eds.), *Cultural diversity in the schools* (Vol. 2, pp. 231–256). London: Falmer Press.

**Aronson, J., Lustina, M.J., Good, C., Keough, K., Steele, C.M., & Brown, J.** (1998). When white men can't do math: Necessary and sufficient factors in stereotype threat. *Journal of Experimental Social Psychology, 35,* 29–46.

**Aschenbrenner, K.M., & Schaefer, R.E.** (1980). Minimal group situations: Comments on a mathematical model and on the research paradigm. *European Journal of Social Psychology, 10,* 389–398.

**Ashmore, R.D., & Del Boca, F.K.** (1981). Conceptual approaches to stereotypes and stereotyping. In D.L. Hamilton (Ed.), *Cognitive processes in stereotyping and intergroup behavior* (pp. 1–35). Hillsdale, NJ: Erlbaum.

**Ayers, L.** (1992). Perceptions of affirmative action among its beneficiaries. *Social Justice Research, 5,* 223–238.

**Ayres, I., & Siegleman, P.** (1995). Race and gender discrimination in bargaining for a new car. *American Economic Review, 85,* 304–321.

**Banaji, M.R.** (1996). Automatic and contolled processes in stereotype priming. *Journal of Personality and Social Psychology, 70,* 1126–1141.

**Banaji, M.R., & Greenwald, A.G.,** (1994). Implicit stereotyping and prejudice. In M.P. Zanna & J.M. Olson (Eds.), *The psychology of prejudice: The Ontario symposium, Vol. 7.* Hillsdale, NJ: Erlbaum.

**Banaji, M.R., Hardin, C., & Rothman, A.I.** (1993). Implicit stereotyping in person judgment. *Journal of Personality and Social Psychology, 65,* 272–281.

**Barcus, F.** (1963). The world of Sunday comics. In D. White & R. Abel (Eds.), *The funnies: An American idiom.* New York: Free Press.

**Bargh, J.A.** (1994). The four horsemen of automaticity: Awareness, intention, efficiency, and control in social cognition. In R.S. Wyer, Jr. & T.K. Srull (Eds.), *Handbook of social cognition* (2nd ed.). Hillsdale, NJ: Erlbaum.

**Bargh, J.A.** (1997). The automaticity of everyday life. In R.S. Wyer, Jr. (Ed.), *Advances in social cognition* (Vol. 10, pp. 161). Mahwah, NJ: Erlbaum.

**Bargh, J.A., & Chen, M.** (1996). Automaticity of social behavior: Direct effects of trait construct and stereotype activation on action. *Journal of Personality and Social Psychology, 71,* 230–244.

**Batson, C.D., & Burris, C.T.** (1996). Personal religion: Depressant or stimulant of prejudice and discrimination? In C.Seligman, J.M. Olson, and M.P. Zanna (Eds.), *The psychology of values: The Ontario symposium* (Vol. 8, pp.149–169). Mahwah, NJ: Erlbaum.

**Batson, C.D., Flink, C.H., Schoenrade, P.A., Fultz, J., & Pych, V.** (1986). Religious orientation and overt versus covert racial prejudice. *Journal of Personality and Social Psychology, 50,* 175–181.

Batson, C.D., & Ventis, W.L. (1982). *The religious experience: A social psychological perspective*. New York: Oxford University Press.

Bayton, J.A., McAlister, L.B., & Hamer, J. (1956). Race-class stereotypes. *Journal of Negro Education, 41,* 75–78.

Bell, A.P., & Weinberg, M.S. (1978). *Homosexualities*. New York: Simon & Schuster.

Bell, A.P., Weinberg, M.S., & Hammersmith, S.K. (1981). *Sexual preference: Its development in men and women*. Bloomington: Indiana University Press.

Bem, D. (1996). Exotic becomes erotic: A developmental theory of sexual orientation. *Psychological Review, 103,* 320–335.

Bem, S.L. (1993). *The lenses of gender*. New Haven, CT: Yale University.

Benbow, C.P., & Stanley, J.C. (1980). Sex differences in mathematical ability: Fact or artifact? *Science, 210,* 1262–1264.

Bergen, D.J., & Williams, J.E. (1991). Sex stereotypes in the United States revisited: 1972–1988. *Sex Roles, 24,* 413–424.

Berry, J.W. (1984). Cultural relations in plural societies: Alternatives to segregation and their sociopsychological implications. In N. Miller & M.B. Brewer (Eds.), *Groups in contact: The psychology of desegregation* (pp. 11–27). New York: Academic Press.

Best, D.L., & Williams, J.E. (1993). A cross-cultural viewpoint. In A.E. Beall & R.J. Sternberg (Eds.), *The psychology of gender* (pp. 215–247). New York: Guilford Press.

Bettencourt, B.A., Brewer, M.B., Croak, M.R., & Miller, N. (1992). Cooperation and reduction of intergroup bias: The role of reward structure and social orientation. *Journal of Experimental Social Psychology, 28,* 301–319.

Bierly, M.M. (1985). Prejudice toward contemporary outgroups as generalized attitude. *Journal of Applied Social Psychology, 15,* 189–199.

Biernat, M., Manis, M., & Nelson, T.E. (1991). Stereotypes and standards of judgment. *Journal of Personality and Social Psychology, 60,* 484–499.

Biernat, M., Vescio, T.K., Theno, S.A., & Crandall, C.S. (1996). Values and prejudice: Toward understanding the impact of American values on outgroup attitudes. In C. Seligman, J.M. Olson, & M.P. Zanna (Eds.), *The psychology of values: The Ontario symposium*, Vol. 8 (pp. 153–190). Mahwah, NJ: Erlbaum.

Billig, M.(1973). Normative communication in a minimal intergroup situation. *European Journal of Social Psychology, 3,* 27–52.

Billig, M. (1985). Prejudice, categorization and particularization: From a perceptual to a rhetorical approach. *European Journal of Social Psychology, 15,* 79–104.

Billig, M.G., & Tajfel, H. (1973). Social categorization and similarity in intergroup behaviour. *European Journal of Social Psychology, 3,* 27–52.

Birenbaum, A. (1970). On managing a courtesy stigma. *Journal of Health and Social Behavior, 11,* 196–206.

Birt, C.M., & Dion, K.L. (1987). Relative deprivation theory and responses to discrimination in a gay male and lesbian sample. *British Journal of Social Psychology, 27,* 139–145.

Blair, I.V., Blanchard, F.A., Crandall, C.S., Brigham, J.C., & Vaughn, L.E. (1994). Condemning and condoning racism: A social context approach to interracial settings. *Journal of Applied Psychology, 79,* 993–997.

Blanchard, F.A., Lilly, T., & Vaughn, L.E. (1991). Reducing the expression of racial prejudice. *Psychological Science, 2,* 101–105.

Blaney, N., Stephan, C., Rosenfield, D., Aronson, E., & Sikes, J. (1977). Interdependence in the classroom: A field study. *Journal of Educational Psychology, 69,* 121–128.

Blascovich, J., Wyer, N.A., Swart, L.A., & Kibler, J.L. (1997). Racism and racial categorization. *Journal of Personality and Social Psychology, 72,* 1364–1372.

Bleier, R. (1984). *Science and gender: A critique of biology and its theories on women*. New York: Pergamon Press.

Block, J., & Block, J. (1950). An investigation of the relationship between intolerance of ambiguity and ethnocentrism. *Journal of Personality, 19,* 303–311.

**Blumer, H.** (1955). Attitudes and the social act. *Social Problems, 3,* 59–65.

**Bobo, L.** (1988). Group conflict, prejudice, and the paradox of contemporary racial attitudes. In P.A. Katz & D.A. Taylor (Eds.), *Eliminating racism: Profiles in controversy* (pp. 85–116). New York: Plenum.

**Bobo, L., Kluegel, J.R., & Smith, R.A.** (1997). Laissez-faire racism: The crystallization of a kinder, gentler, antiblack ideology. In S.A. Tuch & J.K. Martin (Eds.), *Racial attitudes in the 1990s: Continuity and change.* Westport, CT: Praeger.

**Bobocel, D.R., Son Hing, L.S., Davey, L.M., Stanley, D.J., & Zanna, M.P.** (1998). Justice-based opposition to social policies: Is it genuine? *Journal of Personality and Social Psychology, 75,* 653–669.

**Bodenhausen, G.V.** (1988). Stereotypic biases in social decision making and memory: Testing process models of stereotype use. *Journal of Personality and Social Psychology, 55,* 726–737.

**Bodenhausen, G.V.** (1993). Emotions, arousal, and stereotypic judgments: A heuristic model of affect and stereotyping. In D.M. Mackie & D.L. Hamilton (Eds.), *Affect, cognition and stereotyping: Interactive processes in group perception* (pp. 13–37). San Diego, CA: Academic Press.

**Bodenhausen, G.V., & Lichtenstein, M.** (1987). Social stereotypes and information processing strategies. *Journal of Personality and Social Psychology, 52,* 871–880.

**Bodenhausen, G.V., & Macrae, C.N.** (1996). The self-regulation of intergroup perception: Mechanisms and consequences of stereotype suppression. In C.N. Macrae, C. Stangor, & M. Hewstone (Eds.), *Stereotypes and stereotyping* (pp. 227–253). NY: Guilford.

**Bodenhausen, G.V., Macrae, C.N., & Garst, J.** (1998). Stereotypes in thought and deed: Social-cognitive origins of intergroup discrimination. In C. Sedikides, J. Schopler, & C.A. Insko (Eds.), *Intergroup cognition and intergroup behavior* (pp. 311–335). Mahwah, NJ: Lawrence Erlbaum.

**Bodenhausen, G.V., Mussweiler, T., Gabriel, S., & Moreno, K.N.** (in press). Affective influences on stereotyping and intergroup relations. In J.P. Forgas (Ed.), *Handbook of affect and social cognition.*

**Bodenhausen, G.V., Sheppard, L.A., & Kramer, G.P.** (1994). Negative affect and social judgment: The differential impact of anger and sadness. *European Journal of Social Psychology, 24,* 45–62.

**Bonvillain, N.** (1998). *Women and men: Cultural constructs of gender.* Upper Saddle River, NJ: Prentice Hall.

**Bourhis, R.Y., Sachdev, I., & Gagnon, A.** (1994). Intergroup research with the Tajfel matrices: Methodological notes. In M.P. Zanna & J.M. Olson (Eds.), *The psychology of prejudice: The Ontario symposium,* Vol. 7 (pp. 209–232). Hillsdale, NJ: Erlbaum.

**Brand, E.S., Ruiz, R.A., & Padilla, A.M.** (1974). Ethnic identification and preference: A review. *Psychological Bulletin, 81,* 860–890.

**Branscombe, N.R., & Ellemers, N.** (1998). Coping with group-based discrimination: Individualistic versus group-level strategies. In J.K. Swim and C. Stangor (Eds.), *Prejudice: The target's perspective.* New York: Academic Press.

**Branscombe, N., Schmitt, M.T., & Harvey, R.D.** (1999). Perceiving pervasive discrimination among African Americans: Implications for group identification and well-being. *Journal of Personality and Social Psychology, 77,* 135–149.

**Branscombe, N.R., & Wann, D.L.** (1992). Role of identification with a group, arousal, categorization processes, and self-esteem in sports spectator aggression. *Human Relations, 45,* 1013–1033.

**Branscombe, N., & Wann, D.L.** (1994). Collective self-esteem consequences of outgroup derogation when a valued social identity is on trial. *European Journal of Social Psychology, 24,* 641–657.

**Brewer, M.B.** (1979). In-group bias in the minimal intergroup situation: A cognitive-motivational analysis. *Psychological Bulletin, 86,* 307–324.

Brewer, M.B. (1988). A dual process model of impression formation. In T.K. Srull & R.S. Wyer (Eds.), *Advances in social cognition* (Vol. 1). Hillsdale, NJ: Erlbaum.

Brewer, M.B. (1991). The social self: On being the same and different at the same time. *Personality and Social Psychology Bulletin, 17,* 475–482.

Brewer, M.B., & Brown, R.J. (1998) Intergroup relations. In D.T. Gilbert, S.T. Fiske, & G. Lindzey (Eds.), *The handbook of social psychology* (4th ed., Vol. 2, pp. 554–594), New York: McGraw-Hill.

Brewer, M.B., Manzi, J., & Shaw, J. (1993). Ingroup identification as a function of depersonalization, distinctiveness, and status. *Psychological Science, 4,* 88–92.

Brewer, M.B., & Weber, J.G. (1994). Self-evaluation effects of interpersonal versus intergroup social comparison. *Journal of Personality and Social Psychology, 66,* 268–275.

Brickman, P., Rabinowitz, V.C., Karuza, J., Coates, D., Cohn, E., & Kidder, L. (1982). Models of helping and coping. *American Psychologist, 37,* 368–384.

Brigham, J.C. (1971). Ethnic stereotypes. *Psychological Bulletin, 76,* 15–38.

Brink, T.L. (1988). Obesity and job discrimination: Mediation via personality stereotypes? *Perceptual and Motor Skills, 66,* 494.

Bronner, E. (1998, January 20). Inventing the notion of race. *The New York Times,* p. B9.

Broverman, I.K., Vogel, S.R., Broverman, D.M., Clarkson, F.E., & Rosenkrantz, P.W. (1972). Sex-role stereotypes: A current appraisal. *Journal of Social Issues, 28,* 59–78.

*Brown v. Board of Education of Topeka* (1954), 347 U.S. 483.

Brown, L.M. (1998). Ethnic stigma as a contextual experience: A possible selves perspective. *Personality and Social Psychology Bulletin, 24,* 163–172.

Brown, R. (1965). *Social psychology.* New York: Macmillan.

Burnstein, P. (1978). Equal employment opportunity legislation and the income of women

and nonwhites. *American Sociological Review, 44,* 367–391.

Butler, D., & Geis, F.L. (1990). Nonverbal affect responses to male and female leaders: Implications for leadership evaluations. *Journal of Personality and Social Psychology, 58,* 48–59.

Button, J.W., Rienzo, B.A., & Wald, K.D. (1997). *Private lives, public conflicts: Battles over gay rights in American communities.* Washington, D.C.: Congressional Quarterly.

Campbell, C.P. (1995). *Race, myth, and the news.* Thousand Oaks, CA: Sage.

Carmichael, S., & Hamilton, C.V. (1967). *Black power: The politics of liberation in America.* New York: Vintage Books.

Carrier, I.M. (1980). Homosexual behavior in cross-cultural perspective. In J. Marmor (Ed.), *Homosexual behavior* (pp. 100–122). New York: Basic Books.

Carver, C.S., Glass, D.C., & Katz, I. (1978). Favorable evaluations of Blacks and the handicapped: Positive prejudice, unconscious denial, or social desirability? *Journal of Applied Social Psychology, 8,* 97–106.

Center for the American Woman and Politics, Rutgers University. (2000). Women in elected office 2000. World Wide Web, *http://www.rci.rutgers.edu/~cawp/facts/cawpfs.html*

Chen, M., & Bargh, J.A. (1997). Nonconscious behavioral confirmation processes: The self-fulfilling consequences of automatic stereotype activation. *Journal of Experimental Social Psychology, 33,* 541–560.

Christie, R. (1954). Authoritarianism re-examined. In R. Christie and M. Jahoda (Eds.), *Studies in the scope and method of "The Authoritarian Personality."* Glenco, Il: Free Press.

Christie, R. (1993). Some experimental approaches to authoritarianism: II. Authoritarianism and punitiveness. In W.F. Stone, G. Lederer, & R. Christie (Eds.), *Strength and weakness: The authoritarian personality today* (pp. 99–118). New York: Springer-Verlag.

Claire, T., & Fiske, S.T. (1998). A systemic view of behavioral confirmation: Counterpoint to the individualist view. In C. Sedikides, J. Schopler, & C.A. Insko, *Intergroup cognition and intergroup behavior* (pp. 205–231). Mahwah, NJ: Erlbaum.

Clark, K.B., & Clark, M.P. (1947). Racial identification and racial preference in Negro children. In T.M. Newcomb & E.L. Hartley (Eds.), *Readings in social psychology* (pp. 239–252). New York: Holt, Rinehart, & Winston.

Cloud, J. (1999, March 8). Trading white sheets for pinstripes. *Time*, Vol. 30.

Cohen, C.E. (1981). Person categories and social perception: Testing some boundaries of the processing effects of prior knowledge. *Journal of Personality and Social Psychology, 40,* 441–452.

Cohen, G.L. Steele, C.M., & Ross, L.D. (1999). The mentor's dilemma: Providing critical feedback across the racial divide. *Personality and Social Psychology Bulletin, 25,* 1302–1318.

Cole, S.W., Kemeny, M.E., Taylor, S.E., Visscher, B.R., & Fahey, J.L. (1996). Accelerated course of human immunodeficiency virus infection in gay men who conceal their homosexual identity. *Psychosomatic Medicine, 58,* 219–231.

Cook, S.W. (1962). The systematic analysis of socially significant events. *Journal of Social Issues, 18,* 66–84.

Cook, S.W. (1978). Interpersonal and attitudinal outcomes in cooperating interracial groups. *Journal of Research in Developmental Education, 12,* 97–113.

Cook, S.W. (1984). The 1954 social science statement and school desegregation: A reply to Gerard. *American Psychologist, 39,* 819–832.

Cook, S.W. (1985). Experimenting on social issues: The case of school desegration. *American Psychologist, 40,* 452–460.

Cooley, C.H. (1956). *Human nature and the social order.* New York: Free Press.

Craig, R.S. (1992). The effect of television day part on gender portrayals in television commercials: A content analysis. *Sex Roles, 26,* 197–211.

Crandall, C.S. (1994). Prejudice against fat people: Ideology and self-interest. *Journal of Personality and Social Psychology, 66,* 882–894.

Crandall, C.S. (1995). Do parents discriminate against their heavyweight daughters? *Personality and Social Psychology Bulletin, 21,* 724–735.

Crandall, C.S., & Biernat, M.R. (1990). The ideology of anti-fat attitudes. *Journal of Applied Social Psychology, 20,* 227–243.

Crandall, C.S., & Cohen, C. (1994). The personality of the stigmatizer: Cultural worldview, conventionalism, and self esteem. *Journal of Research in Personality, 28,* 461–480.

Crandall, C.S., Glor, J., & Britt, T.W. (1997). AIDS-related stigmatization: Instrumental and symbolic attitudes. *Journal of Applied Social Psychology, 27,* 95–123.

Crocker, J. (1999). Social stigma and self-esteem: Situational construction of self-worth. *Journal of Experimental and Social Psychology, 35,* 89–107.

Crocker, J., Cornwell, B., & Major, B. (1993). The stigma of overweight: Affective consequences of attributional ambiguity. *Journal of Personality and Social Psychology, 64,* 60–70.

Crocker, J., Luhtanen, R., Blaine, B., & Broadnax, S. (1994). Collective self-esteem and psychological well-being among White, Black, and Asian college students. *Personality and Social Psychology Bulletin, 20,* 502–513.

Crocker, J., & Major, B. (1989). Social stigma and self-esteem: The self-protective properties of stigma. *Psychological Review, 96,* 608–630.

Crocker, J., & Major, B. (1994). Reactions to stigma: The moderating role of justifications. In M.P. Zanna & J.M. Olson (Eds.), *The psychology of prejudice: The Ontario symposium,* vol. 7 (pp. 289–314). Mahwah, NJ: Lawrence Erlbaum.

Crocker, J., Major, B., & Steele, C. (1998). Social stigma. In D. Gilbert, S.T. Fiske, & G. Lindsey (Eds.), *The handbook of social psychology,* 4th ed. (Vol. 2, pp. 504–553). New York: McGraw-Hill.

Crocker, J., Voelkl, K., Testa, M., & Major, B. (1991). Social stigma: The affective consequences of attributional ambiguity. *Journal of Personality and Social Psychology, 60,* 218–228.

Croizet, J.C., & Claire, T. (1998). Extending the concept of stereotype threat to social class: The intellectual underperformance of students from low socioeconomic backgrounds. *Personality and Social Psychology Bulletin, 24,* 588–594.

Crosby, F. (1976). A model of egotistical relative deprivation. *Psychological Review, 83,* 85–113.

Crosby, F.J. (1982). *Relative deprivation and working women.* New York: Oxford University Press.

Crosby, F.J. (1984). The denial of personal discrimination. *American Behavioral Scientist, 27,* 371–386.

Crosby, F.J., Pufall, A., Snyder, R., O'Connel, M., & Whalen, P. (1989). The denial of personal disadvantage among you, me, and all the other ostriches. In M. Crawford & M. Gentry (Eds.), *Gender and thought* (pp. 79–99). New York: Springer-Verlag.

Darley, J.M., & Gross, P.H. (1983). A hypothesis-confirming bias in labeling effects. *Journal of Personality and Social Psychology, 44,* 20–33.

Darwin, C. (1871). *The descent of man.* London: J. Murray.

Dator, J.A. (1969). What's left of the economic theory of discrimination? In S. Shulman & W. Darity (Eds.), *The question of discrimination: Racial inequality in the U.S. labor market* (pp. 335–374). Middletown, CT: Wesleyan University Press.

Deaux, K. (1996). Social identification. In E.T. Higgins & A.W. Kruglanski (Eds.), *Social psychology: Handbook of basic principles* (pp. 777–798). New York: Guilford.

Deaux, K., & Lewis, L.L. (1983). Components of gender stereotypes. *Psychological Documents, 13,* 25–34.

Deaux, K., & Lewis, L.L. (1984). Structure of gender stereotypes: Interrelationships among components and gender label. *Journal of Personality and Social Psychology, 46,* 991–1004.

DeFleur, M.L., & Westie, F.R. (1963). Attitude as a scientific concept. *Social Forces, 42,* 17–31.

D'Emilio, J., & Freedman, E.B. (1988). *Intimate matters: A history of sexuality in America.* New York: Harper and Row.

Desforges, D., Lord, C., Ramsey, S., Mason, J., Van Leeuwen, M., West, S., & Lepper, M. (1991). Effects of structured cooperative contact on changing negative attitudes toward stigmatized social groups. *Journal of Personality and Social Psychology, 60,* 531–544.

Deutscher, I. (1966). Words and deeds: Social science and social policy. *Social Problems, 13,* 235–254.

Devine, P.G. (1989). Stereotypes and prejudice: Their automatic and controlled components. *Journal of Personality and Social Psychology, 56,* 5–18.

Devine, P.G., & Elliot, A.J. (1995). Are racial stereotypes really fading? The Princeton trilogy revisited. *Personality and Social Psychology Bulletin, 11,* 1139–1150.

Devine, P.G., Evett, S.R., & Vasquez-Suson, K.A. (1996). Exploring the interpersonal dynamics of intergroup contact. In R.M. Sorrentino & E.T. Higgins, (Eds.), *Handbook of motivation and cognition* (Vol. 3). 423–465. New York: Guilford.

Devine, P.G., & Monteith, M.I. (1993). The role of discrepancy associated affect in prejudice reduction. In D.M. Mackie & D.L. Hamilton (Eds.), *Affect, cognition, and stereotyping: Interactive processes in group perception* (pp. 317–344). New York: Academic Press.

Devine, P.G., Monteith, J.J., Zuwerink, J.R., & Elliot, A.J. (1991). Prejudice with and without compunction. *Journal of Personality and Social Psychology, 60,* 817–830.

Devine, P.G., Plant, E.A., & Harrison, K. (1999). The problem of "us" versus "them" and AIDS stigma. *American Behavioral Scientist, 42,* 1212–1228.

Diamond, M. (1993). Homosexuality and bisexuality in different populations. *Archives of Sexual Behavior, 11,* 181–186.

Dijker, A.J.M. (1987). Emotional reactions to ethnic minorities. *European Journal of Social Psychology, 17,* 305–325.

Dijksterhuis, A., Knippenberg, A.V., Kruglanski, A.W., & Schaper, C. (1996). Motivated social cognition: Need for closure effects on memory and judgment. *Journal of Experimental Social Psychology, 32,* 254–270.

**DiPlacido, J.** (1998). Minority stress among lesbians, gay men, and bisexuals: A consequence of heterosexism, homophobia, and stigmatization. In G.M. Herek (Ed.), *Stigma and sexual orientation: Understanding prejudice against lesbians, gay men, and bisexuals* (pp. 138–159). Thousand Oaks, CA: Sage.

**Doty, R.M., Winter, D.G., Peterson, B.E., & Kemmelmeier, M.** (1997). Authoritarianism and American students' attitudes about the Gulf War, 1990–1996. *Personality and Social Psychology Bulletin, 23,* 1133–1143.

**Dovidio, J.F., Brigham, J.C., Johnson, B.T., & Gaertner, S.L.** (1996). Stereotyping, prejudice, and discrimination: Another look. In C.N. Macrae, C. Stangor, & M. Hewstone (Eds.), *Stereotypes and Stereotyping* (pp. 276–319). NY: Guilford.

**Dovidio, J.F., Evans, N., & Tyler, R.B.** (1986). Racial stereotypes: The contents of their cognitive representations. *Journal of Experimental Social Psychology, 22,* 22–37.

**Dovidio, J.F., & Gaertner, S.L.** (1991). Changes in the expression of racial prejudice. In H. Knopke, J. Norrell, & R. Rogers (Eds.), *Opening doors: An appraisal of race relations in contemporary America* (pp. 119–148). Tuscaloosa: University of Alabama Press.

**Dovidio, J.F., & Gaertner, S.L.** (1999). Reducing prejudice: Combating intergroup biases. *Current Directions in Psychological Science, 8,* 101–105.

**Dovidio, J.F., & Gaertner, S.L.** (2000). Aversive racism and selection decisions: 1989 and 1999. *Psychological Science, 11,* 315–319.

**Dovidio, J.F., Gaertner, S.L., Isen, A.M., & Lowrance, R.** (1995). Groups representations and intergroup bias: Positive affect, similarity, and group size. *Personality and Social Psychology Bulletin, 21,* 856–865.

**Dovidio, J.F., Gaertner, S.L., Isen, A.M., Rust, M., & Guerra, P.** (1998). Positive affect, cognition, and the reduction of intergroup bias. In C. Sedikides & J. Schopler (Eds.), *Intergroup cognition and intergroup behavior.* Mahwah, NJ: Erlbaum.

**Dovidio, J.F., Gaertner, S.L., & Validzic, A.** (1998). Intergroup bias: Status, differentiation, and a common in-group identity. *Journal of Personality and Social Psychology, 75,* 109–120.

**Dovidio, J.F., Kawakami, K., Johnson, C., Johnson, B., & Howard, A.,** (1997). On the nature of prejudice: Automatic and controlled processes. *Journal of Experimental Social Psychology, 33,* 510–540.

**Duckitt, J.** (1992a). Psychology and prejudice: A historical analysis and integrative framework. *American Psychologist, 47,* 1182–1193.

**Duckitt, J.** (1992b). *The social psychology of prejudice.* New York: Praeger.

**Duckitt, J., & Farre, B.** (1994). Right-wing authoritarianism and political intolerance among whites in the future majority-rule South Africa. *Journal of Social Psychology, 134,* 735–741.

**Duncan, B. L.** (1976). Differential social perception and attribution of intergroup violence: Testing the lower limits of stereotyping of blacks. *Journal of Personality and Social Psychology, 34,* 590–598.

**Duncan, L.E., Peterson, B.E., & Winter, D.G.** (1997). Authoritarianism and gender roles: Toward a psychological analysis of hegemonic relationships. *Personality and Social Psychology Bulletin, 23,* 41–49.

**Eagly, A.H.** (1987). *Sex differences in social behavior: A social-role interpretation.* Hillsdale, NJ: Erlbaum.

**Eagly, A.H., & Chaiken, S.** (1993). *The psychology of attitudes.* New York: Harcourt Brace Jovanovich.

**Eagly, A.H., Karau, S.I., & Makhijani, M.G.** (1995). Gender and the effectiveness of leaders: A meta-analysis. *Psychological Bulletin, 117,* 125–145.

**Eagly, A.H., Makhijani, M., & Klonsky, B.G.** (1992). Gender and the evaluation of leaders: A meta-analysis. *Psychological Bulletin, 111,* 3–22.

**Eagly, A.H., & Mladinic, A.** (1989). Gender stereotypes and attitudes toward women and men. *Personality and Social Psychology Bulletin, 15,* 543–558.

**Eagly, A.H., & Mladinic, A.** (1994). Are people prejudiced against women? Some answers from research on attitudes, gender stereotypes, and judgments of competence. In W. Stroebe & M. Hewstone (Eds.), *Europoean Review of Social Psychology,* (Vol. 5, pp. 1–36). New York: Wiley.

**Eagly, A.H., Mladinic, A., & Otto, S.** (1991). Are women evaluated more favorably than men? An analysis of attitudes, beliefs, and emotions. *Psychology of Women Quarterly, 15,* 203–216.

**Eagly, A.H., Mladinic, A., & Otto, S.** (1994). Cognitive and affective bases of attitudes toward social groups and social policies. *Journal of Experimental Social Psychology, 30,* 113–137.

**Eagly, A.H., & Steffen, V.J.** (1984). Gender stereotypes stem from the distribution of women and men into social roles. *Journal of Personality and Social Psychology, 46,* 735–374.

**Eagly, A.H., & Steffen, V.J.** (1986). Gender stereotypes, occupational roles, and beliefs about part-time employees. *Psychology of Women Quarterly, 10,* 252–262.

**Eagly, A.H., & Wood, W.** (1982). Inferred sex differences in status as a determinant of gender stereotypes about social influence. *Journal of Personality and Social Psychology, 43,* 915–928.

The effect of segregation and the consequences of desegregation: A social science statement. Appendix to appellants' briefs: *Brown v. Board of Education of Topeka, Kansas* (1953). *Minnesota Law Review, 37,* 427–439.

**Ellemers, N.** (1993). The influence of socio-structural variables on identity management strategies. In W. Stroebe & M. Hewstone (Eds.), *European Review of Social Psychology,* Vol. 4 (pp. 27–58). New York: Wiley & Sons.

**Ellemers, N., Wilke, H., & Van Knippenberg, A.** (1993). Effects of the legitimacy of low group or individual status on individual and collective identity enhancement strategies. *Journal*

of *Personality and Social Psychology, 74,* 766–778.

**Entman, R.M.** (1994). Representation and reality in the portrayal of blacks on network television news. *Journalism Quarterly, 71,* 509–520.

**Erikson, E.** (1956). The problem of ego-identity. *Journal of the American Psychoanalytic Association, 4,* 56–121.

**Esses, V.M., Haddock, G., & Zanna, M.P.** (1993). Values, stereotypes, and emotions as determinants of intergroup attitudes. In D.M. Mackie & D.L. Hamilton (Eds.), *Affect, cognition, and stereotypinq: Interactive processes in group perception* (pp. 137–166). New York: Academic Press.

**Esses, V.M., & Seligman, C.** (1996). The individual-group distinction in assessments of strategies to reduce prejudice and discrimination: The case of affirmative action. In R.M. Sorrentino & E.T. Higgins (Eds.), *Handbook of motivation and cognition: The interpersonal context* (Vol. 3, pp. 570–590). New York: Guilford.

**Eysenck, H.J.** (1971). Social attitudes and social class. *British Journal of Social and Clinical Psychology, 10,* 210–212.

**Ezekiel, R.S.** (1995). *The racist mind.* New York: Viking.

**Farley, J.E.** (1995). *Majority-minority relations.* Englewood Cliffs, NJ: Prentice Hall.

**Fausto-Sterling, A.** (1992). *Myths of gender: Biological theories about women and men.* New York: Basic Books.

**Fausto-Sterling, A.** (1998). The five sexes: Why male and female are not enough. In D.L. Anselmi & A.L. Law (Eds.), *Questions of gender: Perspectives and paradoxes.* New York: McGraw-Hill.

**Fazio, R.H., Jackson, J.R., Dunton, B.C., & Williams, C.J.** (1995). Variability in automatic activation as an unobtrusive measure of racial attitudes: A bona fide pipeline? *Journal of Personality and Social Psychology, 69,* 1013–1027.

**Feagin, J.R., & Feagin, C.B.** (1993). *Racial and ethnic relations.* Englewood Cliffs, NJ: Prentice Hall.

**Feather, N.T.** (1996). Reactions to penalties for an offense in relation to authoritarianism, values, perceived responsibility, perceived seriousness, and deservingness. *Journal of Personality and Social Psychology, 71,* 571–587.

Fein, S., & Spencer, S.J. (1997). Prejudice as a self-image maintenance: Affirming the self through derogating others. *Journal of Personality and Social Psychology, 73,* 31–44.

Feldman, J.M. (1972). Stimulus characteristics and subject prejudice as determinants of stereotype attribution. *Journal of Personality and Social Psychology, 21,* 333–340.

Festinger, L. (1954). A theory of social comparison processes. *Human Relations, 7,* 117–140.

Festinger, L. (1957). *A theory of cognitive dissonance.* Stanford, CA: Stanford University Press.

Fish, J.M. (1995a, November). Mixed blood. *Psychology Today,* 55–62 .

Fish, J.M. (1995b). Why psychologists should learn some anthropology. *American Psychologist, 50,* 44–45.

Fishbein, H.D. (1996). *Peer prejudice and discrimination: Evolutionary, cultural, and developmental dynamics.* Boulder, CO: Westview.

Fishbein, M. & Ajzen, I. (1972). Attitudes and opinions. *Annual Review of Psychology, 23,* 487–544.

Fisher, R.D., Derison, D., Polley, C.F., Cadman, J., & Johnston, D. (1994). Religiousness, religious orientation, and attitudes toward gays and lesbians. *Journal of Applied Social Psychology, 24,* 614–630.

Fiske, S.T. (1980). Attention and weight in person perception: The impact of negative and extreme behavior. *Journal of Personality and Social Psychology, 38,* 889–906.

Fiske, S.T. (1989). Examining the role of intent: Toward understanding its role in stereotyping and prejudice. In J.S. Uleman & J.A. Bargh (Eds.), *Unintended thought* (pp. 253–283). New York: Guilford.

Fiske, S.T. (1992). Stereotypes work . . . but only sometimes: Comment on how to motivate the "unfinished mind." *Psychological Inquiry, 3,* 161–162.

Fiske, S.T. (1993). Controlling other people: The impact of power on stereotyping. *American Psychologist, 48,* 621–628.

Fiske, S.T. (1998). Stereotyping, prejudice, and discrimination. In D.T. Gilbert, S.T. Fiske, & G. Lindzey, *The handbook of social psychology* (4th ed., Vol. 2, pp. 357–411). New York: McGraw-Hill.

Fiske, S.T., & Depret, E. (1995). Ambivalence and stereotypes cause sexual harassment: A theory with implications for organizational change. *Journal of Social Issues, 51,* 97–115.

Fiske, S.T., & Neuberg, S.L. (1990). A continuum model of impression formation, from category-based to individuating processes: Influence of information and motivation on attention and interpretation. In M.P. Zanna (Ed.), *Advances in experimental social psychology* (Vol. 23). New York: Academic Press.

Fiske, S. T., & Taylor, S. E. (1991). *Social cognition.* New York: McGraw-Hill.

Fiske, S.T., & Von Hendy, H.M. (1992). Personality feedback and situational norms can control stereotyping processes. *Journal of Personality and Social Psychology, 62,* 577–596.

Foucault, M. (1978). *The history of sexuality, Vol. 1: An introduction.* New York: Random House.

Fox, R. (1992). Prejudice and the unfinished mind: A new look at an old failing. *Psychological Inquiry, 3,* 137–152.

Frable, D. (1993). Dimensions of marginality: Distinctions among those who are different. *Personality and Social Psychology Bulletin, 19,* 370–380.

Frable, D.E.S., Blackstone, T., & Scherbaum, C. (1990). Marginal and mindful: Deviants in social interactions. *Journal of Personality and Social Psychology, 74,* 909–922.

Frable, D.E.S., Platt, L., & Hoey, S. (1998). Concealable stigmas and positive self-perceptions: Feeling better around similar others. *Journal of Personality and Social Psychology, 74,* 909–922.

Franco, F., & Maass, A. (1996) Implicit vs. explicit strategies of outgroup discrimination: The role of intentional control in biased language use and reward allocation. *Journal of Language and Social Psychology, 15,* 335–359.

**Freund, T., Kruglanski, A.W., & Shpitajzen, A.** (1985). The freezing and unfreezing of impression primacy: Effects of the need for structure and the fear of invalidity. *Personality and Social Psychology Bulletin, 11,* 479–487.

**Frey, D., & Gaertner, S.L.** (1986). Helping and the avoidance of inappropriate interracial behavior: A strategy that can perpetuate a nonprejudiced self-image. *Journal of Personality and Social Psychology, 50,* 1083–1090.

**Friedman, M.A., & Brownell, K.D.** (1995). Psychological correlates of obesity: Moving to the next research generation. *Psychological Bulletin, 117,* 3–20.

**Gaertner, S.L.** (1973). Helping behavior and discrimination among liberals and conservatives. *Journal of Personality and Social Psychology, 25,* 335–341.

**Gaertner, S.L., & Dovidio, J.** (1977). The subtlety of white racism, arousal, and helping behavior. *Journal of Personality and Social Psychology, 117,* 69–77.

**Gaertner, S.L., & Dovidio, J.** (1986). The aversive form of racism. In J. Dovidio & S.L. Gaertner (Eds.), *Prejudice, discrimination, and racism* (pp. 61–89). New York: Academic Press.

**Gaertner, S.L., Dovidio, J.F., Anastasio, P.A., Bachman, B.A., & Rust, M.C.** (1993). The common ingroup identity model: Recategorization and the reduction of intergroup bias. In W. Stroebe & M. Hewstone (Eds.), *European review of social psychology* (Vol. 4, pp. 1–26). Chichester, England: Wiley.

**Gaertner, S.L., Mann, J., Dovidio, J., Murrell, A., & Pomare, M.** (1990). How does cooperation reduce intergroup bias? *Journal of Personality and Social Psychology, 59,* 692–704.

**Gaertner, S.L., Mann, J., Murrell, A., & Dovidio, J.** (1989). Reducing ingroup bias: The benefits of recategorization. *Journal of Personality and Social Psychology, 57,* 239–249.

**Gaertner, S.L., Rust, M., Dovidio, J., Bachman, B., & Anastasio, P.** (1994). The contact hypothesis: The role of a common ingroup identity on reducing intergroup bias. *Small Group Research, 25,* 224–229.

**Gagnon, A., & Bourhis, R.Y.** (1996). Discrimination in the minimal group paradigm: Social identity or self-interest? *Personality and Social Psychology Bulletin, 22,* 1289–1301.

**Gaines, S.O., & Reed, E.S.** (1995). Prejudice: From Allport to DuBois. *American Psychologist, 50,* 96–103.

**Garcia, L.T., Erskine, N., Hawn, K., & Casmay, S.R.** (1981). The effect of affirmative action on attributions about minority group members. *Journal of Personality, 49,* 427–437.

**Gardner, R.C.** (1973). Ethnic stereotypes: The traditional approach, a new look. *Canadian Psychologist, 14,* 133–148.

**Gardner, R.C.** (1994). Stereotypes as consensual beliefs. In M.P. Zanna & J.M. Olson (Eds.), *The psychology of prejudice: The Ontario symposium,* Vol. 7 (pp. 1–32). Hillsdale, NJ: Erlbaum.

**Gentile, D.A.** (1998). Just what are sex and gender, anyway? A call for a new terminological standard. In D.L. Anselmi & A.L. Law (Eds.), *Questions of gender: Perspectives and paradoxes* (pp. 14–17). New York: McGraw Hill.

**Gerard, H.B., & Hoyt, M.F.** (1974). Distinctiveness of social categorization and attitude toward ingroup members. *Journal of Personality and Social Psychology, 29,* 836–842.

**Gergen, K.J., & Jones, E.E.** (1963). Mental illness, predictability, and affective consequences as stimulus factors in person perception. *Journal of Abnormal and Social Psychology, 67,* 95–105.

**Gibbons, F.X., Stephan, W.G., Stephenson, B., & Petty, C.R.** (1980). Reactions to stigmatized others: Response amplification vs. sympathy. *Journal of Experimental Social Psychology, 16,* 591–605.

**Gilbert, D.T.** (1989). Thinking lightly about others: Automatic components of the social inference process. In J.S Uleman & J. Bargh (Eds.), *Unintended thought: Limits of awareness, intention and control* (pp. 189–211). New York: Guilford.

**Gilbert, D.T., & Hixon, J.G .** (1991). The trouble of thinking: Activation and application of stereotypic beliefs. *Journal of Personality and Social Psychology, 60,* 509–517.

Gilbert, D.T., Pelham, B.W., & Krull, D.S. (1988). On cognitive busyness: When person perceivers meet persons perceived. *Journal of Personality and Social Psychology, 54,* 733–740.

Gilbert, G.M. (1951). Stereotype persistence and change among college students. *Journal of Abnormal and Social Psychology, 46,* 245–254.

Gladue, B.A. (1994). The biopsychology of sexual orientation. *Current Directions in Psychological Science, 5,* 150–154.

Glass, R. (1964). Insiders-outsiders: The position of minorities. *Transactions of the Fifth World Congress of Sociology. Vol 3.* Louvain: International Sociological Association.

Glazer, N., & Moynihan, D.P. (1975). *Ethnicity: Theory and experience.* Cambridge, MA: Harvard University Press.

Glick, P., & Fiske, S.T. (1996). The ambivalent sexism inventory: Differentiating hostile and benevolent sexism. *Journal of Personality and Social Psychology, 70,* 491–512.

Glick, P. & Fiske, S.T. (1997). Hostile and benevolent sexism: Measuring ambivalent sexist attitudes toward women. *Psychology of Women Quarterly, 21,* 119–135.

Glick, P., & Fiske, S.T. (2001). An ambivalent alliance: Hostile and benevolent sexism as complementary justifications for gender inequality. *American Psychologist, 56,* 109–118.

Goffman, E. (1963). *Stigma: Notes on the management of spoiled identity.* Englewood Cliffs, NJ: Prentice Hall.

Goldberg, P. (1968). Are women prejudiced against women? *Transaction, 5,* 28–30.

Goldstein, S. (1997). Institutional discrimination exercise. Available: *Spssi_pr@field.uor.edu.*

Goldstein, S., & Johnson, V.A. (1997). Stigma by association: Perceptions of the dating partners of college students with physical disabilities. *Basic and Applied Social Psychology, 19,* 495–504.

Gordan, R.A. (1990). Attributions for blue-collar and white-collar crime: The effects of subject and defendant race on simulated juror decisions. *Journal of Applied Social Psychology, 20,* 971–983.

Gordon, M.M. (1964). *Assimilation in American life.* New York: Oxford University Press.

Gould, S.J. (1981). *The mismeasure of man.* New York: W.W. Norton.

Grant, M. (1916). *The passing of the great race.* New York: Scribner's.

Gray-Little, B., & Hafdahl, A.R. (2000). Factors influencing racial comparisons of self-esteem: A quantitative review. *Journal of Personality and Social Psychology, 126,* 26–54.

Green, A. (1997). Discrimination against overweight people still widely practiced. *Panama City News Herald.*

Green, D.P., Glaser, J., & Rich, A. (1998). From lynching to gay bashing: The elusive connection between economic conditions and hate crime. *Journal of Personality and Social Psychology, 75,* 82–92.

Green, J.A. (1972). Attitudinal and situational determinants of intended behavior toward blacks. *Journal of Personality and Social Psychology, 22,* 13–17.

Greenberg, J., Solomon, S., Veeder, M., Pyszczynski, T., Rosenblatt, A., Kirkland, S., & Lyon, D. (1990). Evidence for terror management theory II: The effects of mortality salience on reactions to those who threaten or bolster the cultural worldview. *Journal of Personality and Social Psychology, 58,* 308–318.

Greenwald, A.G., & Banaji, M.R. (1995). Implicit social cognition: Attitudes, self-esteem, and stereotypes. *Psychological Review, 102,* 4–27.

Greenwald, A.G., McGhee, D.E., & Schwartz, J.L.K. (1998). Measuring individual differences in implicit cognition: The implicit association test. *Journal of Personality and Social Psychology, 74,* 1464–1480.

Grieve, P.G., & Hogg, M.A. (1999). Subjective uncertainty and intergroup discrimination in the minimal group situation. *Personality and Social Psychology Bulletin, 25,* 926–940.

Guimond, S., & Dube-Simard, L. (1983). Relative deprivation theory and the Quebec nationalist movement: The cognition-emotion distinction and the personal-group deprivation issue. *Journal of Personality and Social Psychology, 526*–535.

Gup, T. (1997, April 21). Who is a whiz kid? Because my sons are Asian-American, people jump to conclusions about their academic gifts. *Newsweek*, p. 21.

Gupta, N., Jenkins, G.D., & Geehr, T.A. (1983). Employee gender, gender similarity, and supervisor-subordinate crossevaluations. *Psychology of Women Quarterly, 8*, 174–184.

Gurr, T.R. (1970). *Why men rebel*. Princeton, NJ: Princeton University Press.

Hacker, A. (1992). Two nations: Black and white, separate, hostile, and unequal. New York: Scribner.

Haddock, G., & Zanna, M.P. (1994). Preferring "housewifes" to "feminists": Categorization and the favorability of attitudes toward women. *Psychology of Women Quarterly, 18*, 25–52.

Haddock, G., & Zanna, M.P. (1998a). Authoritarianism, values, and the favorability and structure of antigay attitudes. In G.M. Herek (Ed.), *Stigma and sexual orientation: Understanding prejudice against lesbians, gay men, and bisexuals*. Thousand Oaks, CA: Sage.

Haddock, G., & Zanna, M.P. (1998b). In G.M. Herek (Ed.), *Stigma and sexual orientation: Understanding prejudice aqainst lesbians, gay men, and bisexuals* (pp. 82–107). Thousand Oaks, CA: Sage.

Haddock, G., Zanna, M.P., & Esses, V.M. (1993). Assessing the structure of prejudicial attitudes: The case of attitudes toward homosexuals. *Journal of Personality and Social Psychology, 65*, 1105–1118.

Hamilton, D. L. (1981). *Cognitive processes in stereotyping and intergroup behavior*. Hillsdale, NJ: Erlbaum.

Hamilton, D.L., & Gifford, R.K. (1976). Illusory correlation in interpersonal perception: A cognitive basis of stereotypic judgments. *Journal of Experimental Social Psychology, 12*, 392–407.

Hamilton, D.L., & Sherman, S.J. (1996). Perceiving persons and groups. *Psychological Review, 103*, 336–355.

Hamilton, D.L., Stroessner, S.J., & Driscoll, D.M. (1994). Social cognition and the study of stereotyping. In P.G. Devine, D.L. Hamilton, &

T.M. Ostrom (Eds.), *Social cognition: Impact on social psychology*. New York: Academic Press.

Harris, M.B., Harris, R.J., & Bochner, S. (1982). Fat, four-eyed, and female: Stereotypes of obesity, glasses, and gender. *Journal of Applied Social Psychology, 12*, 503–516.

Hass, R.G., Katz, I., Rizzo, N., Bailey, J., & Eisenstadt, D. (1991). Cross-racial appraisal as related to attitude ambivalence and cognitive complexity. *Personality and Social Psychology Bulletin, 17*, 83–92.

Heilman, M.E., Block, C.J., & Lucas, J.A. (1992). Presumed incompetent? Stigmatization and affirmative action effects. *Journal of Applied Social Psychology, 77*, 536–544.

Helmreich, W.B. (1997). *The things they say behind your back: Stereotypes and the myths behind them*. New Brunswick: Transaction.

Hense, R.L., Penner, L.A., Nelson, D.L. (1995). Implicit memory for age stereotypes. *Social Cognition, 13*, 399–415.

Hepworth, J.T., & West, S.G. (1988). Lynchings and the economy: A time-series reanalysis of Hovland and Sears (1940). *Journal of Personality and Social Psychology, 55*, 239–247.

Herdt, G. (1981). *Guardians of the flute: Idioms of masculinity*. New York: McGraw-Hill.

Herdt, G., & Boxer, A. (1995). Bisexuality: Toward a comparative theory of identities and culture. In R.G. Parker & J. Gagnon (Eds.), *Conceiving sexuality: Approaches to sex research in a postmodern world* (pp. 69–83). New York: Routledge.

Herek, G.M. (1984). Beyond "homophobia": A social psychological perspective on attitudes toward lesbians and gay men. *Journal of Homosexuality, 10*, 1–21.

Herek, G.M. (1988). Heterosexuals' attitudes toward lesbians and gay men: Correlates and gender differences. *Journal of Sex Research, 25*, 451–477.

Herek, G.M. (1989). Hate crimes against lesbians and gay men: Issues for research and policy. *American Psychologist, 44*, 948–955.

Herek, G.M. (1990a). Gay people and government security clearances: A social science perspective. *American Psychologist, 45,* 1035–1042.

**Herek, G.M.** (1990b). The context of anti-gay violence: Notes on cultural and psychological heterosexism. *Journal of Interpersonal Violence, 5,* 316–333.

**Herek, G.M.** (1991). Stigma, prejudice, and violence against lesbians and gay men. In J.C. Gonsiorek & J.D. Weinrich (Eds.), *Homosexuality: Research implications for public policy* (pp. 60–80). Newbury Park, CA: Sage.

**Herek, G.M.** (1993). On heterosexual masculinity: Some psychological consequences of the social construction of gender and sexuality. In L.D. Garnets & D.C. Kimmel (Eds.), *Psychological perspectives on lesbian and gay male experiences* (pp. 316–330). New York: Columbia University Press.

**Herek, G.M.** (1993). Sexual orientation and military service: A social science perspective. *American Psychologist, 48,* 538–549.

**Herek, G.M.** (1999). AIDS and stigma. *American Behavioral Scientist, 42,* 1106–1116.

**Herek, G.M.** (2000). The psychology of sexual prejudice. *Current Directions in Psychological Science, 9,* 19–22.

**Herek, G.M., & Capitanio, J.P.** (1995). Black heterosexuals, attitudes toward lesbians and gay men in the United States. *Journal of Sex Research, 32,* 95–105.

**Herek, G.M., & Capitanio, J.P.** (1996). "Some of my best friends": Intergroup contact, concealable stigma, and heterosexuals' attitudes toward gay men and lesbians. *Personality and Social Psychology Bulletin, 22,* 412–424.

**Herek, G.M., & Capitanio, J.P.** (1999). AIDS stigma and sexual prejudice. *American Behavioral Scientist, 42,* 1130–1147.

**Herek, G.M., Gillis, J.R., & Cogan, J.C.** (1999). Psychological sequelae of hate crime victimization among lesbian, gay, and bisexual adults. *Journal of Consulting and Clinical Psychology, 67,* 945–951.

**Herrnstein, R.A., & Murray, C.** (1994). *The bell curve.* New York: Grove Press.

**Hertz-Lazarowitz, R., & Miller, N.** (1992). *Interaction in cooperative groups.* New York: Cambridge University Press.

**Hewstone, M.** (1990). The "ultimate attribution error"? A review of the literature on intergroup causal attribution. *European Journal of Social Psychology, 20,* 311–335.

**Hewstone, M.** (1996). Contact and categorization: Social psychological interventions to change intergroup relations. In C.N. Macrae, C. Stangor, & M. Hewstone (Eds.), *Foundations of stereotypes and stereotyping* (pp. 323–368). New York: Guilford.

**Hewstone, M., & Brown, R.** (1986). Contact is not enough: An intergroup perspective on the "contact hypothesis." In M. Hewstone & R. Brown (Eds.), *Contact and conflict in intergroup encounters* (pp. 1–44). Oxford: Basil Blackwell.

**Hinkle, S., Taylor, L.A., Fox-Cardamone, L, & Ely, P.G.** (1998). Social identity and aspects of social creativity: Shifting to new dimensions of intergroup comparison. In S. Worchel, J.F. Morales, D. Paez, & J. Deschamps (Eds.), *Social identity: International perspectives* (pp. 166–179). Thousand Oaks, CA: Sage.

**Hirschfeld, L.A.** (1998). *Race in the making: Cognition, culture, and the child's construction of human kinds.* Cambridge, MA: MIT Press.

**Hoffman, C., & Hurst, N.** (1990). Gender stereotypes: Perception or rationalization? *Journal of Personality and Social Psychology, 58,* 197–208.

**Hogg, M.A., & Abrams, D.A.** (1988). *Social identifications: A social psychology of intergroup relations and group processes.* London: Routledge.

**Hogg, M., & Abrams, D.** (1990). Social motivation, self-esteem and social identity. In D. Abrams & M. Hogg (Eds.), *Social identity theory: Constructive and critical advances* (pp. 28–47). London: Harvester Wheatsheaf.

**Hooker, E.** (1957). The adjustment of the male overt homosexual. *Journal of Projective Techniques, 21,* 18–31.

**Hornsey, M.J., & Hogg, M.A.** (2000a). Assimilation and diversity: An integrative model of subgroup relations. *Personality and Social Psychology Review, 4,* 143–156.

Hornsey, M.J., & Hogg, M.A. (2000b). Intergroup similarity and subgroup relations: Some implications for assimilation. *Personality and Social Psychology Bulletin, 26,* 948–958.

Hornsey, M.J., & Hogg, M.A. (2000c). Subgroup relations: A comparison of mutual intergroup differentiation and common ingroup identity models of prejudice reduction. *Personality and Social Psychology Bulletin, 26,* 242–256.

Hovland, C., & Sears, R.R. (1940). Minor studies in aggression. VI: Correlation of lynchings with economic indices. *Journal of Psychology, 9,* 301–310.

Hughes, E.C. (1945). Dilemmas and contradictions of status. *American Journal of Sociology, 50,* 353–359.

Hunsberger, B. (1995). Religion and prejudice: The role of religious fundamentalism, quest, and right-wing authoritarianism. *Journal of Social Issues, 51,* 113–129.

Hyde, J.S., Fennema, E., & Lamon, S.J. (1990). Gender differences in mathematics performance: A meta-analysis. *Psychological Bulletin, 107,* 139–155.

Hyman, H.H., & Sheatsley, P.B. (1954). "The Authoritarian Personality": A methodological critique. In R. Christie & M. Jahoda (Eds.), *Studies in the scope and method of "The Authoritarian Personality."* Glencoe, IL: Free Press.

"It isn't fair": A federal grand jury steps in. *Time,* Nov 14, 1983, v122, p46.

Jackman, M.R., & Crane, M. (1986). "Some of my best friends are black...": Interracial friendship and whites' racial attitudes. *Public Opinion Quarterly, 19,* 700–710.

Jackson, L. A. (1992). In what way is the unfinished mind unfinished? *Psychological Inquiry, 3,* 163–165.

Jackson, L.A., & Cash, T.F. (1985). Components of gender stereotypes: Their implications for inferences on stereotypic and nonstereotypic dimensions. *Personality and Social Psychology Bulletin, 11,* 326–344.

Jackson, L.A., & Ervin, K.S. (1991). The frequency and portrayal of black females in fashion advertisements. *The Journal of Black Psychology, 18,* 67–70.

Jackson, L.A., Sullivan, L.A., Harnish, R., & Hodge, C.N. (1996). Achieving positive social identity: Social mobility, social creativity, and permeability of group boundaries. *Journal of Personality and Social Psychology, 70,* 241–254.

James, S. (1994). John Henryism and the health of African-Americans. *Culture, Medicine, and Psychiatry, 18,* 163–182.

James, S., Harnett, S., & Kalsbeek, W. (1983). John Henryism and blood pressure differences among black men. *Journal of Behavioral Medicine, 6,* 259–278.

Jefferson, T. (1787). *Notes on the state of Virginia.* Edited by W. Peden (1955). Chapel Hill: University of North Carolina Press.

Johnson, D.W., & Johnson, R.T. (1992). Social interdependence and cross-ethnic relationships. In J. Lynch, C. Modgil, & S. Modgil (Eds.), *Cultural diversity in the schools* (Vol. 2, pp. 179–190). London: Falmer Press.

Jones, E.E., Farina, A., Hastorf, A.H., Markus, H., Miller, D.T., & Scott, R.A. (1984). *Social stigma: The psychology of marked relationships.* New York: W.H. Freeman.

Jones, J.M. (1988). Racism in black and white: A bicultural model of reaction and evolution. In P.A. Katz & D.A. Taylor (Eds.), *Eliminating racism: Profiles in controversy* (pp. 117–158). New York: Plenum Press.

Jones, M. (1991). Stereotyping Hispanics and Whites: Perceived differences in social roles as a determinant of ethnic stereotypes. *Journal of Social Psychology, 131,* 469–476.

Jones, M. (1997). Preventing the application of stereotypic biases in the courtroom: The role of detailed testimony. *Journal of Applied Social Psychology, 27,* 1767–1784.

Jost, J.T., & Banaji, M.R. (1994). The role of stereotyping in system-justification and the production of false consciousness. *British Journal of Social Psychology, 33,* 1–17.

Judd, C.M., & Park, B. (1988). Out-group homogeneity: Judgments of variability at the individual and group levels. *Journal of Personality and Social Psychology, 54,* 778–788.

Judd, C.M., Park, B., Ryan, C.S., Brauer, M., & Kraus, S. (1995). Stereotypes and ethnocentrism: Diverging interethnic perceptions of African Americans and White urban youth. *Journal of Personality and Social Psychology, 69*, 460–481.

Judd, C.M., Ryan, C.S., & Park, B. (1991). Accuracy in the judgment of in-group and out-group variability. *Journal of Personality and Social Psychology, 61*, 366–379.

Jussim, L., & Fleming, C. (1996). Self-fulfilling prophecies and the maintenance of social stereotypes: The role of dyadic interactions and social forces. In C.N. Macrae, C. Stangor, & M. Hewstone (Eds.), *Stereotypes and stereotyping.* New York: Guilford.

Jussim, L., Nelson, T. E., Manis, M., & Soffin, S. (1995). Prejudice, stereotypes, and labeling effects: Sources of bias in person perception. *Journal of Personality and Social Psychology, 68*, 228–246.

Karlins, M., Coffman, T.L., & Walters, G. (1969). On the fading of social stereotypes: Studies in three generations of college students. *Journal of Personality and Social Psychology, 13*, 1–16.

Karpinski, A., & von Hippel, W. (1996). The role of the linguistic intergroup bias in expectancy-maintenance. *Social Cognition, 14*, 141–163.

Katz, D., & Braly, K. (1933). Racial stereotypes in one hundred college students. *Journal of Abnormal and Social Psychology, 28*, 280–290.

Katz, I. (1979). Some thoughts about the stigma notion. *Personality and Social Psychology Bulletin, 5*, 447–460.

Katz, I., Cohen, S., & Glass, D. (1975). Some determinants of cross-racial helping behavior. *Journal of Personality and Social Psychology, 32*, 964–970.

Katz, I., Glass, D., & Cohen, S. (1973). Ambivalence, guilt, and the scapegoating of minority group victims. *Journal of Experimental Social Psychology, 9*, 423–436.

Katz, I., Glass, D., Lucido, D.J., & Farber, J. (1977). Ambivalence, guilt and the denigration of a physically handicapped victim. *Journal of Personality, 45*, 419–429.

Katz, I., & Hass, R.G. (1988). Racial ambivalence and American value conflict: Correlational and priming studies of dual cognitive structures. *Journal of Personality and Social Psychology, 55*, 893–905.

Katz, I., Wackenhut, J., & Glass, D.C. (1986). An ambivalence-amplification theory of behavior toward the stigmatized. In S. Worchel and W. G. Austin (Eds.), *Psychology of Intergroup Relations.* Chicago: Nelson-Hall.

Katz, I., Wackenhut, J., & Hass, R.G. (1986). Racial ambivalence, value duality, and behavior. In J.F. Dovidio & S.L. Gaertner (Eds.), *Prejudice, discrimination and racism* (pp. 35–59). New York: Academic Press.

Katz, J.N. (1992). *Gay American history: Lesbians and gay men in the U.S.A.* New York: Meridian.

Katz, P.A., & Zalk, S.R. (1974). Doll preferences: Index of racial attitudes? *Journal of Educational Psychology, 66*, 663–668.

Kawakami, K., Dovidio, J.F., Moll, J., Hermsen, S., & Russin, A. (2000). Just say no (to stereotyping): Effects of training in the negation of stereotypic associations on stereotype activation. *Journal of Personality and Social Psychology, 78*, 871–888.

Keenan, K.L. (1996). Skin tones and physical features of blacks in magazine advertisements. *Journalism and Mass Communication Quarterly, 73*, 905–912.

Kern-Foxworth, M. (1992, June 4). Colorizing advertising: Challenges for the 1990s and beyond. *Black Issues in Higher Education*, 64.

Kessler, S.J., & McKenna, W. (1985). *Gender: An ethnomethodological approach.* Chicago: University of Chicago Press.

Kinder, D.R. (1986). The continuing American dilemma: White resistance to racial change 40 years after Myrdal. *Journal of Social Issues, 42*, 151–172.

Kinder, D.R., & Sears, D.O. (1981). Prejudice and politics: Symbolic racism versus racial threats to the good life. *Journal of Personality and Social Psychology, 40*, 414–431.

King, M.L., Jr. (1962, August 5). The case against tokenism. *The New York Times Magazine.*

Kinsey, A.C., Pomeroy, W., & Martin, C. (1948). *Sexual behavior in the human male.* Philadelphia: Saunders.

Kirby, R. & Corzine, J. (1981). The contagion of stigma: Fieldwork among deviants. *Qualitative Sociology, 41*, 3–20.

Kite, M.E., & Deaux, B.E. (1987). Gender belief systems: Homosexuality and the implicit inversion theory. *Psychology of Women Quarterly, 11*, 83–96.

Kite, M.E., & Whitley, B.E. (1996). Sex differences in attitudes toward homosexual persons, behaviors, and civil rights: A meta-analysis. *Personality and Social Psychology Bulletin, 22*, 336–353.

Kite, M.E., & Whitley, B.E. (1998). Do heterosexual women and men differ in their attitudes toward homosexuality: A conceptual and methodological analysis. In G.M Herek (Ed.), *Stigma and sexual orientation: Understanding prejudice against lesbians, gay men and bisexuals* (pp. 39–61). Thousand Oaks, CA: Sage.

Kleck, R., Ono, H., & Hastorf, A.H. (1966). The effects of physical deviance upon face-to-face interaction. *Human Relations, 21*, 19–28.

Kleck, R.E., & Strenta, A. (1980). Perceptions of the impact of negatively valued physical characteristics on social interactions. *Journal of Personality and Social Psychology, 38*, 861–873.

Kleinpenning, G., & Hagendoorn, L. (1993). *Social Psychology Quarterly, 56*, 21–36.

Kling, K.C., Hyde, J.S., Showers, C.J., & Buswell, B.N. (1999). Gender differences in self-esteem: A meta-analysis. *Journal of Personality and Social Psychology, 125*, 470–500.

Kohn, W. (1994, Nov. 6). Service with a sneer. *The New York Times Magazine*, pp. 43–47, 58, 78, 81.

Konrad, A.M., & Linnehan, F. (1995). Race and sex differences in line managers' reactions to equal employment opportunity and affirmative action interventions. *Group and Organization Management, 20*, 409–439.

Kopvillem, P. (1996, March 11). Guilty as charged: James Keegstra reaches the end of the legal line. *Maclean's*, p. 24.

Kramer, R.M., & Brewer, M.B. (1984). Effects of group identity on resource utilization in a simulated common dilemma. *Journal of Personality and Social Psychology, 46*, 1044–1057.

Krieger, N., & Sidney, S. (1996). Racial discrimination and blood pressure: The CARDIA study of young black and white adults. *American Journal of Public Health, 8b*, 1370–1378.

Kruglanski, A.W., & Freund, T. (1983). The freezing and unfreezing of lay-inferences: Effects on impressional primacy, ethnic stereotyping, and numerical anchoring. *Journal of Experimental Social Psychology, 19*, 448–468.

Kruglanski, A.W, & Webster, D.M. (1996). Motivated closing of the mind: "Seizing" and "freezing." *Psychological Review, 103*, 263–283.

Kulick, D. (1997). The gender of Brazilian transgendered prostitutes. *American Anthropologist, 99*, 574–585.

Kutner, B., Wilkins, C., & Yarrow, P. R. (1952). Verbal attitudes and overt behavior involving racial prejudice. *Journal of Abnormal and Social Psychology, 47*, 649–652.

Lachman, M.E., & Weaver, S.L. (1998). The sense of control as a moderator of social class differences in health and well-being. *Journal of Personality and Social Psychology, 74*, 763–773.

Lambert, A.J., & Chasteen, A.L. (1997). Perceptions of disadvantage versus conventionality: Political values and attitudes toward the elderly versus Blacks. *Personality and Social Psychology Bulletin, 23*, 469–481.

Langer, E.J., & Imber, L. (1980). Role of mindlessness in the perception of deviance. *Journal of Personality and Social Psychology, 39*, 360–367.

LaPiere, R. T. (1934). Attitudes vs. actions. *Social Forces, 13*, 230–237.

Larkin, J.E., & Pines, H.A. (1979). No fat persons need apply. *Sociology of Work and Occupations, 6*, 312–327.

Lee, Y., Jussim, I., & McCauley, C.R. (Eds.). (1995). *Stereotype accuracy.* Washington, DC: American Psychological Association.

Leippe, M.R., & Eisenstadt, D. (1994). Generalization of dissonance reduction: Decreasing prejudice through induced compliance. *Journal of Personality and Social Psychology, 67,* 395–413.

Lenthall, B., (1998). Outside the panel—race in America's popular imagination: Comic strips before and after World War II. *Journal of American Studies, 32,* 39–61.

Lepore, L., & Brown, R. (1997). Category and stereotype activation: Is prejudice inevitable? *Journal of Personality and Social Psychology, 72,* 275–287.

Lepowsky, M. (1998). The influence of culture on behavior: The case of aggression. In D.L. Anselmi & A.L. Law (Eds.), *Questions of gender: Perspectives and paradoxes* (pp. 170–178). New York: McGraw-Hill.

Leslie, M. (1995). Slow fade to ?: Advertising in Ebony magazine, 1957–1989. *Journalism and Mass Communication Quarterly, 72,* 426–435.

LeVay, S. (1991). A difference in hypothalamic structure between heterosexual and homosexual men. *Science, 253,* 1034–1037.

Levin, S., & Dyer, E. (1998, February 28). A racial divide: Young whites, blacks find little common ground. *Pittsburgh Post-Gazette,* A-16.

LeVine, R.A., & Campbell, D.T. (1972). *Ethnocentrism: Theories of conflict, ethnic attitudes and group behavior.* New York: Wiley.

Levy, J. (1972). Lateral specialization of the human brain: Behavioral manifestations and possible evolutionary basis. In J.A. Kiger (Ed.), *The biology of behavior.* Corvallis: Oregon State University Press.

Liebert, R.M., & Sprafkin, J. (1988). *The early window.* New York: Pergamon Press.

Linn, L. S. (1965). Verbal attitudes and overt behavior: A study of racial discrimination. *Social Forces, 43,* 353–364.

Linville, P.W., Fischer, F.W., & Salovey, P. (1989). Perceived distributions of characteristics of ingroup and outgroup members: Empirical evidence and a computer simulation. *Journal of Personality and Social Psychology, 57,* 165–188.

Linville, P.W., & Jones, E.E. (1980). Polarized appraisal of out-group members. *Journal of Personality and Social Psychology, 38,* 689–703.

Lippman, W. (1922). *Public opinion.* New York: Harcourt, Brace, and World.

Locke, V., & MacLeod, C., & Walker, I. (1994). Automatic and controlled activation of stereotypes: Individual differences associated with prejudice. *British Journal of Social Psychology, 33,* 9–46.

Loehlin, J.C., Lindzey, G., Spuhler, I.N. (1975). *Race differences in intelligence.* San Francisco, CA: W.H. Freeman.

Lott, J.T.(1998). *Asian Americans: From racial category to multiple identities.* Walnut Creek, CA: Altamira Press.

Louderback, L.A., & Whitley, B.E., Jr. (1997). Perceived erotic value of homosexuality and sex-role attitudes as mediators of sex differences in heterosexual college students' attitudes toward lesbians and gay men. *Journal of Sex Research, 34,* 175–182.

Maass, A. (1999). Linguistic intergroup bias: Stereotype perpetuation through language. In M.P. Zanna (Ed.), *Advances in Experimental Social Psychology, Vol. 31.* New York: Academic Press.

Maass, A., & Arcuri, L. (1996). Language and stereotyping. In C.N. Macrae, C. Stangor, & M. Hewstone (Eds.), *Stereotypes and stereotyping.* New York: Guilford.

Maass, A., Ceccarelli, R., & Rudin, S. (1996). The linguistic intergroup bias: Evidence for ingroup-protective motivation. *Journal of Personality and Social Psychology, 71,* 512–526.

Maass, A., Corvino, P., & Arcuri, L. (1994). Linguistic intergroup bias and the mass media. *Revue de Psychologie Sociale, 1,* 31–43.

Maass, A., Milesi, A., Zabini, S., & Stahlberg, D. (1995). The linguistic intergroup bias: Differential expectancies or ingroup protection? *Journal of Personality and Social Psychology, 68,* 116–126.

MacDonald, T.K., & Zanna, M.P. (1998). Cross-dimension ambivalence toward social groups: Can ambivalence affect intentions to hire feminists? *Personality and Social Psychology Bulletin, 24,* 427–441.

Mackie, D.M., Hamilton, D.L., Susskind, J., & Rosselli, F. (1996). Social psychological foundations of stereotype formation. In C.N. Macrae,

C. Stangor, & M. Hewstone (Eds.), *Stereotypes and stereotyping* (pp.41–78). NY: Guilford.

Mackie, D.M., Queller, S., Stroessner, S.J., & Hamilton, D.L. (1996). Making stereotypes better or worse: Multiple roles for positive affect in group impressions. In R.M. Sorrentino & E.T. Higgins (Eds.), *Handbook of motivation and cognition* (Vol. 3, pp. 371–396). New York: Guilford.

Mackie, D.M., & Smith, E.R. (1998a). Intergroup cognition and intergroup behavior: Crossing the boundaries. In C. Sedikides, J. Schopler, & C.A. Insko (Eds.), *Intergroup cognition and intergroup behavior* (pp. 423–450). Mahwah, NJ: Lawrence Erlbaum.

Mackie, D.M., & Smith, E.R. (1998b). Intergroup relations: Insights from a theoretically integrative approach. *Psychological Review, 105,* 499–529.

Macrae, C.N., Bodenhausen, G.V., & Milne, A.B. (1995). The dissection of selection in person perception: Inhibitory processes in social stereotypes. *Journal of Personality and Social Psychology, 69,* 397–407.

Macrae, C.N., Bodenhausen, G.V., & Milne, A.B. (1998). Saying no to unwanted thoughts: Self-focus and the regulation of mental life. *Journal of Personality and Social Psychology, 74,* 578–589.

Macrae, C.N., Bodenhausen, G.V., Milne, A.B., & Ford, R.L. (1997). On the regulation of recollection: The intentional forgetting of stereotypical memories. *Journal of Personality and Social Psychology, 72,* 709–719.

Macrae, C.N., Bodenhausen, G.V., Milne, A.B., & Jetten, J. (1994). Out of mind but back in sight: Stereotypes on the rebound. *Journal of Personality and Social Psychology, 67,* 808–817.

Macrae, C.N., Bodenhausen, G.V., Milne, A B., Thorn, T.M.J., & Castelli, L. (1997). On the activation of social stereotypes: The moderating role of processing objectives. *Journal of Experimental Social Psychology, 33,* 471–489.

Macrae, C.N., Milne, A.B., & Bodenhausen, G.V. (1994). Stereotypes as energy-saving devices: A peek inside the cognitive toolbox. *Journal of Personality and Social Psychology, 66,* 37–47.

Maio, G.R., & Esses, V.M. (1998). The social consequences of affirmative action: Deleterious effects on perceptions of groups. *Personality and Social Psychology Bulletin, 24,* 65–74.

Major, B., & Crocker, J. (1993). Social stigma: The consequences of attributional ambiguity. In D.M. Mackie & D. L. Hamilton (Eds.), *Affect, cognition, and stereotyping: Interactive processes in group perception* (p. 370). New York: Academic Press.

Major, B., Feinstein, J., & Crocker, J. (1994). Attributional ambiguity of affirmative action. *Basic and Applied Social Psychology, 15,* 113–141.

Major, B., & Gramzow, R.H. (1999). Abortion as stigma: Cognitive and emotional implications of concealment. *Journal of Personality and Social Psychology, 77,* 735–745.

Major, B., Spencer, S., Schmader, T., Wolfe, C., & Crocker, J. (1998). Coping with negative stereotypes about intellectual performance: The role of psychological disengagement. *Personality and Social Psychology Bulletin, 24,* 34–50.

Marcus, F.F. (1983, July 6). Louisiana repeals black blood law. *The New York Times,* p. A10.

Marin, G. (1984). Stereotyping Hispanics: The differential effect of reseach method, label, and degree of contact. *International Journal of Intercultural Relations, 8,* 17–27.

Marks, J. (1995). *Human biodiversity: Genes, race, and history.* New York: Aldine De Gruyter.

Maroney, D., & Golub, S. (1992). Nurses' attitudes toward obese persons and certain ethnic groups. *Perceptual and Motor Skills, 75,* 387–391.

Marsiglio, W. (1993). Attitudes toward homosexual activity and gays as friends: A national survey of heterosexual 15- to 19-year-old males. *Journal of Sex Research, 30,* 12–17.

Martin, M.K., & Voorhies, B. (1975). *Female of the species.* New York: Columbia University Press.

Martin, P.Y. (1992). Gender, interaction, and inequality in organizations. In C.L. Ridgeway (Ed.), *Gender, interaction, and inequality* (pp. 208–231). New York: Springer-Verlag.

Marx, D.M., Brown, J.L., & Steele, C.M. (1999). Allport's legacy and the situational press of stereotypes. *Journal of Social Issues, 55,* 491–502.

McCauley, C., & Stitt, C. L. (1978). An individual and quantitative measure of stereotypes. *Journal of Personality and Social Psychology, 36,* 929–940.

McConahay, J.B. (1986). Modern racism, ambivalence, and the modern racism scale. In J. Dovidio & S.L. Gaertner (Eds.), *Prejudice, discrimination, and racism* (pp. 91–125). New York: Academic Press.

McConahay, J.B., Hardee, B.B., & Batts, V. (1981). Has racism declined in America? It depends on who is asking and what is asked. *Journal of Conflict Resolution, 25,* 563–579.

McConahay, J.B., & Hough, J.C., Jr. (1976). Symbolic racism. *Journal of Social Issues, 32,* 23–45.

McFarland, S.G., Ageyev, V.S., & Djintcharadze, N. (1996). Russian authoritarianism two years after communism. *Personality and Social Psychology Bulletin, 22,* 210–217.

Mead, G.H. (1934). *Mind, self, and society.* Chicago: University of Chicago Press.

Meertens, R.W., & Pettigrew, T.F. (1997). Is subtle prejudice really prejudice? *Public Opinion Quarterly, 61,* 54–71.

Meloen, J.D. (1991). The fortieth anniversary of "the authoritarian personality": Is there new evidence to consider the authoritarian personality to be the backbone of "left" as well as "right wing" dictatorships? *Politics and the Individual, 1,* 119–127.

Meloen, J.D., Van der Linden, G., & De Witte, H. (1996). A test of the approaches of Adorno et al., Lederer and Altemeyer of authoritarianism in Belgian Flanders: A research note. *Political Psychology, 17,* 643–656.

Messick, D.M., & Mackie, D.M. (1989). Intergroup relations. *Annual Review of Psychology, 40,* 51–81.

Miller, C.T., & Myers, A.M. (1998). Compensating for prejudice: How heavyweight people (and others) control outcomes despite prejudice. In J.T. Swim & C.Stangor (Eds.), *Prejudice: The target's perspective* (pp. 191–218). New York: Academic Press.

Miller, C.T., Rothblum, E.D., Barbour, L., Brand, P.A., Felicio, D. (1990). Social interactions of obese and nonobese women. *Journal of Personality, 58,* 365–380.

Miller, C.T., Rothblum, E.D., Brand, P.A., & Felicio, D.M. (1995). Do obese women have poorer social relationships than nonobese women? Reports by self, friends, and coworkers. *Journal of Personality, 63,* 65–85.

Miller, C.T., Rothblum, E.D., Felicio, D., & Brand, P. (1995). Compensating for stigma: Obese and nonobese women's reactions to being visible. *Personality and Social Psychology Bulletin, 21,* 1093–1106.

Miller, N. & Brewer, M.B. (1984). *Groups in contact: The psychology of desegregation.* New York: Academic Press.

Miller, N., Brewer, M.B., & Edwards, K. (1985). Cooperative interaction in desegregated settings: A laboratory analogue. *Journal of Social Issues, 41,* 63–79.

Millman, M. (1980). *Such a pretty face: Being fat in America.* New York: Norton.

Minard, R.D. (1952). Race relationships in the Pocahontas coal field. *Journal of Social Issues, 8,* 29–44.

Molnar, S. (1992). *Human variation: Races, types, and ethnic groups.* Englewood Cliffs, NJ: Prentice Hall.

Monello, L.F., & Mayer, J. (1963). Obese adolescent girls: An unrecognized "minority" group? *American Journal of Clinical Nutrition, 13,* 35–39.

Montagu, A. (1963). *Race, science, and humanity.* Princeton, NJ: Van Nostrand.

Monteith, M.J. (1993). Self-regulation of prejudiced responses: Implications for progress in prejudice reduction efforts. *Journal of Personality and Social Psychology, 65,* 469–485.

Monteith, M.J. (1996). Contemporary forms of prejudice-related conflict: In search of a nutshell. *Personality and Social Psychology Bulletin, 22,* 461–473.

Monteith, M.J., Deneen, N.E., & Tooman, G.D. (1996). The effect of social norm activation on the expression of opinions concerning gay men and blacks. *Basic and Applied Social Psychology, 18*, 267–288.

Monteith, M.J., Sherman, J.W., & Devine, P. G. (1998). Suppression as a stereotype control strategy. *Personality and Social Psychology Review, 2*, 63–82.

Monteith, M.J., Spicer, C.V., & Tooman, G.D. (1998). Consequences of stereotype suppression: Stereotypes on and not on the rebound. *Journal of Experimental Social Psychology, 34*, 355–377.

Monteith, M.J., & Walters, G.L. (1998). Egalitarianism, moral obligation, and prejudice-related personal standards. *Personality and Social Psychology Bulletin, 24*, 186–199.

Monteith, M.J., Zuwerink, J.R., & Devine, P.G. (1994). Prejudice and prejudice reduction: Classic challenges, contemporary approaches. In P.G. Devine, D.L. Hamilton, & T.M. Ostrom (Eds.), *Social cognition: Contributions to classic issues in social psychology* (pp. 323–346). San Diego, CA: Academic Press.

Morris, T.D. (1996). *Southern slavery and the law, 1619–1860*. Chapel Hill: University of North Carolina Press.

Moskowitz, G.B., Gollwitzer, P.M., Wasel, W., & Schaal, B. (1999). Preconscious control of stereotype activation through chronic egalitarian goals. *Journal of Personality and Social Psychology, 77*, 167–184.

Moskowitz, G.B., Salomon, A.R., & Taylor, C.M. (2000). Preconsciously controlling stereotyping: Implicitly activated egalitarian goals prevent the activation of stereotypes. *Social Cognition, 18*, 151–177.

Mullen, B., Brown, R.J., & Smith, C. (1992). Ingroup bias as a function of salience, relevance, and status: An integration. *European Journal of Social Psychology, 22*, 103–122.

Murrell, A.J., & Jones, R. (1996). Assessing affirmative action: Past, present and future. *Journal of Social Issues, 52*, 77–92.

Muslims continue to feel apprehensive (1995, April 24). *The New York Times*, p. B10.

National Committee on Pay Equity. (1994). *Newsnotes, 15*, 113.

Neimann, Y.F., Jennings, L., Rozelle, R.M., Baxter, J.C., & Sullivan, E. (1994). Use of free responses and cluster analysis to determine stereotypes of eight groups. *Personality and Social Psychology Bulletin, 20*, 370–390.

Nelson, T.E., Acker, M., & Manis, M. (1996). Irrepressible stereotypes. *Journal of Experimental Social Psychology, 32*, 13–38.

Neuberg, S.L. (1989). The goal of forming accurate impressions during social interactions: Attenuating the impact of negative expectancies. *Journal of Personality and Social Psychology, 56*, 374–386.

Neuberg, S.L., & Newson, J.T. (1993). Personal need for structure: Individual differences in the desire for simple structure. *Journal of Personality and Social Psychology, 65*, 113–131.

Neuberg, S. L., Smith, D. M., Hoffman, J. C., & Russell, F. J. (1994). When we observed stigmatized and "normal" individuals interacting: Stigma by association. *Personality and Social Psychology Bulletin, 20*, 196–209.

Neuberg, S.L., West, S.G., Judice, T.N., & Thompson, M.M. (1997). On dimensionality, discriminant validity, and the role of psychometric analyses in personality theory and measurement: Reply to Kruglanski et al.'s (1997) defense of the need for closure scale. *Journal of Personality and Social Psychology, 73*, 1017–1029.

Noel, J.G., Wann, D.L., & Branscombe, N.R., (1995). Peripheral ingroup membership status and public negativity toward outgroups. *Journal of Personality and Social Psychology, 68*, 127–137.

Nolen-Hoeksema, S. (1987). The emergence of gender differences in depression during adolescence. *Psychological Bulletin, 115*, 424–443.

Oakes, P.J. (1987). The salience of social categories. In J. Turner, M. Hogg, P. Oakes, S. Reicher, & M. Wetherell (Eds.), *Rediscovering the social group* (pp. 117–141). Oxford: Basil Blackwell.

Ogbu, J. (1986). The consequences of the American caste system. In U. Neisser (Ed.), *The school achievement of minority children: New perspectives* (pp. 19–56). Hillsdale, NJ: Erlbaum.

Olson, J.M., Roese, N.M., Meen, J., & Robertson, D.J. (1995). The preconditions and consequences of relative deprivation: Two field studies. *Journal of Applied Social Psychology, 25,* 944–964.

Omi, M. (1989). In living color: Race and American culture. In I. Agnus & S. Jhally (Eds.), *Cultural politics in contemporary America* (pp. 111–122). New York: Routledge.

Overbey, M.M. (1997, October). AAA tells feds to eliminate "race." *Anthropology Newsletter, 38,* 1.

Palardy, J. (1969). What teachers believe—What students achieve. *Elementary School Journal, 69,* 370–374.

Paludi, M.A., & Bauer, W.D. (1983). Goldberg revisited: What's in an author's name? *Sex Roles, 9,* 387–390.

Park, B., & Judd, C.M. (1990). Measures and models of perceived group variability. *Journal of Personality and Social Psychology, 59,* 173–191.

Pendry, L.F., & Macrae, C.N. (1994). Stereotypes and mental life: The case of the motivated but thwarted tactician. *Journal of Experimental Social Psychology, 30,* 303–325.

Peplau, L.A., Garnets, L.D., Spalding, L.R., Conley, T.D., Veniegas, R.C. (1998). A critique of Bem's "exotic becomes erotic" theory of sexual orientation. *Psychological Review, 105,* 387–394.

Perdue, C.W., Dovidio, J.F., Gurtman, M.B., & Tyler, R.B. (1990). Us and them: Social categorization and the process of intergroup bias. *Journal of Personality and Social Psychology, 59,* 475–486.

Perdue, C.W., & Gurtman, M.B. (1990). Evidence for the automaticity of ageism. *Journal of Experimental Social Psychology 26,* 199–216.

Perreault, S., & Bourhis, R.Y. (1999). Ethnocentrism, social identificaiton, and discrimination. *Personality and Social Psychology Bulletin, 25,* 92–103.

Peters, M. (1995). Race differences in brain size. *American Psychologist, 50,* 947.

Peterson, B.E., Doty, R.M., & Winter, D.G. (1993). Authoritarianism and attitudes toward contemporary social issues. *Personality and Social Psychology Bulletin, 19,* 174–184.

Pettigrew, T.F. (1958). Personality and sociocultural factors in intergroup attitudes: A cross national comparison. *Journal of Conflict Resolution, 2,* 29–42.

Pettigrew, T.F. (1979). The ultimate attribution error: Extending Allport's cognitive analysis of prejudice. *Personality and Social Psychology Bulletin, 5,* 461–476.

Pettigrew, T.F. (1980). Prejudice. In S. Thernstrom et al. (Eds.), *Harvard encyclopedia of American ethnic groups.* Cambridge, MA: Harvard University Press.

Pettigrew, T.F. (1986). The intergroup contact hypothesis reconsidered. In M. Hewstone & R. Brown (Eds.), *Contact and conflict in intergroup encounters* (pp. 169–195). Oxford: Blackwell.

Pettigrew, T. F. (1997). Generalized intergroup contact effects on prejudice. *Personality and Social Psychology Bulletin, 23,* 173–185.

Pettigrew, T. (1998). Intergroup contact theory. *Annual Review of Psychology, 49,* pp. 65–85. Palo Alto, CA: Annual Reviews, Inc.

Phillips, S.T., & Ziller, R.C. (1997). Toward a theory and measure of the nature of nonprejudice. *Journal of Personality and Social Psychology, 72,* 429–434.

Phinney, J.S. (1996). When we talk about American ethnic groups, what do we mean? *American Psychologist, 51,* 918–927.

Plous, S., & Neptune, D. (1997). Racial and gender biases in magazine advertising: A content analytic study. *Psychology of Women Quarterly, 21,* 627–644.

Plous, S., & Williams, T. (1995). Racial stereotypes from the days of American slavery: A continuing legacy. *Journal of Applied Social Psychology 25,* 795–817.

Posner, J. (1976) Death as a courtesy stigma. *Essence, 1,* 39–50.

Posner, M.I., & Snyder, C.R.R. (1975). Attention and cognitive control. In R.L. Solso (Ed.), *Information processing and cognition: The Loyola symposium,* pp. 52–82. Hillsdale, NJ: Erlbaum.

Pratkanis, A.R., & Turner, M.E. (1996). The proactive removal of discriminatory barriers: Affirmative action as effective help. *Journal of Social Issues, 52,* 111–132.

Pratto, F., Liu, J.H., Levin, S., Sidanius, J., Shih, M., & Bachrach, H. (1998). Social dominance orientation and legitimization of inequality across cultures. Unpublished manuscript, Stanford University.

Pratto, F., Sidanius J., Stallworth, L.M., & Malle, B.F. (1994). Social dominance orientation: A personality variable predicting social and political attitudes. *Journal of Personality and Social Psychology, 67,* 741–763.

Pratto, F., Stallworth, L.M., & Sidanius, J. (1997). The gender gap: Differences in political attitudes and social dominance orientation. *British Journal of Social Psychology, 36,* 49–68.

Quattrone, G.A., & Jones, E.E. (1980). The perception of variability within ingroups and outgroups: Implications for the law of small numbers. *Journal of Personality and Social Psychology, 38,* 141–152.

Quinn, D.M., & Crocker, J. (1998). Vulnerability to the affective consequences of the stigma of overweight. In J. Swim & C. Stangor (Eds.), *Prejudice: The target's perspective* (pp. 125–143). San Diego, CA: Academic Press.

Quinn, D.M., & Crocker, J. (1999). When ideology hurts: Effects of belief in the Protestant ethic and feeling overweight on the psychological well-being of women. *Journal of Personality and Social Psychology, 77,* 402–414.

Quinn, K.A., Roese, N.J., Pennington, G.L., & Olson, J.M. (1999). The personal/group discrimination discrepancy: The role of informational complexity. *Personality and Social Psychology Bulletin, 25,* 1430–1440.

Quinton, W.J., Cowan, G., & Watson, B.D. (1996). Personality and attitudinal predictors of support of Proposition 187—California's anti-illegal immigrant initiative. *Journal of Applied Social Psychology, 26,* 2204–2223.

Raab, E.R., & Liset, S.M. (1959). *Prejudice and society.* New York: Anti-Defamation League.

Rabbie, J.M., Benoise, F., Oosterbaan, H., & Visser, L. (1974). Differential power and effects of expected competitive and cooperative intergroup interaction on intergroup and out-group attitudes. *Journal of Personality and Social Psychology, 30,* 45–56.

Reitzes, D.C. (Spring, 1959). Institutional structure and race relations. *Phylon,* 48–66.

Reskin, B., & Padavic, I. (1994). *Women and men at work.* Thousand Oaks, CA: Forge Press.

Richardson, L. (1988). *The dynamics of sex and gender.* New York: Harper & Row.

Rodin, M., & Price, J. (1995). Overcoming stigma: Credit for self-improvement or discredit for needing to improve? *Personality and Social Psychology Bulletin, 21,* 172–181.

Roe, D.A., & Eickwort, K.R. (1976). Relationships between obesity and associated health factors with unemployment among low income women. *Journal of American Medical Women's Association, 31,* 193–204.

Rohan, M.J., & Zanna, M.P. (1996). Value transmission in families. In C. Seligman, J.M. Olson, & M.P. Zanna (Eds.), *The psychology of values: The Ontario symposium,* (Vol. 8, pp. 253–274). Mahwah, NJ: Erlbaum.

Rokeach, M. (1960). *The open and closed mind.* New York: Basic Books.

Romo, H., & Falbo, T. (1995). *Latino high school graduation: Defying the odds.* Austin, TX: University of Texas Press.

Rosenbluth, S. (1997). Is sexual orientation a matter of choice? *Psychology of Women Quarterly, 21,* 595–610.

Rosenfield, D., & Stephan, W.G. (1981). Intergroup relations among children. In S. Brehm, S. Kassin, & F. Givvons (Eds.), *Developmental social psychology* (pp. 271–297). New York: Oxford University Press.

Rosenkrantz, P.S., Vogel, S.R., Bee, H., Broverman, I.K., & Broverman, D.M. (1968). Sex role stereotypes and self-concepts in college students. *Journal of Consulting and Clinical Psychology, 32,* 287–295.

Rosenthal, R., & Jacobson, L. (1968). *Pygmalion in the classroom.* New York: Holt, Rinehart & Winston.

Rothbart, M., & John, O.P. (1985). Social categorization and behavioral episodes: A cognitive analysis of the effects of Intergroup contact. *Journal of Social Issues, 41*, 81–104.

Rothbart, M., & Lewis, S. (1994). Cognitive processes and intergroup relations: A historical perspective. In P.G. Devine, D.L. Hamilton, & T.M. Ostrom (Eds.), *Social cognition: Impact on social psychology.* New York: Academic Press.

Rothbart, M., Sriram, N., & Davis-Stitt, C., (1996). The retrieval of typical and atypical category members. *Journal of Experimental Social Psychology, 32*, 309–336.

Rozin, P., & Nemeroff, C. (1990). The laws of sympathetic magic: A psychological analysis of similarity and contagion. In J. E. Stigler, R. A. Schweder, & G. Herdt (Eds.), *Cultural psychology: Essays on comparative human development* (pp. 205–232). Cambridge, England: Cambridge University Press.

Rubin, M., & Hewstone, M. (1998). Social identity theory's self-esteem hypothesis: A review and some suggestions for clarification. *Personality and Social Psychology Review, 2*, 40–62.

Rudman, L.A., & Kilanski, S.E. (2000). Implicit and explicit attitudes toward female authority. *Personality and Social Psychology Bulletin, 26*, 1315–1328.

Ruggiero, K.M., & Major, B.N. (1998). Group status and attributions to discrimination: Are low- or high-status group members more likely to blame their failure on discrimination? *Personality and Social Psychology Bulletin, 24*, 821–838.

Ruggiero, K.M., & Marx, D.M. (1999). Less pain and more to gain: Why high-status group members blame their failure on discrimination. *Journal of Personality and Social Psychology, 77, 774–784.*

Ruggiero, K.M., & Taylor, D.M. (1995). Coping with discrimination: How minority group members perceive the discrimination that confronts them. *Journal of Personality and Social Psychology, 68*, 826–838.

Ruggiero, K.M., & Taylor, D.M. (1997). Why minority group members perceive or do not perceive the discrimination that confronts them: The role of self-esteem and perceived control. *Journal of Personality and Social Psychology, 72*, 373–389.

Runciman, W.C. (1966). *Relative deprivation and social justice.* London: Routledge & Kegan Paul.

Rushton, J.P. (1995). Construct validity, censorship, and the genetics of race. *American Psychologist, 50*, 40–41.

Rushton, J.P. (1996). Race differences in brain size. *American Psychologist, 51*, 556.

Sack, W.H., Seidler, J., & Thomas, S. (1976). The children of imprisoned parents: A psychosocial exploration. *American Journal of Orthopsychiatry, 46*, 618–628.

Sadker, M., & Sadker, D. (1994). *Failing at fairness: How our schools cheat girls.* New York: Touchstone.

Sarup, G. (1976). Gender, authoritarianism, and attitudes toward feminism. *Social Behavior and Personality, 4*, 57–64.

Schaller M., Boyd, C., Yohannes, J., & O'Brien, M. (1995). The prejudiced personality revisited: Personal need for structure and formation of erroneous group stereotypes. *Journal of Personality and Social Psychology, 68*, 544–555.

Schermerhorn, R.A. (1970). *Comparative ethnic relations: A framework for theory and research.* New York: Random House.

Schimel, J., Simon, L., Greenberg, J., Pyszczynski, T., Solomon, S., Waxmonsky, J., Arndt, J. (1999). Stereotypes and terror management: Evidence that mortality salience enhances stereotypic thinking and preferences. *Journal of Personality and Social Psychology, 77*, 905–926.

Schneider, D.J., (1996). Modern stereotype research: Unfinished business. In C.N. Macrae, D. Stangor, & M. Hewstone (Eds), *Stereotypes and stereotyping* (pp. 419–453). New York: Guilford.

Schneider, W., & Shiffrin, R.M. (1977). Controlled and automatic human information processing: I. Detection, search, and attention. *Psychological Review, 84*, 1–66.

Schultz, P.W., Stone, W.F., & Christie, R. (1997). Authoritarianism and mental rigidity: The Einstellung problem revisited. *Personality and Social Psychology Bulletin, 23*, 3–9.

Schuman, H., Steeh, C., & Bobo, L. (1985). *Racial attitudes in America: Trends and interpretations.* Cambridge, MA: Harvard.

Sears, D.O. (1988). Symbolic racism. In P.A. Katz & D.A. Taylor (Eds.), *Eliminating racism: Profiles in controversy.* New York: Plenum Press.

Sears, D.O., & Citrin, J. (1985). *Tax revolt: Something for nothing in California.* Cambridge, MA: Harvard University.

Sears, D.O., & Jessor, T. (1996). Whites' racial policy attitudes: The role of white racism. *Social Science Quarterly, 77,* 751–759.

Sears, D.O., Van Laar, C., Carrillo, M., & Kosterman, R. (1997). Is it really racism? The origins of white America's opposition to race-targeted policies. *Public Opinion Quarterly, 61,* 16–53.

Selvin, P. (1991). The raging bull of Berkeley. *Science, 252,* 368–371.

Shepherd, J.M. (1980). The portrayal of black women in the ads of popular magazines. *Western Journal of Black Studies, 4,* 179–182.

Sherif, M. (1966). *In common predicament.* Boston: Houghton Mifflin.

Sherif, M., Harvey, O.J., White, B.J., Hood, W.R., & Sherif, C.W. (1961). *Intergroup conflict and cooperation: The Robbers Cave experiment.* Norman: University of Oklahoma Press.

Sherif, M., Harvey, O.J., White, B.J., Hood, W.R., & Sherif, C.W. (1988). *The Robbers Cave experiment.* Middletown, CT: Wesleyan University Press.

Sherman, J.W., Stroessner, S.J., Loftus, S.T., & Deguzman, G. (1997). Stereotype suppression and recognition memory for stereotypical and nonstereotypical information. *Social Cognition, 15,* 205–213.

Sherman, S.J., Hamilton, D.L., & Lewis, A.C. (1999). Perceived entitativity and the social identity value of group memberships. In D. Abrams & M.A. Hogg (Eds.), *Social identity and social cognition.* Oxford: Blackwell.

Sherrill, K. (1996). The political power of lesbians, gays, and bisexuals. *PS: Political Science and Politics, 24,* 469–471.

Sidanius, J. (1993). The psychology of group conflict and the dynamics of oppression: A social dominance perspective. In S. Iyengar & W.J. McGuire (Eds.), *Explorations in political psychology* (pp. 183–219). Durham, NC: Duke University Press.

Sidanius, J., & Liu, J.H. (1992). The Gulf War and the Rodney King beating: Implications of the general conservatism and social dominance perspectives. *Journal of Social Psychology, 132,* 685–700.

Sidanius, J., Pratto, F., & Bobo, L. (1994). Social dominance orientation and the political psychology of gender: A case of invariance? *Journal of Personality and Social Psychology, 67,* 998–1011.

Sidanius, J.F., Pratto, F., & Bobo, L. (1996). Racism, conservatism, affirmative action, and intellectual sophistication: A matter of principled conservatism or group dominance? *Journal of Personality and Social Psychology, 70,* 476–490.

Sigall, H., & Page, R. (1971). Current stereotypes: A little fading, a little faking. *Journal of Personality and Social Psychology, 18,* 247–255.

Signorielli, N., McLeod, D., & Healy, E. (1994). Gender stereotypes in MTV commercials: The beat goes on. *Journal of Broadcasting and Electronic Media, 38,* 91–101.

Siller, J. (1986). The measurement of attitudes toward physically disabled persons. In C. P. Herman, M. P. Zanna, & E. T. Higgins (Eds.), *Physical appearance, stigma, and social behavior: The Ontario symposium, Vol. 3.* Hillsdale, NJ: Erlbaum.

Simon, A. (1995). Some correlates of individuals' attitudes toward lesbians. *Journal of Homosexuality, 29,* 89–103.

Simon, B., & Brown, R.J. (1987). Perceived intragroup homogeneity in minority-majority contexts. *Journal of Personality and Social Psychology, 53,* 703–711.

Simpson, G.E., & Yinger, J.M. (1965). Racial and cultural minorities: An analysis of prejudice and discrimination. New York: Harper and Row.

Sinclair, L., & Kunda, Z. (1999). Reactions to a Black professional: Motivated inhibition and activation of conflicting stereotypes. *Journal of Personality and Social Psychology, 77,* 885–904.

Skinner, B.F. (1953). *Science and human behavior.* New York: Macmillan.

Slavin, R.E. (1978). Student teams and achievement divisions. *Journal of Research and Development in Education, 12,* 381–387.

Smart, L., & Wegner, D.M. (1999). Covering up what can't be seen: Concealable stigma and mental control. *Journal of Personality and Social Psychology, 77,* 474–486.

Smedley, A. (1997, November). Origins of "race." *Anthropology Newsletter,* p. 52.

Smith, E.R. (1993). Social identity and social emotions: Toward new conceptualizations of prejudice. In D.M. Mackie & D.L. Hamilton (Eds.), *Affect, cognition and stereotyping: Interactive processes in group perception* (pp. 297–316). New York: Academic Press.

Smith, E.R., & Zarate, M.A. (1992). Exemplar-based model of social judgment. *Psychological Review, 99,* 3–21.

Smith, J., & Welch, F. (1984). Affirmative action and labor markets. *Journal of Labor Economics, 2,* 269–301.

Sniderman, P.M., Paizzo, T., Tetlock, P.E., & Kendrick, A. (1991). The new racism. *American Journal of Political Science, 35,* 423–447.

Sniderman, P.M., & Tetlock, P.E. (1986a). Symbolic racism: Problems of political motive attribution. *Journal of Social Issues, 42,* 129–150.

Sniderman, P.M., & Tetlock, P.E. (1986b). Reflections on American racism. *Journal of Social Issues, 42,* 173–188.

Snyder, M. (1992). Motivational foundations of behavioral confirmation. *Advances in Experimental Social Psychology, 25,* 67–114.

Snyder, M., & Miene, P. (1994). On the functions of stereotypes and prejudice. In M. P. Zanna and J. M. Olson (Eds.), *The psychology of prejudice: The Ontario symposium, Vol. 7.* Hillsdale, NJ: Lawrence Erlbaum.

Snyder, M., & Swann, W.B., Jr. (1978). Behavioral confirmation in social interaction: From social perception to social reality. *Journal of Experimental Social Psychology, 14,* 148–162.

Snyder, M., Tanke, E.D., & Berscheid, E. (1977). Social perception and interpersonal behavior: On the self-fulfilling nature of social stereotypes. *Journal of Personality and Social Psychology, 35,* 656–666.

Snyder, M.L., Kleck, R.E., Strenta, A., & Mentzer, S.J. (1979). Avoidance of the handicapped: An attributional ambiguity analysis. *Journal of Personality and Social Psychology, 37,* 2297–2306.

Soder, M. (1990). Prejudice or ambivalence? Attitudes toward persons with disabilities. *Disability, Handicap, & Society, 5,* 227–241.

Southern Poverty Law Center (1997). Antihomosexual crime: The severity of the violence shows the hatred. *Intelligence Report, 88,* 16–17.

Spencer, S.J., Fein, S., Wolfe, C.T., Fong, C., & Dunn, M.A. (1998). Automatic activation of stereotypes: The role of self-image threat. *Personality and Social Psychology Bulletin, 24,* 1139–1152.

Spencer, S.J., Steele, C.M., & Quinn, D.M. (1999). Stereotype threat and women's math performance. *Journal of Experimental and Social Psychology, 35,* 4–28.

Stangor, C. (1995). Content and application inaccuracy in social stereotyping. In Y. Lee, L. Jussim, & C.R. McCauley (Eds.), *Stereotype accuracy: Toward appreciating group differences* (pp. 275–292). Washington, DC: American Psychological Association.

Stangor, C., & Lange, J.E. (1994). Mental representations of social groups: Advances in understanding stereotypes and stereotyping. In Zanna, M.P. (Ed.), *Advances in experimental social psychology* (pp. 357–418). New York: Academic Press.

Stangor, C., Lynch, L., Duan, C., & Glass, B. (1992). Categorization of individuals on the basis of multiple social features. *Journal of Personality and Social Psychology, 62,* 207–281.

Stangor, C., & McMillan, D. (1992). Memory for expectancy-congruent and expectancy-incongruent information: A review of the social and social developmental literatures. *Psychological Bulletin, 111,* 42–61.

**Stangor, C., & Schaller, M.** (1996). Stereotypes as individual and collective representations. In C.N. Macrae, C. Stangor, & M. Hewstone (Eds.), *Stereotypes and stereotyping* (pp. 3–37). New York: Guilford.

**Stangor, C., Sullivan, L.A., & Ford, T.E.** (1991). Affective and cognitive determinants of prejudice. *Social Cognition, 9,* 350–380.

**Stanush, P., Winfred, A., & Doverspike, D.** (1998). Hispanic and African American reactions to a simulated race-based affirmative action scenario. *Hispanic Journal of Behavioral Sciences, 20,* 3–16.

**Stapel, D.A., & Koomen, W.** (1998). When stereotype activation results in (counter) stereotypical judgments: Priming stereotype-relevant traits and exemplars. *Journal of Experimental Social Psychology, 34,* 136–163.

**Staub, E.** (1990). Moral exclusion, personal goal theory, and extreme destructiveness. *Journal of Social Issues, 46,* 47–64.

**Staub, E.** (1996). Cultural-societal roots of violence: The examples of genocidal violence and of contemporary youth violence in the United States. *American Psychologist, 51,* 117–132.

**Steele, C.M.** (1992). Race and the schooling of black Americans. *Atlantic Monthly,* pp. 68–78.

**Steele, C.M.** (1997). A threat in the air: How stereotypes shape intellectual identity and performance. *American Psychologist, 52,* 613–629.

**Steele, C.M., & Aronson, J.** (1995). Stereotype threat and the intellectual test performance of African Americans. *Journal of Personality and Social Psychology, 69,* 797–811.

**Steele, S.** (1991). *The content of our character.* New York: St. Martin's Press.

**Stephan, W.G.** (1978). School desegregation: An evaluation of predictions made in Brown vs. The Board of Education. *Psychological Bulletin, 85,* 217–238.

**Stephan, W.G., Ageyev, V., Coates-Shrider, L., Stephan, C.W., Abalakina, M.** (1994). On the relationship between stereotypes and prejudice: An international study. *Personality and Social Psychology Bulletin, 20,* 277–284.

**Stephan, W.G., Ageyev, V.S., Stephan, C.W., Abalakina, M., Stefanenko, T., & Coates-Shrider, L.** (1993). Soviet and American stereotypes: A comparison of methods. *Social Psychology Quarterly, 56,* 54–64.

**Stephan, W., & Stephan, C.W.** (1984). The role of ignorance in intergroup relations. In N. Miller & M.B. Brewer (Eds.), *Groups in contact: The psychology of desegregation* (pp. 229–256). Orlando, FL: Academic Press.

**Stephan, W.G., & Stephan, C.W.** (1985). Intergroup anxiety. *Journal of Social Issues, 41,* 157–175.

**Sternglanz, S.H., & Serbin, L.A.** (1974). Sex-role stereotyping in children's television programs. *Developmental Psychology, 10,* 710–715.

**Stoker, L.** (1998). Understanding whites' resistance to affirmative action: The role of principled commitments and racial prejudice. In J. Hurwitz & M. Peffley (Eds.), *Perception and prejudice: Race and politics in the United States.* New Haven: Yale University Press.

**Stone, J., Lynch, C.I., Sjomeling, M., & Darley, J.M.** (1999). Stereotype threat effects on Black and White athletic performance. *Journal of Personality and Social Psychology, 77,* 1213–1227.

**Strack, F., Erber, R., & Wicklund, R.A.** (1982). Effects of salience and time pressure on ratings of social causality. *Journal of Experimental Social Psychology, 18,* 581–594.

**Stringer, C., & McKie, R.** (1997). *African exodus.* New York: Holt.

**Stroh, L.K., Brett, J.M., & Reilly, A.H.** (1992). All the right stuff: A comparison of female and male managers' career progression. *Journal of Applied Psychology, 77,* 251–260.

**Summers, R.J.** (1991). The influence of affirmative action on perceptions of a beneficiary's qualifications. *Journal of Applied Social Psychology, 21,* 1265–1276.

**Swim, J.K., Aikin, K.J., Hall, W.S., & Hunter, B.A.** (1995). Sexism and racism: old-fashioned and modern prejudices. *Journal of Personality and Social Psychology, 68,* 199–214.

**Swim, J.K., Borgida, E., Maruyama, G., & Myers, D.G.** (1989). Joan McKay versus John McKay: Do gender stereotypes bias evaluations? *Psychological Bulletin, 105,* 409–429.

Swim, J., & Stangor, C. (1998). *Prejudice: The target's perspective.* New York: Academic Press.

Tajfel, H. (1969). Cognitive aspects of prejudice. *Journal of Social Issues, 25,* 79–97.

Tajfel, H. (1970). Experiments in intergroup discrimination. *Scientific American, 223,* 96–102.

Tajfel, H. (1978a). *Differentiation between social groups: Studies in the social psychology of intergroup relations.* London: Academic Press.

Tajfel, H. (1978b). *The social psychology of minorities.* New York: Minority Rights Group.

Tajfel, H. (1981). Social stereotypes and social groups. In J.C. Turner & H. Giles (Eds.), *Intergroup behavior* (pp. 144–167). Chicago: University of Chicago Press.

Tajfel, H. (1982). *Social identity and intergroup relations.* Cambridge, England: Cambridge University Press.

Tajfel, H., Billig, M., Bundy, R.P., & Flament, C. (1971). Social categorization and intergroup behavior. *European Journal of Social Psychology, 1,* 149–178.

Tajfel, H., & Turner, J.C. (1986). The social identity theory of intergroup behaviour. In S. Worchel & W.G. Austin (Eds.), *Psychology of intergroup relations* (pp. 7–24). Chicago: Nelson.

Tavris, C. (1992). *The mismeasure of woman.* New York: Touchstone.

Taylor, S.E. (1981). A categorization approach to stereotyping. In D. L. Hamilton (Ed.), *Cognitive processes in stereotyping and intergroup behavior* (pp. 83–114). New York: Erlbaum.

Taylor, S.E., & Fiske, S.T. (1978). Salience, attention, and attribution: Top of the head phenomena. In L. Berkowitz (Ed.), *Advances in experimental social psychology* (Vol. 11, pp. 249–288). San Diego, CA: Academic Press.

Taylor, D.M., & Jaggi, V. (1974). Ethnocentrism and causal attribution in a South Indian context. *Journal of Cross-Cultural Psychology, 5,* 162–171.

Taylor, D.M., Wright, S.C., Moghaddam, F.M., & Lalonde, R.N. (1990). The personal/group discrimination discrepancy: Perceiving my group, but not myself, to be a target for discrimination. *Personality and Social Psychology Bulletin, 16,* 254–262.

Taylor, D.M., Wright, S.C., & Porter, L.E. (1994). Dimensions of perceived discrimination: The personal/group discrimination discrepancy. In M.P. Zanna & J.M. Olson (Eds.), *The psychology of prejudice: The Ontario symposium* (Vol. 7, pp. 233–255). Hillsdale, NJ: Erlbaum.

Taylor, M.C. (1994). Impact of affirmative action on beneficiary groups: Evidence from the 1990 general social survey. *Basic and Applied Social Psychology, 15,* 143–178.

Teitelbaum, S., & Geiselman, R.E. (1997). Observer mood and cross-racial recognition of faces. *Journal of Cross Cultural Psychology, 28,* 93–106.

Terborg, J.R. (1977). Women in management: A research review. *Journal of Applied Psychology, 62,* 647–664.

Thayler, P. (1997). *The spectacle: Media and the making of the O.J. Simpson story.* Westport, CT: Praeger.

Thompson, T.L., & Zerbinos, E. (1995). Gender roles in animated cartoons: Has the picture changed in twenty years? *Sex Roles, 32,* 651–673.

Tougas, F., Brown, R., Beaton, A.M., & Joly, S. (1995). Neosexism: Plus ça change, plus c'est pareil. *Personality and Social Psychology Bulletin, 21,* 842–849.

Traux, K., Cordova, D.I., Wood, A., Wright, E., & Crosby, F. (1998). Undermined? Affirmative action from the targets' point of view. In J. Swim & C. Stangor (Eds.), *Prejudice: The target's perspective.* San Diego: Academic Press.

Trimble, J.E. (1988). Stereotypic images, American Indians, and prejudice. In P.A. Katz & D.A. Taylor (Eds.), *Eliminating racism: Profiles in controversy* (pp. 181–202). New York: Plenum Press.

Tripathi, R.C., & Srivastava, R. (1981). Relative deprivation and intergroup attitudes. *European Journal of Social Psychology, 11,* 313–318.

Tuch, S.A., & Hughes, M. (1996). Whites' racial policy attitudes. *Social Science Quarterly, 77,* 723–745.

Turner, J.C. (1978). Social categorization and social discrimination in the minimal group paradigm. In H. Tajfel (Ed.), *Differentiation between social groups*, pp. 101–140. London: Academic Press.

Turner, J.C. (1981). The experimental social psychology of intergroup behaviour. In J.C. Turner and H. Giles (Eds.), *Intergroup behaviour* (pp. 66–101). Oxford, England: Blackwell.

Turner, J.C. (1982). Toward a cognitive redefinition of the social group. In H. Tajfel (Ed.), *Social identity and intergroup relations* (pp. 14–40). Cambridge, England: Cambridge University Press.

Turner, J.C. (1984). Social identification and psychological group formation. In H. Tajfel (Ed.), *The social dimension: European developments in social psychology* (Vol. 2, pp. 518–540). Cambridge, England: Cambridge University Press.

Turner, J.C. (1999). Some current issues in research on social identity and self-categorization theories. In N. Ellemers, R. Spears, and B. Doosje (Eds.), *Social identity: Context, commitment, content*. Oxford, England: Blackwell.

Turner, J.C., Hogg, M., Oakes, P., Reicher, S., & Wetherell, M. (1987). *Rediscovering the social group: A self-categorization theory*. Oxford, England: Basil Blackwell.

Tyler, T.R., & Smith, H.J. (1998). Social justice and social movements. In D.T. Gilbert, S.T. Fiske, & G. Lindzey (Eds.), *The handbook of social psychology* (Vol. 2). Boston: McGraw-Hill.

Unger, R.K., &: Crawford, M. (1998). Sex and gender: The troubled relationship between terms and concepts. In D.L. Anselmi & A.L. Law (Eds.), *Questions of gender: Perspectives and paradoxes*. New York: McGraw-Hill.

U.S. Bureau of the Census (1996). *Population projections of the United States by age, sex, race, and Hispanic origin: 1995 to 2050.* (Publication No. P25-1130). Washington, DC: U.S. Government Printing Office.

U.S. Bureau of the Census (1999). *Current Population Reports, Consumer Income*. Series P-60, no. 206. *Money Income in the United States, 1998*. Washington, DC: U.S. Government Printing Office.

U.S. Commission on Civil Rights (1981). *Affirmative action in the 1980s: Dismantling the process of discrimination*. Washington, D.C.: U.S. Government Printing Office.

U.S. Department of Labor (1999). *Highlights of women's earnings in 1998*. Washington, D.C.: U.S. Government Printing Office.

Van den Berghe, P. (1967). *Race and racism: A comparative perspective*. New York: Wiley.

Vanman, E.J., & Miller, N. (1993). Applications of emotion theory and research to stereotyping and intergroup relations. In D.M. Mackie & D.L. Hamilton (Eds.), *Affect, cognition, and stereotyping: Interactive processes in group perception* (pp. 213–238). New York: Academic Press.

Vanneman, R.D., & Pettigrew, T.F. (1972). Race and relative deprivation in the urban United States. *Race, 13,* 461–486.

Veilleux, F., & Tougas, F. (1989). Male acceptance of affirmative action programs for women: The results of altruistic or egoistical motives? *International Journal of Psychology, 24,* 485–496.

Von Hippel, W., Sekaquaptewa, D., & Vargas, P. (1995) . On the role of encoding processes in stereotype maintenance. *Advances in Experimental Social Psychology, 27,* 177–254.

Von Hippel, W., Sekaquaptewa, D., & Vargas, P. (1997). The linguistic intergroup bias as an implicit indicator of prejudice. *Journal of Experimental Social Psychology, 33,* 490–509.

Walker, W.D., Rowe, R.C., & Quinsey, V.L. (1993). Authoritarianism and sexual aggression. *Journal of Personality and Social Psychology, 65,* 1036–1045.

Walston, B.S., & O'Leary, V.E. (1981). Sex makes a difference: Differential perceptions of women and men. In L. Wheeler (Ed.), *Review of personality and social psychology*, Vol. 2 (pp. 9–41). Beverly Hills, CA: Sage.

Wann, D.L., & Branscombe, N.R. (1990). Die-hard and fair-weather fans: Effects of identification on BIRGing and CORFing tendencies. *Journal of Sport and Social Issues, 14,* 103–117.

Weber, J.G. (1994). The nature of ethnocentric attribution bias: Ingroup protection or enhancement? *Journal of Experimental Social Psychology, 30*, 482–504.

Webster, D.M., & Kruglanski, A.W. (1994). Individual differences in need for cognitive closure. *Journal of Personality and Social Psychology, 67*, 1049–1062.

Webster, D.M., Kruglanski, A.W., & Pattison, D.A. (1997). Motivated language use in intergroup contexts: Need-for-closure effects on the linguistic intergroup bias. *Journal of Personality and Social Psychology, 72*, 1122–1131.

Weeks, J. (1977). *Coming out: Homosexual politics in Britain, from the nineteenth century to the present.* London: Quartet.

Wegner. D.M. (1994). Ironic processes of mental control. *Psychological Review, 101*, 961–977.

Wegner, D.M., & Wenzlaff, R.M. (1996). Mental control. In E.T. Higgins & A.W. Kruglanski (Eds.), *Social psychology: Handbook of basic principles* (pp. 466–488). New York: Guilford.

Weigel, R.H., & Howes, P.W. (1985). Conceptions of racial prejudice: Symbolic racism reconsidered. *Journal of Social Issues, 41*, 117–138.

Weigel, R.H., Kim, E.L., & Frost, J.L. (1995). Race relations on prime time television reconsidered: Patterns of continuity and change. *Journal of Applied Social Psychology, 25*, 223–236.

Weigel, R.H., Wiser, P.L., & Cook, S.W. (1975). The impact of cooperative learning experiences on cross-ethnic relations and helping. *Journal of Social Issues, 31*, 219–244.

Weiner, B., Perry, R.P., & Magnusson, J. (1988). An attributional analysis of reactions to stigmas. *Journal of Personality and Social Psychology, 55*, 738–748.

Westie, F.P. (1964). Race and ethnic relations. In R.E.L. Faris (Ed.), *Handbook of modern sociology* (pp. 576–618). Chicago: Rand McNally.

White, K.R. (1982). The relation between socioeconomic status and academic achievement. *Psychological Bulletin, 91*, 461–481.

Whitley, B.E. (1990). The relationship of heterosexuals' attributions for the causes of homosexuality to attitudes toward lesbians and gay men. *Personality and Social Psychology Bulletin, 16*, 369–377.

Whitley, B.E. (1999). Right-wing authoritarianism, social dominance orientation, and prejudice. *Journal of Personality and Social Psychology, 77*, 126–134.

Whitley, B.E., & Kite, M.E. (1995). Sex differences in attitudes toward homosexuality: A comment on Oliver and Hyde (1993). *Psychological Bulletin, 117*, 146–154.

Wicker, A.W. (1969). Attitude versus actions: The relationship of verbal and overt behavioral responses to attitude objects. *Journal of Social Issues, 25*(4), 41–78.

Wigboldus, D.H.J., Semin, G.R., & Spears, R. (2000). How do we communicate stereotypes? Linguistic biases and inferential consequences. *Journal of Personality and Social Psychology, 78*, 5–18.

Williams, J.E. & Best, D.L. (1982). *Measuring sex stereotypes: A thirty-nation study.* Newbury Park, CA: Sage.

Williams, W. (1986). *The spirit and the flesh: Sexual diversity in American Indian culture.* Boston: Beacon Press.

Wilson, C.C., & Gutierrez, F. (1985). *Minorities and media: Diversity and the end of mass communication.* Beverly Hills, CA: Sage.

Wilson, T.C. (1996). Compliments will get you nowhere: Benign stereotypes, prejudice, and anti-Semitism. *Sociological Quarterly, 37*, 465–479.

Wirth, L. (1945). The problem of minority groups. In R. Linton (Ed.), *The science of man in the world crisis* (pp. 347–372). New York: Columbia University Press.

Wittenbrink, B., Hilton, J.L., & Gist, P.L. (1998). In search of similarity: Stereotypes as naive theories in social categorization. *Social Cognition, 16*, 31–55.

Wittenbrink, B., Judd, C.M., & Park, B. (1997). Evidence for racial prejudice at the implicit level and its relationship with questionnaire measures. *Journal of Personality and Social Psychology, 72*, 262–274.

Wolf, M.A., & Kielwasser, A.P. (Eds.). (1991) *Gay people, sex, and the media.* Binghamton, NY: Haworth Press.

Wolsko, C., Park, B., Judd, C.M., & Wittenbrink, B. (2000). Framing interethnic ideology: Effects of multicultural and color-blind perspectives on judgments of groups and individuals. *Journal of Personality and Social Psychology, 78,* 635–654.

Worchel, S. (1986). The role of cooperation in reducing intergroup conflict. In S. Worchel and W. Austin (Eds.), *Psychology of intergroup relations* (pp. 288–304). Chicago: Nelson-Hall.

Worchel, S., & Andreoli, V.A. (1978). Facilitation of social interaction through deindividuation of the target. *Journal of Personality and Social Psychology, 36,* 549–556.

Worchel, S., Andreoli, V.A., & Folger, R. (1977). Intergroup cooperation and intergroup attraction: The effect of previous interaction and outcome of combined effort. *Journal of Experimental Social Psychology, 13,* 131–140.

Worchel, S., & Rothgerber, H. (1997). Changing the stereotype of the stereotype. In R. Spears, P. Oakes, N. Ellemers, & S. Haslam (Eds.), *The social psychology of stereotyping and group life: Emphasizing the side of group perceptions* (pp. 72–93). London: Sage.

Word, C.O., Zanna, M.P., & Cooper, J. (1974). The nonverbal mediation of self-fulfilling prophecies in interracial interaction. *Journal of Experimental Social Psychology, 10,* 109–120.

Wyer, N.A., Sherman, J.W., & Stroessner, S.I. (1998). The spontaneous suppression of racial stereotypes. *Social Cognition, 16,* 340–352.

Yang, A.S. (1997). The polls—trends: Attitudes toward homosexuality. *Public Opinion Quarterly, 61,* 477–507.

Yee, A.H., Fairchild, H.H., Weizmann, F., & Wyatt, G.E. (1993). Addressing psychology's problems with race. *American Psychologist, 48,* 1132–1140.

Yinger, J. (1995). *Closed doors, opportunities lost: The continuing costs of housing discrimination.* New York: Russell Sage Foundation.

Young-Bruehl, E. (1995). *The anatomy of prejudices.* Cambridge, MA: Harvard University Press.

Yzerbyt, V.Y., Leyens, J.P., & Corneille, O. (1998). Social judgability and the bogus pipeline: The role of naive theories of judgment in impression formation. *Social Cognition, 16,* 56–77.

Zanna, M.P. (1994). On the nature of prejudice. *Canadian Psychology, 35,* 11–23.

Zebrowitz, L. (1996). Physical appearance as a basis for stereotyping. In C.N. Macrae, C. Stangor, & M. Hewstone (Eds.), *Stereotypes and stereotyping* (pp.79–120). New York: Guilford Press.

Zuwerink, J.R., Devine, P.G., Monteith, M.I., & Cook, D.A. (1996). Prejudice toward Blacks: With and without compunction? *Basic and Applied Social Psychology, 18,* 131–150.

# INDEX